B. F. Skinner
and Behaviorism
in American Culture

B. F. Skinner
and Behaviorism
in American Culture

Edited by
Laurence D. Smith
and
William R. Woodward

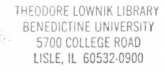

Lehigh
University
Press

Bethlehem
Lehigh University Press
London: Associated University Presses

Associated University Presses
440 Forsgate Drive
Cranbury, NJ 08512

Associated University Presses
16 Barter Street
London WC1A 2AH, England

Associated University Presses
P.O. Box 338, Port Credit
Mississauga, Ontario
Canada L5G 4L8

The paper used in this publication meets the requirements
of the American National Standard for Permanence of Paper
for Printed Library Materials Z39.48-1984.

Library of Congress Cataloging-in-Publication Data

B.F. Skinner and behaviorism in American culture / edited by Laurence
D. Smith and William R. Woodward.
    p.   cm.
Includes bibliographical references and index.
ISBN 0-934223-40-8 (alk. paper)
    1. Skinner, B. F. (Burrhus Frederic), 1904–90.   2. Behaviorism
(Psychology)—United States—History.   I. Smith, Laurence D., 1950–
BF109.S55B33   1996
150.19′.434′092—dc20   95-42466
                                                            CIP

SECOND PRINTING 1997

PRINTED IN THE UNITED STATES OF AMERICA

Contents

Introduction
Skinner and Behaviorism as Cultural Icons: From Local Knowledge to Reader Reception

WILLIAM R. WOODWARD

BEHAVIORISM is perhaps best known through B. F. Skinner's 1948 book *Walden Two*, a fictional account of a behaviorist utopia. His 1971 best-seller *Beyond Freedom and Dignity* brought the scientific utopia to popular attention again. So well-known are its maxims of child-rearing and education that we nod in familiarity to the common coin of setting behavioral objectives, breaking learning into sequential steps, shaping through immediate reinforcement, eschewing punishment except to establish limits, learning by consequences, and achieving "stimulus control" by re-arranging the place and time of our behavior.

Misunderstandings of behaviorism abound, nevertheless, and that is one reason for this book. The authors represented here are not blind devotees of an ideology but rather critical students of a tradition. The tradition we describe goes far beyond a single experimental icon—the pigeon; beyond a single cult figure—B. F. Skinner; and beyond a single method—conditioning. We are interested in facets of a cultural phenomenon—behaviorism—that has long since emerged from the laboratory to permeate daily life around the world.

One need only consult the innumerable introductory textbooks of psychology to find the accepted canon of the scientific "discovery" of the behavioral principles of learning and conditioning: the pivotal figures are Thorndike, Pavlov, Watson, and Skinner. History of psychology texts expand the canon to include Darwin as precursor, Hull and Tolman as contemporaries, Sigmund Koch as critic, and Skinner and his followers. In this hagiography of "great men," the lives are not so important as the legitimizing function they perform: each figure represents an iconographic "method" of naturalistic observation, classical conditioning, instrumental conditioning, maze learning, operant conditioning, and critique of the learning paradigm. At issue is the "discovery" of nomothetic "laws" of

7

learning. Expressed in the physicalistic language of stimulus and response, the "discovered" regularities in nature include the power of positive reinforcement and the fact that much of our lives unfortunately remain under the control of aversive stimuli.[1]

By taking one of these founders, the most successful one, and contextualizing him in a gendered cultural space, the authors of the present volume seek historical objectivity. Objectivity of this sort comes from altogether different realms of discourse than that created by scientific methods. In fact, objectivity of the kind that behaviorists seek, based on observations guided by theory-laden instruments, seems to have been purchased at a certain ideological price. Even more ideologically inspired, though, is much of the criticism of behaviorism from uninformed sources.

Historians take for granted that the discovery of historical "truth" reflects a writer's "theory-laden" interests. The task of historians, as witnessed in this book, consists of bringing appropriate evidence to bear on their contentions. Consider, for example, the familiar icon of a pigeon pecking a key in a box. Despite the seemingly mechanical language of stimulus and response, a fundamentally psychological metaphor (rather than a logical or physical one) underlies the application of Skinner's operant chamber to human situations—namely, an organism behaving in a more or less regular fashion.[2] Skinner's simple psychological recipe—change behavior by stimulus control and schedules of reinforcement—enabled others to purvey skillful experiments and therapies, behavior management and self-help into cultural reform on a broad scale.

As works consciously constructed during a period of technological optimism in American life, Skinner's writings convey a peculiarly "hands-on" social philosophy. They extend to the social and personal realms a philosophy of technology that, however problematic in the eyes of some critics, has long been engrained in the American penchant for making and remaking the environment. Skinner's astounding reception in wide circles of education, medicine, business, and science reflects his embodiment of a technological ideal. Somehow, he managed to capitalize on a growth industry—behavioral technology—and to become the spokesperson for it in many nations. How did he achieve this surprising feat? And, in light of criticisms of Skinner's hands-on techniques and the technological orientation that underlay them, how shall the public as well as behaviorism's devotees adjust to the possible dangers of social engineering—including behavioral technology?

To help make sense of the remarkable cultural dissemination of Skinner's ideas, the present essay draws upon literature from diverse quarters: biography as a nonnomothetic discipline, literary analysis of Skinner's social philosophy, the sociology of experimental practice, an artificial intelligence debate, the reception of Skinnerian behaviorism in a socialist country, and its proliferation in many parts of the world.

THE IDIOSYNCRASY OF BIOGRAPHICAL OBJECTIVITY

Critical biography is one starting point that helps us understand a famous person, for it splendidly illustrates the strengths, and the limits, of critical history. Replacing earlier idolatry toward great persons and great texts, good biography now seeks to understand scientists' lives, warts and all, in textured cultural contexts. Born in 1904, Burrhus Frederic Skinner majored in English language and literature at Hamilton College in upstate New York; studied psychology at Harvard until 1934; and rose from assistant to associate to full professor successively at the Universities of Minnesota in 1936, Indiana in 1945, and Harvard in 1948. He finished raising a family in Cambridge and remained there for the duration of his life, some forty-two more years. Yet these biographical markers actually tell us little about, say, the kind of husband and father he was, or where his crusading spirit came from; they may in fact hide these realities.[3]

Some may think that biography is not necessary when an extensive autobiography—in Skinner's case, three volumes' worth—tells it all. Such a judgment would fail to take into account the motives a person has in telling his or her life story, the selection of the evidence, and the style in which it is told. Consider merely the titles of Skinner's autobiographical works: "A Case History in Scientific Method" (1956), *Particulars of My Life* (1976), *The Shaping of a Behaviorist* (1979), and *A Matter of Consequences* (1983).[4] The motive is transparent: Skinner intended to depict his life as an example of his theory of scientific method.

Skinner's autobiography revealed little about the ups and downs of his marriage. Despite his evident fondness for child-rearing, he hid his vulnerability to human emotions.[5] Closer inspection by Rhonda Bjork sheds some light on his affectionate devotion to his wife, Eve, and to their daughters. Elizabeth Jordan compares the Skinners' permissive approach to parenting favorably with others in the 1930s and 1940s. The motive for inventing and marketing the "Aircrib"—a glorified playpen with a sheet that could be cranked—was simply to lighten a parent's work for a few hours a day. Yet even the sparing use it received in the Skinners' household evoked widespread rumors of mistreatment of their children. Never mind the controversy: the Skinner that emerges from these chapters was dedicated to his family life.

How do biographers capture scientists in their culture? In part, by plumbing the odd details of their lives, private and public, that so often prove revealing:

> The literary biographer must utilize original research that casts new light on the subject; have a thorough mastery of the material; give a complete and accurate synthesis of all the facts about the private as well as the public life: friendships, conversation, dress, habits, tastes, food, money.[6]

Such aspects of the Skinners' social world yield telling detail that has hitherto remained chiefly in the family memory.

For example, Fred and Eve enjoyed monthly Sundays together performing amateur theater.[7] They gathered in the spacious living rooms of Babs and John Spiegel (a psychiatrist), Amos (brother of Thornton) and Katherine Wilder, Martha Van Lennep and her husband William (head of the theater collection at Harvard), and Gardner Cox (a portrait painter). Two couples would direct, shortening the play to permit rehearsal and performance in one day, reading instead of memorizing, whispering stage instructions from behind the imaginary "fourth wall." Aside from these thespians, Eve's closest friends remained Lou Mulligan (the Skinners lived with her and the lawyer Ken Mulligan when they first came to Harvard), Elena Levin (married to Harry Levin, the English professor), and Nancy Homans (wife of George Homans, the sociologist). A biographer would weave a fabric of the Skinners' personal world from such threads, informed by the insights that our authors provide about Fred Skinner's own overlapping personal and professional worlds as "social inventor" (Daniel Bjork), "Baconian" (Laurence Smith), "intellectual" (John Cerullo), "husband" (Rhonda Bjork), and "father" (Elizabeth Jordan).

The use of archival sources (including unpublished letters and notebooks) constitutes one prerequisite of the new biography. It is the idiosyncratic events that adumbrate the person most "objectively" in our authors' accounts: Skinner's conviction by age thirty that reform of the social sciences requires "the principal medium" of language, or the late-blooming fine arts career of Eve Skinner, or the tireless attempts to develop and promote teaching machines.[8] Interview evidence, like archival evidence, must be used with circumspection. Those who interviewed Skinner in later life heard the same anecdote about the dog he trained, on a challenge from a reporter for *Look* magazine, to stand on its hind legs.[9] The story sounds apocryphal, serving Skinner's aim of illustrating the power of his method for the public. That a dog could be trained so quickly is plausible enough that it goes unchallenged. Skinner employed the anecdote because he assumed that it would convince the novice. Actually, there are sufficient data about the human effectiveness of behavior therapy, behavioral medicine, and rehabilitation through token economies to convince most skeptics.

At home Skinner inclined to converse about cultural topics, especially music, theater, and French and British literature. The Skinners' living room was lined with books of literature, while his psychology library stayed in the basement. Paintings—some by their daughter Deborah—adorned the walls of their modest designer-built modern home with a concrete swimming pool. Their private life sheds reflected light on their public one, for Fred wrote often about the design of culture, and Eve explained paintings to children and adults at the Boston Museum of Fine Arts.

Those who met Skinner often remarked on his sense of humor, which ranged from gentle wit to a legendary capacity for practical jokes. He repeatedly told the story of posting bogus handbills announcing the arrival of Charlie Chaplin in his college town (the crowds came, but the famous comedian did not). Throughout his life, humor carried over into scholarship, sometimes in pointed ways that reflected a waggish dedication to his cause. Upon hearing rumors that his (nonbehaviorist) doctoral thesis committee bore him a grudge, Skinner offered to undertake operational definitions of psychological concepts in exchange for leniency at his final oral examination. Or again, toward the end of his life, he began an essay on emotions in the staid *Times Literary Supplement* with a story of two behaviorists who have just made love (one says to the other, "That was fine for you. How was it for me?").[10] Skinner used humor in his role as the enfant terrible of Harvard psychology during his graduate school days and later in his career to soften his status as an intellectual provocateur. It is perhaps tempting to view his behaviorism in a similar light, as an "iconoclastic" bid for attention through novelty and exaggeration.[11] But such an approach would fail to consider his dead-earnest conviction that the principles of behavior—reinforcement and extinction without punishment—could make a better world.

Somerset Maugham wrote that "in most biographies it is the subject's death which is most interesting. The last inevitable step has a fascination and even a practical interest which no previous event can equal."[12] Skinner apparently died calmly on 18 August 1990. He faced life objectively to the end.[13]

THE LOCAL KNOWLEDGE OF SKINNER'S SCIENTIFIC WORLD

Surprisingly, even historians of science have only recently begun to pay attention to the way in which facts are constructed in experiments.[14]

Recent sociological approaches to experimental, or investigative, practice help to situate Skinner's scientific work. For example, some sociologists of scientific knowledge approach the laboratory as an anthropologist would a primitive tribe.[15] We, too, are interested in reconstructing the culture of a laboratory. Culture refers to shared beliefs and actions, and for the behavioral scientist, this means belief both in instruments that deliver certain kinds of information about the world and in certain kinds of experimental designs used to study learning.

How was the work of a behaviorist done? In the 1930s, as Stephen R. Coleman has shown through exquisite detective work, Skinner was seeking both a way of collecting data and a way of analyzing its quantitative order.[16] The cumulative recorder enabled him to go home on weekends instead of remaining in the laboratory to endlessly record data and refill the food bin for the behaving animal. Bruno Latour and Steve Woolgar call such an apparatus that transforms a material phenomenon (an animal eating or moving) into a written record an "inscription device." The originality of a kymograph that collected data continuously, recording rat lever presses (later pigeon key pecks) on a graph on a revolving drum, was that it conveyed some semblance of the temporal aspects of ongoing behavior. The experiment itself became a psychologistic model for the ongoing reciprocal interaction of organism and environment. Neither the laboratory experiments of Thorndike, nor Pavlov, nor even Crozier allowed for this detailed recording of behavior over time.

Skinner is said to have worked alone, not sharing the result of his efforts until it was done. To be sure, Fred Keller became his lifelong scientific friend in the 1930s, though always with a distinctive interest in the human side of research—in programmed instruction and introductory psychology. Then it was Charles Ferster who ran the laboratory in the late 1940s and early 1950s, as Skinner gradually withdrew from active experimentation.[17] Essentially, Skinner experimented alone, tinkering and bringing prototypes of apparatus to the machine shop for Ralph Gerbrands to construct. In the 1940s, Skinner's problem shifted to engineering a guidance system for bombs. Eager to make use of his proven ability to train animals, Skinner changed the local setting of his "inscription device" from the laboratory to the nose cone of a missile. Here, as James Capshew indicates, the patriotic dedication to delivering a practical result is very revealing of Skinner's long-term aims, especially in regard to the possibilities for cultural engineering. Instruments became "social inventions" for him, suggests Daniel Bjork. As Kurt Danziger has stated, "the distinctive nature of Skinner's utopia is that it is *imposed*."[18] Later on, Skinner became a decided peace and environmental advocate, writing with compassionate pessimism about "why we are not acting to save the world" and despairing that our political leaders do not implement the lessons of behaviorism. Skinner's instrument-centered approach to problems large and small contrasts with the more typical reluctance of laboratory scientists to take it upon themselves to find applications for their work (indeed, mental tests are the usual example of a psychological "technology"). Nikolas Rose has recommended that we not assume a unidirectional slide from laboratory to application, however.[19] In many cases, Skinner included, the apparatus seems to have arisen in the social context of a perceived need for a technological solution. In the examples mentioned, it is the problem of continuously collecting data in animal experiments or of guiding a missile to its goal.[20]

Another instance of apparatus design is the teaching machine. Skinner devoted over a decade to an extremely frustrating correspondence with manufacturers in the hope of mass-producing the simple teaching machine. His doggedness, and his polite good humor, impress the reader of his archival letters.[21] Here the "pragmatic perspective" noted by sociologists of scientific knowledge shines through: tinkering, designing, testing of equipment all go on long before the reported data are collected. In this sense, a behavioral experiment is open-ended; even replications sufficiently different in their circumstances do not eliminate alternative interpretations, as in the controversy over single-trial learning of predators to avoid poisoned bait.[22] Historians of science, reports Jan V. Golinski, willingly admit the importance of experimental skills without entirely conceding that practice is adequately described thereby. They see the researcher as confronting nature such that its constraints restrict the possible outcomes.[23]

Sociologists of scientific knowledge refer to these experimental skills as producing "local knowledge." Local knowledge involves a radical departure from the notion of science as a theoretical system of statements, tested by "problem-solving" empirical work. Returning to Thomas Kuhn and Nancy Cartwright, Joseph Rouse suggests that theories may be taken not as testable statements but as "extendable models." Scientific models depend upon skills, equipment, and funding in particular local contexts. But science also proceeds by moving and adapting to new local contexts: (a) from laboratory to technological applications, and (b) from laboratory into the scientific literature. This is the universalizing side, in which science is "decontextualized" from local knowledge.[24]

Skinner exemplifies both aspects. His first book in 1938 was filled with diagrams and graphs of learning and extinction curves.[25] Like other scientists, he employed a wide variety of experimental, discursive, and representational strategies to present his results to audiences and to persuade them of the reality of the natural phenomena of conditioning.[26] Skinner's figures, tables, and diagrams became an integral part of the behavioral science he fostered.[27] Early on, Skinner attempted to move his work into the public arena, with increasing success. A check of introductory psychology texts in the 1990s shows that these very Skinner boxes, learning curves, and reinforcement schedules are still common coin and worthy of coveted textbook space.[28] Why? Because they bear the weight of collective authority as a scientific invention that has borne applied fruit.

FROM LITERARY FORMALISM TO RECEPTION THEORY

The legends of Skinner's *Atlantic Monthly* essay on Gertrude Stein and his encouragement in college by Robert Frost serve as symbolic memories of his literary aspirations.[29] But by far the most persuasive evidence of his literary acumen are his rhetorical strategies themselves. Skinner's writings, taken as a whole, attempt to communicate something of "value" to a wide variety of audiences. At the microlevel of rhetorical style, he often began with an admonition to replace one set of positive reinforcers with another.

Skinner once wrote for an audience of teachers on "how to motivate a student." Students are under the control of pictures and the media. "Knowing how to read is less valuable when pictures and recorded speech replace texts." What Skinner wanted to argue is that reading is more valuable than viewing pictures. He typically tried to persuade his reader by beginning with an undesirable state of affairs. "A news magazine which refers to 'the English novelist Charles Dickens' . . . deprives the reader of some of what he gained from his education if he would have responded just as well to 'Dickens'." Again, the statement is about control by the wrong set of reinforcers. Finally, Skinner lists the advantages of another set of reinforcers. "The student joins the company of educated men and women with its honors and cabalistic practices; he understands its allusions, enjoys its privileges, shares its *esprit de corps*."[30] Reading is more valuable than viewing pictures because understanding literary allusions gives entry into socially privileged company.[31]

The American school of reception theory traced its lineage to a break with New Criticism's scientific exegesis of texts that prevailed from the 1920s to the 1960s. New Critics distinguished between science and poetry viewing them as different endeavors.[32] They considered poetry and other good writing unique; the text was objective in some sense; and the task of the New Criticism—drawing from structuralism, phenomenology, and psychoanalysis—was to decipher what the author was trying to say. Exponents railed against the psychologistic fallacy of examining the effect of a literary work on readers' affective experiences.

Given that Skinner studied English, worked throughout his life at verbal behavior, and became an American writer and scientific analyst of writing, it is not out of place to locate him in twentieth-century literary criticism. Among its founders and early critics was I. A. Richards, who believed (with Skinner) that the function of literature was to "save us" as civilized persons. In his 1924 book *Science and Poetry,* Richards separated the feelings evoked by poetry from the knowledge to which science aspires. Thus "reader-response criticism could be said to have started with I. A. Richards' discussions of emotional response in the 1920s."[33]

Skinner too was applying science to literature, grounding literature on its effects. One of our authors, Terry J. Knapp, elsewhere noted this affinity for literature (so well documented in the Wiklander chapter here): "The whole tenor of *Verbal Behavior* is much more in keeping with the rhetorical or literary tradition than it is with the psychology of the 1940s or 50s."[34] What if we were to generalize this statement to the entire Skinnerian corpus?

In a book that Skinner owned and underlined, coauthored by his friend Ivor A. Richards, appeared the statement: "Words, as every one now knows, 'mean' nothing by themselves. . . . It is only when a thinker makes use of them that they stand for anything, or, in one sense, have 'meaning.' They are instruments."[35] Later literary movements since the 1970s—termed *reception theory, reader-response theory, deconstructionism,* and *postmodernism*—tried to anchor this meaning by historicizing texts; they downplayed pretentions to objectivity beyond a certain time and situation.[36] Above all, they signaled a move away from the "autonomy of the text" in the direction of "audience-oriented criticism."[37]

In a real sense, Skinner belonged to both of these literary movements. He applied science to writing, performing word counts and other measures of texts.[38] Yet he also wrote of "having a poem," an apt metaphor for relativizing the authorial and audience standpoints, and he explicitly acknowledged that his own writing aimed not at recording the truth but at producing a certain effect on his readers.[39] Long before Skinner took this stance, the anthropologist Bronislaw Malinowski credited Ogden and Richards for the definition of words by their functions.[40] Skinner, in fact, drew from this larger tradition in English literary theory, logic, and anthropology.[41] He rewrote his manuscript of *Verbal Behavior* in the mid-1950s when, it might be argued, interaction and reader-response were on the horizon. His scientific behaviorism in fact paralleled the advent of literary and cultural behaviorism, known under other names.

READING SKINNER'S TEXTS

Skinner aimed his first book at a scientific public. In 1938 at age thirty-four, he explained the two methods of conditioning to the reader of *The*

Behavior of Organisms. Looked at as rhetorical strategy, we note his device of always contrasting the wrong approach with the right one.

> One outstanding aspect of the present book, which can hardly be overlooked, is the shift in emphasis from respondent to operant behavior. The definition of behavior as a whole given in Chapter One may not be altogether acceptable to the reader.[42]

Why did he want the reader to know that he was departing from the Watsonian definition of behavior in terms of reflex? He explained that the voluntarily emitted responses called operants differed fundamentally from respondent behavior that is elicited (i.e., Pavlovian conditioned reflexes). The operant concept, he freely acknowledged, came from Thorndike's puzzle-box experiments, in which a cat learned by escaping from the box to repeat the performance of pulling a latch. The important difference consisted in this: the cat's escapes occurred one at a time, whereas the rat's lever press (or, later, the pigeon's peck) repeated itself again and again, producing reinforcement according to an ongoing schedule. A world of difference separates "elicited" and "emitted" behavior, as subsequent psychologists have shown. The one emphasizes antecedent stimuli, the other the consequences of the response. Taken together, they operationally define the way in which learning occurs.

Nikolas Rose's *Governing the Soul: The Shaping of the Private Self* draws on Michel Foucault's writings to describe the psychological technologies in our society. These provide regulatives that free the citizens of liberal democracies to mold themselves.[43] As Rose remarks, the search for psychological regularities and the attempt to improve society went together, while the directionality of influence receded in importance. Thus in 1938, Skinner had already glimpsed a cultural mission. "The importance of a science of behavior derives largely from the possibility of an eventual extension to human affairs"; yet he also defended science for its own sake: it "treats behavior as a subject matter in its own right." The link between the supposedly "natural" laws revealed by the controlled interventions of the laboratory and the implementation of novel forms of social control would become the (arguably precarious) keystone of Skinner's social mission.[44]

A decade later in 1948, *Walden Two* employed dialogue as a literary device. This text aimed at a lay public, which allowed Skinner to frame the issue of social control, as well as its potential dangers, in a favorable light. Skinner engaged the reader of his utopian novel by presenting an obvious dreamer, the former psychologist T. E. Frazier, under questioning by someone more down-to-earth, Prof. Augustine Castle. Castle was forever posing the commonsense questions, the questions that the "mock reader" postulated by reception theorists would have had. Called upon to explain why *Walden Two* was not a fascist dictatorship, Frazier replied:

> It's a little late to be proving that a behavioral technology is well advanced. How can you deny it? . . . Look at [its] frightful misuse in the hands of the Nazis! . . . My question is, have you the courage to take up and wield the science of behavior for the good of mankind?[45]

Skinner was no doubt speaking sincerely here. He exhorts his audience to draw on science for salvation. To escape the damnation of our ways, we must reform by using human technology to our benefit. He belongs, as Smith shows and as Skinner attested, to a Baconian melioristic line of Anglo-Saxon thought.[46] Knowledge and practice are fused through the bridge of practical regulatives, social technologies available to every man, woman, and child.

Here lies the force of Skinner's rhetoric: its link to the authority of the laboratory and to the validation of social practice. But to what end? The technologies of individual self-control that arose readily from laboratory work on single organisms would soon spread into myriad realms of practice. But Skinner's call for explicitly planned social controls on a broad scale evoked a different and serious question: Were the proclaimed benefits of deliberately engineered forms of society equal to their risks, actual or perceived? On this score, Skinner (along with other behaviorists) often spoke as if they had failed to put their message across, perhaps with good reason.[47] When their ideological scruples are set aside, however, the pervasive presence of behaviorism in our culture comes to light.

Other books by Skinner reached different audiences. He wrote *Science and Human Behavior* in 1953 for undergraduate students, a book that also helped college faculty members around the country understand the principles of behaviorism. Then *Verbal Behavior* in 1957 reached out to persons in psycholinguistics and literary criticism. His *Technology of Teaching* and *Skinner for the Classroom* reached an audience of teachers, and, indeed, behavioral techniques have become important to the practices of varied fields of education. His best-seller *Beyond Freedom and Dignity* in 1971 sold mightily to the general public. His three-volume autobiography reached the shelves of literature. He wrote *Upon Further Reflection* in 1987 as a set of broadly gauged essays, as he had done with *Reflections on Behaviorism and Society*. His audiences thus stretched from psychology to social science, humanities, and the lay public. He even wrote a technical report for a vital piece of military hardware, as described by James Capshew. All told, Skinner was his own master marketer, acutely aware of the audiences for whom he wrote.

The Artificial Intelligence Debates:
Using and Abusing Skinnerian Language

A recent example of the cultural penetration of Skinnerian behaviorism beyond psychology into other disciplines is its role in modern discourse *about* the sociology of scientific knowledge. Peter Slezak of Australia has argued that the artificial intelligence of computers refutes the behavioristic "strong program" in the sociology of scientific knowledge (SSK). In characterizing the strong program, Slezak wrote:

> Construed as the causal effects of an external (that is, social) stimulus, scientific beliefs are to be taken as analogous to Skinner's "respondents" or "operants." In short, the fundamental insight of the strong programme is that the discovery of scientific theories is to be explained as comparable to a rat's barpressing in response to food pellets![48]

The strong program emphasizes the social origins of science while downplaying internal logical and intrascientific factors. By slotting SSK and behaviorism together, Slezak aimed to contrast their deterministic approach with his "teleological model" of artificial intelligence and to uphold Chomsky's psycholinguistics and the "cognitive revolution."

Behaviorist psychology serves here as a straw man, a rhetorical device used to attack a very powerful school of science studies. Not that the SSK school is monolithic, but Slezak went on to pin his argument ad hominem on one of its chief advocates, David Bloor of Edinburgh. In his book on Wittgenstein, Bloor "confirms what has always been implicit in his strong programme: the notion that theories and beliefs might have external, social causes is essentially a commitment to the stimulus control of behaviour."[49] Never mind that Bloor ignored Skinner and cited Hull's use of Markov chains and Tolman's purposive behavior of animals, specimens of behaviorism from half a century ago. Behaviorism of the Skinnerian vintage finds use as the whipping boy of a computer intelligence advocate against the sociology of scientific knowledge.

Bloor did not reply to this allegation, but two young North Americans did. Steve Fuller, founding editor of the new journal *Social Epistemology,* defended Skinner's *Verbal Behavior* by a new historical line of argument. He attacked the "folk valorization of Chomsky's significance," alluding to Slezak's praise for the rise of psycholinguistics and supposed demise of behaviorism. Fuller replied that

Bloor is to be congratulated for reviving SSK interest in Skinner's *Verbal Behavior,* since it is clear that Chomsky had hardly delved into the work when he wrote the review that launched him into stardom. . . . Lost on Chomsky was the comprehensiveness of Skinner's theory, which incorporated into the behaviourist repertoire the early version of reader-response theory proposed by I. A. Richards as well as the emotivist theories of language use found in logical positivism and general semantics.[50]

This is not surprising, considering that Skinner and Richards were personal friends.[51] Moreover, Fuller confirms the literary approach to Skinner adopted here.

The significant issue for us is rhetorical. A modern social epistemologist discovers in Skinner a progenitor of a social-behavioral theory of language. "In effect, Skinner had made great strides toward 'socializing' the behaviourist bias toward the isolated organism by transforming the concept of a text's 'meaning' into a network of operant responses that has the text as the nodal stimulus, and which in turn enables efficient communication between an author and multiple readers at once."[52]

Beyond identifying behaviorism with SSK (Slezak) and reader-response theory (Fuller), another author contrasts Skinner's work with "cognitive behaviorism." Michael E. Gorman suggests that

behaviourists treated the mind as a "black box" and simply ignored it; Langley, Simon and others at Carnegie Mellon try to study the mind by building one, based on the idea that the fundamental building blocks of thought are production systems.[53]

So here we have three kinds of rhetorical reception of behaviorism: straw man for a dead school of science (Slezak); herald of a new literary direction with social epistemological ramifications (Fuller); and point of departure for a new psychological specialty of artificial intelligence (Gorman). Both sides in this debate overlook the fact that rule-governed behavior has become the central issue for Skinnerians interested in language.[54] But enough said: Skinnerian behaviorism clearly informs the rhetoric in the sociology of scientific knowledge.

Ideology and an East German Reception of Skinner

One of our authors, Daniel W. Bjork, observes that people attack Skinner for opposing the "liberator" heritage of individual freedom. He links Skinner's emphasis on social controls and environment with the "traditionalist" heritage of institutional controls over individuals.[55] Is this ideology or utopia? Perhaps we can come to an answer by considering how critics of fascism and adherents of Freudo-Marxist utopias view behaviorism and Skinner. In doing so, we will see further evidence of the cultural penetration of behaviorism, even beyond the confines of its country of origin.

Behaviorism has long been a pejorative term in certain circles in Europe, as it has often been in the United States.[56] "Behavioral" connotes dehumanization to many ears, especially in Europe. Already in 1936, Karl Mannheim referred to Watsonian behaviorism as "a technique of thought by means of which all that was only meaningfully intelligible was excluded."[57] Obviously he was more concerned with German fascism, leading to his own flight as a Hungarian Jew to England. Perhaps he saw elements of Watsonian social control in Hitler's Reich.

Other critiques of behaviorism as ideology followed. The Frankfurt School psychoanalyst in West Germany, Alfred Mitscherlich, wrote in 1970, "Now the interest in spectacular healing has been displaced from psychoanalysis to behavioral therapy, which makes do with a primitive psychology comparable to hypnosis."[58] The East German Klaus-Peter Noack noted that "the behavioristic program must be conceived as mistaken methodologically since it leaves no space for a dialectical consideration of the relations of inner mental features (e.g., personality characteristics) and observable behavior."[59] Against the perspective of centuries of dialectical thought (since Plato), behaviorism comes across the Atlantic as incredibly naive.

The East German Lothar Bisky subjected neobehavioral mass communications research to extensive criticism, objecting especially to the intervening variable as employed by Carl Hovland on persuasion, R. P. Abelson on attitudes, and Leon Festinger on cognitive dissonance.[60] Bisky does not directly implicate Skinner but attacks neobehaviorism broadly conceived to include American empirical social psychology of the 1950s and 1960s. Serving to clear up possible confusions of Skinner with neobehaviorism is Eckart Scheerer's chapter in this volume.[61]

Marxists were particularly interested in the social behavioral anthropology of George Homans at Harvard, a friend of Skinner who used behavioral ideas. The East German Walter Friedrich alleges that Homans begins "from an ahistorical abstract individual whose behavior is determined by the principle of utility or profit maximization."[62] Skinner is an "ideologist of imperialistic society" who is "theoretically and ideologically programmed to the concept of adaptation of the 'organism' (animal as well as human) to his environment."[63] Skinner allegedly contributed to the economic success of the Federal Republic of Germany through "manipulation strategies."[64] Skinner's most "unreserved propagandist" in West Germany is Werner Correll, who sought "to reduce class struggle, exploitation, social oppression, etc. to the reinforced reactions of individuals"; his objective, concludes Friedrich, is clearly "to stabilize the social system by means of the theory and technology of adapted behavior."[65]

The claims of these East Germans must be understood in the context of their own academic culture, a culture that the unification of Germany and the opening of the Communist world to Western sources has since dismantled.[66] Their own Marxist-Leninist doctrines about the imminent decline of "bourgeois" forms of thought already seem obsolete. Yet similar negative attitudes toward behaviorism continue in Western Europe, posing a challenge to its North American exponents.[67] European culture may underestimate precisely the kind of self-control afforded by behavioral technologies.

The Proliferation of Behaviorism

Behavior analysis has become a field within the discipline of psychology, and as such, one can view it in terms of "the diffusion of knowledge in scientific communities."[68] It participates actively in both academic and professional psychology. Membership in professional associations draws from the psychological community, as well as from medicine, education, social work, and business. In fact, many behavior analysts do not retain membership in the umbrella organization of psychologists, the American Psychological Association (about 80,000 members) and its Division for the Experimental Analysis of Behavior (about 900 members). Instead, they find their professional identity in the small, more active coterie of behavior analysts themselves. The directory of the Association for Behavior Analysis lists some 2,000 members, each of whom receives its journal *The Behavior Analyst*. Countries of origin include Australia, Belgium, Brazil, Canada, Chile, Columbia, Costa Rica, the Dominican Republic, France, Germany, Greece, Iceland, Ireland, Israel, Italy, Japan, Jordan, Korea, Mexico, the Netherlands, New Zealand, Norway, Peru, Portugal, Puerto Rico, Spain, Sweden, the United Kingdom, the United States, Uruguay, and Venezuela.[69]

Journals constitute overlapping networks of official scientific communication. The prestigious mainstream experimental journal of Skinnerian behaviorism is the *Journal of the Experimental Analysis of Behavior,* founded in 1958. Some newer journals cover applications (the *Journal of Applied Behavior Analysis,* since 1968), behavioral biology (*Behavior Analysis Letters,* ed. J. E. R. Staddon, since 1980), and economics (*Behavioral Economics,* ed. Leonard Green, 1980s). In the realm of social activism, a journal once called *Behavior and Social Action* was renamed *Behavior and Social Issues,* while in philosophy the journal *Behaviorism* (ed. Willard Day, then Robert Epstein) received a new name, *Behavior and Philosophy,* under new editorship (George Graham, then Max Hocutt). Not all journals with "behavior" in the title are Skinnerian, however. Outside of the special-interest journals just cited lie other behavioral journals in clinical practice (*Behavior Therapy,* ed. Cyril Franks, 1970; *Behavior Modification,* 1977), personality testing (*Behavioural Research and Therapy,* 1963, ed. Hans Eysenck), sociobiology (*Behavior Genetics,* 1971), and ethology (*Behaviour,* 1964). On the margins are *Behavioral Medicine,* the *Journal of Pharmacology and Experimental Therapeutics,* and *Psychopharmacologia.*

Training sites for applied behavior analysis serve not only to bring practitioners to the marketplace but to give authority to experimental programs. The Universities of Kansas and Western Michigan have earned reputations in this regard, and private facilities exist in Florida, Massachusetts, and elsewhere. Psychology departments for studying the experimental analysis of behavior include Columbia University, Duke University, Indiana University, the State University of New York at Stony Brook, the University of New Hampshire, the University of Arizona, Temple University, the University of Pennsylvania, the University of California at San Diego, and many more. The University of Nevada at Reno upholds the wing of "interactional behaviorism," inspired by Jacob Kantor. The University of West Virginia espouses behavior analysis in education and verbal behavior. Marvin Harris stands for behavioral anthropology at the University of Florida.

Fostering public interest beyond the scientific community is the Cambridge Center for Advancement of Behavioral Studies. Spawned in tribute to Skinner, this institution exists through the patronage of friends of behaviorism. Its mandate is a publicist one: (1) to advance applied and basic research, and (2) to apply behavioral analysis on behalf of human well-being. For example, it offers workshops on topics of general interest.

CONCLUSION

Science and practice are inextricably bound to specific local contexts. Experiments and clinics, while undeniably local, serve larger goals. Skinner's operant chamber far transcends its homely beginnings, and its modern-day exponents have long since abandoned the single-key chambers of the 1950s for multiple keys and computer-controlled experimental events. The goal has remained, though, to advance human welfare. Far from awaiting a distant utopia, Skinner succeeded in bringing his ideas into widespread discourse. His rejection of the narrowly physicalist language of Watsonian behaviorism in favor of the biological idiom of action and consequence helped bring behaviorism into the mainstream of Ameri-

can pragmatism.[70] From there, it has won a voice in the paramount contemporary debate—how we can cooperate globally to bring about
appropriate technologies to sustain life on Earth.[71]

The adherents of dialectical and empirical philosophies alike have perhaps slighted one key to the behaviorism of Skinner. The linguistic foundations of behaviorism have gone virtually unnoticed, despite the fact
that Skinner worked continuously on them for over two decades. He
continually returned to words. In employing the insights of literary analysis, Skinner emphasized audience reactions; he himself wrote to exert
specific effects on his readers and listeners.

If we want to understand the proliferation of behaviorism in modern
culture, we do well to consider the individual texts that Skinner wrote,
as well as their audiences. We also need to understand how the local
knowledge of operant laboratories came to be transformed into social
instruments and utopian appeals. This book offers a step in that direction.

NOTES

1. Undergraduate public opinion incorrectly considers Skinner an advocate
of aversive social controls. My colleague Peter S. Fernald helped me to appreciate
that Skinner, in *Walden Two,* tried to remove aversive control. In a sense, Skinner
agreed with Freud's view of the importance of eliminating early childhood trauma.
Skinner's rejection of punishment as an effective procedure in applied settings
has been widely endorsed by other behavioral scientists, partly on the grounds
that the emotional responses it evokes interfere with the acquisition of beneficial
responses. However, Skinner's early skepticism about the effectiveness of punishment even in controlled laboratory settings has not been borne out by subsequent
research; see John A. Nevin, "Research: Recent Advances in the Experimental
Analysis of Behavior," in *Progress in Behavioral Studies,* vol. 1, ed. Aaron J.
Brownstein (Hillsdale, N.J.: Erlbaum, 1989), pp. 18–28. Skinner's views of punishment are laid out in his *Science and Human Behavior* (New York: Macmillan,
Free Press, 1953), chap. 12.

2. Laurence D. Smith, *Behaviorism and Logical Positivism: A Reassessment
of the Alliance* (Stanford, Calif.: Stanford University Press, 1986); Thomas H.
Leahey, "More Mythinformation Corrected," review of *Behaviorism and Logical
Positivism,* by Laurence D. Smith, *Behaviorism* 16 (1988): 163–66. Skinner himself considered metaphors acceptable in literature but not in science, even though
his own scientific writings contained numerous metaphorical expressions. See
Smith, "Metaphors of Knowledge and Behavior in the Behaviorist Tradition," in
Metaphors in the History of Psychology, ed. David E. Leary (Cambridge: Cambridge University Press, 1990), pp. 239–66, on p. 262; and A. J. Soyland, *Psychology as Metaphor* (London: Sage, 1994).

3. Fortunately, a superb biography by one of our authors does address family
and cultural milieu: Daniel W. Bjork, *B. F. Skinner: A Life* (New York: Basic,
1993). Cf. David Jackson, *Unmasking Masculinity* (Boston and London: Unwin
Hyman, 1990), especially p. 272; and Victor Seidler, *Rediscovering Masculinity:
Reason, Language, and Sexuality* (London: Routledge, 1989).

4. Skinner, "A Case History in Scientific Method," *American Psychologist* 11 (1956): 221–23; Skinner, *Particulars of My Life* (New York: Knopf, 1976); Skinner, *The Shaping of a Behaviorist* (New York: Knopf, 1979); Skinner, *A Matter of Consequences* (New York: Knopf, 1983).

5. Skinner was, of course, not unlike other men of his time in this respect. Ursula Owen (*Fathers: Reflections by Daughters* [New York: Pantheon, 1983]) writes of her own father, "I recognised that much of this vulnerability lay in the fact that, like many men, he seemed ill at ease with his own emotions" (p. ix). Cf. Jackson, *Unmasking Masculinity,* especially chaps. 4 and 8.

6. Jeffrey Meyers, introduction to *The Craft of Literary Biography,* ed. Jeffrey Meyers (New York: Macmillan, 1985), p. 2.

7. Author's interview with Yvonne Blue Skinner, 19 December 1988, who long ago chose to call herself Eve.

8. Rhonda K. Bjork, "The Personal Culture of Yvonne Blue Skinner," this volume; Nils Wiklander, "From Hamilton College to Walden Two: An Inquiry into Skinner's Early Social Philosophy," this volume; E. A. Vargas and Julie S. Vargas, "B. F. Skinner and the Origins of Programmed Instruction," this volume.

9. Author's interviews with Skinner, October and December 1988, and May 1989.

10. Skinner, "Outlining a Science of Feeling," *London Times Literary Supplement,* 8 May 1987; reprinted as "The Place of Feeling in the Analysis of Behavior," in Skinner, *Recent Issues in the Analysis of Behavior* (Columbus, Ohio: Merrill, 1989), pp. 3–11. On Skinner's practical jokes, see Skinner, *Particulars,* pp. 235–38; and Skinner, *Shaping,* pp. 337–38. His offer to his thesis committee is described in Skinner, *Shaping,* pp. 74–75.

11. On Skinner's iconoclasm, see S. R. Coleman, "B. F. Skinner: Systematic Iconoclast," *The Gamut* 6 (1982): 53–75.

12. Somerset Maugham, quoted in John A. Weigel, *B. F. Skinner* (Boston: G. K. Hall, 1977), pp. 68–69.

13. As our author Nils Wiklander remarked to me after visiting him the day before his death. Cf. Julie S. Vargas, "B. F. Skinner—The Last Few Days," *Journal of the Experimental Analysis of Behavior* 55 (1991): 1–2.

14. Peter Galison, *How Experiments End* (Chicago: University of Chicago Press, 1987); David Gooding, Trevor Pinch, and Simon Schaffer, eds., *The Uses of Experiment: Studies in the Natural Sciences* (Cambridge: Cambridge University Press, 1989).

15. Karin Knorr-Cetina, *The Manufacture of Knowledge. An Essay on the Constructivist and Contextual Nature of Science* (Oxford: Pergamon Press, 1981) [German trans. *Die Fabrikation von Erkenntnis: Zur Anthropologie der Wissenschaft* (Frankfurt: Suhrkamp, 1984)]; cf. Bruno Latour and Steve Woolgar, *Laboratory Life: The Construction of Scientific Facts* (London: Sage, 1979); see the reprint (Princeton: Princeton University Press, 1986, pp. 45–53) for an exposition of "literary inscriptions."

16. S. R. Coleman, "Quantitative Order in B. F. Skinner's Early Research Program, 1928–1931," *Behavior Analyst* 10 (1987): 47–65; Coleman, "Skinner's Progress During the 1930s: Reflexes, Operants, and Apparatuses," this volume.

17. Richard J. Herrnstein, "Reminiscences Already?" *Journal of the Experimental Analysis of Behavior* 48 (1987): 448–53.

18. Kurt Danziger, *Constructing the Subject: Historical Origins of Psychological Research* (Cambridge: Cambridge University Press, 1990), p. 246 n. 26. Cf. James H. Capshew, "Engineering Behavior: Project Pigeon, World War II, and

the Conditioning of B. F. Skinner," this volume; and Daniel W. Bjork, "B. F. Skinner and the American Tradition: The Scientist as Social Inventor," this volume. See Skinner, "Why Are We Not Acting to Save the World?" in *Upon Further Reflection* (Englewood Cliffs, N.J.: Prentice-Hall, 1986), pp. 1–14.

19. Nikolas Rose, "Engineering the Human Soul: Analyzing Psychological Expertise" (paper presented at the annual meeting of Cheiron-Europe, September 1990); expanded in Nikolas Rose, *Governing the Soul: The Shaping of the Private Self* (London: Routledge, 1990).

20. Likewise, Skinner's long involvement with building and refining teaching machines began when he visited his daughter's classroom at the Shady Hill School in Cambridge and observed the inefficiency of classroom learning. See Vargas and Vargas, "Origins of Programmed Instruction," this volume.

21. The archival correspondence on this subject at the Harvard University Archives is extensive.

22. Cf. Harry Collins, *Changing Order: Replication and Induction in Scientific Practice* (London: Sage, 1985). Cf. Ian Lubek, "Neo-Behaviorism and the Garcia Effect: A Social Psychology of Science Approach to the History of a Paradigm Clash," in *Psychology in Twentieth-Century Thought and Society,* ed. Mitchell G. Ash and William R. Woodward (Cambridge: Cambridge University Press, 1987), pp. 59–91.

23. Jan V. Golinski, "The Theory of Practice and the Practice of Theory: Sociological Approaches in the History of Science," *Isis* 81 (1990): 492–505.

24. Joseph Rouse, *Knowledge and Power: Toward a Political Philosophy of Science* (Ithaca, N.Y.: Cornell University Press, 1987), pp. 95, 112; see also in ibid., chap. 1, introduction, pp. 1–25, and chap. 4, "Local Knowledge," pp. 69–126.

25. Skinner, *The Behavior of Organisms: An Experimental Analysis* (New York: Appleton-Century, 1938).

26. See Gordon Fyfe and John Law, eds., *Picturing Power: Visual Depiction and Social Relations* (London: Routledge, 1988).

27. On the use of visual displays in scientific rhetoric, see Alan G. Gross, *The Rhetoric of Science* (Cambridge: Harvard University Press, 1990), pp. 74–80.

28. Carole Wade and Carol Tavris, *Psychology,* 2d ed. (New York: Harper, 1990); Henry Gleitman, *Psychology,* 3d ed. (New York: Norton, 1990).

29. Skinner, "Has Gertrude Stein a Secret?" *Atlantic Monthly* 153 (January 1934): 50–57; reprinted in *Cumulative Record,* enl. ed. (New York: Appleton-Century-Crofts, 1961), pp. 261–71. On Frost's encouragement of Skinner's literary ambitions, see Skinner, *Particulars,* pp. 227–28, 248–51.

30. Skinner, "The Motivation of the Student," in *The Technology of Teaching* (New York: Appleton-Century-Crofts, 1968), pp. 145–68, on pp. 146, 147.

31. Hans Robert Jauss, *Aesthetic Experience and Literary Hermeneutics,* trans. Michael Shaw (Minneapolis: University of Minnesota Press, 1982), pp. 34–36. On the thespian experience of Fred Skinner, see the transcript of my 1988 interview with Eve Skinner.

32. Susan R. Suleiman, introduction to *The Reader in the Text: Essays on Audience and Interpretation,* ed. Susan R. Suleiman and Inge Crosman (Princeton: Princeton University Press, 1980), pp. 5, 27–29.

33. Frederick C. Crews, "Literature, the Art of Literary Criticism," *Encyclopedia Brittanica,* Macropedia, vol. 23, pp. 202–7. On Richards's view of literature and linguistic analysis as a source of salvation, see John Paul Russo, "I. A. Richards in Retrospect," *Critical Inquiry* 8 (1982): 743–60, especially pp. 744–46.

34. Terry J. Knapp, "Beyond *Verbal Behavior,*" *Behaviorism* 8 (1980): 187–94, on p. 191.

35. C. K. Ogden and I. A. Richards, *The Meaning of Meaning* (New York: Harcourt, 1938), pp. 9–10 (original work published 1923). Skinner's affinity for the approach laid out by Ogden and Richards no doubt stemmed from its adoption of a behaviorist slant on literary criticism. On the friendship between Richards and Skinner, see n. 51.

36. Jane P. Tompkins, introduction to *Reader-Response Criticism: From Formalism to Post-Structuralism,* ed. Jane P. Tompkins (Baltimore, Md.: Johns Hopkins University Press, 1984).

37. Robert C. Holub, *Reception Theory: A Critical Introduction* (London: Methuen, 1984), pp. xii–xiii. Note especially chap. 7 on "The Audience" in Skinner, *Verbal Behavior* (New York: Appleton-Century-Crofts, 1957), pp. 172–84.

38. See, for example, Skinner, "The Alliteration in Shakespeare's Sonnets: A Study in Literary Behavior," *Psychological Record* 3 (1939): 186–92.

39. Skinner, "A Lecture on 'Having a Poem'," in *Cumulative Record,* 3d ed. (New York: Appleton-Century-Crofts, 1972), pp. 345–55. Cf. Skinner, "How to Discover What You Have to Say—A Talk to Students," in *Upon Further Reflection* (Englewood Cliffs, N.J.: Prentice-Hall, 1986), pp. 131–43. On Skinner's having written for an effect on his readership, see the epilogue of *Verbal Behavior.*

> Stating the matter in the most selfish light, I have been trying to get the reader to behave verbally as I behave. What teacher, writer, or friend does not? . . . [My analysis] seems to me to be a better way of talking about verbal behavior, and that is why I have tried to get the reader to talk about it in this way too. But have I told him the truth? Who can say? A science of verbal behavior probably makes no provision for truth or certainty (but we cannot even be certain of the truth of that). (pp. 455–66)

See also Skinner's anecdote in *Shaping.*

> The question of truth had come up years before when I was discussing my thesis with Boring. I had said that I was not writing to state truths but to have an effect on my reader. He sent me a note the next day telling me that he was shocked. But my subsequent analysis led to much the same conclusion. Wittgenstein would later say the same thing: "I am in a sense making propaganda for one style of thinking as opposed to another." (p. 336)

For a more recent analysis of the effects of verbal behavior on audiences, see Skinner, "The Listener," in *Recent Issues in Behavior,* pp. 35–47.

40. Bronislaw Malinowski, "The Problem of Meaning in Primitive Languages," appendix in Ogden and Richards, *Meaning of Meaning,* pp. 296–336, cited in n. 35. See the citation in Skinner, *Verbal Behavior,* p. 432.

41. In *Verbal Behavior* alone, Skinner cited the literary critics I. A. Richards, Ezra Pound, T. S. Eliot, George Rylands, H. W. Fowler, William Empson, A. E. Housman, and L. P. Smith. He referred to the logicians Rudolph Carnap, Bertrand Russell, Gilbert Ryle, and W. V. Quine. In the field of language and behavior, he acknowledged Niko Tinbergen, Karl von Frisch, Grace DeLaguna, Florence Goodenough, Sigmund Freud, Carl G. Jung, and R. A. Paget.

42. Skinner, *Behavior of Organisms,* p. 438.

43. Rose, *Governing the Soul.*

44. Skinner, *Behavior of Organisms,* p. 441. Laurence D. Smith, "On Prediction

and Control: B. F. Skinner and the Technological Ideal of Science," *American Psychologist* 47 (1992): 216–23.

45. B. F. Skinner, *Walden Two* (New York: Macmillan, 1976), p. 241 (original work published 1948).

46. Laurence D. Smith, "Knowledge as Power: The Baconian Roots of Skinner's Social Meliorism," this volume.

47. Several of my conversations with Skinner attest to this pessimism. Cf. Thomas McCarthy, "Private Irony and Public Decency," *Critical Inquiry* 16 (1990): 355–70. For other examples of behaviorists who find grounds for pessimism (though not unalloyed) on the prospects for behaviorist social reform, see James A. Dinsmoor, "Setting the Record Straight: The Social Views of B. F. Skinner," *American Psychologist* 47 (1992): 1454–63; and Richard F. Rakos, "Achieving the Just Society in the 21st Century: What Can Skinner Contribute?" *American Psychologist* 47 (1992): 1499–1506.

48. Peter Slezak, "Scientific Discovery by Computer as Empirical Refutation of the Strong Programme," *Social Studies of Science* 19 (1989): 563–600, on p. 590.

49. Ibid., p. 591. Cf. David Bloor, *Wittgenstein: A Social Theory of Knowledge* (New York: Columbia University Press, 1983).

50. Steve Fuller, "Of Conceptual Intersections and Verbal Collisions: Towards the Routing of Slezak," *Social Studies of Science* 19 (1989): 625–38, on p. 631.

51. Aspects of the friendship between I. A. Richards and Skinner are recorded in Skinner, *Shaping*, pp. 92, 125, 130, 213, 334; Skinner, *Matter of Consequences*, pp. 39, 142, 231–33, 254, 347.

52. Fuller, "Routing of Slezak," p. 631. Cf. Fuller, *Social Epistemology* (Bloomington: Indiana University Press, 1988).

53. Michael E. Gorman, "Beyond Strong Programmes: How Cognitive Approaches Can Complement SSK," *Social Studies of Science* 19 (1989): 643–53, on p. 647.

54. See, for example, Peter Slezak, "Computers, Contents and Causes: Replies to My Respondents," *Social Studies of Science* 19 (1989): 671–95. Seemingly oblivious to the Skinnerian concept of rule-governed behavior, Slezak answered his respondents by defending Chomsky's review of Skinner's *Verbal Behavior* as "a line-by-line, page-by-page criticism," calling it "a successful demonstration of the vacuity of Skinner's theory," and praising Herbert Simon for having helped to bring about the downfall of behaviorism (hence also ignoring Gorman's depiction of Simon's work as a horse of a different color, more akin to behaviorism than to artificial intelligence). Slezak explained that Chomsky's Cartesianism, like Simon's artificial intelligence program BACON, depends on "internally represented formal rules" to provide the grammatical constraints within which creativity must operate. For a recent exposition of Skinner's notion of rule-governed behavior, see Marc N. Richelle, *B. F. Skinner: A Reappraisal* (Hillsdale, N.J.: Erlbaum, 1993), chap. 11.

55. Bjork, "Skinner and the American Tradition," this volume.

56. Sven-Eric Liedmann, *Arbetsfördelning självmord och nytta* (Division of labor, suicide and value) (Örebro, Sweden: Högskolan, 1983). This slights the very pervasive impact of behavioral therapy in Europe. See Angela Schorr, *Die Verhaltenstherapie: Ihre Geschichte von den Anfängen bis zur Gegenwart* (Behavior therapy: Its history from the beginning to the present) (Weinheim, Germany: Beltz, 1984). See also Christoph Kraiker, ed., *Handbuch der Verhaltenstherapie* (Handbook of behavior therapy) (Munich: Kindler, 1974). For a bibliography of

German translations of Skinner's works, see Eckart Scheerer, *Die Verhaltensanalyse* (Behavior analysis) (Heidelberg, Germany: Springer, 1983), pp. 178–92.

57. Karl Mannheim, *Ideology and Utopia: An Introduction to the Sociology of Knowledge*, trans. Louis Wirth and Edward Shils (New York: Harcourt, 1936) p. 43 (original work published 1929).

58. Alfred Mitscherlich, 1970, p. 126, cited in Christoph Kraiker, "Bemerkungen über die empirischen und theoretischen Grundlagen der Verhaltenstherapie" (Comments on the empirical and theoretical foundations of behavior therapy), in *Handbuch der Verhaltenstherapie*, ed. Christoph Kraiker (Munich: Kindler, 1974), p. 11.

59. Klaus-Peter Noack, "Zur Kritik der Methodologie des Behaviorismus" (Toward a critique of the methodology of behaviorism), in *Zur Kritik des Behaviorismus*, ed. Walter Friedrich et al., (Cologne, Germany: Pahl-Rugenstein Verlag, 1979), pp. 66–197.

60. Lothar Bisky, "Uber den Neobehaviorismus in der bürgerlichen Kommunikationsforschung" (On neobehaviorism in bourgeois communication research), in ibid., p. 284. Cf. Lothar Bisky, *Zur Kritik der bürgerlichen Massenkommunikationsforschung* (Toward a critique of bourgeois mass communication research) (Berlin: Deutscher Verlag der Wissenschaften, 1976).

61. Eckart Scheerer, "Radical Behaviorism: Excerpts From a Textbook Treatment," this volume.

62. Walter Friedrich, "Zur Lerntheorie Skinners und zu ihrer Rezeption in den bürgerlichen Sozialwissenschaften" (On Skinner's learning theory and its reception in bourgeois social sciences), in *Zur Kritik des Behaviorismus*, pp. 227–28. Friedrich cites George Homans, *The Human Group* (London: Routledge & Kegan Paul, 1951) [German trans. *Theorie der sozialen Gruppe*, 1960] and Homans, *Social Behavior: Its Elementary Forms* (New York: Harcourt, 1961) [German trans. *Elementarformen sozialen Verhaltens* (Cologne, Germany: Opladen, 1972)].

63. Friedrich, "Zur Lerntheorie Skinners," in *Zur Kritik des Behaviorismus*, p. 199.

64. Ibid., p. 201.

65. Ibid., pp. 220–21. Cf. Werner Correll, *Denken und Lernen: Beiträge der Lernforschung zur Methodik des Unterrichts* (Thought and learning: Contributions of learning research to instructional method) (Braunschweig, Germany: Georg Westermann Verlag, 1967); Skinner, *The Technology of Teaching* [German trans. *Erziehung als Verhaltensformung*, introduction by Werner Correll (München-Neubiberg, Germany: E. Keimer Verlag, 1971)] (Englewood Cliffs, N.J.: Prentice-Hall, 1968).

66. William R. Woodward, "How GDR Science Studies Contributed to the Fall of the Wall," in *World Views and Scientific Discipline Formation*, ed. William R. Woodward and Robert S. Cohen (Dordrecht, The Netherlands: Kluwer, 1991). An example of an excellent introductory psychology textbook with a sophisticated treatment of behavior analysis is the textbook by Roger Brown and Richard J. Herrnstein, which appeared in German in the 1980s.

67. For a sampling of Europeans' harsh verdicts on behaviorism, see Richelle, *A Reappraisal*, pp. 4–5. Richelle's own comments are instructive. "European critics often discard Skinner's contribution as a typical product of American society, which does not fit in the context of European culture, or that should be looked at with suspicion in order to avoid contamination" (p. 5). Richelle adds that these critics "tend to ignore the fact that, like it or not, things which originate

in the USA eventually invade Europe sooner or later . . . only because of a persistent European illusion of being at the start of everything important" (p. 6).

68. Diana Crane, *Invisible Colleges: Diffusion of Knowledge in Scientific Communities* (Chicago: University of Chicago Press, 1972); David Krantz, "Schools and Systems: The Mutual Isolation of Operant and Non-Operant Psychology as a Case Study," *Journal of the History of the Behavioral Sciences* 8 (1972), 86–102; reprinted in Mary Henle, Julian Jaynes, and John J. Sullivan, eds., *Historical Conceptions of Psychology* (New York: Springer, 1973), pp. 116–28.

69. For an interesting indication of the diffusion of Skinnerian behaviorism to parts of the Arab world, see Jamal M. S. Yousef, "Arabic Students' Understanding of Skinner's Radical Behaviorism," *Psychological Reports* 71 (1992): 51–56. According to Yousef, Skinner is discussed and mentioned by name in 14 of 20 recently published Arabic introductory psychology textbooks. However, in contrast with Freud (most of whose books have, perhaps surprisingly, been translated into Arabic), *Beyond Freedom and Dignity* is the only book by Skinner to have appeared in Arabic translation.

70. Smith, *Behaviorism and Logical Positivism*.

71. See the discussion in Smith, "Skinner and the Technological Ideal"; Smith, "Natural Science and Unnatural Technology," *American Psychologist* 48 (1993): 588–89; and Smith, "Situating B. F. Skinner and Behaviorism in American Culture," this volume.

B. F. Skinner
and Behaviorism
in American Culture

Part One
Skinner as Social Philosopher

1

B. F. Skinner and the American Tradition: The Scientist as Social Inventor

Daniel W. Bjork

At the conclusion of his three-volume autobiography B. F. Skinner wrote, "by tracing what I have done to my environmental history rather than assigning it to a mysterious, creative process, I have relinquished all chance of being called a Great Thinker."[1] Perhaps. Few commentators would presently place him among such Old World luminaries as Plato, Aristotle, Newton, Marx, Darwin, and Freud. But Skinner may already be a "Great" American, a figure whose science and social innovations evoke a fundamental reassessment of what we imagine to be our native traditions.

I would like to propose that the criticism of Skinner by a sizable group of American academics and intellectuals is culturally and intellectually significant, for such generally negative opinion suggests that Skinner—regardless of the truth or error of his position—has touched something that focuses attention on much that is worth knowing about American values, or more concretely, the American predicament. My object is not so much to support or critique Skinner as to juxtapose his science and social perspective against the traditions that his detractors claim they are defending—traditions that are understood as being within a broad American humanitarian past. To begin to understand Skinner's legacy within a larger American intellectual context, a short historical digression is necessary.

The Ideologies of Memory and Hope

The discussion of American thinkers whatever their literary philosophical, scientific, political, or social persuasion is obviously a complex matter; the divergences of content, emphasis, and era are subtle and important. Yet an argument can be ventured that even given this formidable array of particulars major generalizations are still possible and are indeed worth making.

The literary historian R. W. B. Lewis, taking his cue from Ralph Waldo Emerson, maintained that nineteenth-century American thinkers were divided into two camps, "a split in culture between two polarized parties: 'the party of the Past and the party of the Future,' . . . or the parties 'of Memory and Hope.'" Lewis went on to suggest that before the Civil War these two "parties" carried on a fruitful national dialogue with each other in politics and literature. But since that great conflict one party had emerged triumphant.

> The dismissal of the past has been only too effective: America, since the age of Emerson, has been persistently a one-generation culture. Successive generations have given rise to a series of staccato intellectual and literary movements with ever slighter trajectories. . . . We regularly return, decade after decade and with the same pain and amazement, to all the old conflicts, programs and discoveries. We consume our powers in hoisting back to the plane of understanding reached a century ago and at intervals since.[2]

On the eve of the Civil War "the party of hope," or as I would like to call them, the liberators, was in command. It did not matter whether one had the transcendental perspective of an Emerson or the reformist stance of a William Lloyd Garrison: their intellectual and social victory over the "party of memory," which I call the traditionalists, seemed complete.

The crux of the issue between the two groups was the place of institutions in society, or rather the relationship of the individual to institutions. The liberators insisted that institutions and by implication, society, corrupted the individual. Ideally, the free individual was in a position to make correct moral choices and in time, one by one, could perfect society. But the traditionalists argued that history showed the free individual to be a menace to social health. Only if individuals were restrained within institutional boundaries could a beneficial society be maintained. Few intellectuals in the North were listening: American individualism reigned supreme.[3]

The crisis of the Civil War itself, however, gave the traditionalists renewed intellectual and social leverage. As the historian George Fredrickson has illustrated, the sheer magnitude of the conflict, the necessity of an "organized response to suffering," revived the authority of the traditionalists' social dictates. The industrialists who shaped a modern America owed far more to the traditionalist plea for institutional discipline, order, and efficiency than to the liberator cry for anti–institutional individualism and Good Samaritan humanitarianism.[4]

The liberators, however, were only temporarily routed. Persistent advocates of individualistic humanitarianism such as Mark Twain, William James, and Horatio Alger kept this perspective in the near background, while advocates of a more socially oriented and politically active creed such as Edward Bellamy, Henry George, and Lester Frank Ward injected a new social vision into the liberator ranks. Indeed, the social-reform frame of reference seemed to provide a fresh format for interpreting the American scene.[5] Yet despite these social innovators, a humanitarian individualism was still the bedrock of the social creeds of liberator-oriented American intellectuals. By the early twentieth century, American individualism was defended more and more as a birthright, a heritage, and an indelible national traditional, regardless of how far the liberators wanted to extend social reform. Two world wars, a great depression, and looming environmental, population, and nuclear crises have not diminished the liberator dominance. Indeed, the ideology of individualism is stronger than ever.[6]

SKINNER AND THE AMERICAN DIALOGUE

Skinner is maligned for being against the liberator heritage that puts individualized expectations for justice, equality, and the good life at the forefront of the truly American and humanitarian ethic; he is rarely attacked as a defender of individualism.[7] Usually, he is criticized as being the enemy of the individual's creative role in society. As one of Skinner's earliest critics, Joseph Wood Krutch, remarked in the early 1950s, *Walden Two* "for all practical purposes [made] man . . . merely the product of society."[8] And the psychologist Carl Rogers in a Skinner-Rogers symposium in 1956 echoed Krutch by approvingly quoting John Dewey, one of the most visible twentieth-century liberators. "Science has made its way by releasing, not by suppressing, the elements of variation, of novel creation in individuals."[9]

Not all liberator critics have been so restrained. Ayn Rand, the late philosopher-novelist, aimed pure invective at *Beyond Freedom and Dignity*. She likened it to "Boris Karloff's embodiment of Frankenstein's monster: a corpse patched with nuts, bolts and screws from the junkyard of philosophy, Darwinism, Positivism, Linguistic Analysis, with some nails by Hume, threads by Russell, and glue by the *New York Post*." Carrying the unflattering analogy a bit further, she concluded that "the book's voice, like Karloff's, is an emission of inarticulate moaning growls—directed at a special enemy: 'Autonomomous Man.'" Skinner was obsessed with a "hatred of man's mind and virtue (with everything they entail: reason, achievement, independence, enjoyment, moral pride, self-esteem)—so intense and consuming a hatred that it consumes itself,

and what we read is only its gray ashes, with feeble, snickering obsceni-
ties (such as the title) as a few last smoking, stinking coals."[10] Such unqualified language of destruction suggests that Skinner had reminded
Rand of other historical conditions, conditions in which "autonomous
man" was regarded as dangerous to social health—an article of faith
among socialists with whom Rand also quarreled.[11]

If Skinner is placed in the broad context of an ongoing dialogue between liberators and traditionalists in American intellectual history, the
negative reactions to his social thinking become more culturally understandable.[12] By the same measure, Skinner's own social thinking takes on
a distinctive cultural coloring. He may in fact serve to remind many
American thinkers that the traditionalist perspective—now operating in
the guise of behavioral science—has not yet been thoroughly routed.
For Skinner, knowingly or unknowingly, forces a reconsideration of the
essential ingredient in the traditionalist perspective—the older view that
pushes back through the expansive nineteenth century to the Republican
eighteenth and Puritan seventeenth centuries, back to American efforts
to build into the fabric of their New World society the obligation of civic
duty and social responsibility.

This is a venerable American theme. Puritan jeremiads and Republican
moral tirades warned repeatedly against the loss of social cohesion. Ex-
hortations defending society *as* social responsibility were delivered as
part and parcel of an ideology that emphasized that the American future
was nothing if not the fulfillment of a sacred social mission—whether to
establish a "city on a hill" or Republican virtue.[13]

Skinner's social utopia, *Walden Two,* suggests a return to the older
tradition of social responsibility. As Frazier, the committed leader of the
fictional community remarked, "By a careful cultural design, we control
not the final behavior, but the *inclination* to behave—the motives, the
desires, the wishes. The curious thing is that in that case *the question of
freedom never arises.*"[14] If the Puritan clergy had heard such a pro-
nouncement they undoubtedly would have been pleased. Yet for the liberators the question of the "desire" or "wish" for freedom not only must
arise, it must be at the very heart of the meaning of America's future and
the interpretation of her past. It is not simply Skinner's behavioral science
but his social intention of replacing individualism with social responsibility—a vision which the liberators have largely rejected since at least the
late eighteenth century—that irritates, even infuriates critics.

Consider, for example, Skinner's concluding comments in *Beyond Freedom and Dignity* (1971). Death was "the final assault on freedom and
dignity," the last affront to the individual. And at the end of life,

> the individualist can find no solace in reflecting upon any contribution which
> will survive him. He has refused to act for the good of others and is therefore

not reinforced by the fact that others whom he has helped will outlive him. He has refused to be concerned for the survival of his culture and is not reinforced by the fact that the culture will long survive him. In defense of his own freedom and dignity he has denied the contributions of the past and must therefore relinquish all claim upon the future.

"Science," he concluded, "has probably never demanded a more sweeping change in the traditional way of thinking about a subject [i.e., society], nor has there ever been a more important subject."[15] In effect, Skinner seems to be asking behavioral science to de-emphasize the prevailing self-indulgence of liberator individualism and thereby return to an American past in which the individual behaved in ways that benefited the well-being of the social whole.

But such a past was never firmly established. The emphasis on self-sacrifice for the social whole was slipping away even as it was being defended.[16] Skinner's implicit appeal to a New World social past that never sank long-lasting American roots can be understood as a rather exceptional contemporary lament that echoes the jeremiads of Puritan clergy. Skinner takes his place beside the likes of Cotton Mather, John Adams, George Templeton Strong, Henry Demarest Lloyd, Jane Addams, and Norman Thomas who—despite considerable temporal and philosophical differences—all wanted individualism to be subsumed for the greater good of society. The further one travels from the seventeenth century, the less real appeal this social vision has. The liberator position is now so entrenched that the very mention of these personages together evokes quaintness and makes it tempting to treat Skinner as an anachronism.

But Skinner would not want to return to a society in which social responsibility was maintained through aversive control, the very controls that the liberators throughout much of American history had fought to eliminate. He would maintain, as he did in *Science and Human Behavior* (1953), that controls were never really absent. "A doctrine of personal freedom appeals to anyone to whom release from coercive control is important." Nonetheless, "we all control, and we are all controlled. As human behavior is further analyzed, control will become more effective. Sooner or later the problem must be faced."[17]

Inexorably bound with the problem of control, however, was the matter of building for future social responsibility; and Skinner insisted that in order to achieve the latter the former need not be removed but shaped through arranging environmental contingencies in socially desirable ways. "The important thing is that institutions last longer than individuals and arrange contingencies which take a reasonably remote future into account."[18] Yet to the liberators the plea for social control was more easily associated with long-standing opposition to those individuals and groups who manipulated power—a theme that has obsessed American intellectuals and politicians from before the American Revolution.[19]

Carl Rogers struck at the heart of the liberator concern when he remarked, "I believe that in Skinner's presentation here [the 1956 symposium] and in his previous writings, there is a serious underestimation of the problem of power." Rogers's own understanding of recent history was juxtaposed against Skinner's historical naïveté.

> To hope that the power which is being made available by the behavioral sciences will be exercised by the scientists . . . seems to me a hope little supported by either recent or distant history. It seems far more likely that behavioral scientists, holding their present attitudes, will be in the position of German rocket scientists specializing in guided missiles. First they worked devotedly for Hitler to destroy the U.S.S.R. and the United States. Now, . . . they worked devotedly for the U.S.S.R. in the interest of destroying the United States, or devotedly for the United States in the interest of destroying the U.S.S.R. If behavioral scientists are concerned solely with advancing their science, it seems most probable that they will serve the purposes of whatever individual or group has the power.[20]

In the Cold War atmosphere of the mid-1950s Rogers's concern about government manipulation of scientists of whatever persuasion or however well-meaning had special force.

But Skinner was not put off by the question of power. The end of behavioral engineering was social survival, and social survival implied social responsibility. The major issue was not *who* had the power, but *how* society was to be shaped. "'Who *should* control?'" Skinner asserted in 1953 "is a spurious question. . . . If we look to the long-term effect upon the group the question becomes, 'Who should control if the culture is to survive?'" This was the equivalent of asking "Who *will* control in the group which does survive?"[21] Hence, it is the survival of the group— "the culture"—that is the larger issue. The intent to use science to insure group survival linked Skinner to the long-standing American concern about using power to shape social destiny. And Skinner was partly misleading when he concluded his debate with Rogers by claiming, "We look to the future, not the past, for the test of goodness or acceptability."[22]

THE SCIENTIST AS INVENTOR

While Skinner's public reputation as a social critic climaxed with the reaction to *Beyond Freedom and Dignity,* his interest in social engineering seemed to appear quite suddenly in the summer of 1945 when in a "white heat" of zeal he wrote *Walden Two*.[23] Actually, he had some interest in social questions in the 1920s and 1930s.[24] Nonetheless, the slightly more than two decades between his most widely recognized publications, 1948–71, were the crucial years in the development of his social perspective. This was the period in which he and other radical behaviorists began to apply the laws of behavior discovered in rats and pigeons during the 1930s and 1940s to humans.

Skinner once stated that his most significant accomplishment lay perhaps not so much in discovering the laws of operant conditioning as in his career as a social inventor.[25] This is important not only because it confirms the obvious shift from experimental work with rats and pigeons to humans, but also because it indicates that a more in-depth understanding of Skinner's professional career may need another emphasis. To interpret him simply as a "psychologist," a "behaviorist," or a "scientist" misleads if he also understood himself as a social inventor. Indeed, one could even venture to state that behaviorism itself helped shift American psychology from an intellectual enterprise to an inventive, hands-on science, shifted it from introspection to manipulation, from observation to demonstration. And in this changed emphasis is a subtle progression to the world of action and interrelationships, a world in which science finds it more difficult *not* to be involved in social invention.

Obviously scientists and inventors have similar concerns. The understanding of natural phenomena often requires the invention of new apparatus. Franklin showed that lightning discharge is an electrical phenomenon in the invention of the lightning rod.[26] Edison's "sound writer," the phonograph, dramatically translated natural sound waves into audible music.[27] Robert Oppenheimer demonstrated the awesome force of the basic building block of nature in the invention of the atomic bomb.[28] American inventors have abounded; and they have been particularly adept at making technological translations of nature.[29]

The historian of American science, Robert V. Bruce, has reflected that New World scientists and inventors have shared important traits. "They [both] were born puzzle solvers, sought glory in priority, and prided themselves on helping mankind." Inventors, however, tended to avoid close analysis of the theories of others (certainly characteristic of Skinner) and drew more exclusively from personal experiences. Then, too, their "mode of thought" was less "verbal, symbolic, linear and sequential" than scientists' (not the case with Skinner who was, of course, highly verbal); and they, especially mechanical inventors, concentrated on problems of spatial relationship.[30]

Certainly the point is not that Skinner was simply an academic Edison. It is rather to suggest that he may have been acting within another context than one defined exclusively as "scientific," and that the scientist-as-inventor seems especially a product of the American context.

Invention in the American setting has powerful cultural resonance. There is a grass-roots quality about it, an Americanism, that does not emerge when we simply consider American science. It is easier to think of modern America as a "building site" than an abstract experiment.[31] And, notwithstanding Skinner's formidable verbal accomplishment, it is culturally more fitting to think of him as a builder than an experimenter—although there are overlaps and interrelationships.

I do not want to argue, however, that Skinner was completely culturally bound, that his inventive science was wholly wrapped in an American cocoon. The historian of science Laurence Smith has persuasively linked Skinner to the Baconian and Machian traditions in the history of science, both of which emphasize the inventive dimension of scientific activity.[32] Science evolved as craftmanship to solve problems, the solution of which gave humans a survival advantage. Indeed, Skinner himself viewed his contributions within those traditions.[33] He also remembered that "the world of my childhood taught me to build things—toys, shacks, and eventually apparatus."[34]

Early in his career as a Harvard graduate student Skinner plied his inventive bent in the Psychology Department's machine shop in Emerson Hall—and not initially in the approved way.

> The shop became my center of activity. I had bought a *caffe espresso* brewer and made a tripod to hold it over an alcohol lamp, using strips of brass hammered to an attractive finish, but a remark or two and a few glances among my fellow students alerted me to the fact that the shop and supplies were there only to advance the science of psychology. I was ready to advance it. The ship models I had made in that dark year in Scranton had been digressions for which I was openly criticized; now I had good reasons to build things.
> One of the first things I made was a silent release box.[35]

The series of improvisations that eventually became the Skinner box began in the Emerson Hall machine shop.

Like Edison and Alexander Graham Bell, who early in their careers used Charles Williams's machine shop in Count Street in Boston, Skinner needed a hands-on environment where he could invent in relative independence.[36] In the spring of his first year at Harvard he recalled that psychology "clinched my loyalty" by providing him with a room that served as an office-laboratory.[37] There, Skinner brought squirrels in order to study separate reflexes and to simplify maze behavior. By 1928 the department laboratory had moved to Boylston Hall, where "the shop was much smaller than in Emerson, . . . but it was all I needed."[38] At Boylston he continued to modify the maze and studied the behavior of individual rats which were released from an enclosure he called "my soundless starting box."[39]

After graduating in June 1931, a Walker fellowship enabled him to continue working at Boylston Hall. During that year he applied for and received a National Research Council (NRC) fellowship in General Physiology. The NRC fellowship gave him access to an office in the recently completed Biology Building, as well as the use of "a special suite of rooms two floors underground which were practically soundproof."[40] Here Skinner completed the box that bears his name, the heart of which was a "lever and dispenser only" which he called a "repeating problem box."[41] Long after he had ceased to work with rats and pigeons, indeed after he retired, he continued to use a workshop in the basement of his Cambridge residence. When his daughter, Julie S. Vargas, was asked what her father enjoyed most, she said he liked to tinker—she remembers him doing so incessantly.[42] Clearly, Skinner fashioned his science by hand as well as by mind; without the inventor there would not have been a scientist.

SOCIAL INVENTION

When we think of Skinner's inventions, the "Skinner box"—despite his protestations about the name—comes quickly to mind. The fascinating tale of how he came to build it has been told by Skinner himself—and amended by the historian of science Stephen Coleman.[43] Refinements such as the nonelectric "problem box" and innovations such as the pigeon-guided Pelican missile also show his inventive talent.[44] Yet, if we take Skinner at his word and look at his accomplishments as a "social inventor," it is clear that making devices to facilitate the investigation of pigeons and rats was not the climatic inventive story.

Many of his inventions had direct social application. *Walden Two* may have been cast in fictional form, but Skinner did not think of it that way. "I am much more a Frazierian now than when I wrote *Walden Two*," he said in 1956. "I am sure it can be done [building a real Walden Two], and that it will be the most reinforcing experiment of the century."[45] The Aircrib or baby-tender, the verbal summator, and the teaching machine were explicitly designed to facilitate social functioning.

Skinner's career as a social inventor was most active during the 1950s. It was a remarkably productive decade which saw the publication of three books—*Science and Human Behavior* (1953), *Verbal Behavior* (1957), and, with Charles Ferster, *Schedules of Reinforcement* (1957). It was the decade when behavioral techniques were first used on psychotic patients at Metropolitan State Hospital.[46] It was, most of all, the period when

Skinner became absorbed with the educational potential and commercial development of teaching machines. Skinner reported that he was so completely involved in these various projects and pushed himself so unsparingly that in retrospect he was amazed he did not suffer a collapse.[47]

Skinner did not simply drift into social invention during the 1950s. His excitement about the social uses of behavioral technology rose as the data on schedules of reinforcement with pigeons began to accumulate. In a long letter to the Stanford University psychologist Ernest R. Hilgard, Skinner outlined the scientific advantages of the Skinner-Ferster experimental results. "With the degree of rigor we have achieved, we can generally give an account of the moment-to-moment behavior of the organism rather than, as in 'The Behavior of Organisms,' the general course of change in behavior over an experimental period or a series of experimental sessions." The work with pigeons demonstrated "the potentiality of a program of research which is not theoretically oriented."

> In other words, this is a sort of Baconian analysis in which we have undertaken to explore all the relevant conditions which have turned up in the course of our work, to fill in the gaps in the analysis of such conditions, and eventually emerge with a more generalized account which seems to me to be the only kind of theory warranted or advisable at this stage of our science.[48]

But "Baconian analysis" for what? Skinner was not content to let the new, more precise behavioral controls speak for themselves. He could not "resist adding another word or two in defense of this particular program." The "extraordinarily increased degree of control achieved over the organism . . . has already been put to extremely practical use." Investigations on the effect of drugs on behavior, on obesity in mice, and on adaptations to light were proceeding. He also, however, told Hilgard that "my own immediate future interests lie first in completing my book on 'Verbal Behavior' and then in putting the analysis of verbal behavior to practical use by designing new classroom techniques."[49] Though he did not explicitly say so, the juxtaposition of the Ferster-Skinner results with his educational hopes for verbal behavior gives the impression that the former increased his optimism about the application of the latter.

To remove any lingering suspicion that the pigeon business was science for science's sake, an excuse to indulge in theoretical discussion, he announced: "You won't find papers in journals from my pen arguing whether Hull, Tolman or anyone else was right about the nature of learning. I have always felt that the only real test would be a practical one."[50] In 1954 "practical" meant shifting behavioral techniques from pigeons to persons. That, in turn, meant social invention; and the heart of social invention was to be the development of a "technology of teaching."[51]

INVENTION IN EDUCATION

Skinner's understanding of social invention was not utopian, at least not utopian in the sense that it depended upon a visionary scheme. It was true that *Walden Two* created an imaginary community, one that he expected to be transformed from fiction to life. But Skinner's hopes for social progress through behavioral science focused in the mid-1950s on a firm conviction that his experimental work and that of collaborators had conclusively shown that "the species of the organism has made surprisingly little difference." Reinforcement could now be used to shape an astonishing variety of behaviors; and "comparable results have been obtained with pigeons, rats, dogs, monkeys, human children and . . . human psychotic subjects."[52] Behavioral techniques were universally valid, and that was a boon for social invention.

The American classroom in the 1950s seemed ripe for radical reform. Education had been historically steeped in a "welter of aversive consequences, [where] getting the right answer is in itself an insignificant event, any effect of which is lost amid the anxieties, the boredom and the aggressions which are the inevitable by-products of aversive control." The teacher was not at fault. Neither was the student. The basic problem was "the relative infrequency of reinforcement." Skinner noted that "since the pupils are usually dependent upon the same teacher, the total number of contingencies which may be arranged during, say, the first four years, is of the order of only a few thousand." But in order to produce, for example, in an arithmetic class "efficient mathematical behavior," it would necessitate "something of the order of 25,000 contingencies." The hard fact was that "an organism is affected by subtle details of contingencies which are beyond the capacity of the human organism to arrange. Mechanical and electrical devices must be used."[53]

Skinner was not merely transferring reinforcement theory to the classroom; in a broad cultural sense he was also acting within the American tradition of using technology to solve social problems, in this case educational ones. Edison, for instance, had believed that "motion pictures can be applied to the scientific, systematic course of memory training in the schools, taking the children at an early age when the mind is plastic enough to adapt itself most readily to new habits of thought."[54] The Menlo Park inventor was certain that "the introduction of kinetoscope pictures in schools" would make those institutions so attractive that "you couldn't keep the children away even by the police."[55]

Yet whereas Edison had only a vague sense of the historical context of educational failure, Skinner developed a sharper picture. "In any other field a demand for increased production would have led at once to the invention of labor-saving capital equipment. Education has reached this stage very late, possibly through a misconception of its task." He also realized that Edison's dream for kinetoscopes in the classroom was being realized as "film projectors, television sets, phonographs, and tape recorders are finding their way into American schools and colleges." The danger in audiovisual aids, however, was in making "the student . . . more and more a passive receiver of instruction," a result the teaching machine avoided because the students were conditioned to construct the correct answers for themselves.[56]

The fear that machines would replace teachers was groundless. "On the contrary, they are the capital equipment to be used by teachers to save time and labor." Indeed, the use of teaching machines was only a very important trend within a larger historical progression. "Not only education but Western culture as a whole is moving away from aversive practices." Earlier in the century John Dewey had correctly turned from aversive practices toward "positive and humane methods"; but Dewey failed to exploit the potential of technology to make education truly progressive.[57]

Skinner's faith in the ability of technology, properly used in accordance with the findings of behavioral science, to raise educational performance is an interesting facet of what James Beniger has recently called the "control revolution." The great challenge of the twentieth century, according to Beniger, has been the effort to extend and integrate technological control through advances in information processing.[58] Because it helped American students process information more efficiently, the teaching machine—like its more sophisticated successor, the computer—can be viewed as one of many information technologies that have socially completed the fundamental economic transformations of nineteenth-century industrialization.

It is also important to underscore that Skinner's America, from graduate school at Harvard in the 1920s through the 1950s, not only accepted the automobile, the airplane, and the electrification of cities as progressive modernization; it assumed as a matter of course that humans could control their environment through the efforts of inventors and industrial scientists. Skinner's hope for an industrial revolution in education exemplified the modern American mentality and its cultural assumptions that were shared in common with persons as diverse as William Taylor, Henry Ford, John Dewey, and Lewis Mumford.[59] Skinner in this sense was fully in step with many American industrialists and intellectuals who, regardless of disagreement, believed wholeheartedly in the social progress that would result from continued technological advancement.

RECASTING FREEDOM AND CONTROL

Optimism about teaching machines did not mean that mechanical devices would be the exclusive way to effect educational reform. By the late 1950s and even more so in the 1960s, Skinner turned toward shaping the total classroom environment, toward "contingency management" and programming personalized instruction.[60] He also became interested in writing a book-length essay about his broad cultural hopes for a social future engineered by behavioral science. In 1957 he wrote a friend at the University of Virginia that "you are quite right that I have in mind something in book form as an expansion of my article on Freedom and the Control of Men and some of the material in the Rogers Debate."[61]

"Freedom and the Control of Men" is interesting not only as a precursor of *Beyond Freedom and Dignity,* but as a telling statement of Skinner's historical frame of reference. His career as a social inventor assumed a particular interpretation of the Western past. Even though Frazier asserted in *Walden Two* that "history tells us nothing,"[62] Skinner fit his social invention, his cultural designing, into a particular historical perspective, one that allows further insight into the relationship between Skinner-the-social-inventor and his American legacy.

As Skinner recognized, his gathering hopes for successful social invention were not unprecedented. "[The] immediate practical implication of a science of behavior has a familiar ring, for it recalls the doctrine of human perfectibility of eighteenth- and nineteenth-century humanism." Although "History" had recorded "many foolish and unworkable schemes for human betterment, . . . almost all the great changes in our culture which we now regard as worthwhile can be traced to perfectionistic philosophies." Moreover, regardless of the workability of utopian designs, they all had shared a common expectation: "The underlying hypothesis is always the same: that a different physical or cultural environment will make a different and better man." Behavioral science shared that commitment to environmental change, but "it promises new and better hypotheses."[63] Social progress in history—the making of "a different and better man"—meant successful environmental manipulation.

It is significant that Skinner chose to connect behaviorism with the utopianism of the eighteenth and nineteenth centuries, especially the latter. He remembered having been interested in communitarianism as a youngster growing up in Susquehanna, a town not far removed from the perfectionist excitement in New York State during the Jacksonian era. "As a child I had read stories about the Shakers and other perfectionist sects, and I had grown up only two or three miles from the spot where Joseph Smith had dictated the Book of Mormon. I had gone to college near the site of the Oneida Community."[64] He also remarked that he remembered Susquehanna as a town that lacked obvious aversive social controls, one that may have suggested the congeniality of Walden Two. He did not remember knowing where the local jail was located; and he recalled that the community social structure encouraged face-to-face social interaction—as did Walden Two.[65]

But utopian cultural design began much earlier in America. Skinner made no mention of religious perfectionism in the seventeenth century, most notably in Puritan New England. That tradition as well as that of the Quakers in Pennsylvania emphasized perfecting the relationship between the individual and God. The Puritans, for example, would never have argued that the natural and social environment was unimportant; but it was thought secondary to the true source of a reformed spiritual relationship, the Bible. By the nineteenth century, perfectionist communities were in general more secular, less based in the authority of the written word, and more reflective of the larger transformations of the age, in particular the early stages of industrial capitalism. In America, perfectionism was in moral and social tension with, and symptomatic of, the growth of a national market and the rise of democratic individualism.[66]

The main point is that Skinner identified his perfectionism with an era in American history when the liberator persuasion was in full swing—when perfectionists, religious and secular, were trying to free the individual from the constraints of the past. "In rallying men against tyranny it was necessary that the individual be strengthened, that he be taught that he had rights and could govern himself," Skinner explained. "To give the common man a new conception of his worth, his dignity, and his power to save himself, both here and hereafter, was often the only resource of the revolutionist."[67] A Jacksonian reformer would not have quarreled with such opinion, but a seventeenth century Puritan would have objected to the lack of social deference, to the assumption that the individual was supreme.

Yet unlike many of the nineteenth-century "humanitarian perfectionists," Skinner was not attempting to change the environment to free the individual from the social constrictions of the past; rather he wanted to transform the environment so the individual "may learn at last to control himself."[68] And by emphasizing the theme of control in social invention, Skinner was identifying himself with the earlier American perfectionism, with the Puritans, and with the traditionalist persuasion that had consistently viewed the "free" individual with alarm.

In Skinner's view, the stress on individual freedom, while historically necessary, had brought misunderstanding. "We do not oppose all forms of control because it is 'human nature' to do so." Such a presumption was "an attitude which has been carefully engineered, in large part by what we call the 'literature' of democracy." The point that Skinner-as-social-inventor insisted upon was the inevitable existence of control whatever its disguises. "Through a masterful piece of misrepresentation, the illusion is fostered that . . . [social institutions] do not involve the control of behavior." But in truth "analysis reveals not only the presence of well-defined behavioral processes, it demonstrates a kind of control no less inexorable, though in some ways more acceptable, than the bully's threat of force."[69] He appeared sympathetic to the liberator heritage of individualism and democracy, while simultaneously insisting that science had now revealed personal freedom to be illusory.

Skinner was involved in a delicate balancing act. On the one hand, he recognized the importance of the evolution of Western democracy, the historic fight against political tyranny, and the growth of the freedom of the individual. On the other hand, through the findings of behavioral science, he recognized the "illusion" of freedom, and the necessity of shaping a social system with humane but inevitable controls. Yet his emphasis was clear: he was saying that future social progress rested not with politicians who would continue the quest for the freedom of the individual, but with behavioral scientists who would continue "man's long struggle to control nature and himself."[70] In the "liberator" versus "traditionalist" historical dialogue, Skinner seems to side with the latter: he would never be comfortable using science to free the individual from society; indeed such a state only masked social controls that were inevitably present.

Nonetheless, Skinner presents an interesting variation of the ambivalence Americans have long expressed about the relationship of freedom to control. The Puritans wanted to free themselves from the corruptions of the Church of England by establishing a special kind of social and intellectual control in America. The revolutionary generation wanted to free itself from the tyranny of the British Parliament and to build a "Republican" society based on personal sacrifice for the good of the nation. The South seceded from the Union to preserve its slave society. Postbellum Americans sought to arrange the emerging industrial nation to "order" society without giving up individual freedoms. Twentieth-century inventors, scientists, and industrial leaders have embraced technology as a boon to personal freedom. And countercultural thinkers have lambasted the technological order for destroying natural freedoms. The canvas of our history has been painted with large and small stories testifying to recurrent difficulties in defining a stable relationship between freedom and control, between liberation and tradition, between the individual and society. Indeed, the lack of a stable relationship has been an enduring American dilemma.[71]

Skinner, however, would use behavioral science to cast this predicament in new form, and by social invention resolve it. One reviewer of *Beyond Freedom and Dignity,* writing one of the few favorable reviews, suggested that the counterculture upheaval of the late 1960s and early 1970s was as much a search for control as for freedom. Skinner reminded us "that human beings need not only freedom but mutual control as well." "Maybe this is what our alienated youth are asking for: the right to control others . . . in return for being controlled to some extent." And he concluded the review with a statement Skinner surely would have endorsed. "Revolutions should be about the business of replacing aversive controls .'. . with positive fulfilling ones."[72] Skinner, of course, had been making just that point since the midfifties.

CONCLUSION

Skinner presented an interesting and, I believe, novel synthesis of the liberator and traditionalist perspectives in American intellectual history. The methods of behavioral science were applied to the individual, whether rat, pigeon, psychotic, or student. Behavioral engineering—"the design of culture"—was a matter of positively reinforcing the individual so that the environmental contingencies would be supportive of social invention. Skinner viewed his work within the liberator "party of hope" perspective of removing aversive social and political conditions and replacing them with positively reinforcing ones. In this sense, Skinner falls squarely within the liberator frame of reference. He would seem to support the extension of democracy and individual autonomy.

As just noted, however, his objective was not to "free" the individual from social controls; that result is not possible and it certainly is not desirable. Rather, by manipulating the environmental variables of which individual behavior is a function—or more generally by social invention—the individual becomes socially responsible. The individual does not have to depend on a personal "conscience" or a social "mission" to be a good citizen; one does not do one's civic duty for fear of consequences whether they be personal or social retribution. In other words, Skinner-as-social-inventor rejected the usual American solutions—both individualistic and social—that have historically promoted social responsibility in America. Neither a personal conscience, nor a social crusade, nor traditional institutional restraints will effectively promote the *survival* of a responsible social culture.

Hence, Skinner stepped outside both "the party of hope" and "the party of memory," outside of liberation and tradition. His social invention was radical not so much because it fell within the American utopian heritage as because the findings of behavioral science left Skinner with only a behavioral social solution.

But there is another consideration. The historically dramatic interaction of Americans with their environment has evolved into a national trait. American history is the saga of sloughing off Old World restraints; and that, in turn, is the story of a natural frontier that shaped an exceptionally individualistic, democratic, and technologically oriented culture. Skinner can be profitably considered as an exceptionally articulate and innovative example of that native tradition. He was not, however, simply an interesting cultural specimen; few, if any, twentieth-century Americans ever so tellingly translated our social predicament. For if the individual and the environment are the great focuses of the American experience, then Skinner not only urged us to consider them in relation to each other, but also insisted that we consider the relation *scientifically.* This is behavioral science with innovative cultural application: Skinner challenged Americans to recognize the radical potential in the American experience, to face the *possibility* of fashioning a responsible society without relying on either the liberator or the traditional heritage. It is in this sense that his social invention became his American legacy. And it may well be the very novelty of that legacy that has shaped the reaction of his critics.

Notes

1. B. F. Skinner, *A Matter of Consequences* (New York: New York University Press, 1984), p. 411.

2. See R. W. B. Lewis, *The American Adam: Innocence, Tragedy, and Tradition in the Nineteenth Century* (Chicago: University of Chicago Press, 1964), p. 7. Lewis also discusses a smaller but intellectually incisive "party of irony" represented by intellectuals with a "tragic understanding" such as Hawthorne and Melville (pp. 110–55). Whatever the ironic complexity of these literary thinkers, I believe they are generally more sympathetic to the party of memory.

3. George M. Fredrickson, *The Inner Civil War: Northern Intellectuals and the Crisis of the Union* (New York: Harper, 1968), pp. 7–35.

4. Ibid., pp. 98–112, 183–216.

5. See, for example, Daniel Aaron, *Men of Good Hope: A Story of American Progressives* (New York: Oxford University Press, 1961).

6. Ralph Ketcham has crafted a fine discussion of both the development and contemporary dominance of American individualism in *Individualism and Public Life: A Modern Dilemma* (New York: Basil Blackwell, 1987), pp. 1–70, 134–219.

7. For an interesting exception, see the historical sociologist Richard Sennett's scathing review of *Beyond Freedom and Dignity* in the *New York Times Book Review,* 17 October 1971. Sennett accused Skinner of having a "hidden agenda," the purpose of which was to defend "the articles of faith in Nixonian America, of the small-town businessman who feels life has degenerated, has got-

ten beyond his control, and who thinks things will get better when other people learn how to behave."

8. Joseph Wood Krutch, *The Measure of Man: On Freedom, Human Values, Survival and the Modern Temper* (New York: Grossett, 1954), p. 61.

9. Carl R. Rogers and Skinner, "Some Issues Concerning the Control of Human Behavior: A Symposium," *Science* 124 (1956): 1063.

10. Ayn Rand, *Philosophy: Who Needs It?* (New York: Signet, 1984), pp. 137–38. Rand's review of *Beyond Freedom and Dignity* was originally unpublished, but probably was written sometime between 1971 and 1973. See Leonard Peikoff's introduction in ibid., p. x.

11. Rand, *The Virtue of Selfishness* (New York: New American Library, 1964), pp. 86–91.

12. Lewis Hartz brilliantly questioned the political strength of a liberator-traditionalist exchange in American political history in *The Liberal Tradition in American: An Interpretation of American Political Thought Since the Revolution* (New York: Harcourt, 1955). More recently, scholars have argued that a political dialogue about political philosophy continued to the Civil War and even beyond. See Major Wilson, "The Concept of Time and the Political Dialogue in the United States, 1828–1848," *American Quarterly* 19 (winter 1967): 629–64; and Russell L. Hanson, *The Democratic Imagination in America: Conversations With Our Past* (Princeton: Princeton University Press, 1985). One should underscore, however, that Hartz's critical point about the triumph of the liberal tradition (in our language the triumph of the liberators) remains viable, if qualified. For a version of the liberator-traditionalist dialogue in biographical context, see Daniel W. Bjork, *B. F. Skinner: A Life* (New York: Basic, 1993), pp. 191–213.

13. Perry Miller was one of the first to recognize the central place of community cohesion in the social thinking of the Puritan clergy. See his *New England Mind: The Seventeenth Century* (Boston: Beacon, 1954), especially the chapter "The Social Covenant," pp. 398–431. Other notable treatments of this theme include Sacvan Bercovitch, *The American Jeremiad* (Madison: University of Wisconsin Press, 1978); Loren Baritz, *City on a Hill: A History of Ideas and Myths in America* (New York: Wiley, 1964); and Gordon Wood, *The Creation of the American Republic, 1776–1787* (Chapel Hill: University of North Carolina Press, 1969). For a good overview to the historiography of this theme see Robert E. Shalhope, "Toward a Republican Synthesis," *William and Mary Quarterly* 3d ser., 39 (1982): 334–56.

14. Skinner, *Walden Two* (New York: Macmillan, 1948), p. 262 (Skinner's italics).

15. Skinner, *Beyond Freedom and Dignity* (New York: Knopf, 1971), p. 201.

16. The slippage of social cohesion even in the seventeenth century has been the subject of not a few excellent works. Two of the best are Perry Miller, *The New England Mind: From Colony to Province* (Boston: Beacon, 1961); and Kenneth Lockridge, *A New England Town: The First One Hundred Years* (New York: Norton, 1970).

17. Skinner, *Science and Human Behavior* (New York: Macmillan, 1953), p. 438.

18. Skinner, *About Behaviorism* (New York: Vintage, 1976), p. 222.

19. The classic study of the American obsession with the manipulation of power in the prerevolutionary period is Bernard Bailyn's *Ideological Origins of the American Revolution* (Cambridge: Harvard University Press, 1967). The theme is chronologically extended through the establishment of the Constitution by Bai-

lyn's student, Gordon S. Wood, in *Creation of the American Republic* (Chapel Hill: University of North Carolina Press, 1969).

20. Rogers and Skinner, "Control of Behavior," p. 1061.

21. Skinner, *Science and Human Behavior*, pp. 445–46 (Skinner's italics).

22. Rogers and Skinner, "Control of Behavior," p. 1063.

23. Skinner relates how he came to write *Walden Two* in *The Shaping of a Behaviorist* (New York: New York University Press, 1984), pp. 292–93, 295–99.

24. See Nils Wiklander, "From Hamilton College to Walden Two: An Inquiry into B. F. Skinner's Early Social Philosophy," this volume.

25. Conversation between Skinner and author, 19 July 1988.

26. For a concise statement of the interplay between science and invention in Franklin, see I. Bernard Cohen, *Benjamin Franklin: Scientist and Statesman* (New York: Scribner, 1975).

27. See Robert Conot, *Thomas A. Edison: A Streak of Luck* (New York: Da Capo Press, 1979), pp. 97–116.

28. Of course building the atomic bomb was a group endeavor that depended on developments in theoretical physics and laboratory experiments stretching over nearly half a century. Nonetheless, Oppenheimer was indispensable to its actual construction. See Richard Rhodes, *The Making of the Atomic Bomb* (Boston: Little, Brown, 1986), pp. 119–27, 415–20, 447–50.

29. Indeed, Thomas P. Hughes has recently asserted that by the twentieth century Americans had fashioned a culture that viewed "the world as artifact." See Hughes, *American Genesis: A Century of Invention and Technological Enthusiasm. 1870–1970* (New York: Viking, 1989), pp. 1–12; also useful is Brook Hindle, *Emulation and Invention* (New York: Random, 1973).

30. Robert V. Bruce, *The Launching of American Science, 1846–1876* (New York: Knopf, 1987), pp. 151–55.

31. Thomas P. Hughes reminds us that American technology itself is "value laden." Hughes, *American Genesis*, p. 5.

32. See Laurence D. Smith, *Behaviorism and Logical Positivism: A Reassessment of the Alliance* (Stanford, Calif.: Stanford University Press, 1986); and Smith, "Knowledge as Power: The Baconian Roots of Skinner's Social Meliorism," this volume.

33. Skinner, *Science and Human Behavior*, pp. 12–14; and Skinner, *Matter of Consequences*, pp. 406–7, 412–13. For a classic description of Skinner's nontheoretical, "grass roots" approach to scientific method, see his "Case History in Scientific Method," *American Psychologist* 11 (1956): 221–33.

34. Skinner, *Matter of Consequences*, pp. 406–7.

35. Skinner, *Shaping of a Behaviorist*, p. 32.

36. Hughes, *American Genesis*, pp. 41–43.

37. Skinner, *Shaping of a Behaviorist*, p. 32.

38. Ibid., p. 50.

39. Ibid., p. 51.

40. Ibid., pp. 85–86.

41. Ibid., p. 88.

42. Conversation between Julie S. Vargas and author, 23 September 1988.

43. See Skinner, "Case History," pp. 221–33; and S. R. Coleman, "Quantitative Order in B. F. Skinner's Research Program, 1928–1931," *Behavior Analyst* 10 (spring 1987): 47–65.

44. Skinner discusses the problem box that he designed and that Ralph Gerbrands built in *Shaping of a Behaviorist*, pp. 169–70. For the Pigeon-in-a-Pelican

project, see ibid., pp. 257–74, and Skinner, "Pigeon in a Pelican," *American Psychologist* 15 (1960): 28–37. For an interpretation of the project by an historian of psychology, see James H. Capshew, "Engineering Behavior: Project Pigeon, World War II, and the Conditioning of B. F. Skinner," this volume.

45. Skinner to Matthew Israel, 16 August 1956, B. F. Skinner Papers (hereafter referred to as BFSP), Harvard University Archives, Cambridge, Mass. This letter is included in the first and only issue of the *Walden Two Bulletin* 1 (20 August 1956). Israel was a Harvard Psychology Department graduate student who, along with several other students from Harvard and the Massachusetts Institute of Technology, were seriously considering the feasibility of building a Walden Two in rural Massachusetts. So far as I know the project never got beyond the planning stage.

46. For a detailed description of this project see the Harvard Medical School, Department of Psychiatry, "Status Report I, Studies in Behavior Therapy," Metropolitan State Hospital, BFSP.

47. Conversation between Skinner and author, 12 December 1988.

48. Skinner to Ernest R. Hilgard, 28 December 1954, BFSP.

49. Ibid.

50. Ibid.

51. From 1954 to the appearance of *The Technology of Teaching* in 1968, Skinner published eleven essays dealing with teaching machines and programmed instruction—more than on any other subject. For citations see Robert Epstein, "A Listing of the Published Works of B. F. Skinner, with Notes and Comments," *Behaviorism* 5 (1977): 106–7.

52. Skinner, "The Science of Learning and the Art of Teaching," *Harvard Educational Review* 24 (spring 1954): 89.

53. Ibid., pp. 90–91, 94.

54. Dagobert D. Runes, ed., *The Diary and Sundry Observations of Thomas Alva Edison* (New York: Philosophical Library, 1948), p. 145.

55. Quoted in Conot, *Edison,* p. 412.

56. Skinner, "Teaching Machines," *Science* 128 (October 1958): 969–77, on p. 969.

57. Ibid., pp. 976–77.

58. James Beniger, *The Control Revolution: Technological and Economic Origins of the Information Society* (Cambridge: Harvard University Press, 1986), pp. 1–27.

59. Hughes, *American Genesis,* pp. 295–309.

60. See Skinner, "Contingency Management in the Classroom," *Education* 90 (December 1969): 93–100; and Skinner, *The Technology of Teaching* (Englewood Cliffs, N.J.: Prentice-Hall, 1968).

61. Skinner to Frank W. Finger, 23 May 1957, BFSP.

62. Skinner, *Walden Two* (New York: Macmillan, 1976), p. 194 (original work published 1948).

63. Skinner, "Freedom and the Control of Men," *American Scholar* 25 (1956): 47–48.

64. Skinner, *Shaping of a Behaviorist,* p. 292.

65. Conversation between Skinner and author, 19 December 1988.

66. For an astute study of the interrelationship between Jacksonian capitalism and utopian communities, see Whitney R. Cross, *The Burned-Over District: The Social and Intellectual History of Enthusiastic Religion in Western New York* (New York: Harper, 1965).

67. Skinner, "Freedom and Control," p. 53.

68. Ibid., p. 49.

69. Ibid., p. 54.

70. Ibid., p. 65.

71. The difficulty Americans have had in establishing social and intellectual balance between freedom and control is one of the crucial interpretative problems of American history. Among a multitude of works that center or touch upon it, there are several ones that I noted earlier. Perry Miller et al. have interpreted this theme in the seventeenth and eighteenth centuries (see nn. 13, 16, and 19). George Fredrickson has examined it in the Civil War era (see n. 3).

For a presentation of the problem in the late nineteenth and early twentieth centuries, see Robert Wiebe, *The Search for Order* (New York: Hill and Wang, 1967). Wiebe broadened his canvas to include the whole of American history in *The Segmented Society: An Introduction to the Meaning of America* (New York: Oxford University Press, 1975).

72. Don Browning, "Pro Controls," *Christian Century* 88 (September 1971): 1116.

2

Knowledge as Power: The Baconian Roots of Skinner's Social Meliorism

LAURENCE D. SMITH

> We can best understand the cultural designer, not by guessing
> at his goals or asking him to guess at them for us, but by study-
> ing the earlier environmental events which have led him to ad-
> vocate a cultural change.
>
> —B. F. Skinner (1953)[1]

ONE of the conspicuous features of B. F. Skinner's life and work is the contrast between the cautious experimental research that brought him recognition as a laboratory scientist and the expansive social philosophy that later brought him wider renown. Indeed, Skinner's call for the redesign of culture on the basis of experiments with lower organisms in contrived environments has struck many of his critics as presumptuous or even bizarre. Yet, given the presuppositions that Skinner operated under, the relationship between laboratory experiments and cultural experiments was not so farfetched. The goals of this chapter are to elucidate Skinner's belief in a close link between experimental research and social philosophy; to trace that belief to his early exposure to a particular outlook on science and society first expressed by the seventeenth-century philosopher Francis Bacon; and to consider the implications of Skinner's Baconian beliefs for the reception of his social philosophy in postmodern culture.

Few scholars have delved into Skinner's Baconian roots,[2] but Skinner himself made no secret of his lifelong fascination with Bacon. He recounted in his autobiography that he read Bacon's major works as a teenager and came to view himself as an "ardent Baconian"—so much so that he proceeded to read biographies of Bacon and books on his philosophy. Later in his life Skinner would return often to Bacon, finding comfort and inspiration in Bacon's lofty plans for the betterment of the human condition. The final pages of Skinner's autobiography were devoted to the Baconian principles that had characterized his life: that one should study nature, not books; that knowledge is power; that nature, to be commanded, must be obeyed; and that for a better world to come about, it must be planned and built. Skinner's writings contain numerous references to Bacon, and his utopian novel *Walden Two* was both inspired by and patterned after Bacon's own utopian work, *New Atlantis*.[3]

To understand Bacon's significance requires an appreciation of his role in promulgating a novel conception of science. Historians of science have discerned in the Western tradition two broad ideal-types of science.[4] The first, dating back to Aristotle, is the contemplative ideal, which seeks to understand the natural world and its causes. The second is the technological ideal, first championed by Bacon, which seeks the means of controlling, making, and remaking the world. The contemplative ideal focuses on passive observation, classification of natural phenomena, and systematic description. In contrast, the technological ideal emphasizes active experimentation and the hands-on manipulation of both natural materials and experimental variables. The long-standing motto of Baconian scientists is that Knowledge Is Power. For them, knowledge is not merely the passive contemplation of nature but rather the capacity to control the ways of nature and to direct them to human ends. Intervention in the course of nature is held by Baconians to be deeply revealing of natural processes, but it is also the key to remaking the world with an eye toward improving the human condition. Not surprisingly, the reformism inherent to the Baconian tradition has long held great appeal in America, where the technological mind-set became integral to the national identity through the nation's history of taming a wild continent.[5]

Skinner was certainly not the first American to relate the experimental method of science to the experimental reform of society. For example, John Dewey's philosophy had already made explicit the view of culture as an ongoing experiment, and Skinner's behaviorist predecessor John B. Watson was but one of several American psychologists who had offered utopian visions based on scientific psychology.[6] Within psychology proper, the twin focus on experimentation and social reform was embodied in the 1913 emergence of behaviorism. Indeed, the avowed aim of behaviorism to control behavior, both in the laboratory and outside it, made it the most characteristically American of all approaches to psychology. Behaviorism's adherence to the technological ideal was noted from its very beginning—E. B. Titchener's 1914 objection to Watsonian behaviorism was that it traded a science for a technology—and has been discussed ever since.[7] But if the linking of Skinner directly with Francis Bacon constitutes part of a larger story, it is nonetheless a crucial part of that story, for Skinner was unique in casting the technological reform of society in terms that were readily apprehended (with various degrees of sympathy and antipathy) by large segments of American society.

An understanding of Skinner's Baconian roots will shed light not only on behaviorism's commitment to the technological ideal but also on its status as a modern movement for the reform of culture. As we shall see, the fate of Skinner's utopian social philosophy is entangled with Western culture's growing struggle to come to grips with its own technology and with those vexing questions about the artificial and the natural that so regularly exercise thinkers at the end of the twentieth century. The curiously pessimistic turn that Skinner's writings took toward the end of his life cannot be understood without seeing that his program for the melioration of society, grounded in the traditional Baconian faith in technological solutions, had come to be undermined by postmodern society's skepticism toward technological fixes.

BACONIAN SCIENCE

Making Knowledge

In twentieth-century philosophy of science, Bacon's name is most often associated with his advocacy of the inductive method. But, as recent historical scholarship has shown, Bacon's more fundamental contribution was a distinctive vision of science as a process of human construction. For Bacon, knowledge was something made by manipulating natural materials in a process not unlike that by which artisans and technicians manufacture implements and artifacts. As Antonio Perez-Ramos has argued at length, Bacon's conception of science as a form of productive knowledge was premised on the belief that what we know best is that which we can make. Knowledge of nature is, for Bacon, identified with the ability to produce and reproduce phenomena at will. According to Perez-Ramos:

> The capacity of (re)producing Nature's "effects" was perceived as the epistemological guarantee of man's knowledge of the natural processes of the external world. On this interpretation, man can become knower only *qua* maker.[8]

In promoting the tradition of "maker's knowledge," Bacon opposed the dominant scholastic philosophy of his day which embraced Aristotle's priority of theory over praxis. Aristotle's ranking of *theoretical* (or contemplative) knowledge over the lower forms of *practical* and *productive* knowledge reflected the denigration of the manual arts in the Greek world and its belief that the full understanding of nature was attainable only through theoretical contemplation. By Bacon's time, however, a series of remarkable technical innovations (gunpowder, the printing press, and the compass) had begun to suggest a certain superiority of technology over mere contemplation, particularly in regard to its seemingly steady accretion of knowledge and its promise of improving human life. With the rise to prominence of the technical arts and their incorporation in the early stages of the Scientific Revolution, Bacon was prepared to reverse the Aristotelian priorities and embrace the technical arts as both a noble form of activity and a new paradigm of knowing. The implications of this shift have been described by Robert Proctor.

> Nature was for Aristotle that which creates itself—that which is essential, as opposed to that which is incidental or the product of human artifice. With the rise of seventeenth-century science, . . . this essentialist, respectful view of nature begins to decline. Nature is seen as raw material, as stuff waiting to be transformed by the artifice of man. The calling of humankind is now a productive one—to carry forth God's creation in the form of works and deeds; to bring to perfection the work that God has left undone.[9]

In elevating the role of the artisan above that of the theoretician, Bacon often cited the biblical sanction of Adam's dominion over nature and spoke of human creations as "imitations of divine works." In his view, anxieties over the unnaturalness of technological innovation were a needless hindrance to the rightful use of science for the relief of the human condition.[10]

For Bacon, the power of operation that permits humans to reproduce nature brings with it the power to redirect natural processes toward the production of novel effects. Bacon's classic dictum, cited approvingly by Skinner, that "human knowledge and human power meet in one" was an affirmation, not that contemplative knowledge can be put to human use, but that to truly know anything is to be able to create it.[11] In this sense, artifacts (the products of power over nature) take precedence over facts (the traditional objects of knowledge), and the artificial assumes more value than the natural. With Bacon,

> there arises a curious reversal of the order of art and nature. Art becomes the standard against which nature is judged. Francis Bacon's "nature in distress"— nature distraught by experiment—is as genuine as nature left alone. "The artificial," writes Bacon, "does not differ from the natural either in form or in essence, but only in the efficient."[12]

Indeed, for Bacon, the human power to produce and reproduce artifacts at will made artifacts the most convenient objects of investigation and hence the favored subjects of scientific study.

At the same time, Bacon recognized that human dominion over nature is constrained by nature's own ways—natural objects can be transformed but nature has its preferences for the forms that its objects can assume. According to Bacon, the understanding of nature's preferred forms requires "a very diligent dissection and anatomy of the world" in order to reveal those "true and exquisite lines" by which underlying order is manifested in nature.[13] The control of nature thus necessitates due regard for its inherent causal structure—a notion expressed by Bacon (and reiterated by Skinner) in the well-known aphorism that "nature to be commanded must be obeyed."[14]

In Bacon's view, knowledge of causes entails the ability to produce effects: "that which in contemplation is as the cause is in operation as the rule."[15] Accordingly, Bacon identified two great sides of the scientific enterprise. The first—referred to by Bacon as the "Inquisition of Causes"—involves "searching into the bowels of nature" to learn of its causal structure and preferred forms. The second—the "Production of Effects" (also referred to as "the Operative" aspect of science)—involves "shaping nature as on an anvil."[16] But because knowledge and power are one for Bacon, the Inquisition of Causes is ultimately fused with the Production of Effects, the two being united in their common reliance on experimental interventions in the course of nature. The discovery of causes may be aided by naturalistic observation, said Bacon, but discovery is most efficiently pursued through the experimental method—that is, through the production and reproduction of effects. In Bacon's words, we learn best from nature "forced out of her natural state, and squeezed and moulded," because "the nature of things betrays itself more readily under the vexations of art [i.e., experiments] than in its natural freedom."[17] Thus, for Bacon, the skilled manipulation of nature spans the range of scientific activity. It is essential both at the outset when nature is "squeezed and molded" by experiments to reveal its order and at the end when scientific laws, conceived as rules of operation, permit the "shaping" of nature for the promotion of human welfare. In either case, for Bacon, "the experimental method was not only experimental, but interventionist. It advocated active interference with Nature."[18]

Playing God

While important in its own right for its epistemological implications, Bacon's identification of knowledge with the power to produce effects also stood at the root of the reformist and utopian aspects of the Baconian tradition. Bacon himself believed that due regard for the value of the technical arts and their recognition as a new model of knowing would inevitably produce beneficial changes in society, including continuous improvements in the fulfillment of human needs and the emergence of social harmony. Assuming that social strife could be attributed to shortages of material goods, Bacon felt that directing the control of nature to the "relief of man's estate" would provide sufficient material well-being to guarantee the benevolent reform of society.[19] For Bacon, the experimental control of nature thus projected readily into the reform of society through remaking the world. It was this vision of the future that Bacon portrayed in his utopian work the *New Atlantis*.[20]

Located on the remote island of Bensalem, the New Atlantis was an advanced technological culture in which productive knowledge was accorded due respect and nature was experimented upon and remade for the benefit of its inhabitants. The central feature of the society was a scientific institute called Solomon's House (later to serve as the model for the Royal Society of London). Research teams at the institute worked in an intricate division of labor to plumb the ways of nature and to create it anew, producing effects for the common good. The goal of the institute, Bacon declared, was nothing less than "the enlarging of the bounds of human empire, to the effecting of all things possible."[21] Conspicuously absent from the culture were the institutions of government. As Carolyn Merchant describes it:

> In the *New Atlantis,* politics was replaced by scientific administration. No real political process existed in Bensalem. Decisions were made for the good of the whole by the scientists, whose judgment was to be trusted implicitly, for they alone possessed the secrets of nature.[22]

In testimony to the presumed beneficence of science, the power to decide which inventions and discoveries would be revealed to the citizenry was entrusted to the hierarchy of Solomon's House.[23]

For the scientists of New Atlantis, the effecting of all things possible involved the active reworking of nature's materials, whether physical or biological, toward human ends. On the physical side, the culture had produced such marvels as synthetic dyes, artificial gemstones, newly compounded metals, perpetual motion machines, telephones, submarines, methods of flight, and means of artificially synthesizing and reproducing human speech. On the biological side, there were synthetic food and drink, new medicines, methods of surgically transplanting organs, and artificial means of extending the life span. Most remarkably, the New Atlantis's biological laboratories had succeeded in producing new life forms through "commixtures and copulations of divers kinds" in such a way that they varied in "color, shape, and activity." "Neither do we this by chance," Bacon wrote, "but we know beforehand of what matter and commixture, what kind of those creatures will arise."[24]

The *New Atlantis* marked a turning point in the Western tradition and became the prototype of the scientific and technological utopias that followed. By providing the license for humans to play God in their earthly domain, Bacon attempted to allay medieval fears of human-wrought novelty and to nurture the alternative belief that human benefits would automatically ensue from technological innovation. It has often been remarked that, with the advent of modern physical and chemical technologies in the last one hundred fifty years, the prophecies of the *New Atlantis* have been largely realized. And with the more recent emergence of biotechnology, Bacon's prescient writings on the creation of new species are seen as being singularly prophetic of genetic engineering. But if one believes, along with the behaviorists, that an organism *is* what an organism does—that a creature is defined by its behavior—then creating new behavior is tantamount to creating a new organism. For those who, like Skinner, were convinced that behavioral engineering was at hand even in the 1940s, there would be no need to wait for genetic engineering to re-create the human species for the benefit of all.

Skinner's Behavioral Technology

Baconian Ideology in Skinner

As we have seen, Skinner acknowledged that Baconian thought pervaded his life's work. He drew on Bacon, in fact, not only for his orienting attitudes toward science but also for the language in which those attitudes were couched—such idioms as the "production of effects," the "shaping" of nature, and the "operative" side of science with its "rules of operation." Following Bacon's reverence for the manual arts, Skinner traced the origins of science to the skilled repertoires of craftworkers and artisans, and to the rules used by them in constructing artifacts.[25] He argued that knowledge is nothing more than effective behavior and, in particular, that the exalted laws of science are merely rules for successful action.[26] He also, of course, spoke of the "shaping" of that part of nature called behavior, noting that the process could be carried out in much the same way that "a sculptor shapes a lump of clay."[27] As a devout Baconian, Skinner often lapsed into the language of engineering in describing his work, referring to behavior as a "product" that could be "constructed" and "manufactured to specifications."[28] Sharing the Baconian preference for productive knowledge over contemplative knowledge, Skinner wrote that "science is not concerned with contemplation" and that his own interest in psychology was "not so much in understanding behavior as in changing it."[29]

Skinner has been characterized as a "psychologist with the soul of an engineer," a designation that aptly captures his thoroughgoing allegiance to the technological ideal of science.[30] In its most basic conceptions, the operant psychology he devised is inherently technological, portraying both the subject and the investigator as technological creatures by nature. The rat and scientist alike are seen as manipulators and controllers of their environments: just as the rat operates a lever to produce an effect on the environment (reinforcement), so too the scientist operates on the environment, manipulates variables, and shapes the behavior of organisms in it. Both are hands-on interveners in the course of nature, or, as Skinner conceived it, both are systems of variables defined by their *effects on* the environment.[31] In one of his later works on the philosophy of behaviorism, Skinner endorsed the Baconian equation of knowledge with power, and proceeded to characterize operant behavior as follows:

> Operant behavior is essentially the exercise of power: it has an effect on the environment. . . . That an organism should act to control the world around it is as characteristic of life as breathing or reproduction. . . . We can no more stop controlling nature than we can stop breathing or digesting food.[32]

In biologizing the technological imperative in this way, Skinner offered a Darwinian license for the Baconian drive to control nature, replacing the authority of Bacon's God with that of natural necessity. In doing so, he also raised the ironic possibility that the "natural" drive to control the world would eventuate in the transformation of nature itself.

The effects of Skinner's immersion in the Baconian ideology are everywhere evident in his work. For example, Bacon's veneration of the manual arts is reflected in Skinner's notable achievements in the fabrication of laboratory artifacts, such as the Skinner box and the cumulative recorder, as well as in his more notorious feats of domestic technology, such as the Aircrib.[33] Likewise, the Baconian fascination with constructing novelties found expression in Skinner's lifelong practice of demonstrating his knowledge of the causes of behavior through the construction of novel behaviors shaped by hand. Viewed in a Baconian context, these demonstrations of novelties represent Skinner's most characteristic achievements. They include the well-publicized rat Pliny who was trained to earn and spend token "money"; the pigeons who played Ping-Pong or performed on a toy piano; and the "Columban simulations" in which pigeons were trained to display "insight behavior" by solving complex problems of the sort previously studied in primates.[34] Most tellingly, given Skinner's ambitions to apply behavioral technology to the construction of a society, the behavioral novelties he fabricated also included what he called "synthetic social relations" in which pigeons were made to exhibit competition, cooperation, and even communication with one other about important events in their shared laboratory environment.[35]

From the perspective of the natural scientist, Skinner's demonstrations of behavioral novelties may seem trivial, serving as no more than a parlor game for behavioral engineers; after all, such demonstrations of artificial behavior afford no understanding of the nature of rats or pigeons as species or the role of their natural capacities in the economy of their native environments.[36] But from the perspective of a Baconian scientist, for whom the production of novel phenomena is the best way to demonstrate the artificer's knowledge of causes, such demonstrations are all the more significant for their artificiality. Writing about the transformation of biology from a natural science to an engineering science in the hands of the Baconian biologist Jacques Loeb, one historian of science has written:

> As biologists' power over organisms increased, their experience with them as "natural" objects declined. And as the extent of possible manipulation and construction expanded, the original organization and normal processes of organisms no longer seemed scientifically privileged; nature was merely one state among an indefinite number of possibilities, and a state that could be scientifically boring. This transformation . . . was a generalization from biologists' practice as they saw the extent of artificialization taking place in laboratories.[37]

Skinner, who counted himself among the devotees of Loeb,[38] was bringing the same transformation to psychology. Given the power of operant conditioning to shape behavior, organisms could be viewed as the raw materials for creative artifice. The naturally occurring differences between species that had long interested students of natural history could be safely downplayed as mere problems of engineering.

Faith in the human capacity to improve upon nature would become a hallmark of Skinner's writings. Discussing his monumental work on schedules of reinforcement, Skinner once remarked that "the behavioral scientist does not confine himself to the schedules of reinforcement which happen to occur in nature: he constructs a great variety of schedules, some of which might never arise by accident."[39] To create novel contingencies of reinforcement was, of course, to create novelty in the organisms subjected to them. "Our present understanding of the so-called 'contingencies of reinforcement' is undoubtedly incomplete," Skinner wrote, "but it nevertheless permits us to construct new forms of behavior, . . . often with surprising ease." The question that inevitably loomed was: "What might human beings do if we could build a more favorable environment for them?"[40]

Skinner's facile transition from laboratory to practice rested on his conviction that the operant represented nature's preferred form for behavioral events. His own "inquisition of causes"—the basic research published in 1938 as the *Behavior of Organisms*—consisted of experimental investigations in which nature had been forced out of its usual course in such a way as to reveal its inherent causal structure of stimulus, response, and consequence. Echoing Bacon's notion of the "true and exquisite lines" of natural order, Skinner wrote that he had demonstrated the "experimental reality" of the operant by taking into account those "*natural lines of fracture* along which behavior and environment actually break."[41] To respect those lines—to use operant conditioning—was to obey nature. Now nature was ready to be commanded. In the *Behavior of Organisms,* Skinner had declined to extend his findings with laboratory animals to the human species. "Let him extrapolate who will," he wrote. But as he would later admit, "I was soon extrapolating," and a mere seven years later he sat down to compose *Walden Two.*[42]

From Laboratory to Utopia

From the publication of *Walden Two* until his death, Skinner's chief preoccupation would be the application of the experimental method to the construction of a better society. As in the case of his activist view of laboratory research, Skinner eagerly acknowledged the Baconian roots of his utopianism.

A third Baconian theme completes [my] story. The *New Atlantis* was the first utopia I read. A better world was possible, but it would not come about by accident. It must be planned and built, and with the help of science. . . . By its very nature an experimental analysis of behavior spawns a technology because it points to conditions which can be changed to change behavior. I said as much in my own *New Atlantis, Walden Two.*[43]

If the *New Atlantis* had alluded to the possibilities of controlling life, Bacon nonetheless did not incorporate the actual engineering of humans into his utopian plan; such a completion of the Baconian trajectory would not arrive for some time. Commenting on the role of social engineering in the transformation of utopia into a "scientifically feasible construction," one utopian scholar remarked that with the twentieth century "the House of Solomon is finally ready to turn its creative talents back upon the civilization from which it emanated."[44]

This was precisely Skinner's plan. In directing the experimental tradition toward social planning, Skinner invested his Walden Two community with an unrelenting experimentalism in all phases of life. In the words of Frazier, the community's designer and Skinner's alter ego,

> the main thing is, we encourage our people to view every habit and custom with an eye to possible improvement. A constantly experimental attitude toward everything—that's all we need. Solutions to problems of every sort follow almost miraculously.[45]

Here as elsewhere in the work, Frazier gave voice to an uncompromising faith that human benefits would ensue from the adoption of the experimental attitude. Faith in scientific method was such that political institutions were neither needed nor desired. Like the New Atlantis, Walden Two was a pure technocracy in which decision-making was invested in scientific managers. Questions about the ends of society or what constitutes the good life could safely be ignored, in Skinner's view, because there was more than enough consensus on such issues to justify launching the process of social melioration without hesitation.

> To confuse and delay the improvement of cultural practices by quibbling about the word *improve* is itself not a useful practice. Let us agree, to start with, that health is better than illness, wisdom better than ignorance, love better than hate, and productive energy better than neurotic sloth.[46]

Skinner's faith in method thus obviated the need for political discourse about ends. In a lengthy assessment of Skinner's utopianism, Krishan Kumar fittingly characterized Walden Two as "a utopia of means—a 'methodological utopia'."[47] The real problems, for Skinner, were not political but methodological; they were matters of engineering.

As discussed by Daniel W. Bjork in the preceding chapter, Skinner drew the rationale for Walden Two from the perfectionistic philosophies of the past. "The underlying principle is always the same: that a different physical or cultural environment will make a different and better man."[48] Because people are products of their surroundings, engineered environments provide an entering wedge for the remaking of humankind. "It is here," writes Krishan Kumar, "in this boundless confidence in the human power to reshape the world . . . that Skinner's utopianism shines through most strongly."[49] The God-like powers of creation that Bacon had extolled three centuries earlier had devolved into Frazier's hands in the form of behavioral technology. "I like to play God," he confessed. "Who wouldn't under the circumstances?"[50] Skinner's wartime experience with Project Pigeon had convinced him that individual behavior could be shaped by hand to any specification, however precise the requirements.[51] For him, the design of an entire culture to specification was no less a hands-on exercise in productive knowledge. Evincing his roots in the Baconian reverence for the manual arts, Skinner tellingly analogized the creation of a culture to the turning of a physical artifact on a lathe, resulting in a "smoothly turned" society.[52]

As a hands-on exercise in human power, the design and construction of a better culture was viewed by Skinner as a feasible goal "within the reach of intelligent men of goodwill."[53] However, the sharply critical reception that greeted *Walden Two* showed that the feasibility of cultural design was perceived more as cause for alarm than as grounds for optimism. Although critics predictably attacked *Walden Two* for its antidemocratic themes, the deeper concern they voiced was that the deliberate, artificial control of culture somehow seemed dangerously unnatural.[54]

In response to the perceived artificiality of cultural design, Skinner defended cultural engineering in a series of works beginning in the 1950s. In one way or another, all made the same Baconian point: that in matters of cultural design, as elsewhere, there is no reason to prefer the natural to the artificial. One argument advanced by Skinner was that in regard to the origin of cultures there is no virtue in accident. The historical process of cultural evolution that had produced existing cultures was due to a series of accidents; by seizing control, humans could do better. To reinforce this point, Skinner drew on analogies from physical technology.

> The experimental method is superior to simple observation just because it multiplies "accidents" in a systematic coverage of the possibilities. Technology offers many familiar examples. We no longer wait for immunity to disease to develop from a series of accidental exposures, nor do we wait for natural mutations in sheep and cotton to produce better fibers.[55]

Similar arguments are scattered through Bacon's writings, as when Bacon urged that the products of unconstrained natural processes (the "births of time") are no worthier that those of human art (the "births of wit").[56] For Skinner and Bacon alike, timidity toward the rightful exercise of human dominion over nature could only jeopardize the prospects for human progress.

A second argument that Skinner brought to bear against his critics was that, despite appearances to the contrary, an artifactual culture would not subject its members to more control than a naturally evolved one. All behavior is controlled anyway, he argued, and to leave culture undesigned was simply to leave the control of behavior to other sources.[57] Such sources could be largely accidental—in which case they would have no advantage over deliberate control—or they could be designed haphazardly without the aid of science—again losing any advantage over scientific forms of control. In urging his readers to reject "the verbal devices of democracy," Skinner even turned the tables on his opponents, speaking of widespread opposition to all forms of control as itself "an attitude which has been *carefully engineered*" through existing prescientific forms of political discourse.[58] The lesson was plain: if control cannot be escaped, then let it be engineered with the aid of science.

Finally, Skinner challenged the artificial/natural distinction by arguing that, in reality, *all* cultures are experiments. Whether designed or not, cultures are nothing more than ways of living that are being tried out and subjected to selection by consequences.

> A given culture is, in short, an experiment in behavior. . . . The experimental test of a given culture is provided by competition between groups under the conditions characteristic of a particular epoch.[59]

Utopias, said Skinner, are like any other cultural experiment, except for their being *better-controlled* by virtue of their smaller size and their isolation from the larger culture.

> A utopian community is a pilot experiment, like the pilot plant in industry or the pilot experiment in science, where principles are tested on a small scale to avoid the risks and inconvenience of size. Utopias have usually been isolated geographically because border problems can then be neglected. . . . Given these helpful simplifications and the demonstrated power of a behavioral technology, a successful utopia is not too hard to imagine.[60]

Once deliberate cultural experimentation is understood as equivalent to, but more efficient than, the wider process of unplanned cultural experimentation, its advantages become evident: cultural reforms represent mutations in cultural evolution, and to increase the rate of mutations is to enhance the possibilities for progress.[61]

Underlying Skinner's response to *Walden Two's* detractors was his belief that a designed culture would operate more efficiently because it would be easier to control. A culture remade as a human artifact would possess the crucial Baconian advantage of any artifact, that of being better understood and better controlled than its naturally occurring counterpart. Skinner lamented the spurious plausibility that objections to cultural engineering gained from appearing to "champion the natural against the artificial," but he hoped that a proper understanding of cultural design might "allay our traditional anxieties and prepare the way for the effective use of man's intelligence in the construction of his future."[62] As we have seen, that future would be constructed by applying the Baconian experimental attitude both to the overall design and production of a culture and to the daily details of its ongoing operation. All that was required was an openness to social experimentation; fears that cultural design was some-how unnatural could be dismissed on Baconian grounds as baseless.

SKINNER AND THE CRITIQUE OF TECHNOLOGY

The Decline of Baconian Ideology

Skinner's Baconian aspirations to apply behavioral technology to the melioration of the human condition represented the continuation of long-standing Western faith in technology. Viewed in the larger context of the history of technology, however, his proposals for behavioral engineering arrived at an inopportune time. The manuscript for *Walden Two* was completed just weeks before the bombing of Hiroshima, an event that aroused unprecedented levels of suspicion about the consequences of technological creations. Even before Hiroshima, the prospects for unlim-ited technological expansion were not favorable: the great century of American invention had drawn to a close, the "golden age of technological ebullience" was rapidly fading, and the effects of technological innovation were beginning to be perceived as less than uniformly beneficial.[63] In literature, the half-century era of technological utopias had given way to the rise of technological dystopias, a genre that already included such psychological dystopias as Aldous Huxley's *Brave New World* and would soon come to include Anthony Burgess's *Clockwork Orange*.[64] The dec-ades following the publication of *Walden Two* saw continued growth in the critique of technology. In 1962, Rachel Carson's *Silent Spring* pop-ularized antitechnology sentiment by exposing the environmental conse-quences of modern systems of industrial production, including many of those industries whose existence Bacon had optimistically projected in his *New Atlantis*.[65] While popular criticism of technology has continued to find expression in legislated restrictions against genetic and behavioral engineering, scholarly indictments of technology have increasingly traced the predicaments arising from modern technology to the pronouncements of Bacon himself.[66] One result of these developments has been that defenders of technological solutions have given up the technological imperative in its unqualified Baconian form, advocating instead the lim-ited use of technology in small-scale systems of so-called "appropriate technology."[67]

At a minimum, the continuing discovery of untoward effects of techno-logical interventions has shown that the human estate is not always well served by the adoption of the Baconian experimental attitude toward nature. Contrary to the faith of the Bacons and Fraziers of the world, it is now clear that in producing technological creations we are protected

neither by the divine license of Bacon's God nor by the long-held faith
in the inevitability of scientific and technological progress. In his timely
monograph on the evolution of technology, George Basalla has argued
forcefully that no *general* notion of technological progress is defensible,
that technological progress can be ascribed, at best, only to developments
over restricted time intervals and in locally circumscribed conditions
where the relevant dimensions of progress can be clearly specified.[68] The
social ramifications of technological progress pose an even more complex
set of problems, but it is not clear whether the defenders of technology
will find comfort in even the cases of beneficial technologies. Nicholas
Rescher, in his *Unpopular Essays on Technological Progress,* has presented sociological survey data suggesting that self-reports of happiness
have actually declined as technology has advanced, in part, he concludes,
because technology creates expectations of gains in material well-being
that rise faster than technological innovations can satisfy them.[69]

At root, however, the technological crisis stems from the growing realization that—contrary to Bacon's article of faith—the artificial does differ
in critical ways from the natural. It is no longer possible to overlook the
fact that synthetic artifacts do not always have the same overall consequences as their natural counterparts, even though the two may be
equivalent in terms of the narrower ends for which the synthetic version
was designed. In urging the immediate deployment of social engineering
to multiply "accidents" instead of waiting for them to emerge naturally,
Skinner appealed, as we have seen, to seemingly unproblematic analogies
from the realms of medical and synthetic-fiber technology. With hindsight,
the analogies are instructive in ways that Skinner could not have foreseen
when he invoked them during the 1950s: artificial immunity to disease has
often proven less valuable than natural immunity because of the latter's
effectiveness against a wider range of naturally evolved and constantly
changing pathogens; and synthetic fibers, even when they equal or sur-
pass their natural counterparts in specified ways, are produced at the
expense of greater long-term costs to the environment. As long as the
technology is effective, such "births of wit" may achieve their immediate
intended aims, but without contemplative understanding of the complex
systems into which the innovations are introduced, the unintended effects
of interventions are notoriously difficult to predict. In contrast, the
"births of time"—those evolving natural systems that are the subject
matter of contemplative science—often carry the advantages of having
been tested by time and natural circumstances.[70]

With the sobering lessons of history in mind, one can fairly inquire
what the unforeseen consequences of "synthetic social relations" might
be, and whether the "helpful simplifications" of the laboratory might
prove misleading after all.[71] As Mark R. Lepper and David Greene have

shown in their analyses of the "hidden costs of reward," the use of reinforcement in behavioral engineering is not without its risks: though demonstrably effective in producing the intended changes in behavior, the use of reinforcement can have unintended long-term effects on the complex motivational systems of persons to whom the techniques are applied.[72] Others have raised serious questions about the unforeseen consequences of behavioral engineering even on those who do the controlling.[73] In behavioral technology as in physical technologies, there is now good reason to question the Baconian premise that we always understand that which we can produce and reproduce at will. Put simply, the success of technology at providing rules of thumb for the creation of immediate effects neither requires nor yields a contemplative understanding of the natural systems that may be disrupted by those innovations.[74]

As the desirability of technological fixes is increasingly questioned, it is well to remember that Bacon's utopia was itself conceived as a sort of technological fix. The premise of the New Atlantis was that the multiplication of human comforts through technological innovation would bring prosperity and harmony to society. But despite the fact that Bacon's prophecies have been realized in much of the Western world, few Westerners regard themselves as living in utopia; in fact, if Rescher is right in his analysis of the impact of technological growth on social well-being, human happiness may recede as a direct function of technological development. Moreover, as faith in technological means has eroded, it remains far from clear whether the prospects for consensus on the ends of society have fared any better. If anything, the fragmentation characteristic of postmodern culture has lent increased credibility to the view that cultural ends, like individual needs, are socially constructed and highly variable rather than biologically given and fixed.[75] Yet even in the late 1940s and 1950s, a marked failure of consensus on ends was evident in the divergent reactions to *Walden Two*. As several observers have noted, Skinner's utopian book met the same curious fate as many others of its ilk—that of being interpreted by critics both as a serious proposal and as a satirical spoof on such proposals.[76]

Skinner's Rejoinder

By the 1970s, Skinner had spent decades promoting applications of behavioral technology, only to find the status of the technological ideal in decline. As a consequence, he could scarcely ignore the challenge posed to his work by the widespread critique of technology. His response took the form, first, of an apologia for technology along with a reassertion of the technological imperative, and, second, of a renewed emphasis on those aspects of his cultural engineering that were consonant with the new understanding of technology.

In his later writings, Skinner did acknowledge that technology has not always served humans well. "We have no doubt made mistakes," he wrote. Despite the achievements of technology, "things grow steadily worse, and it is disheartening to find that technology itself is increasingly at fault."[77] Yet Skinner was by no means prepared to abandon technology.

> In trying to solve the terrifying problems that face us in the world today, we naturally turn to the things we do best. We play from strength, and our strength is science and technology. . . . It is certainly not difficult to point to the unhappy consequences of many advances in science, but it is not clear how they can be corrected except through a further exercise of scientific power.[78]

In contrast with his writings of the fifties where Skinner had reassured readers by drawing analogies between behavioral engineering and familiar examples of physical technology, Skinner was now eager to dissociate behavioral technology from physical technology in an effort to protect the former from the tarnished reputation of the latter. According to Skinner,

> when we say that science and technology have created more problems than they have solved, we mean physical and biological science and technology. It does not follow that a technology of behavior will mean further trouble. . . . We cannot say that a science of behavior has failed, for it has scarcely been tried.[79]

In Skinner's view, behavioral technology, once implemented, would produce an engineered society in which human self-control would permit the earlier excesses of physical technology to be corrected. The technologically induced problems of pollution, overpopulation, and war, he argued, are now chiefly problems of human behavior rather than problems to be solved by physical and biological technologies. The salvation to be won through behavioral technology would be salvation primarily from technology itself.[80]

Reflecting the Cold War mentality of the 1950s, Skinner's writings of that decade had stressed his concern that other cultures might gain an advantage over our own by preceding the West in adopting behavioral technologies. By the 1970s, however, the imperative to implement behavioral technology had taken on a different flavor, evincing Skinner's heightened concern with issues of global survival. Although the survival of the culture had long figured prominently in Skinner's account of the values against which cultures are judged, the survival of the species as a whole began to take on a new prominence in his works.[81] At the same time, Skinner continued to argue that control over the environment is inherent to the nature of organisms, humans included, and therefore unavoidable.

In response to William Leiss's argument that the West has made a fetish of controlling nature, he wrote that "control is not a passing phase. . . . we cannot choose a way of life in which there is no control."[82] As before, Bacon's technological imperative of the "effecting of all things possible" for the betterment of the human condition was to be grounded in the biology of human nature and human survival. If consensus on the aims of society had failed to emerge in Western political thought, perhaps it could be rediscovered in the kind of global thinking necessitated by threats to the species as a whole.

The second part of Skinner's response to the prevailing critique of technology was designed to underscore those parts of his proposals that accorded with the new antitechnological sentiments. Sometimes obscured by the controversy surrounding *Walden Two* was the realization that the community depicted therein engaged in many practices of the sort that technology's critics would recognize as forms of appropriate technology. During the 1970s and 1980s, Skinner reminded his readers that Walden Two was a community characterized by small scale, harmony with the natural environment, judicious use of natural resources, and planned abstinence from conspicuous consumption.[83] In fact, the creation of artificial markets for consumer products that John B. Watson helped introduce into American culture through his advertising exploits of the 1920s had been deliberately engineered *out* of Walden Two.[84]

The smallness of Walden Two provided Skinner with the opportunity to further explore the virtues of small-scale operations, to link them with the new visions of appropriate technology, and to remind his critics that the experimental method inherently involves small-scale interventions. In a brief 1985 sequel to *Walden Two* titled "News From Nowhere," Skinner portrayed Frazier's encounter with E. F. Schumacher's 1973 book *Small Is Beautiful: Economics as If People Mattered*—a work that played a central role in promoting calls for appropriate technology. After discoursing on the advantages of small communities like Walden Two, Frazier proceeded to draw the parallel with the laboratory.

> Small was also beautiful, Frazier pointed out, in the study of behavior. A laboratory was a small sample of daily life. Philosophers and psychologists had begun with massive samples. . . . You could not expect to get very far that way. 'Small animals in small places,' Frazier exclaimed, patting Schumacher's book, 'and beauty is truth, truth beauty.'[85]

Skinner had long characterized utopias as experiments and cited the benefits of small scale when assessing the effects of interventions; but here was a chance to relate the rationale for utopias to the rationale for all experiments and to tie both to the theme of small scale embraced by technology's critics. As with Bacon, truth would come from experimental interventions—and experiments, for the Baconian scientist, are things both small and beautiful.

CONCLUSION

Skinner's response to the growing criticisms of technology and to the decline of Baconian ideology evinced a certain resourcefulness, and his calls to action do not seem out of place in a world faced with severe challenges. Yet the issues raised by Skinner's advocacy of social engineering remain far from resolution. As recently as *Beyond Freedom and Dignity,* Skinner reiterated his faith in the unimportance of the natural/ artificial distinction,[86] but it seems clear that the issue will not go away. A deep distrust of human artifice as the source of solutions to human problems is by now widespread in the postmodern world. The authority of technology, like that of political institutions, has eroded in the years since *Walden Two* first appeared, and concerns about the artificial design of culture do not appear to have abated during that time. To justify the supposed inevitability of technological implementations on the grounds that "we can no more stop controlling nature than we can stop breathing or digesting food" is unlikely to persuade the postmodern skeptic. Despite its ring of Darwinian plausibility, such a broad statement too easily pre-empts discussion about what *kinds* of control are appropriate during an era in which human stewardship of nature has replaced notions of human dominion over nature.[87]

With the decline of the Baconian ideology, the responsibility would seem to fall on those who advocate technological interventions, whether physical or behavioral, to seek a comprehensive understanding of the consequences of those interventions, and not to be content with mere demonstrations of their immediate effectiveness. However, as with innumerable other technological issues confronting Western culture, there can be divergent perceptions of the risks involved, as well as differing views of exactly where the burden of proof lies. In *Beyond Freedom and Dignity* Skinner wrote:

> A proposal to design a culture with the help of a scientific analysis often leads to Cassandran prophecies of disaster. The culture will not work as planned, and unforeseen consequences may be catastrophic. [But] proof is seldom offered. . . . [88]

Perhaps so. But it is amply clear that Skinner's observation that "proof is seldom offered" would apply no less to the advocates of cultural engineering than to its critics. If behavioral technology is indeed innocent of the excesses of earlier technologies by virtue of its having "scarcely been tried," then it is also necessarily bereft of the sort of history of testing that could assure a wary population of the safety of an untried social technology.

Even though Skinner never quite succeeded in persuading his own culture that a scientifically designed society is worth the risks, he nonetheless gave forceful expression to the current cultural predicament—that of being caught between urgency and inexperience. As Skinner himself realized, urgency calls for large-scale action, while inexperience counsels beginning with small-scale interventions. The renewed emphasis shown in Skinner's later writings on small-scale experiments in living was an apposite concession to the fall of the technological imperative. But he knew that caution comes with a price. At the conclusion of "News From Nowhere," Frazier's companion posed the cardinal question:

"Can we create a culture that has the chance of a future before our present cultures destroy us?"

Frazier stopped. . . . Then he said quickly, "I think there's time," and started to walk on.

I laid my hand on his arm and stopped him. "Do you *really* believe that?" I said. He pulled his arm free and walked on.[89]

NOTES

1. B. F. Skinner, *Science and Human Behavior* (New York: Macmillan, Free Press), p. 428.

2. Brief treatments of the Skinner-Bacon connection may be found in B. R. Hergenhahn, *An Introduction to the History of Psychology* (Belmont, Calif.: Wadsworth, 1986), p. 275; Arnold S. Kaufman, "The Aims of Scientific Activity," *Monist* 52 (1968): 374–89; Thomas H. Leahey, *A History of Psychology,* 2d ed. (Englewood Cliffs, N.J.: Prentice-Hall, 1987), p. 380; Laurence D. Smith, "Inquiry Nearer the Source: Bacon, Mach, and the *Behavior of Organisms,*" in *Modern Perspectives on Classical and Contemporary Behaviorism,* ed. James T. Todd and Edward K. Morris (Westport, Conn.: Greenwood, 1995), pp. 39–50; and Smith, "On Prediction and Control: B. F. Skinner and the Technological Ideal of Science," *American Psychologist* 47 (1992): 216–23. With the exception of the last-cited article, these treatments of Skinner and Bacon have focused more on the inductivist style of science advocated by the two than on the utopian and reformist social themes that Skinner drew from Bacon.

3. Skinner, *Particulars of My Life* (New York: Knopf, 1976), pp. 128–29; Skinner, *A Matter of Consequences* (New York: Knopf, 1983), pp. 398–413.

4. See Thomas S. Kuhn, "Mathematical Versus Experimental Traditions in the Development of Physical Science," in *The Essential Tension* (Chicago: University of Chicago Press, 1977), pp. 31–66; Antonio Perez-Ramos, *Francis Bacon's Idea of Science and the Maker's Knowledge Tradition* (New York: Oxford University Press, 1988), chap. 3; Stephen E. Toulmin, "The Twin Moralities of Science,"

in *Science and Society: Past, Present, and Future,* ed. Nicholas H. Steneck (Ann Arbor: University of Michigan Press, 1975), pp. 111–24; and Edgar Zilsel, "The Sociological Roots of Science," *American Journal of Sociology* 47 (1942): 545–46. For a related distinction between traditional natural science and the "engineering ideal" of science in biology, see Philip J. Pauly, *Controlling Life: Jacques Loeb and the Engineering Ideal in Biology* (New York: Oxford University Press, 1987).

5. For a discussion and references, see Laurence D. Smith, "Situating B. F. Skinner and Behaviorism in American Culture," this volume.

6. On the role of psychology in Deweyian progressivism, see John C. Burnham, *Paths Into American Culture: Psychology, Medicine, and Morals* (Philadelphia: Temple University Press, 1988). The psychological utopias of Watson and of other American psychologists are discussed in J. G. Morawski, "Assessing Psychology's Moral Heritage Through Our Neglected Utopias," *American Psychologist* 37 (1982): 1082–95.

7. Edward B. Titchener, "On 'Psychology as the Behaviorist Views It'," *Proceedings of the American Philosophical Society* 53 (1914): 1–17, on p. 14. For recent discussions, see David Bakan, "Behaviorism and American Urbanization," *Journal for the History of the Behavioral Sciences* 2 (1966): 5–28; Kerry W. Buckley, *Mechanical Man: John Broadus Watson and the Beginnings of Behaviorism* (New York: Guilford, 1989); and John M. O'Donnell, *The Origins of Behaviorism: American Psychology, 1870–1920* (New York: New York University Press, 1985).

8. Perez-Ramos, *Bacon's Idea of Science,* p. 59. In placing Bacon in the tradition of "maker's knowledge," Perez-Ramos links Bacon with a countervailing epistemological tradition that includes the likes of Giambattista Vico in the eighteenth century and Marx Wartofsky in the twentieth (chap. 5). Possibly because of the dominance of positivist thinking in this century, there have been no previous efforts to place Skinner in this tradition, or to explore its relation to the recent social constructionist movement in the philosophy of science.

9. Robert N. Proctor, *Value-Free Science?: Purity and Power in Modern Knowledge* (Cambridge: Harvard University Press, 1991), p. 21. The examples of gunpowder, the printing press, and the compass were often cited by Bacon in attacking the Aristotelian tradition. See, for example, Bacon's 1602–3 essay "Thoughts and Conclusions" in *The Philosophy of Francis Bacon,* ed. and trans. Benjamin Farrington (Chicago: University of Chicago Press, 1964), pp. 73–102, on p. 93. An enlightening treatment of Bacon's assault on his Aristotelian contemporaries is given in Perez-Ramos, *Bacon's Idea of Science,* chaps. 6–11.

10. This was the one of the central themes of Bacon's plan for the "Great Instauration," that is, the restoration of human power over nature through productive science. See Bacon's "Great Instauration," in *The New Organon,* ed. Fulton H. Anderson (Indianapolis: Bobbs, 1960), pp. 1–29. For a further discussion of Bacon's agenda for the instauration, see Lisa Jardine, *Francis Bacon: Discovery and the Art of Discourse* (Cambridge: Cambridge University Press, 1974); and Charles Whitney, *Francis Bacon and Modernity* (New Haven: Yale University Press, 1986).

11. Bacon, *The New Organon,* ed. Fulton H. Anderson (Indianapolis: Bobbs, 1960), p. 39 (original work published 1620); Skinner, *Matter of Consequences,* p. 407.

12. Proctor, *Value-Free Science,* p. 22; on Bacon's denial of the artificial/natural distinction, see Fulton H. Anderson, *The Philosophy of Francis Bacon* (Chicago: University of Chicago Press, 1948), pp. 201–3.

13. Bacon, *New Organon,* pp. 113, 114.

14. Ibid., p. 39.

15. Ibid.

16. Francis Bacon, "De Dignitate et Augmentis Scientiarum" (Of the dignity and advancement of learning), in *Essays, Advancement of Learning, New Atlantis, and Other Pieces,* ed. and trans. Richard Foster Jones (Garden City, N.Y.: Doubleday, Doran, 1937), pp. 377–438, on pp. 413–14 (original work published 1623).

17. Bacon, "Great Instauration," in *New Organon,* p. 25.

18. J. A. Bennett, "The Mechanics' Philosophy and the Mechanical Philosophy," *History of Science* 24 (1986): 1–28, on p. 1.

19. See Benjamin Farrington, *Francis Bacon: Pioneer of Planned Science* (New York: Praeger, 1963).

20. Bacon, "New Atlantis," in *Essays and New Atlantis,* ed. Gordon S. Haight (New York: Walter J. Black, 1942) (original work published 1624).

21. Ibid., p. 288.

22. Carolyn Merchant, *The Death of Nature: Women, Ecology, and the Scientific Revolution* (San Francisco: Harper, 1983), p. 180. It should be noted that, according to Bacon's editor Rawley, Bacon had planned to include a political system in the *New Atlantis,* but died before the work could be completed; see the discussion in J. Weinberger, "Science and Rule in Bacon's Utopia: An Introduction to the Reading of the *New Atlantis," American Political Science Review* 70 (1976): 865–85.

23. For an insightful analysis of the perpetual tension between the innovative tendencies of science and the conservative forces of the state, see J. C. Davis, "Science and Utopia: The History of a Dilemma," in *Nineteen Eighty-Four: Science Between Utopia and Dystopia,* ed. Everett Mendelsohn and Helga Nowotny (Dordrecht, The Netherlands: D. Reidel, 1984), pp. 21–48.

24. Bacon, "New Atlantis," p. 292.

25. For example, Skinner, *Science and Human Behavior,* pp. 13–14; Skinner, *About Behaviorism* (New York: Vintage Books, 1976), pp. 136–37.

26. Skinner, *About Behaviorism;* Skinner, *Contingencies of Reinforcement: A Theoretical Analysis* (New York: Appleton-Century-Crofts, 1969); see G. E. Zuriff, "Radical Behaviorist Epistemology," *Psychological Bulletin* 87 (1980): 337–50.

27. Skinner, "How to Teach Animals," in *Cumulative Record,* enl. ed. (New York: Appleton-Century-Crofts, 1961), pp. 412–19, on p. 413.

28. For example, Skinner, *Science and Human Behavior,* p. 427; Skinner, *Contingencies of Reinforcement,* p. 14.

29. Skinner, *Science and Human Behavior,* p. 14; Skinner, *Matter of Consequences,* p. 407. For a critique of Skinner's emphasis on "cookbook knowledge" at the expense of theoretical understanding, see Richard F. Kitchener's classic essay "B. F. Skinner—The Butcher, the Baker, the Behavior-Shaper," in *PSA 1972,* ed. Kenneth F. Schaffner and Robert S. Cohen (Dordrecht, The Netherlands: D. Reidel, 1974), pp. 87–98.

30. Harvey Mindess, *Makers of Psychology: The Personal Factor* (New York: Human Sciences Press, 1988), p. 108. Cf. the remark of J. E. R. Staddon that Skinner's "lifelong fundamental purpose was not scientific but *meliorative.* He wanted to improve mankind. . . . His aim was better living through behavior analysis" (Staddon, "The Conventional Wisdom of Behavior Analysis: Response to Comments," *Journal of the Experimental Analysis of Behavior* 60 [1993]: 489–94, on p. 494).

31. Skinner, *Verbal Behavior* (New York: Appleton-Century-Crofts, 1957), p. 313; Skinner, "Current Trends in Experimental Psychology," in *Cumulative Record*, pp. 223–41, on p. 236.

32. Skinner, *About Behaviorism*, pp. 154, 208, 209. The noted historian of utopian thought, Frank Manuel, has remarked that such conceptions became commonplace in post-Darwinian thought, to the extent of creating a stereotype of "beast-machines, emotionally impoverished, existing only to exercise power" (see Manuel, "Toward a Psychological History of Utopias," in *Utopias and Utopian Thought*, ed. Manuel [Boston: Houghton, 1966], pp. 69–98, on p. 86).

33. See Daniel W. Bjork, *B. F. Skinner: A Life* (New York: Basic, 1993); Bjork, "B. F. Skinner and the American Tradition: The Scientist as Social Inventor," this volume; S. R. Coleman, "Skinner's Progress During the 1930s: Reflexes, Operants, and Apparatuses," this volume; and Elizabeth A. Jordan, "Freedom and the Control of Children: The Skinners' Approach to Parenting," this volume.

34. For accounts of these projects, see Skinner, *The Shaping of a Behaviorist* (New York: Knopf, 1979), pp. 196–98; *Matter of Consequences*, pp. 25–26, 103, 382–83.

35. Skinner, "Two 'Synthetic Social Relations'," *Journal of the Experimental Analysis of Behavior* 5 (1962): 531–33; Robert Epstein, Robert P. Lanza, and B. F. Skinner, "Symbolic Communication Between Two Pigeons (*Columba livia domestica*)," *Science* 207 (1980): 543–45.

36. This became a fairly standard complaint of ethologists against Skinner's work. Garcia, an advocate of the naturalistic study of animal behavior, has argued that Skinner could demonstrate table tennis in pigeons only because they already do so in the wild: feral pigeons are readily observed tossing leaves back and forth to one another as they try to clear off their respective feeding patches in search of food. The simulation is bogus, since "pigeons play when they are hungry and underweight; they are trying to gain weight. Humans play tennis to lose weight." See Garcia, "Lorenz's Impact on the Psychology of Learning," *Evolution and Cognition* 1 (1991): 31–41, on p. 33.

37. Pauly, *Controlling Life*, p. 199.

38. Ibid., pp. 183–97; Skinner, *Shaping*, p. 220.

39. Skinner, *Beyond Freedom and Dignity* (New York: Knopf, 1971), p. 160. In an intriguing series of essays, Barry Schwartz and his colleagues have raised profound questions about whether schedules of reinforcement play *any* important role in natural settings—and, in effect, whether they can ever be said to arise by accident as opposed to design. They argue that before the emergence of modern wage systems, work was performed chiefly to fulfill social and legal obligations rather than for material benefits or rewards (even though the latter may have been loosely related to the amount of work performed). Only with the advent of factory piecework practices did human activity come under the control of schedules of reward, and the behaviorist "principle" of reinforcement can be viewed as the elevation of a contingent, socially constructed practice to the status of a supposedly universal law of nature. Schwartz and Hugh Lacey (*Behaviorism, Science, and Human Nature* [New York: Norton, 1982]) write:

What we are arguing . . . is that the "fundamental" principle of human nature [reinforcement] was not overlooked prior to the nineteenth century. Simply, it was not a fundamental principle. It has become one over the last 200 years as a result of economic development. What this means is that the fundamental principle that is exemplified by modern factory work is not that human behavior is controlled by contingencies of rein-

forcement. Rather, it is that human behavior *can* be controlled by contingencies of reinforcement. Behavior theory does provide an accurate account of much of what people
do in the modern world. But the question here is whether its success stems from having
discovered a fundamental principle which is exemplified in all contexts or a principle
which is manifest only in contexts that have been *created* in the last 200 years. (p. 243)

This argument parallels, in important respects, the complaints of ethologists that
the ability of behaviorists to control the behavior of animals through reinforcement in laboratory settings says nothing about whether behavior in naturalistic
settings is so controlled. To the extent that operant behaviorists are indeed in the
bioengineering tradition of Bacon and Loeb, they should not find Schwartz and
Lacey's argument particularly disturbing—*except* for the fact that it deprives
them of the rhetorical advantages of claiming to ground their technology in *natural*
science, with its presumed universality and ideological neutrality. Possibly these
advantages are too lucrative to forgo. For a full exposition of their argument, see
Barry Schwartz, Richard Schuldenfrei, and Hugh Lacey, "Operant Psychology
as Factory Psychology," *Behaviorism* 6 (1978): 229–54; supporting analyses are
given in Schwartz, "The Creation and Destruction of Value," *American Psychologist* 45 (1990): 7–15.

40. Skinner, *Matter of Consequences,* p. 47; Skinner, "The Design of Cultures,"
in *Cumulative Record,* pp. 36.01–36.12, on p. 36.03.

41. Skinner, *The Behavior of Organisms: An Experimental Analysis* (New
York: Appleton-Century, 1938), pp. 41, 33 (emphasis added).

42. Ibid., p. 441; Skinner, *"The Behavior of Organisms* at 50," in *Recent Issues
in the Analysis of Behavior* (Columbus, Ohio: Merrill, 1989), pp. 121–35, on p. 131.

43. Skinner, *Matter of Consequences,* p. 412.

44. Helga Nowotny, "Science and Utopia: On the Social Ordering of the Future," in *Nineteen Eighty-Four,* pp. 3–18, on p. 13.

45. Skinner, *Walden Two* (New York: Macmillan, 1976), p. 25 (original work
published 1948).

46. Skinner, "Freedom and Control of Men," in *Cumulative Record,* pp. 3–18,
on p. 6.

47. Krishan Kumar, *Utopia and Anti-Utopia in Modern Times* (London: Basil
Blackwell, 1987), p. 350.

48. Skinner, "Freedom and Control of Men," in *Cumulative Record,* p. 4.

49. Kumar, *Utopia and Anti-Utopia,* p. 372.

50. Skinner, *Walden Two,* pp. 281–82.

51. See James H. Capshew, "Engineering Behavior: Project Pigeon, World War
II, and the Conditioning of B. F. Skinner," this volume.

52. Skinner, *Notebooks,* ed. Robert Epstein (Englewood Cliffs, N.J.: Prentice-
Hall, 1980), p. 199.

53. Skinner, *Contingencies of Reinforcement,* p. 20.

54. Joseph Wood Krutch, *The Measure of Man* (Indianapolis: Bobbs, 1953);
Morris S. Viteles, "The New Utopia," *Science* 122 (1955): 1167–71. Cf. Carl
Rogers's remark to Skinner that in Walden Two "nothing is really genuine. Everything has a 'pseudo' quality to it" (*Carl Rogers: Dialogues,* ed. Howard Kirschen-
baum and Valerie Land Henderson [Boston: Houghton, 1989], p. 126).

55. Skinner, "Freedom and Control of Men," p. 12. In the same paper, Skinner
cited a provision in the Marshall Plan to give atomic energy to developing nations
as an example of sound social engineering.

56. For example, Francis Bacon, "The Masculine Birth of Time," in *The Phi-*

losophy of Francis Bacon, ed. Benjamin Farrington (Chicago: University of Chicago Press, 1964), pp. 61–72.

57. Skinner, *Science and Human Behavior,* chap. 29; Skinner, *Beyond Freedom and Dignity,* chap. 2.

58. Skinner, "Freedom and Control of Men," in *Cumulative Record,* pp. 8, 9 (emphasis added).

59. Skinner, *Science and Human Behavior,* pp. 430–31.

60. Skinner, *Contingencies of Reinforcement,* pp. 37–38.

61. Skinner, *Science and Human Behavior,* p. 434; Skinner, *Contingencies of Reinforcement,* chap. 2.

62. Skinner, "Design of Cultures," in *Cumulative Record,* pp. 36.01, 36.02.

63. Thomas P. Hughes, *American Genesis: A Century of Invention and Technological Enthusiasm, 1870–1970* (New York: Viking, 1989); Joseph W. Slade, review of *Imagining Tomorrow: History, Technology, and the American Future,* by Joseph J. Corn, in *Technology and Culture* 30 (1989): 459–60, on p. 459. See the discussion in Howard P. Segal, *Technological Utopianism in American Culture* (Chicago: University of Chicago Press, 1985).

64. Aldous Huxley, *Brave New World* (Garden City, N.Y.: Doubleday, 1932); Anthony Burgess, *A Clockwork Orange* (New York: Norton, 1963).

65. Rachel Carson, *Silent Spring* (Boston: Houghton, 1962).

66. For example, Merchant, *Death of Nature;* William Leiss, *The Domination of Nature* (New York: Braziller, 1972); Langdon Winner, *Autonomous Technology: Technics-out-of-Control as a Theme in Political Thought* (Cambridge: MIT Press, 1977).

67. See Segal, *Technological Utopianism,* chaps. 8, 9.

68. George Basalla, *The Evolution of Technology* (Cambridge: Cambridge University Press, 1988).

69. Nicholas Rescher, *Unpopular Essays on Technological Progress* (Pittsburgh, Pa.: University of Pittsburgh Press, 1980).

70. Curiously, Skinner himself anticipated this point in the early 1960s when he acknowledged that naturally evolved immunity to disease may have more survival value than artificial immunity (Skinner, "Design of Cultures," in *Cumulative Record,* p. 36.11).

71. The point that the simplifications of the laboratory can blind behavioral technologists to the complexity of the effects of real-world interventions was made forcefully two decades ago by Edwin P. Willems in his insightful essay "Behavioral Technology and Behavioral Ecology," *Journal of Applied Behavior Analysis* 7 (1974): 151–65. In this essay—which is replete with concrete examples of technology, both biological and behavioral, gone awry—Willems notes that "every intervention has its price, no matter how well-intentioned the agent of intervention may be," and decries the "almost child-like irresponsibility" of behavioral engineers in neglecting the need for a deeper understanding of the complex systems in which they intervene (pp. 154, 155). It is noteworthy that Willems's article appeared in the leading journal for applied operant behaviorism; yet the detailed recommendations laid out in the article for grounding behavioral technology on an understanding of behavior's systemic determinants have been largely ignored. For a relevant survey of the literature, see J. R. Lutzker, "'Damn It Burris, I'm Not a Product of Walden Two,' or Who's Controlling the Controllers," in *Perspectives on the Use of Nonaversive and Aversive Interventions for Persons with Developmental Disabilities,* ed. Alan C. Repp and Nirbhay N. Singh (Sycamore, Ill.: Sycamore, 1990), pp. 495–501.

72. Mark R. Lepper and David Greene, *The Hidden Costs of Reward* (Hillsdale, N.J.: Erlbaum, 1978). For an in-depth (though distractingly polemical) review of the literature on the untoward side-effects of reinforcement, see Alfie Kohn, *Punished by Rewards* (Boston: Houghton, 1993). An extension of Kohn's critique to the use of rewards in business practices is in his article "Why Incentive Plans Cannot Work," *Harvard Business Review* 71 (1993): 54–60. One of the surprisingly few serious replies by a behaviorist to the critique of Lepper and Greene is given by Alyce M. Dickinson, "The Detrimental Effects of Extrinsic Reinforcement on 'Intrinsic Motivation'," *Behavior Analyst* 12 (1989): 1–15.

73. David Kipnis, *Technology and Power* (New York: Springer-Verlag, 1990).

74. One renegade member of the Skinnerian tradition has recently argued that Skinner's emphasis on producing immediate effects may actually impede the progress of operant psychologists in achieving their self-proclaimed goal of controlling behavior.

> A real difference between science and craft is the time the practitioner is willing to wait before achieving power over nature. . . . Successful working *now* may be the enemy of much more successful working down the road. The lesson I take from the history of science is that a search for *understanding* (no matter how ill-defined that idea may be) will eventually yield much more control over nature than a shortsighted emphasis on control now. American businesses are often criticized, and contrasted with their counterparts in Japan, for their overemphasis on the next quarter's profits. It would be unfortunate if American behavioral science were to fall victim to the same shortsightedness. (Staddon, "Conventional Wisdom of Behavior Analysis," p. 491)

75. See Ruth Levitas, *The Concept of Utopia* (Syracuse, N.Y.: Syracuse University Press, 1990), p. 164. Cf. Merle Curti's remark that many of Skinner's critics object not to his "creation of social forms more conducive to the satisfaction of human needs, but rather to his dogmatic perception of those needs" (Curti, *Human Nature in American Thought: A History* [Madison: University of Wisconsin Press, 1980], p. 393).

76. See the discussion and examples in Kumar, *Utopia and Anti-Utopia,* especially p. 348; and Levitas, *Concept of Utopia,* which notes the "perennial problem of distinguishing between utopia and dystopia" and cites *Walden Two* as an example of a utopian work sometimes interpreted "in opposition to the author's intention" (Levitas, p. 165). Skinner himself was aware of this phenomenon: "Some readers may take the book as written with tongue-in-cheek, but it was actually a quite serious proposal" (Skinner, *Contingencies of Reinforcement,* p. 29).

77. Skinner, *About Behaviorism,* p. 209; Skinner, *Beyond Freedom and Dignity,* p. 3. For an example of the soul-searching that the decline of the technological ideal has occasioned among Skinner's followers, see E. Scott Geller, "Is Applied Behavior Analysis Technological to a Fault?" *Journal of Applied Behavior Analysis* 24 (1991): 401–6.

78. Ibid., p. 3; Skinner, *About Behaviorism,* p. 154. The issue of whether technology is the best way to correct technologically induced problems is by now a well-exercised one. For a skeptical view regarding the use of narrowly conceived behavioral technologies to this end, see Willems, "Behavioral Technology and Behavioral Ecology," p. 155.

79. Skinner, *About Behaviorism,* p. 276.

80. Skinner, *Beyond Freedom and Dignity,* pp. 3–5.

81. See, for example, Skinner, *About Behaviorism,* p. 226; Skinner, *Beyond Freedom and Dignity,* p. 175; Skinner, *Upon Further Reflection* (Englewood Cliffs,

N.J.: Prentice-Hall, 1987). For Skinner's Cold War concern that other cultures might supersede our own by winning the race for behavioral technology, see, for example, "Freedom and Control of Men," especially pp. 17–18. An analysis of the shifts in Skinner's versions of the technological imperative over the course of his career would make a fascinating study.

82. Skinner, *About Behaviorism,* pp. 209, 281. Leiss's work is cited in n. 66.

83. See Skinner, "Walden Two Revisited," in *Walden Two* (introduction to 1976 reprint), pp. v–xvi; Skinner, "News From Nowhere," in *Upon Further Reflection,* pp. 33–50.

84. See, for example, Skinner, *Walden Two,* pp. 28, 57; on Watson's role in engineering consumer behavior, see Buckley, *Mechanical Man,* chap. 8.

85. Skinner, "News From Nowhere," p. 45; the book referred to is E. F. Schumacher, *Small Is Beautiful: Economics as If People Mattered* (New York: Harper, 1973).

86. Skinner, *Beyond Freedom and Dignity,* pp. 158–59.

87. For discussions of the control of nature without domination over it, see Merchant, *Death of Nature;* Don Ihde, *Technology and the Life-World: From Garden to Earth* (Bloomington: Indiana University Press, 1990); and Evelyn Fox Keller, "Science and Power for What?" in *Nineteen Eighty-Four,* pp. 261–72.

88. Skinner, *Beyond Freedom and Dignity,* p. 161.

89. Skinner, "News From Nowhere," in *Upon Further Reflection,* p. 50.

3

From Hamilton College to Walden Two: An Inquiry Into B. F. Skinner's Early Social Philosophy

NILS WIKLANDER

UTOPIANISM is an expression of both the critical and the constructive impulse. It involves the critique, implicit or explicit, of the existing society, and it offers a solution to various social problems in the form of an overall design for the reconstruction of society. If we take this dual aspect of utopian thinking seriously, utopianism becomes entangled in political theory and social philosophy.[1] Furthermore, the dual character emphasizes the importance of the social and intellectual context in which the utopian tract was written: in the phrase of the utopian scholar Arthur E. Morgan, "nowhere was somewhere."[2] The more general term *social philosophy* implies a set of ideas about the origin and nature of society, including visions of a better way to organize social life. The focus of the present analysis will be on the visionary aspects of utopianism and the role played by science and scientists in the formation of such visions.

Prior to the 1948 publication of his utopian novel *Walden Two,* B. F. Skinner had not publicly shown any concern for social problems. During the 1930s he directed his efforts mainly toward experimentation and the construction of a descriptive science of behavior. In spite of the fact that he did not see his early work as directly useful to human affairs, he nonetheless had a firm belief in its ultimate social value and relevance. But the application of a science of behavior to human affairs had to be postponed until he had reached a better understanding of human behavior itself.

The visionary aspects of a social philosophy deal with the unknown and the possible, whereas science, especially empirical science, is devoted to study the observable and the probable. Skinner combined these two modes of dealing with the world and created an interesting tension, a tension best seen by comparing his first two published books *The Behavior of Organisms: An Experimental Analysis* in 1938 and *Walden Two* in 1948. The experimental book became a document in the formation of a research tradition; it presented a system and a vast amount of experimental research. There Skinner avoided speculation, making no extensions to human behavior. In the novel, however, "recent advances" in a science of behavior became the chief instrument for social improvement.

Skinner's early work on verbal behavior was his first extension to human behavior and, as such, held an intermediate position between the rigorous experimental science and the vision of an ideal social community. The interpretation of verbal behavior with the conceptual tools derived from controlled experiments often seemed to lack face validity, a problem to which we will return. And in *Walden Two*, Skinner took still another speculative step by adopting a literary form and by making a complex real-life laboratory out of a small community.

Walden Two was Skinner's first major step toward a social philosophy. After its appearance, he frequently discussed the implications of a science of behavior for society at large. Analyses of his social philosophy have generally focused on later nonfictional works, especially *Science and Human Behavior* (1953) and *Beyond Freedom and Dignity* (1971). Instead of proceeding back from recent works to *Walden Two*, however, my aim is to move forward from Skinner's early social thinking on up to his utopian novel. I will argue that Skinner was concerned with human behavior and social improvement from the outset of his research. In fact, one could make the case that his desire to save the world motivated his choice of psychology as a field of study in the late 1920s.

If we confine ourselves to Skinner's publications in the 1930s and 1940s, we find almost no material relevant to the issue of his social philosophy. The archival materials similarly yield little of direct relevance. Yet it is still possible to reconstruct Skinner's early notions about science and society by paying careful attention to archival, biographical, and textual clues, in addition to those found in his autobiography.

THE TWENTIES: COLLEGE, WRITING, AND PSYCHOLOGY

In her classic study of American youth in the 1920s, Paula S. Fass observes that other students of the twenties treat the decade in "cultural terms" and describe the periods before and after in terms of social reform and war; in the twenties, it is said, the social reformer was replaced by Big Business, and artists fled to a world of fantasy. In contrast to this simplified picture, Fass argues that the 1920s were crucial years in which "the tension between modern and traditional modes of thought and behavior was finally played out."[3] She goes on to argue that adjustment to change, not escape from it, is the significant contribution of the 1920s to modern American history. In this process, traditional social institutions such as the family, religion, and the school came under attack. This skepticism toward tradition is reflected at a personal level in Skinner's autobiographical account of his college years.

College

In 1922 the Skinner family moved from Susquehanna to Scranton, Pennsylvania. That fall, young Skinner went to Hamilton College in New York. Hamilton College had a reputation for public speaking, and it was distinguished among colleges for its teaching of modern languages.[4] Skinner took courses in English composition, the history of literature, French theater, and creative writing. He also took courses in biology and political science.[5] Literature and language became the dominant theme of his college years, and in the fall of 1925 he decided to become a writer, having spent the summer at Bread Loaf, a writing school in Vermont. He had sent a sample of short stories to Robert Frost and in April 1926 received an encouraging reply which Frost concluded by saying, "You are worth twice anyone else I have seen in prose this year."[6] Skinner's parents reluctantly agreed to support him for a one-year trial at a writing career at the family home in Scranton. In May 1926, he graduated with a major in English literature. Skinner was about to enter what he later called "The Dark Year."[7]

Although Skinner's reading at college mostly involved works of literature, he also read books and magazines that acquainted him with contemporary social thought.[8] Modern literature was antitraditional and iconoclastic, and it emphasized authentic and direct experience.[9] Modernist culture was arriving in the United States via literary figures such as Ezra Pound (a Hamilton alumnus), Carl Sandburg, and Robert Frost, to name just a few of those whom Skinner followed closely and, in the case of Sandburg and Frost, actually met.[10]

During his college years Skinner also manifested a rebellious attitude toward traditional beliefs and values. As a senior, he participated in several hoaxes that put him at risk of expulsion from college.[11] He became skeptical toward religion and the kind of respectable middle-class life his parents represented. He showed signs of dissatisfaction with life both at college and in the family home. In the short stories "The Laugh" and "Elsa," which Skinner wrote during these years, we find a writer describing social discomfort and psychological complexities.[12]

In his senior year, Skinner began to publish reviews of literature and was one among four friends who attracted attention as a writer. He later remarked that "the four of us met frequently, controlled the local media, and were active in what could be called political discussion."[13] Skinner's account reveals nothing, however, about the content of those discussions or about his own political position. In another comment on his college years, he wrote that the Hamilton student culture was not the kind of environment that made one concerned about "how the country was run."[14] The implication is that he did not have political convictions in the 1920s, which, according to Fass, was typical of young people in college at the time ("on the whole, the young were politically apathetic").[15] Yet his father, William A. Skinner, who was a devout Republican and an active public speaker on political matters, worried that his son might turn to socialism. As an antidote, he provided him with a book on free-enterprise economics, titled *The Things that Are Caesar's: A Defense of Wealth,* in an effort to meet this danger.[16]

Literature and Psychology

The yearlong experiment in writing after college soon proved to be a mistake. Skinner noted in *Particulars of My Life* that "nothing in my history had led me to take a position on any important current issue, and the topics I wrote about continued to turn up by accident. . . . The truth was, I had no reason to write anything."[17] In effect, Skinner lacked a stimulating social environment and the critical audience needed to develop his literary talent.[18]

In his choice of reading during the postgraduation period, Skinner appears to have sampled broadly. He did not concentrate on a special style, topic, or author, and he did not exclusively read works of fiction or poetry. His reading included several works by Modernist authors, from Dostoevsky to James Joyce and Ezra Pound. He subscribed to periodicals dealing with Modernist art, music, and literature, including *The Dial, The American Mercury,* and the *Saturday Review of Literature.*[19] Two examples from these sources are telling.

The famous iconoclast H. L. Mencken founded *The American Mercury* in 1922. Using the magazine as a platform, he satirized some aspects of American life and cherished others, becoming a controversial figure in the process. Mencken's agnosticism and scientism were based on Darwin and Huxley, and the *Mercury* addressed a broad range of social, economic, and political questions as well as showing considerable interest in the natural and social sciences.[20] Skinner read the magazine and contributed two items to the "Americana" section which satirized life in America.[21]

A second example is the works of Ezra Pound, whom Skinner had studied and written a major article about at college. Skinner subscribed to Pound's short-lived magazine *Exile* (1927–28), in which Pound engaged in cultural critique and expressed his views of the time on politics and commerce. "I want a new civilization," Pound wrote, and he did not hesitate to extend his notions about order and force from the realms of art, literature, and science to the arena of ethics and politics. For example, he spoke of Mussolini's power as being like that of a magnet which aligns the iron filings in its field—a metaphor reminiscent of Jacques Loeb's tropistic account, already familiar to Skinner, of an animal's forced movement through a field of physical forces.[22]

The historian John Burnham has depicted the 1920s as a decade of critical changes in life-style and public mood. The "new psychologies" of psychoanalysis, glandular theories of human behavior, and behaviorism are representative of these intellectual changes.[23] As a reflection of World War I and the impact of evolutionary thinking, the new psychologies stressed the irrational and animalistic features of human behavior.[24] The iconoclastic tone common to these scientific theories fitted easily with the Modernist culture that triumphed in the 1920s.

Science was an integral part of American Modernism and it was regarded, as a friend of Skinner remarked at the time, as "the art of the twentieth century."[25] The importance of science was also emphasized by the likes of H. G. Wells and Bertrand Russell, both of whom had a decisive influence on Skinner in this period. Wells's novel *The World of William Clissold* (1926), which Skinner read, bore the same message as his earlier utopian fantasies *Men Like Gods* and *The Dream*.[26] Science, and especially social science, were seen as instruments for improving society and solving social problems. Russell was also convinced of the importance of science for an understanding of human action and society in general, and it was Russell's writings that introduced Skinner to John B. Watson and behaviorism. Both Wells and Russell envisioned a central role for science and scientists in the reconstruction of society, a view widely shared among intellectuals of the twenties.[27]

Watson was, of course, *the* behaviorist. In his renowned manifesto of 1913, he had been the first to use the term *behaviorism* and the first to articulate an uncompromising behaviorist position. In his role as founder-leader and as an agent of a scientific reform movement, he was a combative and rebellious figure who enjoyed debating.[28] Watson's behaviorist manifesto stated that the goal of psychology is prediction and control. This carried a special meaning, referring not only to experimental control but to social control—to the manipulation of persons for the sake of a well-functioning society.[29]

The first edition of Watson's *Behaviorism,* which Skinner read in 1927, was a collection of lectures marked by polemical style, exaggerations, and overstatements.[30] Watson began the book with a distinction between the óld and new psychology. The new psychology, behaviorism, regarded the subject matter of psychology as "the *behavior or activities of the human being.*"[31] Watson went on to urge the application of the S-R procedure to social experimentation. In fact, he argued that the social scientist should be the "ruler" of society, because behaviorism is the natural science that deals with human adjustment, and it is crucial to the organization and control of society.[32]

Skinner found in Watson's book more an approach to the study of psychology than a ready-made system. The polemical style, the radical and scientistic perspective, did strike a chord in the mind of a young man searching for social identity. He saw the possibility of entering a new, fresh, and promising field, the scientific study of human behavior. The impact of Watson on Skinner seems to have been largely motivational, especially in the sense of suggesting applications to "big things"; as Skinner would later write, *Behaviorism* allowed him to begin to "glimpse the possibility of technological applications."[33] Yet he did not follow Watson closely: when the latter wrote a short behaviorist utopia published in 1929 in the *Liberty Magazine,* Skinner did not read it.[34]

In the fall of 1927 an article by H. G. Wells in the *New York Times* was instrumental, according to Skinner, in his choice of graduate studies in psychology.[35] Wells argued that if one were forced to choose between science and literature, the former is the more important for the future of humankind. If he had to choose, Wells would save Pavlov over George Bernard Shaw. Skinner's acknowledgment of the influence of Wells's article suggests that it was the aspect of social relevance that carried weight in his choice of a career.[36] The arguments against literature as a method that Skinner was formulating at the time reinforce this suggestion. In Skinner's view, literature could describe human behavior but it could not really explain it.[37]

All in all, Skinner's reading during this two-year period pointed to the importance of social science, and especially psychology, as a potent instrument for improving society. Behaviorism, in the Watsonian version, carried this reform impulse along with a radical, modern, and antitraditional thrust. It shared with psychoanalysis a critical perspective on religion and a certain frankness about sexuality that was easily picked up by the young generation of the twenties. Furthermore, behaviorism was an American product.[38] However, Skinner was not a wholehearted psychologist or behaviorist in 1927, or for that matter during his subsequent first year at Harvard.[39]

The Digest

If Skinner's literary reading was one major preoccupation during this period, it was not to the exclusion of other projects, including one that in fact eventuated in his first published book. In the summer of 1927 Skinner accepted an offer from his father to work on a digest of decisions of the Anthracite Board of Conciliation. The anthracite coal strike of 1902 had resulted in White House involvement. Theodore Roosevelt approved the constitution of an Anthracite Coal Strike Commission, whose main purpose was to "inquire into, consider, and pass upon all questions at issue" between the coal companies and the miners.[40] Acting as both interpreter and arbiter, the Anthracite Board of Conciliation worked out disagreements that arose under the purview of the commission.

The work on the digest was, according to Skinner, a kind of "Baconian classification of scientific facts";[41] he sorted out and classified decisions on 1,148 grievances made by the board and the umpire from 1902 up to the midtwenties. In the present context of inquiry about Skinner's early social philosophy, it is worth noting that this was classificatory work on a subject matter that made young Skinner an expert on grievances and conflicts between miners and operators in the coal district of Pennsylvania. This involved a large scope of subject matters, such as methods of payment, working hours, discipline, and relations between employer and employee, as well as definitions and specifications of different kinds of work and processes in the mine.

In addition to providing the young Skinner with experience in Baconian classification and in grappling with a large range of material (including definitional issues), his work on the digest acquainted him with an important part of recent American labor history that concerned the allocation of rewards for work. The emphasis of the research was on the legislation of the board, and it was intended to give company lawyers an advantage over the union and workers.[42] Skinner worked in the service of his father, and the book was published in February 1928 with William A. Skinner as coauthor.[43]

Skinner had failed as a writer of fiction after college for various reasons. But the two-year period after college familiarized him with major trends in literature, philosophy, and social thinking. Taken together, these activities formed an important part of his preparation for graduate studies in psychology. Skinner stated several times that epistemology was his "first love," and it has often been repeated that he first encountered Watson and behaviorism in this context.[44] But an equally interesting and important context was the contemporary literature—both fiction and nonfiction—that unmasked social life and emphasized the capacity of the social sciences to improve human affairs. In behaviorism, "the new faith of America," there was a youthful readiness for social action.[45]

HARVARD UNIVERSITY, 1928–1936

The years that Skinner spent at Harvard University were a period of social and economic turbulence in society at large. The depression reached its peak in the early thirties. Unemployment, poverty, and disillusionment also affected the educational sphere; colleges closed down and student riots were common.[46] Among intellectuals the search for solutions to this "collapse of the American dream" had priority. The crisis demanded new and fundamental reforms, and planning for a new social order became a predominant theme. The era of laissez-faire and individualism ended in the minds of economists and social thinkers. As *Business Week* reported in 1931, "to plan or not to plan is no longer the question. The real question is, who is to do it?"[47] Scientific planning of a collectivist order was regarded as a necessary approach in order to solve the problems confronting the nation.[48]

Psychology as the science of humans had an important place in this context. Applied and clinical psychology expanded after World War I, as experimental psychologists had extended their research into fields like education, industry, media, and the family.[49] Although not all psychologists concerned with human needs and social improvement turned to applied science, the assumption that psychology was ultimately a science with the mission of improving human relations was shared alike by experimentalists and applied psychologists.[50] In 1929, psychologists, social scientists, and benefactors drew up plans for an Institute of Human Relations at Yale University. This research center was to be devoted to an integrated science of human affairs with eventual practical applications.[51]

Skinner wrote in his autobiography that he did not follow the social and political events of the time. He did not read newspapers or magazines, and "Roosevelt slipped into office almost unobserved by me."[52] Not paying attention to politics during the thirties was, according to Skinner, an explicit decision. To Ivor Richards he used to say that he was gambling on the survival of Western culture, that it would probably survive without his contribution. Meanwhile, he spent most of his time—and more time because of his noninvolvement in politics—working for a better understanding of human behavior in the hope that such an understanding would eventually enable him to accomplish what he could not do effectively by running for office or by supporting candidates.[53]

This is a statement by a social scientist about psychology at a time when it would have been premature to apply it to the world of human affairs. Skinner was concerned with building a research tradition in psychology upon a descriptive and functional analysis of behavior. This involved experimentation, epistemology, scientific method, and terminology. There was no place for social action in this agenda; it had to be postponed. The plans for his future that he drew up in 1932 did not include any area of research with direct social relevance.[54]

At Harvard Skinner devoted himself to experimental research, striving in his dissertation of 1930 to define the basic response unit of a science of behavior. He invented experimental apparatuses and published a number of experimental articles. The outcome of this research was the concept of the operant. Skinner's overriding interest was in the exploration of behavioral orderliness. The approach was mathematical in a sense, but he did not emphasize numerical values or develop mathematical elaborations. Rather, the significance of the research lay in the fact that regularities had actually been exhibited. Skinner's graduate years were characterized by a diversity of research, but the one unifying feature of his work was the search for quantitative regularities and orderliness in the behavior of rats.[55]

What can be said about Skinner's nonexperimental activity at Harvard? The unpublished record shows that as a graduate student he was fascinated by perceptual illusions and associations, Proustian recollections, and Henri Bergson's concept of mental time; he even became interested in the phenomena of self-hypnosis and suggestion.[56] The "books to read" lists that Skinner drew up in the late twenties and early thirties reveal something of his interests, although we cannot ascertain exactly what he read from them. One list contained a collection of scientists and writers working in different fields: Claude Bernard, C. D. Broad, Lawrence J. Henderson, Ivor A. Richards, Wyndham Lewis, Albert Einstein, and Sir Arthur Eddington.[57] The areas he wanted to study comprised physiology, philosophy, physics, and literary criticism, with a general focus on problems of scientific method and broader issues of the scientific conception of the world. The lists show a continued interest in the fields that had caught his attention before coming to Harvard.

Skinner's postgraduate years at Harvard were marked by a revival of his interest in literature. When he made the decision to enter a career in psychology, he rejected literature as a means to understand human behavior. Now having finished his dissertation, Skinner approached literature as a scientist rather than as a young author. Although he had entered the field of psychology with bad feelings toward literature, he kept the literary magazines to which he had subscribed during the "literary days"—such periodicals as *The Dial, Exile,* and *Two Worlds Monthly*.[58]

During this period, Skinner met and discussed literature with James Agee and several other writers.[59] One of these was Ivor A. Richards, whom he met in the fall of 1931. In *The Dial* Skinner had encountered Bertrand Russell's 1926 review of Richards and Ogden's book *The Meaning of Meaning,* and now he found himself discussing literature and behaviorism with one of its authors. Richards was well acquainted with behaviorism, having, for example, reviewed Watson's *Behaviorism* for *The New Criterion.* In his 1926 book *Science and Poetry,* he suggested the use of "the new 'science' of psychology to define poetry." The psychology he referred to in this case was current experimental psychology.

Richards had attempted to make a science out of literary criticism,[60] and
the idea of subjecting poetry to a scientific treatment was not lost on
Skinner, who would later publish an article on alliteration in the sonnets
of Shakespeare.[61]

The "Sketch for an Epistemology"

In addition to Skinner's return to literature, the postdoctoral years at
Harvard were also marked by a concern with epistemological problems.
In the late fall of 1932, Skinner began work on a manuscript intended to
be his first scholarly book: the "Sketch for an Epistemology."[62] The only
part of it ever to be published was the 1935 article "The Generic Nature
of the Concepts of Stimulus and Response," which became an important
position paper of the 1930s.[63]

Skinner admitted in the "Sketch" that the behaviorist could not, at that
time, provide a valid description of complex cases of behavior—certainly
not in terms of quantitative laws or principles. Behaviorism was as speculative as the traditional view. Neither could it be proved right or wrong.
The reason for entering this discussion was that traditional psychology
had had a long history, and it was relatively advanced in dealing with
complex cases. Behaviorism was a new approach and not easily integrated with psychology. The behaviorist was primarily interested in the
logical development of a science of behavior, in which the complex cases
would be tackled at a later stage. But still, the main interest of the behaviorist was, according to Skinner, the field of human behavior. Enough had
been done already in order to say something about the matters with which
traditional psychology dealt, even if this was merely stating a disagreement. Skinner wrote that "the implications of a successful description of
behavior are important, and enough has been done to make them seem
reasonable."[64]

Science is fundamentally simple, Skinner wrote, and there is no aim.
Above all, science is action.[65] But it is action in a special sense. It provides simplicity and it reveals order in nature. The important thing about
sticking to observation is the possibility of controlling the experiment.
Controlling the experiment means that one is able to detect functional
variables which in turn eventually enable one to predict behavior. Behaviorism is not simply a new vocabulary for old terms; it works better and
"it produces order instead of disorder, simplicity instead of piling confusion upon confusion."[66]

As is apparent from the foregoing, the "Sketch" revealed affinities with
notions commonly linked with American pragmatism and with the philosophy of Ernst Mach.[67] Mach argued for science as a complete, consis-

tent, and cohesive world-picture with the greatest stability, to be used as a means of orienting oneself in the world. A central notion in his conception of science is the theory of the economy of thought. The object of science is to communicate facts in an abridged and simple manner.[68] However, it is not a matter of simple fact-gathering. Rather, it is guided by interest; the choice of study of the scientist is related in one way or another to practical concerns.[69] The notion that science originates in the biological needs of humans resonates through Mach's philosophical writings: "All science has its origin in the needs of life."[70]

When Skinner abandoned his plans to publish the "Sketch" as a book on epistemology, he started out on the long road to come to terms with verbal behavior. Skinner had an interest in both literary and scientific language. In the "Sketch" he claimed that scientific research is largely concerned with the verbal behavior of scientists, and very much so in the case of the experimental psychology. A scientific treatment of verbal behavior was called for, and in the summer of 1934 Skinner started work on his book *Verbal Behavior,* published in 1957.

The Murchison Project, 1934

In October 1934 Carl Murchison of Clark University met with Warren Weaver from the Rockefeller Foundation. Weaver asked Murchison for advice about where to fund research in the social sciences during the coming twenty-five years. Murchison took the issue seriously and formed a small group to discuss the matter and prepare a report for Weaver. The members of the chosen group were Clarence Graham, Leonard Carmichael, and Skinner.[71] They prepared position papers, defining fundamental problems and worthwhile projects for the future. Whether or not the report was taken seriously (which Skinner had doubts about), these position papers are interesting as statements about which issues in psychology and the social sciences were viewed as the most important.

In his position paper, Skinner argued that the greatest contribution to social science would be a scientific analysis of language. Skinner wrote that "all of the social sciences are concerned with the study of man's relation with man; and such a study must have for its foundation a description of the principal medium of this relationship—language."[72] The rigorous scientific analysis of language would also, from what Skinner referred to as the practical point of view, enable us to deal with the real but vague notions of human volition, responsibility, social and political motives, emotion, and prejudice. Two lines of approach to this study were discussed: the pure science level and the practical level. Skinner emphasized the importance of the former but claimed that they should develop together.[73]

The Society of Fellows, 1933–1936

When Skinner entered the Harvard Society of Fellows in September 1933, he began a three-year period of regular social interactions with a network of senior scientists and young colleagues. The purpose of the society was to encourage free intellectual exchange in different areas among talented young researchers and a group of established scholars. No protocols or records were taken from these meetings, and a reconstruction from the autobiographies of the participants does not yield a comprehensive picture of the content of the discussions that took place.[74] For example, were there discussions of contemporary politics, the depression, and the New Deal? Of the role of science in society?

Among the Junior Fellows during this three-year period were Willard Quine, George Homans, Henry Guerlac, and Conrad Arensberg, to mention just a few. Among the known topics of the society were logical positivism, behaviorism, and functional anthropology. The Junior Fellows were, according to Homans, far more inclined to favor the New Deal than were undergraduate students. However, none of them were communists, but rather liberal democrats or socialists.[75] Homans and Bailey characterized the discussions at the Junior luncheons in the following way: "Men lived up as Republicans or Democrats, isolationists and interventionists. They came to know each other less as intellectuals than as common Americans."[76]

In the society, Skinner became well acquainted with some of the leading figures at Harvard in the 1930s, among whom the key member was Lawrence J. Henderson (1878–1942), a professor of biological chemistry. Cynthia E. Russett asserts that "to a whole generation of Harvard students he passed on his conception of scientific method, of social science methodology, and specifically of the place of equilibrium in the social sciences."[77] By the end of the twenties, Henderson had brought his methodological and philosophical interests to bear on the social sciences. The work of Vilfredo Pareto (1848–1923) became his entering wedge. The step from organism to society was not difficult for Henderson because "Pareto's work was simply proof to Henderson that the analytical tools and concepts with which he had long been familiar were more widely applicable than he had realized."[78] Pareto used the concept of equilibrium and treated society as a system. This organic metaphor implied that stability and cooperation could be achieved through the management of spontaneous tendencies. Social equilibrium was to Henderson not simply a theoretical construct but something that operated in reality, and he tried to turn his scientific training to social ends during the depression.[79]

In 1927, the Fatigue Laboratory was set up at the Harvard Business School in order to study physical and mental stress in workers. Henderson was the first director of the laboratory, and influenced both physiological work and social research. He was also involved in the problems of industrial relations arising from the Hawthorne experiments and Elton Mayo's work. In 1932 Henderson started a Pareto seminar at Harvard with a group that included Homans, Charles P. Curtis, Joseph Schumpeter, Talcott Parsons, Bernhard DeVoto, Crane Brinton, Elton Mayo, Henry Murray, and Robert Merton. The "Pareto cult" at Harvard became a way to counter attacks from Marxists and liberals, an observation consistent with the conservative bent of Henderson, who was known to be hostile toward the New Deal.[80]

Skinner met with Henderson at least once a week during his time in the Society of Fellows. He had taken a course in the history of science under Henderson in 1929, who then recommended that Skinner read Mach's *Science of Mechanics*.[81] Skinner also served as a guide for foreign visitors in the Fatigue Laboratory in that year. Skinner did not participate in the "Pareto cult" of the 1930s at Harvard, but he had bought a copy of Pareto's book and referred to it in the "Sketch." However, Skinner dismissed Pareto in his autobiography, writing that "Pareto was not a behaviorist, and I wasn't quite sure what to do with him."[82]

Although Skinner may not have been directly influenced by Henderson's views, he was probably not unaffected by Henderson's general support for a scientific methodology focusing on issues of determinism, adaptation, and the relation of organism to environment. Henderson also practiced Machian extensions from scientific facts and concepts to other areas, for example when he discussed social equilibrium in terms derived from his research in physical chemistry.

To what extent can the origins of Skinner's interest in social philosophy be reconstructed up to the mid-1930s? We have seen that during his college years and the two-year period before entering Harvard, Skinner was concerned chiefly with language and literature. But we have also noted that he was interested in studying a scientific conception of the world and that he read books about social reconstructions in which social science was instrumental. After an intense period of experimentation and invention of apparatus Skinner approached literature once again. The "Sketch" was a means to come to terms with epistemology and terminology in an experimental science of behavior. As such, it was an attempt to address such questions as the relation between scientist and subject matter. The "Sketch" and the work on verbal behavior which immediately followed were also Skinner's first extensions to human behavior. The

Society of Fellows provided stimulating intellectual contact that could only have broadened Skinner's interests in societal issues, including exposure to the idea of generalizing from organism to society and treating society as a system in equilibrium.

The foregoing provides only scattered elements of a social philosophy, but it reveals the important social role that Skinner assumed a science of behavior would play in the future. He was concerned with fundamental issues in a science of behavior, a science that would ultimately be of prime significance to individuals and society. The analysis of verbal behavior was a step toward a socially relevant science of behavior. In avoiding politics and concentrating on furthering a science of behavior, Skinner also assigned scientists in the field a crucial role in improving social conditions.

The Turn to Human Affairs at Minnesota and Indiana, 1936–1948

In 1936 Skinner left Harvard for the University of Minnesota, where he had been offered a position as instructor. He had almost completed what was to become *The Behavior of Organisms,* but as we have seen he was also deeply concerned with literature and language. For strategic reasons he chose to publish a full presentation of the system first, the terminology and methodology of a descriptive science of behavior, and a presentation of a vast amount of experimental work.[83] In the book he did not extrapolate to the world of human affairs, although he regarded this as the ultimate value of a science of behavior.

The social and economic problems of the depression, along with the rise of fascism in Europe, had contributed to the growth and relevance of social psychology.[84] In the 1930s an increasing number of psychologists sought to establish applied psychology as a profession and to emphasize the relevance of psychology for addressing social needs. They formed organizations like the American Association for Applied Psychology and the Society for the Psychological Study of Social Issues, although these organizations were subordinate to the science-oriented American Psychological Association. Skinner did not partake in these efforts and seems to have remained rather unaffected by social and political events.[85]

However, Skinner's dedication to "pure" research became harder to defend in the late thirties when events in Nazi Germany became a matter of concern to everyone. In a letter to Edward Freeman in 1937, Skinner showed his concern about intellectuals and their role in society. He worried about nationalism and used terms like *beehive* and *anthill* to describe the phenomenon. Intelligent men, he wrote, must protest and possibly organize themselves to counter the threat of cultural leveling involved in nationalism. He believed that Russia and Germany lift the unintelligent up to a higher position, but in doing so pull down the intelligent.[86]

World War II mobilized the entire psychological community, and experimental psychologists who had been far from the applied realm now delved into work and projects that displayed the important use of psychology for a society at war. Skinner also shifted his activity from research to military projects when the United States entered the war in December 1941. Project Pigeon required total control of the behavior of a pigeon in order to make it capable of guiding a missile. Skinner and his associates worked hard to obtain such complete control by carefully arranging the animals' environment. Although the project was abandoned in May 1944, the result was a revelation to Skinner at the time. The control of behavior was indeed not a new notion to him, but the kind of demonstration of total control found in this project had been lacking. A technology of behavior had been born. According to Skinner, Project Pigeon was one of the main inspirations to the writing of *Walden Two*.[87]

Psychologists' involvement in the war effort was a major event in the history of American psychology. It changed the discipline in a number of ways, and it seemed to assure psychologists of their role as experts in the field of human affairs.[88] Planning for the peace and for the reconstruction period after the war became common themes. In the case of Skinner this impulse was expressed in the form of a utopian novel where Planners and Managers used behavioral technology to design an experimental community.

With *Walden Two* Skinner attempted to influence public opinion in a radical manner by showing how a science of behavior might be used for the benefit of society. Skinner wrote the manuscript during a seven-week period in June and July of 1945. Inspired by the control of behavior displayed in Project Pigeon and by a book on nineteenth-century experiments in communal living, he developed a new mode of attacking social problems. The message was that politics had failed and that experimental communities guided by behavioral scientists were the needed alternative.

The community described in *Walden Two* is a real-life laboratory. There is a thorough study of individual fulfillment, and if dissatisfaction arises, protests are easily effected. Noteworthy is the absence of politics, police, and military. It is a well-run social machinery designed by social and cultural engineers. It also makes possible "*a genuine science of human behavior,*" a full-scale social experiment in which behavioral scientists are experimental leaders.[89] The managerial elite wants the workers to be productive, efficient, and happy, and to feel that they are in command of their work tasks and interests. But they see to it that the workers take interest in the community as a whole and choose just the right activities for the benefit of the group. The crucial task of the Planners is to design a small community that fosters self-control and effective behavior. When this task has been fulfilled, the Planners would no longer be needed, only the Managers.[90]

Skinner compared his vision of society to that of nineteenth-century anarchism. The Walden Two community lacked "any institutionalized government, religion, or economic system," just as in the vision of anarchism.[91] The link with anarchism stemmed mainly from Skinner's knowledge of Henry David Thoreau's work. In addition to some similarities between *Walden* (1854) and *Walden Two,* a significant part of Skinner's critique of democracy (election, voting, and majority rule) was, for example, rather close to Thoreau's arguments in *Civil Disobedience* (1849).[92]

However, it is hard to maintain that the Walden Two community bears any close relation to Thoreau's philosophy. Rather, it seems, that Skinner's vision is more related to the kind of managerial society expressed in the industrial sociology of the time, in business management, and in works like James Burnham's *Managerial Revolution: What Is Happening in the World.*[93] It is likely that Skinner was well acquainted with the work at the Harvard Business School through such persons as Henderson and Homans.[94] Furthermore, commenting on Burnham's book in 1944, he expressed a firm belief in the managerial society but held that scientists had to become better managers, a view in accordance with the Walden Two philosophy.[95]

A common notion in business management and industrial sociology was that cooperation in an industrial society cannot be left to chance or for that matter to the State, but that an elite of social scientists is best equipped to organize and administrate social life. The belief was that the physical sciences had thrown society out of balance, and that a compensatory use of psychology and sociology was needed to develop the societal skills of humans. In his reading during the twenties Skinner had encountered the view that scientists, and especially social scientists, would have an important role to play in social reconstruction. And in *Walden Two,* Skinner did not hesitate to point out the powerful potential of those agents of social reform: "What a few can make of mankind. . . . What kind of world we can build—those of use who understand the science of behavior."[96]

In his contributions to the Pittsburgh conference in March 1947 Skinner wrote that a theory of human behavior is necessary "not only to talk about the problems of the world, but to do something about them, to achieve the sort of control which it is the business of a science of behavior to investigate."[97] The experimental analysis of behavior had obviously reached a stage where it was possible to use a science of behavior for social action. There are several reasons for this outspoken concern about social issues. We have mentioned the optimistic and expansive mood in the psychological profession as an effect of World War II. Furthermore, a research tradition in the field of operant behavior was taking shape after the war: conferences occurred, newsletters circulated, and teachers had begun to introduce Skinner's system in the undergraduate classroom.

However, it should be noted that no major research in the field of human behavior had been performed under the auspices of Skinner's system. The only exception to this was the extension to verbal behavior that became Skinner's main field of research in the period 1944–47. In the fall of 1947 Skinner was the William James lecturer at Harvard, where he presented material from the manuscript on language. Already in the thirties Skinner had stressed the importance of verbal behavior for human affairs. Now he discussed the three major functions of verbal behavior: the personal, the scientific, and the social gain.

In the last lecture of 12 December, half a year before *Walden Two* was published, Skinner remarked: "There is no conflict between the aims of literary and scientific behavior. They are not opposed, but, if anything, complementary, and neither ever appears in pure form."[98] And so it was with Skinner himself. His failure as a writer during the "Dark Year" had, after all, been a temporary failure. The first explicit tract of social philosophy to come from his pen was a literary product rather than a scientific treatise, and with it he would soon enter the ranks of the "visible scientists."[99]

NOTES

1. Barbara Goodwin and Keith Taylor, *The Politics of Utopia: A Study in Theory and Practice* (London: Hutchinson, 1982), pp. 15–37.

2. Arthur E. Morgan, *Nowhere Was Somewhere: How History Makes Utopias and How Utopias Make History* (Chapel Hill: University of North Carolina Press, 1946).

3. Paula S. Fass, *The Damned and the Beautiful: American Youth in the 1920's* (New York: Oxford University Press, 1977), p. 5.

4. B. F. Skinner, *Particulars of My Life* (New York: New York University Press, 1976), p. 195. For revealing accounts of Skinner's college and precollege years, see Daniel W. Bjork, *B. F. Skinner: A Life* (New York: Basic, 1993), chaps. 1–2.

5. Skinner, *Particulars,* pp. 196–97, 215–16, 223–24.

6. Ibid., pp. 248–49, on p. 249. Skinner's letter to Robert Frost is also published in *Selected Letters of Robert Frost,* ed. Lawrence Thompson (London: Jonathan Cape, 1965), pp. 326–27.

7. Skinner gives an account of the "Dark Year" in *Particulars,* pp. 262–87. The period has also been analyzed by S. R. Coleman, "B. F. Skinner, 1926–1928: From Literature to Psychology," *Behavior Analyst* 8 (1985): 77–92; and Alan C. Elms, "Skinner's Dark Year and *Walden Two,*" *American Psychologist* 36 (1981): 470–79.

8. Compilation of authors and books read during his college years according to

Skinner, *Particulars*, pp. 202, 203, 204, 214-16, 224, 226–27, 234–35, 243, 251–52. Skinner makes general references to Stephen Crane, Sherwood Anderson, Robert Frost, Edgar Lee Masters, Ezra Pound, Carl Sandburg, and Herbert Spencer (probably referring to Spencer's *Philosophy of Style: An Essay*, 1873). He also refers to the following books: Joseph Battell, *Ellen; or the Whisperings of an Old Pine;* Maxwell Bodenheim, *Replenishing Jessica;* William C. Brownell, *The Genius of Style;* James B. Cabell, *Jurgen;* Willa Cather, *The Professor's House* and *One of Ours;* Ben Hecht, *Fantazius Mallare;* Percy Lubbock, *The Craft of Fiction;* Edgar A. Poe, *The Philosophy of Composition;* Georges Polti, *The Thirty-Six Dramatic Situations;* Upton Sinclair, *Book of Life;* Louis Untermeyer, *Modern American Poetry* and *Modern British Poetry;* Edith Wharton, *Ethan Frome;* and Elinor Wylie, *The Venetian Glass Nephew.* For the following books I have not been able to identify the authors: *The Diary of a Young Girl* and *Apologia pro Vita Monastica.* For course requirements Skinner read: Homer, Corneille, Racine, Molière, Marivaux, Hervieu, Bernstein, Rostand, Chaucer, and Shakespeare.

9. Sanford Schwartz, *The Matrix of Modernism: Pound, Eliot, and Early Twentieth-Century Thought* (Princeton: Princeton University Press, 1985), pp. 44–49.

10. Skinner, *Particulars*, pp. 226–28. The intention here is not to demonstrate direct influences but rather to show that Skinner was acquainted with Modernist literature and social thinking during the twenties. A further example of his contact with social thinking at the time is Upton Sinclair's *Book of Life* (London: Allan & Unwin, 1923), which he read before going to Bread Loaf. Sinclair was an active socialist, best known for his naturalistic novels. Sinclair's book had, as the title suggests, the character of a worldview presentation discussing wide-ranging questions from the nature of life to love, economy, and political systems, as well as the new world to come.

11. Skinner, *Particulars*, pp. 235–38. Skinner has characterized this sort of activity as "intellectual vandalism" and has commented that "today I should no doubt be protesting. I should be storming the President's office carrying placards. . . . But that was not the fashion, and I was to leave college without ever trying to tell myself or anyone else what was wrong with it" (ibid., p. 256).

12. Coleman, "Skinner, 1926–1928," p. 82.

13. Skinner, *Particulars*, p. 241.

14. Skinner, *Reflections on Behaviorism and Society* (Englewood Cliffs, N.J.: Prentice-Hall, 1978), p. 188.

15. Fass, *Damned and the Beautiful*, p. 328.

16. Guy M. Walker, *Things that Are Caesar's: A Defense of Wealth* (New York: Fowle, 1922). Skinner, *Particulars*, p. 224. William Arthur Skinner took the degree of Bachelor of Laws at New York Law School in 1896 and shortly thereafter began private practice as an attorney. In 1903 he became U.S. commissioner and ran for mayor of Susquehanna as the Republican candidate; one year later he also ran for district attorney. Both these attempts were without success. In 1907 he became local attorney for the Erie Railroad. According to Skinner, his father's political career was ended in 1907 when he defended a strikebreaker who had killed a picketer. William Skinner won the case, but it turned out to be a very unpopular verdict. In 1922 William Skinner was offered the position as junior counsel at the Hudson Coal Company in Scranton. He accepted it with the understanding that he subsequently would replace the general counsel. After this failed to happen, he started a private practice once again in 1926. By this time, Skinner

had published a book titled *The Workmen's Compensation Law of Pennsylvania* (Philadelphia: George T. Bisel, 1924).

17. Skinner, *Particulars,* pp. 263–64.

18. Ibid., pp. 263–64. See also Coleman, "Skinner, 1926–1928," pp. 82, 84.

19. In addition to these he subscribed to *Two Worlds Monthly, Haldeman-Julius Weekly,* and *The Exile.* Skinner, *Particulars,* p. 262.

20. Douglas C. Stenerson, *H. L. Mencken: Iconoclast from Baltimore* (Chicago: University of Chicago Press, 1971), pp. 15–17.

21. Ibid., pp. 5, 19. Skinner, *Particulars,* p. 268.

22. David C. Heymann, *Ezra Pound: The Last Rower* (London: Faber & Faber, 1976), p. 60; Schwartz, *Matrix of Modernism,* p. 126. Pound supported Mussolini as the kind of "donative" intelligence—the projective mind that stood for a new order—which Pound admired. On Jacques Loeb's notion of forced movement, see Loeb, *The Organism as a Whole, From a Physicochemical Viewpoint* (New York: Putnam, 1916). Skinner had read this work as an undergraduate and "was impressed by the concept of tropism or forced movement" (Skinner, *Particulars,* p. 295). On Loeb's influence on Skinner, see Philip J. Pauly, *Controlling Life: Jacques Loeb and the Engineering Ideal in Biology* (New York: Oxford University Press, 1987). Social critics such as Pound evidently had a real presence in Skinner's intellectual landscape; he later reported that while traveling in Europe in the summer of 1928, he thought about what persons like Sinclair Lewis, Ezra Pound, and H. L. Mencken would say about him as an American tourist (Skinner, *Particulars,* p. 313).

23. John C. Burnham, "The New Psychology: From Narcissism to Social Control," in *Change and Continuity in Twentieth Century America: The 1920's,* ed. John Braeman, Robert H. Bremmer, and David Brody (Columbus: Ohio State University Press, 1968), pp. 352, 354–56. As noted by Burnham (p. 356), glandular theories emphasized the role of body chemicals in the entire personality, as in Louis Berman's *Glands Regulating Personality* (New York: Macmillan, 1921).

24. Burnham, "New Psychology," in *Change and Continuity,* pp. 378–80.

25. Skinner, *Particulars,* p. 291. The friend was Alf Evers, an artist and college friend of Skinner's.

26. David C. Smith, *H. G. Wells, Desperately Mortal: A Biography* (New Haven: Yale University Press, 1986), p. 269.

27. For example, Walter Lippman, John Dewey, Lincoln Steffens, and John T. Adams. Skinner read Sinclair Lewis's novel *Arrowsmith* (New York: Grosset & Dunlap, 1925), a book whose subject may well have influenced Skinner a great deal. According to Mark Schorer, the novel introduced something new into American fiction, the description of "a research scientist fighting for his different kind of integrity" (afterword, to Lewis, *Arrowsmith* [New York: New American Library, Signet Classics, 1981], p. 436). The stories of Martin Arrowsmith and Max Gottlieb (the elderly German professor) are portrayed as heroic struggles to maintain a scientific dedication to truth. Gottlieb probably had several features in common with the famous German physiologist Jacques Loeb. Lewis had worked with Paul de Kruif in writing the book, and the latter was a research associate of Loeb (ibid., p. 432).

28. Alexandra W. Logue, "The Origins of Behaviorism: Antecedents and Proclamation," in *Points of View in the Modern History of Psychology,* ed. Claude E. Buxton (Orlando, Fla.: Academic Press, 1985), pp. 158, 163.

29. Franz Samelson, "Struggle for Scientific Authority: The Reception of Wat-

son's Behaviorism, 1913–1920," *Journal of the History of Behavioral Sciences* 17 (1981): 399–425, on p. 417.

30. The lectures were given at the Cooper Institute, 1924. Watson was dissatisfied with this first edition, having been rushed into publishing the lecture pamphlets. David Cohen, *J. B. Watson, The Founder of Behaviourism: A Biography* (London: Routledge & Kegan Paul, 1979), pp. 236–37. In the revised edition of 1930, Watson's final statement of behaviorism, he altered the form and style, and added about 100 pages of new material. John B. Watson, *Behaviorism* (New York: Norton, 1930), p. xi. The point here is that Skinner's first, and for a long time only, acquaintance with Watson's work came from reading the hastily prepared first edition.

31. John B. Watson, *Behaviorism* (New York: People's Institute, 1924), p. 3.

32. Ibid., pp. 11, 35–38.

33. Personal communication with Skinner (1986). Skinner, *Particulars,* p. 299.

34. John B. Watson, "Should a Child Have More Than One Mother?" *Liberty Magazine* (1929): 31–35. Personal communication with Skinner (1986).

35. H. G. Wells, "Mr. Wells Appraises Mr. Shaw," *New York Times Sunday Magazine,* 13 November 1927.

36. Skinner, *Particulars,* pp. 300–301.

37. Skinner, *The Shaping of a Behaviorist* (New York: New York University Press, 1984), p. 353n.

38. David Bakan, "Behaviorism and American Urbanization," *Journal of the History of the Behavioral Sciences* 2 (1966): 5–28.

39. Coleman concludes that "neither in the fall of 1927, when he decided on a field of study, nor in the fall of 1928, when he arrived at Harvard, was he wholeheartedly either a psychologist or a behaviorist" (Coleman, "Skinner, 1926–1928," p. 90).

40. R. J. Cornell, *The Anthracite Coal Strike of 1902* (Washington, D.C.: Catholic University of America Press, 1957), p. 229.

41. Skinner, *Particulars,* p. 287.

42. Ibid., p. 286.

43. B. F. Skinner and W. A. Skinner, *A Digest of Decisions of the Anthracite Board of Conciliation* (Scranton, Pa., 1928).

44. Skinner, *A Matter of Consequences* (New York: Knopf, 1983), p. 395; Skinner, *Reflections,* p. 124.

45. A phrase used by Louis A. Berman in *The Religion Called Behaviorism* (New York: Boni & Liveright, 1927).

46. Donald S. Napoli, *Architects of Adjustment: The History of the Psychological Profession in the United States* (New York: Kennikat Press, 1981), p. 65. Seymour Martin Lipset and David Riesman, *Education and Politics at Harvard* (New York: McGraw-Hill, 1975), pp. 157–63.

47. *Business Week,* 24 June 1931, p. 44.

48. As one historian has described it:

By the early 1930's, the concept of a planned economy was achieving widespread support. Economists and experts in government, business, and the universities were suggesting possible blueprints for comprehensive reform, while spokesmen for industry, labor, and the church were giving their almost unqualified approval to the idea of planning along collectivist lines.

Arthur A. Ekirch, Jr., *The Decline of American Liberalism* (New York: Atheneum, 1967), p. 270.

49. Napoli, *Architects of Adjustment*, pp. 34–36.

50. J. G. Morawski, "Assessing Psychology's Moral Heritage Through Our Neglected Utopias," *American Psychologist* 37 (1982): 1091–92.

51. Jill G. Morawski, "Organizing Knowledge and Behavior at Yale's Institute of Human Relations," *Isis* 77 (1986): 219–42.

52. Skinner, *Shaping*, p. 113.

53. Ibid., p. 230. Also discussed in private communication (1985).

54. Ibid., p. 115. The plans involved the experimental description of behavior, Behaviorism versus Psychology, and theories of knowledge, both scientific and nonscientific.

55. S. R. Coleman, "Quantitative Order in B. F. Skinner's Early Research Program, 1928–1931," *Behavior Analyst* 10 (1987): 47–65, on p. 61.

56. Notes from the later 1920s and early 1930s, B. F. Skinner Papers (hereafter referred to as BFSP), Harvard University Archives, Cambridge, Mass.

57. "Books to read lists," BFSP.

58. Skinner, *Shaping*, p. 90.

59. Skinner's name appeared on the dedication page in James Agee's book of poems *Permit Me Voyage* (New Haven: Yale University Press, 1934). Skinner also reports having discussed literature with the poet John Brooks Wheelwright, the novelist Victoria Lincoln, and the writer Sherry Mangan (*Shaping*, pp. 90–92, 112).

60. The Watson review appeared in *The New Criterion* 4 (1926): 372–78. Ivor A. Richards wrote "if only something could be done in psychology remotely comparable to what has been achieved in physics, practical consequences might be expected even more remarkable than any that the engineer can contrive." Richards, *Poetries and Sciences: A Reissue of Science and Poetry (1926, 1935) with Commentary* (London: Routledge & Kegan Paul, 1970), pp. 18–19.

61. Skinner, "The Alliteration in Shakespeare's Sonnets: A Study in Literary Behavior," *Psychological Record* 3 (1939): 186–92.

62. The "Sketch" is a handwritten 60-page manuscript (pagination added by Skinner several years later), BFSP.

63. Skinner, "The Generic Nature of the Concepts of Stimulus and Response," *Journal of General Psychology* 12 (1935): 40–65. (The paper was submitted to the journal's advisory board in June 1934.)

64. Skinner, "Sketch," p. 51.2.

65. Ibid., pp. 3, 17.

66. Ibid., p. 27.

67. Skinner read C. I. Lewis's *Mind and the World-Order: Outline of a Theory of Knowledge* (New York: Dover, 1929), and wrote running marginal notes. He was also acquainted with works by Charles S. Peirce. Skinner, *Shaping*, pp. 41, 116–17. For a general discussion of the relation between Skinner and Ernst Mach, see Willard F. Day, Jr., "The Historical Antecedents of Contemporary Behaviorism," in *Psychology: Theoretical-Historical Perspectives*, ed. R. W. Rieber and Kurt Salzinger (New York: Academic, 1980), pp. 203–62; and Laurence D. Smith, *Behaviorism and Logical Positivism: A Reassessment of the Alliance* (Stanford, Calif.: Stanford University Press, 1986), pp. 264–75.

68. Ernst Mach, *The Science of Mechanics: A Critical and Historical Account of Its Development* (La Salle, Ill.: Open Court, 1974), p. 577 (original German edition published 1883).

69. Ibid., pp. 90, 578.

70. Ibid., p. 609.

71. Carl Murchison's report to Warren Weaver, 26 November 1934, BFSP. Skinner, *Shaping*, pp. 165–66.

72. Skinner, Murchison project, position paper marked "5B Further BFS," p. 1, BFSP.

73. Ibid., pp. 4–5.

74. The following autobiographies have been studied: George Homans, Willard Quine, Lawrence J. Henderson, and James B. Conant, as well as several secondary sources. Skinner set out to write a notebook on these discussions, but the only entry he actually wrote is for the opening evening on 25 September 1933 (see Skinner, *Shaping*, pp. 129–30). Membership of the society for the relevant years is:
Senior Fellows 1933–36: Lawrence J. Henderson (chairman), Alfred N. Whitehead, J. L. Lowes, A. L. Lowell (former president of Harvard), James B. Conant (president of Harvard), Kenneth Murdoch (dean of faculty of art and sciences), Charles Curtis.
Junior Fellows, 1933– : Skinner (Psychology), W. O. Quine (Philosophy), J. C. Miller (Government), G. D. Birkhoff (Mathematics), T. Chambers (Chemistry), F. Watkins (Government).
Junior Fellows, 1934– : C. M. Arensberg (Anthropology), D. T. Griggs (Geology), G. M. Huss (Medicine), G. C. Homans (Sociology), H. T. Levin (English Literature), E. B. Wilson (Chemistry).
Junior Fellows, 1935– : J. Barden (Physics), I. H. Getting (Astronomy), H. E. Guerlac (Biological Chemistry, later History), G. M. A. Haufmann (Archaeology), P. L. Ward (Medical History).

75. George C. Homans, *Coming to My Senses: The Autobiography of a Sociologist* (New Brunswick, N.J.: Transaction Books, 1985), p. 127.

76. George C. Homans and Orville T. Bailey, *The Society of Fellows* (Cambridge: Harvard University, 1948), p. 104.

77. Cynthia E. Russett, *The Concept of Equilibrium in American Social Thought* (New Haven: Yale University Press, 1966), p. 117.

78. Ibid., p. 118.

79. Stephen J. Cross and William R. Albury, "Walter B. Cannon, L. J. Henderson, and the Organic Analogy," *Osiris* 3 (1987): 165–92, on pp. 180–82.

80. Barbara S. Heyl, "The Harvard 'Pareto Circle'," *Journal of the History of the Behavioral Sciences* (1968): 316–34, on p. 317.

81. Skinner, *Shaping*, p. 66.

82. Ibid., p. 49.

83. Skinner wrote that "it is a serious, though common, mistake to allow questions of ultimate application to influence the development of a systematic science at an early stage." Skinner, *The Behavior of Organisms: An Experimental Analysis* (New York: Appleton-Century, 1938), p. 441.

84. James H. Capshew, "Psychology on the March: American Psychologists and World War II" (Ph.D. diss., University of Pennsylvania, 1986), p. 159.

85. In 1941 Skinner was a member of the American Psychological Association, the American Association for the Advancement of Science, the Midwestern Psychological Association, the Society of Experimental Psychologists, Phi Beta Kappa, and Sigma Xi. See Application for Guggenheim Fellowship, BFSP.

86. "Let intelligence once be established as a determinant of behavior and the goal of the merely instinctive becomes no goal at all." Skinner to (University of Minnesota) Dean Edward M. Freeman, 18 March 1937, BFSP.

87. Skinner, *Shaping*, p. 274.

88. Capshew, "Psychology on the March," p. 289.

89. Skinner, *Walden Two* (New York: Macmillan, 1976), p. 274 (original work published 1948).

90. Ibid., p. 256.

91. Skinner, "News from Nowhere, 1985," *Behavior Analyst* 9 (1985): 5–14, on p. 6; reprinted in Skinner, *Upon Further Reflection* (Englewood Cliffs, N.J.: Prentice-Hall, 1987). Skinner, *Consequences,* pp. 426–427n. Evelyn F. Segal, "Walden Two: The Morality of Anarchy," *Behavior Analyst* 10 (1987): 147–60.

92. Skinner read *Walden* and several other works by Thoreau in the thirties. He bought a second-hand eleven-volume edition of Thoreau's collected works (not complete), and also read Odell Shephard's *Heart of Thoreau's Journals.* Skinner, *Shaping,* p. 296; Skinner, *Reflections,* pp. 188–89.

93. James Burnham, *The Managerial Revolution: What Is Happening in the World* (New York: John Day, 1941).

94. Most famous is the "Hawthorne study," which was directed by Elton Mayo of the Harvard Business School. Mayo, *The Human Problems of an Industrial Civilization* (New York: Macmillan, 1933); Mayo, *The Social Problems of an Industrial Civilization* (Andover, Mass.: Andover Press, 1945). F. J. Roethlisberger and W. J. Dickson, *Management and Worker* (Cambridge: Harvard University Press, 1939).

95. In a letter to Spencer, a National Defense Research Council official, cited in Capshew, "Psychology on the March," pp. 157–58n.

96. Skinner, *Walden Two,* p. 279.

97. Skinner, "Experimental Psychology," in *Current Trends in Psychology,* ed. Wayne Dennis (Pittsburgh: University of Pittsburgh Press, 1947), pp. 16–49, on p. 46.

98. Skinner, "Verbal Behavior, by B. F. Skinner. William James lectures, Harvard University, 1948," p. 170, BFSP.

99. Rae Goodell, *The Visible Scientists* (Boston: Little, Brown, 1977).

Part Two
Skinner as Scientist

4

Skinner's Progress During the 1930s: Reflexes, Operants, and Apparatuses

S. R. Coleman

About B. F. Skinner we know too much and too little. We have an overabundance of personal information, primarily from his autobiographical writings; his research publications are easily obtained, and so are the writings of his associates in behavior analysis and a large, related literature of critical appraisal. And yet there is a dearth of interpretive studies that make historical sense of this material either by offering personological-developmental interpretations[1] or by situating the available information in contexts that are broader than his professional discipline. Consider Skinner's *Particulars of My Life*:[2] the book provides a highly textured account of his family, his childhood activities, and the way of life in his hometown of Susquehanna, Pennsylvania; of his college years at Hamilton College; of his postgraduate efforts to develop a career as a writer, and of the failure of those career plans; and of his subsequent choice of psychology as a substitute career field in 1927–28.[3] Despite the abundance of autobiographical detail, regional factors in Skinner's development still await interpretation; efforts to place his story in "the American experience," specifically in the early twentieth-century, small-town context, have only recently begun.[4]

Psychologists may be willing to consign such material to a neglectable background of regional and national matters, but the same problem—the need for a contextualized, multidimensional understanding—arises also in considering the commencement of Skinner's career in psychology. The relevant years at Harvard saw Skinner in the roles of graduate student and postdoctoral fellow from 1928 to 1936, a period covered in his second autobiographical volume, *The Shaping of a Behaviorist*.[5] In that book too, Skinner's heavily descriptive compositional style created a quiltwork of seemingly independent strands: his personal and social life; his laboratory

activities and discoveries; the Harvard psychology scene; the larger cultural life in Cambridge; his marriage and job responsibilities; psychology
at Indiana and Minnesota; pigeon research on an applied military problem; and so on. These strands are cut and pasted in chronological cross
sections. In this array of circumstances, there are visible landmarks, but
his narrative decidedly favors description over interpretation, a characteristic that again leaves us without a pattern.[6]

The primary objectives of the present chapter are, first, to make more
apparent the order and timing of events in Skinner's development during
his graduate-student and postdoctoral years at Harvard in the mid-1930s;
second, to point out significant gaps in our understanding of this development; and, third, to focus on Skinner's abandonment of reflexes as an
important phase in his intellectual development.

In pursuit of these objectives, it will be useful to have at hand a listing
of important events in Skinner's development that can be apprehended
in one viewing. The timeline that appears in Table 1 begins in 1928, when
Skinner enrolled for graduate study at Harvard, and extends to the end
of 1934. It is organized by categories that are presented as column
headings.[7]

GRADUATE STUDY, HARVARD UNIVERSITY, 1928

In the fall of 1928 Skinner arrived in Cambridge, Massachusetts, with
virtually no knowledge of experimental psychology. He had graduated
from Hamilton College (Clinton, New York) in 1926 with a concentration
in literature and languages, but had failed in his efforts to carve out a
vocation and personal identity as a writer while living at his parents'
home in the Green Ridge section of Scranton, Pennsylvania, in the year
following his graduation. A resolution of his distressing vocational uncer-
tainty and identity problems was begun when, in late November of 1927,
he decided to undertake graduate study in psychology. After several
months of residence in New York City and travel with his parents on a
European trip,[8] he finally applied to, and was accepted by, Harvard in
May of 1928 for graduate study in psychology.[9] Uncertainties regarding
a career were largely resolved in his first year or two at Harvard.

It is arguable that Skinner came to Harvard with primarily epistemological interests;[10] such topics were prominent in his reading late in the
two-year gap between his undergraduate and graduate careers. His reading showed relatively few obvious substantive links from literature to
psychology; available evidence favors the idea that his choice of psychology had been largely circumstantial and, to that extent, accidental.[11] Skinner certainly did not know enough psychology to have recognizably

Table 1
Timeline

Year	Status	Research	Publications and Date of Submission	Books Read	Events
1928					
Spring				*Pavlov,* 1927	
Summer					
Sept.	*grad. student*			*Evans* 1928	
Oct.					
Nov.				*Sherrington,* 1906	
Dec.					
1929					
Jan.		ant research		*Loeb,* 1900	
Feb.					
Mar.					
Apr.		Parthenon			
May					
June					
		posture			
July		research			
Aug.					
					Int. Congress of Physio.
Sept.	*Thayer Fellow*			*Bridgman,*	meets Cuthbert
Oct.				1927	Daniel
		translating			
Nov.		*Magnus,* 1924		*Cannon,* 1929	
Dec.					
1930					
Jan.		tilting runway			
Feb.				*Lashley,* 1929	
		cumulative			
Mar.		record & curve-fitting		*Fearing,* 1930	
Apr.			'Elicitation' 4–21–1930		
May					

Table 1 *(Continued)*
Timeline

Year	Status	Research	Publications and Date of Submission	Books Read	Events
June		lever box			
July			"Review" of *Fearing,* 1930		
Aug.					
Sept.	*Walker Fellow*	writing on history of reflex			
Oct.					Diss. Part 1 to Boring
Nov.			"Concept of Reflex"		
Dec.			11–21–1930		Diss. Part 2 to Boring
1931					Diss. accepted
Jan.		running wheel			1–21–1931 Divisional Exam
Feb.					1–27–1931
Mar.					
Apr.					
May				*Sarton,* 1930	applies to Hist.
June				*Meyerson,* 1930	Sci. Society
July			"Drive"		
Aug.			7–7–1931		
Sept.	*N.R.C. Fellow*	reading in physio. &			"return to lit." I. A. Richards
Oct.		chemistry one-trial	"Drive, II" 10–6–1931	*Taylor,*	Hal Davis
Nov.		theory		1931	member of Hist. Sci. Society
Dec.					
1932					
Jan.		reinf. delay			
Feb.		extinction ratio	"Rate of Form." 2–5–1932		
Mar.					

Table 1 *(Continued)*
Timeline

Year	Status	Research	Publications and Date of Submission	Books Read	Events
Apr.					
May					
June					
July					
Aug.			"Spont. Act."		
Sept.	*N.R.C.* *Fellow*	reversible spinal block	8–23–1932	*Creed et al.,* 1932	C.L.A. House APA/Cornell
Oct.					
Nov.					plan for 30
Dec.					years
1933					
Jan.			"Discrimination" 1–27–1933	*Erkenntnis* *Phil.of Science*	
Feb.					
Mar.					
Apr.			"Resistance" 4–28–1933		selected as Junior Prize
May					Fellow
June		working on			
July		behaviorism book	"Abolishment" 7–21–1933		Monhegan, Maine,
Aug.			"Chronaxie" 8–23–1933		reading books
Sept.	*Society* *of Fellows*				about language
Oct.					
Nov.					
Dec.					
1934			"Gertrude Stein"		
Jan.					
Feb.					
Mar.			"Chained Ref." 3–13–1934	*Lowes,* 1927 *Tooke,* 1786	Whitehead Brown Univ.
Apr.		starts on language book			S.E.P./Harvard Hull's visit

Table 1 *(Continued)*
Timeline

Year	Status	Research	Publications and Date of Submission	Books Read	Events
May					
			"Generic"		
June		completed	"Two Types"		
		classif. of	6–4–1934		
July		verb. beh.	"Discrim."		
			7–2–1934		
Aug.			"Without"	*Wittgenstein*, 1922	
			8–6–1934	*Ogden & Richards,*	
Sept.	*Society*			1934	APA/Columbia
	of Fellows				
Oct.		reflex reserve			Murchison
					Project
Nov.					
					Quine lect.
Dec.			"Disinhibition"		Carnap trans.
			12–28–1934		project

psychological research interests, although it seems that he had some idea about wanting to be a behaviorist, based on a somewhat nebulous interest in behaviorism as a cultural phenomenon.[12]

Of great importance to our concern with his development at Harvard, he arrived with a personal inclination toward unconventional ideas, especially to those critical of the larger culture.[13] The iconoclastic appeal of behaviorism to Skinner may have stemmed largely from this predilection; it seems pertinent that Skinner was aware that Watson appealed to Pavlov and that Watson and Pavlov were separately promoted by two great social critics of the day, Bertrand Russell and H. G. Wells, respectively, whose essays Skinner would have encountered in *The Dial* and elsewhere in his reading.[14]

Skinner's penchant for critical ideas found a vehicle in the hard-headed, positivistic (and mechanistic-behavioristic) viewpoint he adopted at Harvard.[15] *Shaping of a Behaviorist* contains many examples of Skinner's readiness to take an antagonistic stance toward his less hard-nosed professors, and of his attraction to the attitude of rigor, simplicity, and restrictiveness that is characteristic of positivism. An attraction to the metaphysical notion of determinism seems to have been another noteworthy aspect of his intellectual commitment. In the Harvard graduate-school context, he had enough social and personal support (Charles Trueblood and Fred Keller for behaviorism, and W. J. Crozier for biological mechanism) to assume the position of conceptual sniper taking shots at the conventional wisdom of Harvard psychology, particularly as embodied in the person of E. G. Boring.[16] The anachronistic departmental linkage of psychology to philosophy at Harvard may have confirmed Skinner's harsh appraisal of Harvard psychology. However, it would be misleading to attribute Skinner's development during this period *solely* to the expression of personal predispositions; his assumption of a role as outspoken champion of behaviorism at Harvard probably served important social functions for psychology graduate students with behavioral interests,[17] and even for the larger institutional designs of Crozier. Philip Pauly's characterization of the ambitious Crozier suggests that Skinner was a valuable addition to Crozier's circle; that is a matter in need of elaboration, and an adequate treatment would make sense of Crozier's adoption of a mentor role with regard to Skinner.[18] Eventually Skinner went beyond paradigms favored by his mentor[19] (i.e., quantitative depiction of the discharge of a process through time, as in Skinner's study of satiation[20]) and later pursued a different program.

Given the sparse offerings in behavioral psychology in the Department of Philosophy and Psychology, and given the unsympathetic depiction of behaviorism by the senior psychologist of the department (Boring),[21] it is not surprising that Skinner spent much of his time in Crozier's Department of Physiology. The presence of two psychology doctorates (Hoagland and Upton) in Crozier's department supported the accepted option of taking behavioral coursework outside Philosophy and Psychology, so Skinner's coursework choices coincided with accepted practice. As a result, his behavior theory and research developed in a setting that was institutionally and intellectually separate from Harvard psychology, and his contact with the psychological literature was idiosyncratic, fortuitous, and partial.[22]

The importance of Skinner's affiliation with physiology for understanding his psychology should not be underestimated, but our comprehension of the matter is incomplete. What specific concepts, ideas, and models did Skinner borrow from his coursework, reading, and personal contact in physiology? What was borrowed at one time (early) and at another (late in the period)? What was going on during Skinner's postdoctoral retooling in physiology[23] in 1931–32? What unique features typified Harvard physiology or the persons with whom Skinner came into contact, and how was Skinner's theoretical and methodological system thus affected? In short, how can Skinner's work be situated in relation to physiological theory and research? And in what ways did the materials (concepts, facts, examples, style, etc.) that Skinner selectively adopted leave an enduring mark on his behavior system? A detailed treatment of the changing impact of Crozier's research program—and of physiology more generally—on Skinner's research and intellectual commitments has yet to be undertaken.

Evolution of Skinner's Research Apparatuses

Skinner also arrived on the Harvard scene with well developed "shop" skills, which he had acquired while growing up in Susquehanna, an Erie Railroad town in northeastern Pennsylvania. As a boy he had designed and built a number of toys and other devices;[24] hand-tool inventiveness, or at least extensive familiarity with mechanical contrivances, may have been a fairly widely distributed skill among the townfolk. In his first year at Harvard (1928–29), Skinner's repertoire of manual skills made it possible for him to construct several research apparatuses. Indeed, about his decision to remain in the Psychology program rather than to shift over to Physiology sometime in 1929, he says he was swayed by the excellent shop facilities in Psychology; so it is likely that there was a personal enjoyment in apparatus construction that was partly independent of its service to research questions.[25] In his three years as a graduate student he constructed eight or nine different apparatuses for the study of rat behaviors, and he stopped fabricating new apparatuses only when he had devised the lever-press box in 1931.[26] Subsequently he made many small improvements in this prototype "Skinner box" but retained its essential features while pursuing a program of research problems that continued beyond *The Behavior of Organisms*.[27] For our understanding of Skinner's progress, it is an important fact that his shop skills allowed his research findings—that is, his successes and failures in demonstrating quantitative orderliness in the behavior of his animals—to shift his research interests effortlessly and opportunistically from topic to topic, from apparatus to apparatus.[28]

Skinner had no specific, preconceived problem for investigation in his early rat research, other than the open-ended aim of vindicating determinism by showing that (at least some of) the behavior of the freely moving rat was as lawful as the reflexive behavior studied in physiology. Consequently, he thought of his work as part of a broad-scale extension of the concept of the reflex to freely moving organisms.[29] Skinner thought in terms of reflexological constructs such as the interaction of antagonistic reflexes and the chaining of reflexive components of serially complex acts.[30] As a result, he had the flexibility to pursue a succession of investigative topics that were uncovered by accident and curiosity. That indeed is the theme of his retrospective treatment of his research activities as a "case history" of the behavior of scientists.[31]

His research involved a succession of three such topics. In his first-year coursework (1928–29), Skinner read classics of reflexology by Rudolph Magnus and Charles Sherrington[32] (as the timeline shows), and his first research topics involved the analysis of posture and locomotion. Adopting the methods of Magnus as a model, Skinner searched for reflexes in his freely moving rats with the open-ended aim of observing reflexive behavior; in the summer of 1929, he planned, but never actually carried out, a project to photograph reflexive acts in young rats.[33] Skinner also devised tunnels and runways, primarily for the study of locomotion in the freely moving adult rat, thus rejecting the traditional, artifically simplified preparations of reflex physiology that used surgically altered, immobilized animals (typically cats).

The second distinguishable category of Skinner's research concerned hunger-drive and satiation; while investigating this topic, he developed a prototype Skinner box, which he called a "problem box." The third set of topics—conditioning, extinction, and discrimination—was addressed with this newly acquired problem-box methodology. These topics occupied the bulk of Skinner's laboratory research time in the 1930s, and, enlarged greatly by a focused program of research, they were the subjects of his 1938 book *The Behavior of Organisms*. Progress in this three-stage *topical* development was made possible by *apparatus* changes that less talented students would probably have been unable to instrument.

Given the role of curiosity and accident in shifting Skinner's research problems, it is not surprising that his development of the lever-box apparatus seems a bit more fumbling and complicated than he himself suggested in his "Case History." A reexamination of the archival records that have survived from this period supports that impression.[34] In pursuing the three topics of locomotion, drive, and conditioning, Skinner worked in three interlocking avenues of *apparatus development* that unfolded more or less simultaneously in the early 1930s. One involved *running wheels*.[35] A second involved measurement of halt (to an unexpected, calibrated click) in the running of unrestrained rats in *runways,* a line of work that continued beyond the invention of the lever-box.[36] In a third line of research Skinner made labor- and time-saving changes in his runway that turned the discrete-trial runway preparation into the free-responding *lever-box apparatus.*[37]

In his "Case History" written in the early 1950s, Skinner concentrated on this third line of development to make points concerning research practices that had been neglected by philosophical advocates of logical-positivist principles, hypothetico-deductive strategy, and theory-driven motives for research. A brief discussion of the runway-to-box development will shed light on one of the avenues by which Skinner effected his ambivalent departure from a reflexological model.

As Skinner described in his "Case History" (and illustrated with line-drawings), the first step in the runway-to-box development involved adding a return-alley from goal box to start box so that the runway became a continuous circle (a "double runway," he called it) interrupted by presentation of food at a fixed location.[38] Although it appears—at least from his retrospective "Case History," in which he pointed to this consideration as an important principle of scientific behavior—that this move was prompted *only* by labor-saving concerns, the apparatus modification shifted his methodology from a discrete-trial to a continuous-behavior procedure. Using a clock that ran continuously, he began a session by starting the clock when he released a rat into the apparatus, and then jotted down the time of each return of the rat to its starting point. The list of return-times served as his record, and he looked for an orderly pattern in these scores. (He also kept a naturalistic log of the behaviors each rat exhibited on a run, but this log apparently did not lead to any systematic examination of the variety of behaviors that came and went during successive runs, thus leaving quantitatively recorded behavior as the sole object of study.[39])

Later Skinner eliminated the burdensome chore of recording the return-times by mounting the runway on a rod transverse to the direction of the run, so that the runway tilted like a seesaw when the rat crossed the plane of the rod.[40] The resultant tilting of the runway was made to advance a toothed disc one step at a time (by a ratchet mechanism) so that food pellets that had been placed in separate holes in the disc were automatically dispensed one at a time into a food tray. Simultaneously a recording pen was allowed to drop one step per run on a moving kymographic record, thereby producing a decreasing record of cumulative runs (i.e., returns) against time.[41] Skinner drew lines through relatively straight segments of the record, a practice that suggests he was on the lookout for consistency of rate in a quest that certainly points to Crozier's guidance.

Finally—and this was a decisive change because it removed the reflexological topic of locomotion from Skinner's investigative program—he eliminated the requirement of running and allowed a stationary rat in a small chamber (a "problem box") to press a panel behind which was a food tray. Hunger became the chief topic of interest—Skinner's second topic, as we have seen. The timeline shows that about this time (late 1929) he was reading Walter B. Cannon's classic *Bodily Changes in Pain, Hunger, Fear and Rage*.[42] The arbitrarily chosen behavior of panel-pressing was the target behavior on which food was contingent, and Skinner's apparatus graphically displayed the temporal spacing of its occurrences as a progressive decline in panel-press rate resulting from satiation (of what Skinner called an "ingestive-reflex" sequence!). The panel-pressing was originally recorded as a decreasing function of time, as was just noted in the case of the seesaw apparatus; a small apparatus change reversed the display and enabled him to use the more conventional format of an increasing (concave-down) cumulative function.[43]

FROM MOLECULAR DETERMINISM TO MOLAR LAWFULNESS

Having found similar satiation curves for different rats, Skinner stopped scrapping apparatuses and was content to harvest records whose importance he took for granted. A routine soon emerged,[44] including efforts to identify the kind of function that his records exhibited. Progress consisted of the replacement of one activity (apparatus construction) by an activity that created engaging challenges that thereafter occupied his time and reduced the time available for further apparatus construction. With the help of Cuthbert Daniel, a close acquaintance, graduate student in physics, and housemate during Skinner's postdoctoral period, Skinner explored a variety of data transformations in a search for the function that described his concave-down cumulative records.[45] This quantitative agenda was more congruent with Crozier's research program than with the research of Pavlov, who published only tabular data, of Sherrington, who presented only kymographic-record figures, or of Magnus, who seldom used graphic presentations.[46] The fact that Skinner undertook such a problem with his limited mathematical skills is testimony to the importance of Crozier as an examplar. After exploring alternative transformations of his data, Skinner found that the cumulative data from the panel-press apparatus were closely fit by a power function of time.[47]

Within the year (1931) he made a small apparatus modification by substituting a lever for the panel, and he found that a power function of time with the same exponent fit cumulative records of bar-pressing as well. Finding such uniformity ("lawfulness") despite topographical differences between the sequential act of pushing a panel/grasping and removing a food pellet/and eating, on the one hand, and the sequence of pressing a lever/going to a food tray/and eating, on the other hand, suggested that topographical differences between the sequences were "irrelevant."[48] Such a suggestion was not at all congruent with reflexology, which regarded the molecular constituents of a complex act as determiners of the act's molar features. Thus Skinner's allegiance to a reflex model was seriously weakened by the changes in his methodology, by the shifts in his investigative topics, and by his discoveries in examining food-motivated behavior. Crozier was apparently not committed to reflexology anyway, Sherrington and Magnus being the relevant figures for Skinner, but Crozier's role in Skinner's conceptual shifts during this period has not been fully comprehended.

Another step in Skinner's development occurred at about the same time. He had noticed that his rats pressed the lever in a heterogeneous variety of ways, an observation that had previously disturbed him because of its implications of indeterminism. But his demonstrations of regular ("smooth") changes in rate as a function of such manipulations as satiation showed that lever-pressing (i.e., the response *class* that includes a variety of individual lever-presses) "behaves experimentally as a unitary thing" (i.e., exhibits "lawfulness") in spite of inexplicable topographical variation from occasion to occasion.[49] This point, which Skinner enunciated in his 1935 paper on "The Generic Nature of Stimulus and Response," amounted to a defense of a molar behaviorism against molecular viewpoints such as those of psychological theorists who were influenced by reflex-physiological ideas.[50] Thus by mid-1934 (when he submitted his manuscripts on the generic nature of reflexes and on two types of conditioned reflexes [see the timeline]), Skinner had completed *part of* his emancipation from the physiological ideas that had been major components of his investigative model of behavior.

Recapitulation and Implications

First. Skinner's discoveries were, for him, a watershed, but only in the animal-learning field. The eventual importance of *The Behavior of Organisms* as a landmark in the experimental analysis of behavior may obscure other enterprises on which Skinner worked simultaneously. Skinner's interest in language might well be regarded as far more important to him if his development from 1928 to 1938 were not framed as a laborious preparation for *The Behavior of Organisms*. And yet it would require only a little exaggeration to regard the 1938 book as a pragmatic enterprise suitable for a young assistant professor. Indeed, there is considerable evidence that Skinner's work on verbal behavior was of at least equal importance to him: his undergraduate major in literature and languages; the fact that his epistemological (i.e., language in use) interests remained strong;[51] his retrospective evaluation of *Verbal Behavior* as his most important work;[52] his reading, indicated in the timeline, especially after 1933;[53] his own autobiographical comments;[54] finally, his publications on language from 1934 to the early 1940s (not all shown in the timeline). All these indicate that the significance of verbal behavior is misleadingly overshadowed if we fasten on *Behavior of Organisms* as the publication that alone defines the character of the decade from 1928 to 1938.

Second. It is tempting to treat Skinner's development as though his ideas and discoveries had a life of their own; although the resulting intellectual history is a one-dimensional story, such a strategy for understanding is a time-honored option in the history of psychology, and we have used it extensively here. But that constrictive approach cannot provide a contextual and varied portrait of Skinner. Skinner's development was, of course, not simply conceptual and intellectual. He developed confidence,[55] and there occurred a gradual shift from a restrictive, critical, and somewhat defensively aggressive stance in his graduate-school years to an expansive, more tolerant stance later; *Shaping of a Behaviorist* includes abundant illustration of an expansion in his personal life during his postdoctoral years. The year 1934 is a convenient choice for illustrating this shift. He had been selected for the Harvard Society of Fellows, which provided contact with established, mature scholars as well as broadening experiences. He acquired an automobile, which enhanced his social life.[56] Clark Hull's interest in Skinner's research provoked a correspondence,[57] and one of Hull's students at Yale constructed a "Skinner-type" box for a dissertation project.[58] Skinner's research techniques were finally acknowledged by being taken up at other labs, a development that placed his research program in a larger framework of valuation. He gave colloquium presentations at Brown and Clark universities (see the timeline) and delivered a paper at the American Psychological Association (APA) meeting at Columbia University. In other words, he was acquiring a reputation, primarily in East Coast psychology circles. Moreover, his Gertrude Stein article in early 1934 established his versatility and provoked contact with scholars beyond the confines of psychology.[59] He was at work on a "language book" in which the local authorities at Harvard were very interested. Finally, in late 1934 Skinner was chosen to be a consultant in a project directed by the entrepreneurial psychologist Carl Murchison, as the timeline shows; the objective of the project was to assess the relationship between psychology and the biological sciences and to advise in regard to the distribution of Rockefeller Foundation moneys.[60] Such biographical detail supports the point that Skinner's postdoctoral-student development (1931–36) involved a considerable widening of the scope of his contacts and competence. As his sphere of activity enlarged, the field of vision of historians intent on describing that development should expand accordingly.

Third. To return to a primary theme of this chapter, it has been suggested here that Skinner's major problematic through the first half of the 1930s concerned the role of reflexes in the behavior of the freely moving organism. By 1935, Skinner had moved far from his reflexological starting point. He had nearly abandoned the reflexological idea that the orderliness of complex learned behavior depends on an underlying mechanism of individual reflexes composing the complex activity. And yet he was so thoroughly accustomed to reflexological models and constructs that he continued to employ them in the lever-press preparation even though his behavioral rate measure precluded the identification, measurement, and manipulation of reflexes, as he candidly acknowledged.[61] Skinner was still convinced that the behavior he studied was elicited reflex behavior; he continued to write of lever-pressing as a "conditioned reflex" until about 1937; and he retained the concept of reflex up through 1938 as a very abstract umbrella term (for operants and respondents), roughly synonymous with the notion of behavior-environment lawfulness.

Skinner's attachment to reflexological ideas has been emphasized in order to provide a basis for suggesting that some aspects of Skinner's mature psychology owe their existence to that background. Although Skinner went on to stress the *independence* of behavioral psychology from physiology (e.g., in the final chapter of *Behavior of Organisms*), it would be a mistake to regard that claim as an assertion of conceptual independence within the originating historical context of Skinner's major concepts, such as operant and respondent; the claim came only after years of deep involvement with physiology. The involvement makes sense of the centrality of the two-types distinction that Skinner made in 1935 and reframed in 1937,[62] because it suggests that an enduring issue for Skinner was to keep his own enterprise distinct from physiology proper and from reflexes, including Pavlovian conditioned responses. The negative definition of operant behavior as not elicited ("spontaneous") and nonreflexive follows as well. Other residuals of that historical background could probably be added to our list; but the composition of the list requires a more detailed picture of what Skinner demonstrably carried over from the physiology that he had studied. Accomplishments on that front would provide, simply for Skinner's scientific-career development, an important component of the kind of contextualized historical understanding that has been urged here.

NOTES

1. But see Alan C. Elms, "Skinner's Dark Year and *Walden Two*," *American Psychologist* 36 (1981): 470–79.

2. B. F. Skinner, *Particulars of My Life* (New York: Knopf, 1976).

3. S. R. Coleman, "B. F. Skinner, 1926–1928: From Literature to Psychology," *Behavior Analyst* 8 (1985): 77–92.

4. Christopher Lasch, review of *The Shaping of a Behaviorist*, by Skinner, in the *New Republic*, 4–11 August 1979, pp. 36–38. See also Daniel W. Bjork, "B. F. Skinner and the American Tradition: The Scientist as Social Inventor," this volume; *B. F. Skinner: A Life* (New York: Basic, 1993).

5. Skinner, *The Shaping of a Behaviorist* (New York: Knopf, 1979).

6. In his invited address "On Writing an Autobiography" at the American Psychological Association meetings in New York City (3 September 1979), Skinner reported that he took pains to minimize interpretation in composing the first two volumes of his autobiography.

7. Dates for reading most of the books came in the form of flyleaf dates that had been inscribed into the books. The late Professor Skinner graciously permitted me to examine his personal library.

8. Skinner, *Particulars,* pp. 298–319.

9. A copy of his application is in the B. F. Skinner Papers (hereafter referred to as BFSP), Harvard University Archives, Cambridge, Mass.

10. Skinner, *Shaping,* pp. 3–15, 353–55.

11. See Coleman, "Literature to Psychology," pp. 86–87; and Skinner, *Particulars,* pp. 298–302.

12. Skinner, *Particulars,* pp. 298–301.

13. See Skinner, *Particulars,* where unconventional people are mentioned on pp. 149–55; Tom Paine is discussed on p. 9; on Skinner's postgraduate bohemianism, see pp. 302–7.

14. See, for example, Bertrand Russell, "The Meaning of Meaning," *Dial* 81 (1926): 114–21; *Philosophy* (New York: Norton, 1927); and H. G. Wells, "Mr. Wells Appraises Mr. Shaw," *New York Times Sunday Magazine,* 13 November 1927, pp. 1, 16.

15. For examples of his critical bent, see Skinner, *Shaping,* pp. 46, 62–64.

16. See ibid., pp. 48, 80.

17. See ibid., pp. 60–61; Fred S. Keller, "Psychology at Harvard (1926–1931): A Reminiscence," in *Festschrift for B. F. Skinner,* ed. P. B. Dews (New York: Appleton-Century-Crofts, 1970), pp. 29–36.

18. Philip J. Pauly, *Controlling Life: Jacques Loeb and the Engineering Ideal in Biology* (New York: Oxford University Press, 1987). A tone of helpfulness and paternal concern pervades four letters from Crozier to Skinner in the summer of 1931; the letters contain advice on Skinner's paper, then in preparation, and later published as "Drive and Reflex Strength: II," *Journal of General Psychology* 6 (1932): 38–48. The papers are in Box 4 of Accession 9710, BFSP.

19. See Skinner's critique of Crozier in *Shaping,* pp. 170–71.

20. Skinner, "On the Conditions of Elicitation of Certain Eating Reflexes," *Proceedings of the National Academy of Sciences* 16 (1930): 433–38.

21. See Skinner, *Shaping,* p. 80.

22. Ibid., pp. 178–79. Inspection of the reference lists in Skinner's publications prior to *The Behavior of Organisms*—which did not depart greatly from his previous citation practice—shows minimal attention to the animal-conditioning literature, a fact that was not lost on his contemporaries. See David L. Krantz, "Schools and Systems: The Mutual Isolation of Operant and Non-Operant Psychology as a Case Study," *Journal of the History of the Behavioral Sciences* 8 (1972): 86–102, on pp. 98–99; and Gordon H. Bower and Ernest R. Hilgard, *Theories of Learning,* 5th ed. (Englewood Cliffs, N.J.: Prentice-Hall, 1981), p. 209. Among the eventual consequences was an isolation of the operant-conditioning enterprise; see Krantz, "Schools," and S. R. Coleman and S. E. Mehlman, "An Empirical Update (1969–1989) of D. L. Krantz's Thesis that the Experimental Analysis of Behavior Is Isolated," *Behavior Analyst* 15 (1992): 43–49.

23. See Skinner, *Shaping,* pp. 99–101.

24. See Skinner, *Particulars,* for example, pp. 66–69.

25. Skinner, *Shaping,* pp. 31–32.

26. The role played by his shop skills at Harvard can be gleaned from the first 200 pages of Skinner, *Shaping.* For an interpretation of the predoctoral development of Skinner's research program, see S. R. Coleman, "Quantitative Order

in B. F. Skinner's Early Research Program, 1928–1931," *Behavior Analyst* 10 (1987): 47–65.

27. See Skinner, "A Case History in Scientific Method," *American Psychologist* 11 (1956): 221–33.

28. See Coleman, "Quantitative Order," p. 61.

29. See, for example, Skinner, "The Concept of the Reflex in the Description of Behavior," *Journal of General Psychology* 5 (1931): 427–58. There he referred to the enterprise simply as "a science of behavior," but not as "behaviorism" or "psychology."

30. For the concept of antagonistic reflexes, see Skinner, *Shaping*, p. 33. For chaining, see Skinner, "Conditions of Elicitation," pp. 433–34; "Drive and Reflex Strength," *Journal of General Psychology* 6 (1932): 22–37, especially pp. 23, 31–34. See also Skinner, *Shaping*, p. 81; and S. R. Coleman, "Background and Change in B. F. Skinner's Metatheory from 1930 to 1938," *Journal of Mind and Behavior* 5 (1984): 471–500, especially pp. 488–90.

31. Skinner, "Case History." In this essay, Skinner treated as paradigmatic the most exploratory and least programmatic phase of his research career, thus downplaying any guidance by a framework of questions, whether empirical or theoretical.

32. Skinner, *Shaping*, pp. 16–17.

33. Ibid., pp. 36–37; Coleman, "Quantitative Order," p. 51.

34. Skinner, "Case History," pp. 222–25; Coleman, "Quantitative Order," pp. 53–54.

35. On running wheels, see Skinner, "The Measurement of 'Spontaneous Activity'," *Journal of General Psychology* 9 (1933): 3–23.

36. See Coleman, "Quantitative Order," pp. 50–52; and Skinner, "Case History," figures 1, 2, 4, pp. 222–23.

37. See Skinner, "Case History," figures 5 and 8, pp. 224–25; Coleman, "Quantitative Order," pp. 53–56.

38. See the double-runway illustration in Skinner, "Case History," figure 5, p. 224.

39. See Coleman, "Quantitative Order," p. 54.

40. Skinner, "Case History," figure 8, p. 225.

41. Ibid., figures 9 and 10.

42. Walter B. Cannon, *Bodily Changes in Pain, Hunger, Fear and Rage,* 2d ed. (New York: Appleton-Century, 1929).

43. See Skinner, "Case History," figures 10 and 11, pp. 225–26.

44. See Coleman, "Quantitative Order," pp. 62–63.

45. Ibid., pp. 58–61.

46. In Magnus's *Körperstellung,* only 10 of the 263 figures (plus numerous tables) present data graphically. Most of the figures are photographs, kymographic records, and anatomical drawings.

47. Skinner's published data in his 1930 paper, "Conditions of Elicitation," include a figure showing log-transformed data for two rats. The figure is reprinted in Coleman, "Quantitative Order," as figure 8, p. 59.

48. Skinner's argument for irrelevance is given in Skinner, "Drive, II," p. 47.

49. Ibid., p. 46; the quote is from Skinner, "The Generic Nature of the Concepts of Stimulus and Response," *Journal of General Psychology* 12 (1935): 40–65, on p. 45.

50. Though Skinner did not use such terminology, he would have been familiar with Edward C. Tolman's discussion of the distinction in the first chapter of his

classic *Purposive Behavior in Animals and Men* (New York: Century, 1932). Skinner may also have been familiar with John B. Watson's vacillation on the distinction, which appears throughout Watson's *Behaviorism* (New York: Norton, 1925).

51. See, for example, Skinner, *Shaping,* p. 353.

52. See, for example, Skinner, "The Experimental Analysis of Operant Behavior," in *Psychology: Theoretical-Historical Perspectives,* ed. Robert W. Rieber and Kurt Salzinger (New York: Academic Press, 1980), pp. 191–202, on p. 198. See also Skinner's remarks in *Verbal Behavior* (New York: Appleton-Century-Crofts, 1957), preface, and pp. 456–60, and see the timeline.

53. The timeline shows that he was at Monhegan Island in the summer of 1933. There he read several books on language (e.g., *The Meaning of Meaning*) and used a chart to record the time he spent in daily reading, which amounted to exactly six hours.

54. See Skinner, *Shaping,* pp. 90–92, 105–6, 112–13, 138, 149–51 (especially), 158–59, 171, 207–8; cf. pp. 14, 27.

55. See comparable remarks about confidence in the development of Charles Darwin, in Frank J. Sulloway, "Darwin's Early Intellectual Development: An Overview of the *Beagle* Voyage (1831–1836)," in *The Darwinian Heritage,* ed. David Kohn (Princeton: Princeton University Press, 1985), pp. 121–54.

56. Skinner's expanded life-style was made possible in part by generous post-doctoral financial support. As a member of the Society of Fellows, Skinner received a stipend of $1,500 plus room and board. The stipend alone was 137 percent of the average annual earnings of all full-time employees in the United States in 1934 (U. S. Bureau of the Census, *Historical Statistics of the United States, Colonial Times to 1970,* bicentennial ed., part 1 [Washington, D. C.: U. S. Government Printing Office, 1975], ser. D722, pp. 148, 164), so he could afford to enlarge his manner of living.

57. There are 10 letters in the correspondence, primarily from 1934, that are in BFSP.

58. R. E. P. Youtz, "Reinforcement, Extinction, and Spontaneous Recovery in a Non-Pavlovian Reaction," *Journal of Experimental Psychology* 22 (1938): 305–18; Youtz, "The Change with Time of a Thorndikian Response in the Rat," *Journal of Experimental Psychology* 23 (1938): 128–40.

59. Skinner, "Has Gertrude Stein a Secret?" *Atlantic Monthly,* January 1934, pp. 50–57.

60. See Skinner, *Shaping,* pp. 165–67.

61. Skinner, "Drive," p. 23. Skinner's belated abandonment of reflex terminology is discussed in relation to his research of the 1930s in Iver H. Iversen, "Skinner's Early Research: From Reflexology to Operant Conditioning," *American Psychologist* 47 (1992): 1318–28. A theme-based interpretation of Skinner's progress is suggested by S. R. Coleman, "From Critic to Theorist: Themes in Skinner's Development from 1928 to 1938," *Journal of Mind and Behavior* 12 (1991): 509–34.

62. The concept of operant was introduced by Skinner in "Two Types of Conditioned Reflex: A Reply to Konorski and Miller," *Journal of General Psychology* 16 (1937): 272–79. The concept came to serve as a label for the animal-conditioning field begun by Skinner and involving free-responding methodology. For conceptual analysis of operants, see A. C. Catania, "The Concept of Operant in the Analysis of Behavior," *Behaviorism* 1 (1973): 103–16; and Karl Schick, "Operants," *Journal of the Experimental Analysis of Behavior* 15 (1971): 413–23. That Skinner introduced the concept of operant primarily to defend his distinction of two types of conditioning is the theme of Coleman, "Historical Context and

Systematic Functions of the Concept of the Operant," *Behaviorism* 9 (1981): 209–26. That the postulation of operants reflected intellectual shifts that Skinner had undergone during the 1930s is the gist of Judith L. Scharff, "Skinner's Concept of the Operant: From Necessitarian to Probabilistic Causality," *Behaviorism* 10 (1982): 45–54, and also of Coleman, "Background of Skinner's Metatheory."

TIMELINE REFERENCES

The parenthetical word or phrase following an item is the short title that identifies the item in the timeline.

Bridgman, Percy W. *The Logic of Modern Physics.* New York: Macmillan, 1927.
Cannon, Walter B. *Bodily Changes in Pain, Hunger, Fear and Rage.* 2d ed. New York: Appleton-Century, 1929.
Creed, R. S.; Denny-Brown, Derek; Eccles, John C.; Liddell, E. G. T.; and Sherrington, Charles S. *Reflex Activity of the Spinal Cord.* Oxford: Oxford University Press, 1932.
Evans, C. L. *Recent Advances in Physiology.* 3d ed. Philadelphia: Blakiston's, 1928.
Fearing, Franklin. *Reflex Action: A Study in the History of Physiological Psychology.* Baltimore: Williams & Wilkins, 1930.
Lambert, Elizabeth F.; Forbes, Alexander; and Skinner, B. F. "Some Conditions Affecting Intensity and Duration Thresholds in Motor Nerve, with Reference to Chronaxie of Subordination." *American Journal of Physiology* 106 (1933): 721–37. ("Chronaxie")
Lashley, Karl S. *Brain Mechanisms and Intelligence: A Quantitative Study of Injuries to the Brain.* Chicago: University of Chicago Press, 1929.
Loeb, Jacques. *Comparative Physiology of the Brain and Comparative Psychology.* New York: Putnam, 1900.
Lowes, John Livingston. *The Road to Xanadu: A Study in the Ways of the Imagination.* Boston: Houghton Mifflin, 1927.
Magnus, Rudolph. *Körperstellung.* Berlin: Springer, 1924.
Meyerson, Émile. *Identity and Reality.* Translated by Kate Loewenberg. New York: Macmillan, 1930.
Ogden, Charles K.; and Ivor A. Richards. *The Meaning of Meaning.* 2d ed. New York: Harcourt, Brace, 1934.
Pavlov, Ivan P. *Conditioned Reflexes.* Edited and translated by G. Anrep. Cambridge: Cambridge University Press, 1927.
Sarton, George. *The History of Science and the New Humanism.* New York: Holt, 1930.
Sherrington, Charles. *The Integrative Action of the Nervous System.* New Haven: Yale University Press, 1906.
Skinner, B. F. "On the Conditions of Elicitation of Certain Eating Reflexes." *Proceedings of the National Academy of Sciences* 16 (1930): 433–38. ("Elicitation")
———. "The Concept of the Reflex in the Description of Behavior." *Journal of General Psychology* 5 (1931): 427–58. ("Concept of Reflex")
———. "Drive and Reflex Strength." *Journal of General Psychology* 6 (1932): 22–37. ("Drive")
———. "Drive and Reflex Strength: II." *Journal of General Psychology* 6 (1932): 38–48. ("Drive, II")

————. "On the Rate of Formation of a Conditioned Reflex." *Journal of General Psychology* 7 (1932): 274–86. ("Rate of Form.")

————. "The Abolishment of a Discrimination." *Proceedings of the National Academy of Sciences* 19 (1933): 825–28. ("Abolishment")

————. "The Measurement of 'Spontaneous Activity'." *Journal of General Psychology* 9 (1933): 3–23. ("Spont. Act.")

————. "The Rate of Establishment of a Discrimination." *Journal of General Psychology* 9 (1933): 302–50. ("Discrimination")

————. "'Resistance to Extinction' in the Process of Conditioning." *Journal of General Psychology* 9 (1933): 420–29. ("Resistance")

————. "A Discrimination Without Previous Conditioning." *Proceedings of the National Academy of Sciences* 20 (1934): 532–36. ("Without")

————. "The Extinction of Chained Reflexes." *Proceedings of the National Academy of Sciences* 20 (1934): 234–37. ("Chained Ref.")

————. "Has Gertrude Stein a Secret?" *Atlantic Monthly* 153 (January 1934): 50–57. ("Gertrude Stein")

————. "A Discrimination Based upon a Change in the Properties of a Stimulus." *Journal of General Psychology* 12 (1935): 313–36. ("Discrim.")

————. "The Generic Nature of the Concepts of Stimulus and Response." *Journal of General Psychology* 12 (1935): 40–65. ("Generic")

————. "Two Types of Conditioned Reflex and a Pseudo Type." *Journal of General Psychology* 12 (1935): 66–77. ("Two Types")

————. "A Failure to Obtain 'Disinhibition'." *Journal of General Psychology* 14 (1936): 127–35. ("Disinhibition")

————, and Crozier, William J. Review of *Reflex Action: A Study in the History of Physiological Psychology,* by Franklin Fearing. *Journal of General Psychology* 5(1931): 125–29. ("Review")

Taylor, Hugh S., ed. *A Treatise on Physical Chemistry,* 2 vols., 2d ed. New York: Van Nostrand, 1931.

Tooke, John Horne. *Epea Pteroenta. Or, The Diversions of Purley.* Part 1. London: J. Johnson, 1786.

Wittgenstein, Ludwig. *Tractatus Logico-Philosophicus.* London: Routledge, 1922.

5

Engineering Behavior:
Project Pigeon, World War II,
and the Conditioning of B. F. Skinner

JAMES H. CAPSHEW

DURING the Second World War, B. F. Skinner's scientific outlook and professional goals underwent a remarkable metamorphosis. Although he had already glimpsed the possibilities for applying science to society through his early exposure to Francis Bacon, Skinner's conversion to the cause of behavioral engineering did not occur until the contingencies of wartime had reshaped his research agenda. Before the war, Skinner was reluctant to venture very far outside the academic laboratory. He was a scientific purist who resisted extrapolating the results of his animal experimentation to the realm of human behavior. After the war, he attempted to make such connections boldly explicit, arguing that the scientific principles of behaviorism had widespread applicability to human affairs. By the 1950s Skinner had emerged as an advocate of the use of operant conditioning techniques for the control of individual and group behavior in a variety of settings and promoted applications ranging from teaching machines to the design of entire societies.

Skinner's transition from inventive scientist to social inventor can be traced to the circumstances of World War II, which provided him with opportunities to explore the technological ramifications of operant psychology. Years later he noted that three wartime projects had dramatically broadened his intellectual horizons by offering the first evidence that his system of behavioral science could engender a system of behavioral

Reprinted, with minor changes, from *Technology and Culture* 34 (1993): 835–57, by permission of the author and the publisher. Copyright 1993 by The University of Chicago.

engineering.[1] The first was known as Project Pigeon—an attempt to construct a missile guidance system utilizing the conditioned pecking behavior of pigeons. Project Pigeon consumed much of Skinner's energy during the war, and although it was never brought to fruition, it played a pivotal role in reorienting his thinking toward the possibilities of behavioral engineering.[2] The second project was closer to home. Faced with the challenges of raising a second baby daughter, Skinner drew on his manual skills and invented the "baby-tender," a futuristic climate-controlled crib designed to promote the physical and psychological health of infants.[3] Featured in the *Ladies' Home Journal* shortly following the war, the device was later marketed commercially with little success as the "Aircrib."[4] Skinner's third novel project was precisely that—a novel. During the summer of 1945 he drafted the manuscript that would be published three years later as *Walden Two*.[5] The book was Skinner's attempt to conceive a utopian human society based on the principles of reinforcement that he had gleaned from his laboratory research on animal behavior.

Taken together, these efforts represent Skinner's initial forays into the realm of behavioral engineering, and they clearly demonstrate how the technocratic ideals embedded in his research practices found expression in the wartime context. Although Skinner's work was undeniably idiosyncratic, it reflected broader trends in American psychology that reached their fullest expression during the Second World War, with its overriding emphasis on military utility and the virtues of order, control, and effectiveness.[6]

Of the three projects, *Walden Two* became the most famous. It was the first step in Skinner's public transformation from experimental psychologist to social philosopher, and its description of an entire culture molded along behaviorist lines suggested the scope of Skinner's ambitions. As important as the novel was, it was only the most visible manifestation of a more fundamental change that had begun during Project Pigeon, when Skinner first confronted the difficulties associated with conducting research outside the laboratory environment. The history of this unusual project is essential to understanding Skinner's profound intellectual shift from the development of a natural science of behavior in the laboratory toward its technological applications in a variety of real-life contexts. Project Pigeon encouraged Skinner to think about his research in new ways and reinforced his belief in the underlying orderliness of behavior. Skinner's behavioral technology was characterized by the same kind of inventive activity he had engaged in as a professional psychologist, except that it took place beyond the confines of the laboratory.

From the start of his career, Skinner had been an inventor. His experimental work depended significantly on his ability to design, build, and repair laboratory apparatuses. Devices such as the Skinner box were essential in providing the proper conditions for the manipulation of operant behavior; in fact, they can be regarded as machines for the production of behavior. When integrated with other elements of Skinner's research method, such as conditioning techniques, data recording, and interpretive schemes, such devices composed part of a technological system for scientific research.[7] What was notable about Skinner's wartime projects was their common focus on controlling behavior in nonlaboratory settings. Because it was his first serious effort to construct a technological system to address a practical problem, Project Pigeon is worth examining in detail.

THE CONTROL OF BEHAVIOR

In 1938, a year before the war began in Europe, Skinner published his first book, *The Behavior of Organisms: An Experimental Analysis*.[8] The monograph synthesized nearly a decade of laboratory research on the conditioning of white rats and contained Skinner's program for establishing psychology as a natural science alongside biology, chemistry, and physics. The young psychologist was after nothing less than the foundations for a true science of behavior, one that treated behavior as a scientific datum in its own right. He was equally critical of both mentalistic theorizing and neurological reductionism. In his view, the goal of a naturalistic science of behavior was within reach, thanks largely to the legacy of Charles Darwin, Lloyd Morgan, and John B. Watson.

Skinner's scientific ambitions had been shaped by a long apprenticeship in the Laboratory of General Physiology at Harvard University. Arriving at the university as a graduate student in the mid-1920s, Skinner earned his Ph.D. in 1931. Although his degree was in psychology, he did the bulk of his work in physiology, where his primary mentor was W. J. Crozier, the architect of the Harvard laboratory's program. Under the influence of Crozier and other members of the laboratory, Skinner became an adherent of the engineering ideal in biology championed by Jacques Loeb and sought to extend similar principles and techniques to the control of behavior.[9] Following an intellectual agenda outlined in his doctoral dissertation, Skinner virtually lived in the laboratory for five years of postdoctoral research, first as a National Research Council fellow and then as a member of Harvard's Society of Fellows.

Skinner modeled his approach on Ernst Mach's philosophy of science, emphasizing the functional description of observed behavior and rejecting causal explanations as unnecessary. His laboratory practices followed the pattern laid down by Loeb and his disciples, with their characteristic accent on the manipulation of biological organisms, and Skinner adopted "prediction" and "control" as his watchwords.

During this period Skinner gradually refined his concept of the operant. In simple terms, operant behavior was emitted by the organism spontaneously, rather than being elicited by particular stimuli as in the classical conditioning demonstrated by Ivan Pavlov. In classical conditioning, if a neutral stimulus (e.g., a bell) is paired with an unconditioned stimulus (e.g., food), eventually the unconditioned response (salivation) will occur upon presentation of the previously neutral stimulus. Although classical conditioning had yielded useful quantitative analyses of some kinds of behavior, it seemed to be limited to simpler, reflexive behavior. Skinner was interested in exploring the more complex kinds of behavior that were maintained through operant reinforcement.

Skinner developed relatively simple yet powerful experimental procedures for operant conditioning. The basic setup involved a single rat in a standard apparatus (what became known as the Skinner box), in which the animal would press a bar in order to receive reinforcing stimuli in the form of food or water. Measurements of the rat's bar-pressing behavior were recorded mainly in the form of graphs plotting the cumulative number of responses over a given period of time.

Skinner discovered many regularities in the response rates of his subjects under various stimulus protocols and reinforcement schedules. As an example of how an animal's behavior could be radically shaped by operant methods, he trained one rat, named Pliny the Elder, to perform a series of acrobatic tricks with a marble by reinforcing successive approximations of the desired responses. This provided a vivid demonstration of the power of operant conditioning to produce responses that were not in the original behavioral repertoire of the rat. Skinner was well aware of the fact that professional animal trainers relied on similar methods, which they had developed through trial and error rather than through disciplined investigation. Skinner's work with Pliny came to the attention of the national media, and a story about it was published in *Life* magazine in 1937.[10]

By this time Skinner had left his monastic lab-centered existence at Harvard and was an assistant professor of psychology at the University of Minnesota. There he was exposed to the demands of teaching as well as to the array of scientific and professional concerns represented in a large midwestern psychology department. Although Minnesota was a noted center for applied psychology, Skinner hewed to his experimental program. In *The Behavior of Organisms,* he had studiously avoided commenting on the relevance of his work to human behavior until the last pages of the volume, where he admitted that the importance of a science of behavior derives largely from the possibility of an eventual extension to human affairs. But it is a serious, though common, mistake to allow questions of ultimate application to influence the development of a systematic science at an early stage. I think it is true that the direction of the present inquiry has been determined solely by the exigencies of the system. . . . The book represents nothing more than an experimental analysis of a representative sample of behavior. Let him extrapolate who will.[11]

Not long afterward, the Second World War began, and Skinner himself was faced with the opportunity to extrapolate his system. Although a great number of other psychologists mobilized rapidly for the national emergency, nearly all, including those researchers in animal laboratories, addressed problems of human behavior. Skinner was unique, however, in that he found a way to continue working with animals in the unlikely field of guided missile technology.

THE GENESIS OF PROJECT PIGEON

Among the most disturbing aspects of the war in Europe was the emergence of aerial bombing as a terrible new weapon against which there was little reliable defense. Musing about the problem on a train bound for the Midwestern Psychological Association meeting in Chicago in 1940, Skinner was inspired with a solution: why not bomb the bombers with guided missiles dropped from planes flying at higher altitudes? The idea was hardly original—except for the guidance system, which would rely on the discriminative abilities of trained animals. As Skinner described his first thoughts: "I saw a flock of birds lifting and wheeling in formation as they flew alongside the train. Suddenly I saw them as 'devices' with excellent vision and extraordinary maneuverability. Could they not guide a missile? Was the answer to the problem waiting for me in my own backyard?"[12]

Fifty years later Skinner's idea may appear outlandish since guided missile technology has become highly sophisticated, relying on the latest advances in electromechanics and electronics. At the time, however, the United States possessed virtually no expertise in guided missiles. The development of propulsion systems and warheads was confined to a few experimental projects in mechanical and electrical engineering laboratories, and guidance techniques based on servomechanisms were in the early stages of theoretical exploration. Work soon accelerated, however, when U.S. government authorities, realizing that the Nazis were well ahead in the area, started to mobilize American scientists and engineers.[13]

Skinner continued to ponder the idea, and by the spring of 1941 he was actively exploring its feasibility. Deciding that birds would be the most appropriate research subjects, he bought several pigeons and trained them to peck at a bull's-eye target. The birds were harnessed to a movable hoist, and as they pecked their head movements operated electric motors that steered the hoist toward the target. Skinner demonstrated the experiment to John T. Tate, a well-known physicist and dean of the College of Science, Literature, and Art at Minnesota, who passed along the psychologist's "Description of a Plan for Directing a Bomb at a Target" to Richard C. Tolman, head of the Physics Department at the California Institute of Technology and vice chairman of the National Defense Research Committee (NDRC).[14]

Although Tolman called the plan "a new and unconventional approach to the problem," he rejected it, diplomatically claiming that the probable lack of interest by the armed services made it "hardly advisable" for the NDRC to develop it, even though the "suggestion may be perfectly feasible."[15] Skinner thanked Tolman for his interest and told him that he would continue to seek support for what was "admittedly a 'long shot.'"[16]

The entrance of the United States into the war after the attack on Pearl Harbor reactivated Skinner's interest, and on 8 December 1941, he began experiments on the guidance of offensive bombs directed toward stationary targets. With the help of a graduate student, Keller Breland, Skinner harnessed a pigeon in an apparatus that was guided by the bird's neck movements toward a target. After making a film demonstrating the device, he enlisted the aid of some of his colleagues in Washington and again approached the NDRC. Writing to Tolman once more, Skinner suggested that "if the United Nations could suddenly begin to sink ships with high altitude bombing, practically at the rate of one ship per bomb, the war would be won. And this is not a consequence to be sneezed at." He offered to send the demonstration film to the committee, joking that it would "at least . . . prove to be an entertaining 'short.'"[17] Tate also wrote to Tolman, avowing his "great confidence" in Skinner. In support of the unorthodox plan the physicist said, "If you have a steerable bomb, I feel fairly confident that a bird's vision and head movement constitute an instrument for guidance which is probably superior to anything which can be produced by the hand of man."[18]

In March 1942 Skinner traveled to New York to receive the prestigious Warren Medal of the Society of Experimental Psychologists. A chance encounter with a colleague led to a meeting between Skinner and the navy's chief of special devices in Washington. The official was supportive of Skinner's plan but was unable to provide financial backing.[19] Later the same month Tolman again rejected the proposal, in part because of the lack of suitable missiles. At that time only rudimentary research had been conducted on guided missile technology, and the NDRC designated an entire division—Division 5—to foster its development.[20] Tolman encouraged Skinner to contact him if he performed more research and cautioned him against discussing the proposal in public.[21]

Skinner decided to continue on his own. Writing to Dean Tate about recent kamikaze attacks on Allied warships, he said it "looks as if the Japs were using men rather than birds. Perhaps we can get American morale that high, but if not, I can provide perfectly competent substitutes."[22] Through a fortuitous chain of circumstances, Skinner was able to obtain some research money from an unlikely source—the General Mills Company in Minneapolis. His work had come to the attention of the company's vice president for research, Arthur D. Hyde, when it was mentioned by an inspired citizen in support of a scheme to use dogs to steer torpedoes by sound signals.[23] General Mills provided Skinner with a five-thousand-dollar grant to support his work during the summer of 1942.

General Mills also furnished the project with work space in an old flour mill, and another graduate student, Norman Guttman, volunteered to help. Skinner's group began working on an apparatus to translate a pigeon's pecking movements into a signal that could steer a gliding bomb. The pigeon's pecking behavior was shaped to the point where it would respond steadily and precisely to a sample visual target, which in this case was a particular street intersection in an aerial photograph of Stalingrad. At the same time Skinner worked with two more students, William K. Estes and Marian Breland, to carry out supplementary studies of possible environmental influences on the pigeon's behavior, including deprivation levels, reinforcement schedules, noise, and changes in temperature and pressure. The properly trained pigeon proved to be a stable performer under a wide range of conditions.[24]

Another demonstration film was sent to the NDRC, and the committee responded by dispatching an observer to Minnesota. Skinner was then invited to Washington to present his proposal in February 1943. The plan for what Skinner termed the *Bird's-Eye Bomb* was based on principles of operant conditioning, which could easily be applied to pigeons. The birds also made good subjects because of their excellent vision and their imperturbability in the face of acceleration and noise. The steering mechanism was straightforward and fairly simple. A plastic screen was placed behind a lens in the nose cone of the missile. As the bomb pointed downward toward the target, an image of the field was projected upward onto the screen. The bird, trained on a chosen target, would peck at the image on the screen, which was mounted on gimbal bearings. Electrical contacts were activated when the bird pecked at the off-center target image, which then generated signals in order to operate steering controls.[25]

This method simplified the stimulus-response situation. The target pattern appeared directly in front of the bird in such a way as to readily control the desired pecking response. Extraneous stimulation was minimized, and the pigeon's instinctive flight habits were bypassed by the use of a harness that restrained wing movements. Training the bird to peck at a target image, such as a boat or a landscape feature, was easily accomplished by using aerial photographs. (The project was provided with photos of the New Jersey coastline for training purposes.) By using variable-ratio conditioning schedules, Skinner was able to train birds to peck continuously for a period of several minutes, which would be necessary in the actual use of the missile. One bird, for example, made over 10,000 pecks in forty-five minutes without stopping. Factors that might disturb the birds were systematically studied. The pigeons could readily be adapted to loud noises, vibration, and acceleration. Temperature and pressure changes could easily be accommodated in the design of the device. Possible disturbing effects of variations in the target such as brightness and size, as well as of atmospheric interference such as clouds, could be avoided by means of appropriate training procedures.[26]

The proposal and demonstration film favorably impressed NDRC officials, and in March 1943 the chief technical officer of Division 5, an electrical engineer named Hugh S. Spencer, visited Minneapolis along with an assistant for a firsthand look at the project. They were pleased with what they saw, commenting that "aside from the pigeon racket, the organization seems exceptionally able, well staffed, and well equipped."[27] By April, Spencer informed the group that a contract was likely to be approved if quantitative data on the accuracy of the pigeon pecking could be provided. Skinner supplied the data in the form of plaster casts taken from modeling clay used to record the birds' pecking. The pigeons' marksmanship was excellent. Spencer also inquired about the available supply of birds. Skinner replied that practically all varieties of the species were usable and that pigeons could be obtained easily on the commercial market.[28]

An additional visit to the project laboratory by another NDRC staff member, a physicist named Alan C. Bemis, clinched the case for support. After spending a couple of hours with Skinner, Bemis reported, "As seems to be the case with most visitors, I went as a scoffer and came away somewhat converted."[29] Skinner discussed his need for assistance on the mechanical and electrical engineering aspects of the device. The only other visual guidance system under development by Division 5 was one that utilized television, and in consideration of the money spent on it Bemis commented, "Pigeons don't look too bad, but I still wouldn't know whether to vote yes or no on a contract."[30] His ambivalent endorsement epitomized the general attitude toward the project within the National Defense Research Committee (NDRC). Even though the animal homing device had some promise, especially given the state of guidance system technology, the NDRC officials clearly had trouble accommodating a psychological approach to an engineering problem.

By the end of May, Spencer wrote to Vannevar Bush, president of the Carnegie Institution and director of the Office of Scientific Research and Development (OSRD), the NDRC's parent body, to recommend support for the project, citing computations indicating that the system could guide a missile to within 20 feet of its target if the original azimuth error was less than 2,000 feet. Bush thanked Spencer for the project summary, stating, "I have the feeling that this whole subject is now for the first time on a basis of sound scientific examination from the angle of the physical as well as the organic elements."[31] On 1 June the NDRC awarded a $25,000 contract for an "organic homing device" to General Mills for the period from 1 February to 31 December 1943.[32]

REFINING THE DEVICE

Neither Skinner nor the NDRC engineers made much effort to enlist advice about the project from other psychologists. On a programmatic level, Skinner and his group received the endorsement of the Princeton psychologist Charles W. Bray, soon to become head of the OSRD Applied Psychology Panel.[33] The panel, however, was oriented toward manpower and training problems and was preoccupied with the administration of its own contracts. Skinner had mentioned a number of psychologists as potential advisors, but the suggestion was never followed up.[34] Project Pigeon remained isolated both intellectually and institutionally from the tight-knit wartime psychology community.

At General Mills, the project was supervised by Arthur Hyde, vice president and director of research. Hyde, who wanted to channel the company's broad program of engineering research on food-processing machinery into federal contract research, became an enthusiastic supporter of Skinner's group. Bemis, the NDRC official assigned to oversee the project, was located at Division 5's headquarters at the Massachusetts Institute of Technology (MIT). Engrossed in overseeing a number of contracts on servomechanism research and development, he was not particularly interested in the Minnesota project, and its distant location reinforced his laissez-faire attitude. It was clear from the start that General Mills and Project Pigeon were on their own.

Problems soon arose as it became apparent that the main technical obstacles were mechanical rather than psychological. The birds' pecking provided an adequate signal for the servomechanism, but the development of mechanical linkages for translating the signal into steering movements proved difficult. Skinner was disappointed with the slow pace of the mechanical research, saying, "I am not yet used to the low tempo of industry." Unfortunately, collaboration between the project's psychologists and engineers was hampered because the two groups were not under the same roof at General Mills, being housed in separate buildings nearly four miles apart. The NDRC's Spencer also expressed some reservations about the project's low-budget style, which he characterized privately as building on a "hay-wire-screen-door basis."[35]

Within a few months, however, the General Mills group constructed an improved signaling system that used pneumatic valves rather than electrical contacts. The target plate rested on four air valves at its edges. Depending on the location of the bird's pecking, the valves would allow air into the chamber and operate tambours that sent signals to the mechanism. As Skinner described it:

> When the missile was on target, the pigeon pecked the center of the plate, all valves admitted equal amounts of air, and the tambours remained in neutral positions. But if the image moved as little as a quarter of an inch off-center, corresponding to a very small angular displacement of the target, more air was admitted by the valves on one side, and the resulting displacement of the tambours sent appropriate correcting orders directly to the servosystem.[36]

By early September 1943 Project Pigeon had produced a workable model. At that time the project engineer at General Mills tried to get more information concerning the design and performance characteristics of the missile, which was under development at the MIT Servomechanisms Laboratory. The NDRC contract monitor was lackadaisical in responding to the queries, and, without proper specifications for their part of the servomechanism, Project Pigeon workers refined their system as best they could.[37]

The project was discussed at the next general meeting of NDRC Division 5. After hearing a report on its overall progress, the division chief could foresee eventual combat action, "not tomorrow, but in the not indefinite future."[38] This meeting was apparently the first time that many division officials had heard of the project, and Bemis told Hyde that there were favorable notices "in spite of the natural reaction which everyone has when learning about it for the first time to make light of it."[39]

By November contract funds were running out, and Skinner was anxious for NDRC officials to view his working model. In mid-December, shortly before the contract officially expired, Spencer and Bemis made another trip to Minnesota. They reviewed tracking data and observed the simulator—now with a three-bird control system to provide redundancy—following a target in the laboratory. Skinner later reported, "The only questions which arose were the inevitable consequence of our lack of information about the signal required to steer the [missile]."[40] The

Minnesota group, without guidance from the NDRC or its vehicle contractors, had had to make arbitrary engineering decisions, such as com-
promising between smoothness and sensitivity in the vacuum-generated
signal. Unfortunately, the chosen values had produced data that did not
favorably impress the NDRC advisors. Bemis thought the birds' behavior
looked erratic and was skeptical about the mechanics of the device. He
favored extending the contract, "but," as he told Spencer, "let's can the
thing in a hurry if they don't do a neat job on the oscillating target
measurements."[41]

Project Pigeon came up for extended discussion at the next meeting of
the NDRC, in January 1944. The MIT physicist Joseph C. Boyce, chief
of the section, recommended the continuation of three projects, including
the General Mills contract. The other two contracts—totaling $130,000—
were quickly approved. Boyce began discussion of the third by saying,
"I, having been previously skeptical, would now like to recommend an
additional $25,000 for General Mills for the continuation of the studies
on the organic homing project."[42] He noted that the latest version of
the device used three pigeons rather than one for added efficiency and
reliability. Boyce's positive opinion was undercut by Spencer, who told
the group that he and Bemis were disappointed by their observations in
Minnesota the month before. Concerned about the overextension of the
project budget (it had run out of contract funds in November), Spencer
had told Hyde then that the results were "not of sufficient promise to
justify my asking him to go any farther or giving him any expectation of
further support from NDRC."[43] Hyde had asked what kind of data the
NDRC advisors would find conclusive; Spencer replied that they would
like something quantitative that Albert C. Hall, a specialist at the Servomechanisms Lab, could analyze. General Mills complied, Spencer reported, but "unfortunately, the data shows just a little too much hope, so
that you can't drop it out of hand. It is not quite good enough to be
promising; it is not quite bad enough to throw away."[44]

An official from another section who had originally supported the contract changed his mind, saying that "if it doesn't look pretty good by this
time I'm inclined to be a little cool."[45] Another committee member, an
aeronautical scientist named Hugh Dryden who was engaged in missile
development, criticized the control mechanism as a "player piano movement type of thing" of the sort expected in a psychologist's laboratory.[46]
J. C. Hunsaker, the National Advisory Committee on Aeronautics representative, maintained his original opposition. Although his vote did not
count, Bemis, the project's technical monitor, voiced his opposition to
extending the contract. In the face of dwindling support, Boyce was ready

to withdraw his motion for $25,000, but the group went ahead and voted, rejecting the request for more funds for Project Pigeon.[47]

FIGHTING FOR CONTINUATION

Reacting to news of the termination, Skinner exploded with a long letter to Spencer. He began by saying that "the action of the Division regarding our project was very nearly a knockout blow" and that he found it "difficult to understand this decision." He went on to reiterate the rationale for the project and suggested that the device had not been "judged fully on its merits" because the division had not provided complete performance specifications. The signal system gave values within the verbal specifications supplied in November, but those had evidently changed. Skinner complained that "if more rigid specifications are now found to be necessary, we should at least have been given the chance to shoot for them." Responding to another question concerning the bird's accuracy at close range, Skinner told Spencer that the bird could be conditioned to focus on successively smaller details as the target approached. Furthermore, "the extraordinary possibilities of pattern selection could hardly have been correctly represented to the Division at the time action was taken, since we have not reported on them."[48] Skinner provided his own analysis of the decision.

> My guess is that certain technicalities have been invoked to support an underlying doubt concerning the reliability of the birds. I am quite sure that a non-organismic device which gave the same kind of signal with respect to any visual pattern would not be dropped at this stage. As a psychologist I can understand this (I have certainly seen enough of it during the past four years!), but I hate to accept it as the final word of men well acquainted with the history and methods of science. Any valid judgment of reliability must be made on the facts, not on random personal experiences. As you yourself must be able to testify, every competent person who has familiarized himself with our work has passed from a stage of amused skepticism to a serious belief that the scheme deserves to be tried. It is unfortunate that the final decision always seems to rest with men who have not had the benefit of close contact with the project.[49]

Skinner wanted to present his case directly to NDRC officials, hoping to persuade them to reopen the contract "up to the point of a field test." But he left the decision to Spencer, saying to him, "If you feel that such a step is hopeless, that the action would not be reconsidered, please say so frankly. In that case we shall immediately close up shop."[50] Under

Hyde's signature additional supporting materials, including new data on the signal characteristics, were sent to Spencer from General Mills. In that report Hyde estimated that the device could be ready for a drop test in one month, at an estimated cost of $6,000. He repeated the group's plea that their work be more closely coordinated with the vehicle development team at MIT, complaining that "so far we have been working in the dark . . . with rather nebulous guesses and assumptions for guidance." In summary, he listed fourteen distinct advantages of the device, including its resistance to jamming, automatic close-up targeting, wide field of vision and small dead spot, easy construction, and short preparation time.[51]

Hyde also appealed to Spencer's superiors at the National Defense Research Committee. He arranged for the president of General Mills to contact Frank B. Jewett, an NDRC member and president of Bell Laboratories, and sent him a copy of the report. Ten days after the termination Jewett put Spencer "on the griddle" at a general NDRC meeting. Under pressure to justify the decision, Spencer requested more information from General Mills and asked Hall of the MIT Servomechanisms Lab to prepare a statement concerning the proper testing procedures for the device.[52]

The General Mills researchers responded with a three-part plan, covering drop tests, combat tests, and regular field use. The drop tests would use 6 pigeon units, costing $1,000 apiece, and could be ready to go in one week. For combat testing an estimated 200 units—employing 1,000 birds and 50 training devices—would be required, taking about three months of preparation time. Some forty unskilled workers would be needed to condition the pigeons under the supervision of five psychologists. Finally, plans for a regular field program projected 16 units per day. For the necessary output of 50 birds per day, some 3,000 pigeons would participate in a general training program. Upon selection for a mission, they would be conditioned to the specific target. The basic conditioning work could be performed by the elderly or physically unfit, who could learn the procedures in a month or less. Compared to other military logistical operations, personnel requirements would be relatively modest, consisting of 4 experts, 9 skilled group trainers (e.g., graduate students), 100 unskilled trainers, 20 caretakers, 2 repairmen, 1 pigeon specialist, 1 records clerk, 1 secretary, and a part-time installation crew. The report ended with a rhetorical flourish aimed at the NDRC engineers. "We again wish to emphasize our belief that the pigeon—an organism—is essentially an extremely reliable instrument, rugged in construction, simple and economical to obtain, and easily conditioned to be entirely predictable in behavior."[53]

Spencer received a five-page memorandum in early March from Hall regarding the device's technical feasibility. The servomechanism expert seemed impressed with its possibilities and stated that "at the present time I can see nothing which would lead me to believe that such a system should be inoperative."[54] On the basis of the new material Spencer pushed for reconsideration of the project. He wrote Hyde: "If the Division's action in terminating the project at its last meeting was premature, the fault was mine. I did not feel at that time assurance that the results obtainable by the system could be as substantially improved as your later work has shown possible."[55] Soon Spencer sent a memo to Division 5 members asking that the project be reconsidered. Citing the improved results reported by General Mills, Spencer apologized for "misleading" the group at the last meeting and admitted, "I am wholly candid in stating that the material furnished this office in these two reports is definitely more encouraging than anything that I expected to receive."[56] Skinner and his group were invited to present their case at the next meeting of Division 5, in March 1944.[57]

Spencer began the meeting's discussion by saying that he would have supported extension of the contract in January had the improved data been available then. Hall, harboring some doubts about the device, strongly recommended that thorough laboratory testing be completed before field testing. His mathematical calculations of the signal characteristics were inconsistent with the empirical data the project researchers had obtained. Various explanations of the inconsistency were offered, but, whatever the reason for it, the signal seemed adequate for controlling the missile. Skinner thought the discrepancy had been satisfactorily resolved beforehand and was surprised when Hall told the group "that the signal we reported would cause the missile to 'hunt' wildly and lose the target."[58]

Skinner went on to enunciate the unique advantages of the organic device, pointing out the bird's ability to react to patterns rather than to the point sources or fields of force that radar and other systems relied on. Drawing on the language of engineering again, he said, "We have used pigeons, not because the pigeon is an intelligent bird, but because it is a practical one and can be made into a machine, from all practical points of view."[59]

Hoping that a live demonstration would dispel any doubts about the feasibility of the project, Skinner set up a simple simulation. A target was projected on a window in a small black box in which the pigeon was harnessed. A small tube would allow individual observation, but, since time was short, the top was taken off the box. As Skinner described the scene:

> The translucent screen was flooded with so much light that the target was barely visible, and the peering scientists offered conditions much more unfamiliar and

threatening than those likely to be encountered in a missile. In spite of this the pigeon behaved perfectly, pecking steadily and energetically at the image of the target as it moved about on the plate. . . . It was a perfect performance, but it had just the wrong effect. One can talk about phase lag in pursuit behavior and discuss mathematical predictions of hunting without reflecting too closely upon what is inside the black box. But the spectacle of a living pigeon carrying out its assignment, no matter how beautifully, simply reminded the committee of how utterly fantastic our proposal was. I will not say that the meeting was marked by unrestrained merriment, for the merriment was restrained. But it was there, and it was obvious that our case was lost.[60]

Literally and figuratively unable to keep the lid on the black box, Skinner left the group to its deliberations.[61] Spencer suggested an additional $50,000 for the project, including $20,000 to cover the General Mills deficit as well as a budget for six additional months. Much discussion focused on the logistics of field deployment until it was pointed out that the army already used pigeons, as carriers for messages. Pigeons would also be simple to transport compared to other things already routinely moved, such as bombs or electronic equipment. But the officials seemed more interested in laying the matter to rest. It was clear that the project had not received good supervision or adequate technical support. Boyce, the section chief, admitted, "I am perfectly free to confess that I have not supervised the thing in detail." Another official noted that project members were "working in ignorance of what is involved in a guided missile. We have been so long finding out."[62] These statements seemed designed more to assuage possible guilt feelings regarding the project's administration than to promote serious reconsideration. Continued support was voted down, 4 to 2, on the basis of the perceived lack of armed forces interest and the problems of coordination with the missile development team at MIT.[63]

THE DEMISE OF PROJECT PIGEON

Project Pigeon was officially over. As Skinner wrote, "We had to show, for all our trouble, only a loftful [sic] of curiously useless equipment and a few dozen pigeons with a strange interest in a feature of the New Jersey coast."[64] In retrospect, it seems clear that the project failed, not for technical reasons, but because of fundamental differences in disciplinary outlook and research style between the Skinner team and the NDRC engineers. Coming from laboratory psychology, Skinner was at a disadvantage in trying to enter territory that was considered part of electrical and mechanical engineering. He lacked experience in dealing with extramural research funding agencies, even in his own field of psychology.

Furthermore, he failed to mobilize the support of influential psychologists involved in government scientific circles. Instead, Project Pigeon members felt their way, eventually learning to articulate their work in engineering terms, as seen in the use of the metaphor of the bird as a machine. But that rhetorical ploy was tried only after NDRC officials had already begun to lose their initial enthusiasm for the novel guidance system. The contract administrators had tried to be open-minded about the project but proved unable to accommodate its unusual approach and eventually retreated behind traditional professional boundaries. In the official account of the project, NDRC staff members noted the prevailing mood: "Investigators in the physical sciences are inclined to discount unduly the findings of their colleagues in the field of psychological behavior. Such an attitude is far from scientific."[65]

The interests of the NDRC staff members were focused elsewhere, on the development of more conventional hardware, and they devoted a minimum of supervision to Project Pigeon. Although the General Mills contract generated much discussion, it was a marginal item in the budget, receiving only $25,000 of the $13,000,000 spent by the division over the course of the war.[66] Other speculative projects, such as television-guided missiles, received major funding despite little demonstrable utility. None of the officials assigned to oversee the project spent much time doing so; more significant, none of them emerged as advocates for it, which was crucial to continued funding. Finally, logistical problems deepened the gulf between the two groups. The division was headquartered at MIT, a key center of wartime technological innovation, whereas Project Pigeon was isolated in a more limited research environment in the Midwest. The development of the missile vehicle went ahead at MIT without real consideration of the organic-guiding mechanism. Communication between the groups was poor, and the lack of information clearly hampered the General Mills engineers.

The physical scientists and engineers of the National Defense Research Committee succeeded in closing the issue, and their postwar accounts became the official word on Project Pigeon. In *Guided Missiles and Techniques,* the Summary Technical Report of Division 5, less than four pages were devoted to "Organic Target Seeking." Asserting that "recognition by intelligence" was the simplest method of targeting, the report mentioned the effectiveness of Japanese kamikaze attacks as a prime example.[67] The main components of the pigeon device were described, and the summary concluded that the project "was given up because the mechanical engineering problem of developing an appropriate servo link seemed too difficult," especially in light of advances made with other missile systems.[68]

In the official public history of wartime guided missile research and development, the NDRC section chief Joseph Boyce gave a brief but balanced review of Project Pigeon.[69] Another Division 5 member, the physicist Louis N. Ridenour, satirized the project in the pages of the *Atlantic Monthly* in 1947 as one of "the more bizarre problems of wartime research." In a short piece entitled "Doves in the Detonator," he caricatured Skinner (under the pseudonym Ramsay) as an impractical dreamer and misrepresented several key aspects of the project. Among other inaccuracies, Ridenour claimed that homing pigeons were used and placed together in ten-bird units. In dismissing the work, he invoked the ultimate wartime fruit of physical science and engineering by concluding that perhaps "operational problems loomed so large that the Air Forces decided they'd rather wait for the atomic bomb, which you don't have to be very accurate with."[70]

BEYOND THE LABORATORY

With Project Pigeon over, Skinner returned to scholarly pursuits and took up a Guggenheim Fellowship to prepare a monograph dealing with verbal behavior. As he worked on the book during the 1944–45 academic year, Skinner explored other forms of behavioral technology. He built the baby-tender for his second daughter, and described it to the NDRC's Hugh Spencer as "a very different and more peaceful sort of behavioral engineering."[71] Extending his concerns to the rational management of society, Skinner drafted the manuscript for *Walden Two* during the summer of 1945, shortly before the end of the war. He later noted the connection between Project Pigeon and the book, saying "that piece of science fiction was a declaration of confidence in a technology of behavior."[72]

The details of Project Pigeon remained classified for more than a decade following the war. Unable to comment directly on this research, Skinner continued to elaborate on the insights gained from his wartime experiences. In 1947, at a symposium on current trends in psychology, he punctuated his discussion of experimental psychology by stating, "It is not a matter of bringing the world into the laboratory, but of extending the practices of an experimental science to the world at large. We can do this as soon as we wish to do it."[73] Although Skinner resumed his research program in the experimental analysis of behavior, he devoted increasing amounts of time to applied projects, most notably teaching machines.[74] In *Science and Human Behavior,* published in 1953, he took a unified approach to behavioral science and engineering. Arguing that "the methods of science have been enormously successful wherever they have been tried," Skinner proposed to "apply them to human affairs" in the form of operant conditioning techniques.[75]

In 1958, after Project Pigeon was finally declassified, Skinner chose to discuss it in a highly visible forum when he accepted the Distinguished Scientific Contribution Award from the American Psychological Association. Instead of talking about his laboratory research, Skinner presented a history of Project Pigeon, characterizing it as "a crackpot idea, born on the wrong side of the tracks intellectually speaking, but eventually vindicated in a sort of middle class respectability."[76] He claimed that his efforts to develop a pigeon-guided missile generated techniques for shaping behavior that provided the foundation for a "technology of behavior."[77]

Over the course of two decades Skinner's perspective on the relation between his scientific research and its applications had shifted markedly. In the 1930s he had acknowledged that the ultimate worth of a laboratory science of behavior lay in its potential social benefits, but had issued a stern warning against premature extensions to the practical affairs of the world. During World War II Skinner began to link the pursuit of scientific discovery through experimental research to various technical and social problems encountered in the wartime context. By the 1950s, he had integrated the scientific and technological elements in his system and used them to advance a behavioristic view of the world.

Skinner dramatized the consequences of his wartime research in his autobiography, published thirty-five years after the event.

> Project Pigeon was discouraging. Our work with pigeons was beautifully reinforced, but all our efforts with the scientists came to nothing. . . . [However,] the research that I described in *The Behavior of Organisms* appeared in a new light. It was no longer merely an experimental analysis. It had given rise to a technology.[78]

Project Pigeon became the opening wedge in what evolved into a campaign for behavioral engineering. The war provided Skinner with an opportunity to redefine the disparate problems associated with guiding a missile, raising a baby, and managing a society in terms of a common behavioral framework and to propose solutions based on techniques derived from the psychological laboratory. His wartime mechanical devices and literary constructions were designed with the same goals as his experimental apparatus: to control behavior predictably. Although Skinner's inventions received mixed reviews, he became convinced that behaviorism offered scientific methods equally applicable outside as well as inside the experimental workplace. Faced with new contingencies, Skinner changed his behavior as a scientist during the war, and in doing so confirmed firsthand that the laboratory could indeed provide significant leverage in the wider realm of human affairs.[79]

NOTES

I am grateful for the editorial suggestions of Alejandra C. Laszlo, Eliot Hearst, and B. F. Skinner and for the encouragement received from audiences that heard earlier versions of this chapter at Indiana University and at the annual meetings of the Air Force Historical Foundation, the Society for the History of Technology, and the Association for Behavior Analysis.

1. Skinner, "My Years at Indiana" (paper prepared 31 March 1988, for the Indiana University Department of Psychology Centennial Celebration, Bloomington, April 1988, p. 5) ; copy is in the personal collection of the author.
2. Skinner, "Pigeons in a Pelican," *American Psychologist* 15 (1960): 28–37.
3. Skinner, *The Shaping of a Behaviorist* (New York: Knopf, 1979), pp. 275ff.
4. Skinner, "Baby in a Box," *Ladies' Home Journal,* October 1945, pp. 30–31, 135–36, 138. See the discussion in Elizabeth A. Jordan, "Freedom and the Control of Children: The Skinners' Approach to Parenting," this volume.
5. Skinner, *Walden Two* (New York: Macmillan, 1948).
6. See James H. Capshew, "Psychology on the March: American Psychologists and World War II" (Ph.D. diss., University of Pennsylvania, 1986).
7. On the notion that technological systems include people and organizations as well as artifacts and processes, see Thomas P. Hughes, *American Genesis: A Century of Invention and Technological Enthusiasm, 1870–1970* (New York: Viking, 1989), pp. 184ff.
8. Skinner, *The Behavior of Organisms: An Experimental Analysis* (New York: Appleton-Century, 1938).
9. Philip J. Pauly, *Controlling Life: Jacques Loeb and the Engineering Ideal in Biology* (New York: Oxford University Press, 1987), pp. 188–91; see the discussion in Laurence D. Smith, "Knowledge as Power: The Baconian Roots of Skinner's Social Meliorism," this volume.
10. "Working Rat," *Life,* 31 May 1937, pp. 80–81.
11. Skinner, *Behavior of Organisms,* pp. 441–42.
12. Skinner, *Shaping of a Behaviorist,* p. 241. A similar account that is mistakenly dated 1939 is given in Skinner, "Autobiography," in *A History of Psychology in Autobiography,* vol. 5, ed. Edwin G. Boring and Gardner Lindzey (New York: Appleton-Century-Crofts, 1967), pp. 385–413, on p. 402.
13. Leaders of the wartime research and development establishment considered guided missile work a top priority, second only to the atomic bomb project. See Vannevar Bush and James B. Conant, foreword to *Guided Missiles and Techniques,* Summary Technical Report, National Defense Research Committee, Division 5 (Washington, D.C., 1946), p. v.
14. Skinner, "Pigeons in a Pelican," pp. 28–29. Skinner recalled that psychological research using pigeons had hardly been attempted before and that he had bought the birds at a shop that sold them to Chinese restaurants. Skinner to James H. Capshew, 11 August 1986; Skinner to Capshew, 9 August 1990; these letters are in the personal collection of the author. If Tolman was not particularly sympathetic toward psychology, he was certainly not ignorant of it since both his wife, Ruth S. Tolman, and his brother, Edward C. Tolman, were active professional psychologists in California.
15. Tolman to Skinner, 9 June 1941, Record Group 227, Office of Scientific Research and Development (OSRD), National Defense Research Committee

(NDRC), Records of Civilian Members, Tolman Files (hereafter cited as Tolman Files), Sk-Sm, National Archives, Washington, D.C.

16. Skinner to Tolman, [June 1941], Tolman Files.

17. Skinner to Tolman, 11 March 1942, Tolman Files.

18. Tate to Tolman, 19 March 1942, Tolman Files.

19. Skinner, *Shaping of a Behaviorist,* p. 257.

20. See *Guided Missiles and Techniques.*

21. Tolman to Skinner, 31 March 1942, Tolman Files.

22. Quoted in Skinner, *Shaping of a Behaviorist,* pp. 256–57.

23. Skinner remembered only the man's first name—Victor. See Skinner, "Pigeons in a Pelican," p. 29.

24. For technical details, see ibid., p. 30. Skinner noted that the technique of "shaping" behavior (i.e., reinforcing successive approximations of the desired response) had its origins in the flour mill during an attempt to teach a pigeon to bowl. See Skinner, "Reinforcement Today," *American Psychologist* 13 (1958): 94–99.

25. Skinner, K. B. Breland, and N. Guttman, "The Present Status of the 'Bird's-Eye Bomb,'" 1 February 1943, OSRD, NDRC Division 5, Spencer Files (hereafter cited as Spencer Files), 15, General Mills, Special Reports.

26. Ibid.

27. Spencer, "Visit," 16 March 1943, Spencer Files, 15, General Mills Correspondence.

28. Spencer to Hyde, 10 April 1943; Skinner to Spencer, 12 April 1943; Spencer to Skinner, 30 April 1943; Skinner to Spencer, 6 May 1943; all in Spencer Files.

29. Alan Bemis characterized Skinner as "scientifically sound, able in his field though not of great caliber, and certainly a very pleasant individual personally." See Bemis, "Diary," 1 May 1943; OSRD, NDRC Division 5, Bemis Files (hereafter cited as Bemis Files), 91, Diary 1943.

30. Ibid.

31. Spencer to Bush, 27 May 1943; Bush to Spencer, 28 May 1943; both in Spencer Files, 15, General Mills Correspondence.

32. Contract no. OEMsr-1068, Spencer Files, 15, General Mills Contracts and Vouchers.

33. Joseph Boyce, chief of Section 5.5, solicited Bray for some advice on the project, which they had previously discussed at the Cosmos Club in Washington. Bray was glad to oblige but apparently never did. See Boyce to Bray, 13 July 1943; Bray to Boyce, 17 July 1943; Boyce to Bray, 21 July 1943; all in Bemis Files, 96, General Mills Correspondence.

34. Spencer to Bemis, 31 July 1943, Bemis Files, 91, General Mills-Pigeons.

35. Ibid.

36. Skinner, "Pigeons in a Pelican," p. 31.

37. Bemis, perhaps feeling some guilt over his lack of help, was reassured by a visit from Charles Bray and Walter Hunter of the Applied Psychology Panel, who had a "positive opinion" of the project. See Bemis to Hyde, 10 September 1943; Bemis Files, 91, General Mills-Pigeons; and Bemis, "Diary," 15 October 1943, Bemis Files, 91, Diary.

38. Meeting of Division 5, verbatim transcript, 20 October 1943, Richmond quoted on p. 46; OSRD, NDRC Division 5, Richmond Files (hereafter cited as Richmond Files), 62.

39. Bemis to Hyde, 22 October 1943, Spencer Files, 15, General Mills Correspondence.

40. Bemis to Hyde, 20 November 1943, Bemis Files, 91, General Mills-Pigeons; Bemis to Spencer, 3 December 1943, Spencer Files, 15, General Mills Correspondence; Skinner, "Pigeons in a Pelican," p. 33.

41. Bemis to Spencer, 13 December 1943, Spencer Files, 15, General Mills Correspondence.

42. Meeting of Division 5, verbatim transcript, 12 January 1944, Boyce quoted on p. 130, Richmond Files, 62.

43. Ibid., p. 134.

44. Ibid.

45. Ibid., p. 135.

46. Ibid., p. 136.

47. Ibid., p. 140. After the vote, Spencer raised the nagging issue of reimbursing General Mills for its good faith in continuing to fund the project. He thought the NDRC's "no loss/no gain" principle regarding contractors implied some moral commitment to the company and pointed out that most contractors did not know how much they had spent until well past budget. Furthermore, the contract had come up for consideration without a thorough report from the contractor. Skinner and General Mills had complied with requests for data and results from their NDRC advisors, but no summary report had been requested. Apparently the Project Pigeon researchers had not been warned that their funding was in such jeopardy. After discussion, however, the reimbursement issue was dropped without a vote.

48. Skinner to Spencer, 31 January 1944, Spencer Files, 15, General Mills Correspondence.

49. Ibid.

50. Ibid.

51. Hyde to Spencer, 31 January 1944; OSRD, NDRC Division 5, Contractor's Reports (hereafter cited as Contractor's Reports), 648, General Mills Final Report, 31 January 1944.

52. Spencer to Boyce, "Memo," 21 February 1944, Bemis Files, 91, General Mills-Pigeons.

53. Skinner et al., "Cost of Homing Units, Personnel and Organization Required, Discussion and Analysis," 21 February 1944, Contractor's Reports, 648, General Mills Final Report, 21 February 1944. Kuphal to Spencer, 25 February 1944, Bemis Files, 91, General Mills-Pigeons.

54. Hall to Spencer, 6 March 1944, Spencer Files, 15, General Mills Correspondence. Spencer thanked Hall for his reports, commenting that he was sorry that a plan for using a mirror-centering system rather than the pneumatic signal was not picked up by the project. See Spencer to Hall, 10 March 1944, Bemis Files, 91, General Mills-Pigeons.

55. Spencer to Hyde, 10 March 1944, Spencer Files, 15, General Mills, Special Reports.

56. Spencer, "Memo to Division 5 Members," 13 March 1944, OSRD, NDRC Division 5, Dryden Files, 67, General Mills.

57. "Minutes of Section 5.5 Meeting," 21 March 1944, Bemis Files, 91, Minutes of Meetings.

58. Skinner, "Pigeons in a Pelican," p. 33. Meeting of NDRC Division 5, verbatim transcript, 30 March 1944, Richmond Files, 62.

59. Meeting of NDRC Division 5, 30 March 1944, pp. 94–95, Richmond Files, 62.

60. Skinner, "Pigeons in a Pelican," p. 34. In an earlier summary of the project,

Skinner noted only that "the questions which were put to us were random and for the most part trivial. It was clear to us that most of the men present had only the vaguest notion of the proposed system, and we left the meeting with the feeling that any decision, favorable or unfavorable, would have little to do with the facts of the case." See [Skinner], "History of the 'Project Pigeon' Contract with NDRC," HUG 60.20, Box 8, Folder 2, Project Pigeon, p. 5, B. F. Skinner Papers, Harvard University Archives, Cambridge, Mass.

61. On the notion of "black boxes" in the construction of knowledge claims, see Michel Callon and Bruno Latour, "Unscrewing the Big Leviathan: How Actors Macro-structure Reality and How Sociologists Help Them to Do So," in *Advances in Social Theory and Methodology: Toward an Integration of Micro- and Macro-Sociologies,* ed. Karin Knorr-Cetina and Aaron V. Cicourel (Boston: Routledge & Kegan Paul, 1981), pp. 277–303.

62. Meeting of NDRC Division 5, 30 March 1944, pp. 151–53, Richmond Files, 62.

63. Ibid., pp. 154–55.

64. Skinner, "Pigeons in a Pelican," p. 34.

65. *Guided Missiles and Techniques,* p. 201.

66. Irvin Stewart, *Organizing Scientific Research for War: The Administrative History of the Office of Scientific Research and Development* (Boston: Little, Brown, 1948), pp. 86–87.

67. *Guided Missiles and Techniques,* p. 198.

68. Ibid., p. 201.

69. Joseph C. Boyce, ed., *New Weapons for Air Warfare: Fire-control Equipment, Proximity Fuzes, and Guided Missiles* (Boston: Little, Brown, 1947), pp. 247–48.

70. Louis N. Ridenour, "Doves in the Detonator," *Atlantic Monthly,* January 1947, pp. 93–94.

71. Skinner to Spencer, 23 August 1945, Spencer Files, 15, General Mills Correspondence. In an earlier letter Skinner had thanked Spencer for recommending James Burnham's recent book *The Managerial Revolution* (New York: John Day, 1941), and commented, "My faith in the success of a managerial society will not, however, reach a maximum until scientists become better managers." Skinner to Spencer, 31 January 1944, Spencer Files, 15, General Mills Correspondence.

72. Skinner, "Pigeons in a Pelican," p. 37.

73. Skinner, "Experimental Psychology," in *Current Trends in Psychology,* ed. Wayne Dennis (Pittsburgh, Pa.: University of Pittsburgh Press, 1947), pp. 16–49, on p. 24.

74. Skinner, "The Science of Learning and the Art of Teaching," *Harvard Educational Review* 24 (1954): 86–97; and Skinner, "Teaching Machines," *Science* 128 (1958): 969–77. Skinner noted "a direct genetic connection between teaching machines and Project Pigeon." See Skinner, "Pigeons in a Pelican," pp. 36–37. On Skinner's construction of teaching machines, see E. A. Vargas and Julie S. Vargas, "B. F. Skinner and the Origins of Programmed Instruction," this volume.

75. Skinner, *Science and Human Behavior* (New York: Macmillan, 1953), p. 5.

76. Skinner, "Pigeons in a Pelican," p. 28.

77. Ibid., p. 37.

78. Skinner, *Shaping of a Behaviorist,* p. 274. His students Marian Breland and Keller Breland also profited from their experience and in 1947 opened Animal Behavior Enterprises, a business based on the "mass production of conditioned

operant behavior in animals" for circuses and other clients. See Breland and Breland, "A Field of Applied Animal Psychology," *American Psychologist* 6 (1951): 202–4, on p. 202. See also Breland and Breland, *Animal Behavior* (New York: Macmillan, 1966). For a brief account of postwar research on organic control (ORCON, for short) at the Naval Research Laboratory, see U.S. Naval Research Laboratory, "Project ORCON: The Use of Pigeons to Guide Missiles," in *Report of NRL Progress, August 1959* (Washington, D.C.: U.S. Naval Research Laboratory, 1959); and Skinner, "Pigeons in a Pelican," pp. 34–36. For a review of the military uses of animals, see Robert E. Lubow, *The War Animals* (Garden City, N.Y.: Doubleday, 1977). On Skinner's indirect but inspirational role in NASA's use of chimpanzees in Project Mercury test flights see Frederick H. Rohles, Jr., "Orbital Bar Pressing: A Historical Note on Skinner and the Chimpanzees in Space," *American Psychologist* 47 (1992): 1531–33.

79. See Bruno Latour, "Give Me a Laboratory and I Will Raise the World," in *Science Observed: Perspectives on the Social Study of Science,* ed. Karin Knorr-Cetina and Michael Mulkay (London: Sage, 1983), pp. 141–70. In the apt phrase of one historian, Skinner remained "above all a scientific preacher," preferring to proselytize from his university post rather than become a full-time behavioral engineer. See Pauly, *Controlling Life,* p. 196. Since this essay was written, the first major scholarly biography of Skinner has appeared: Daniel W. Bjork, *B. F. Skinner: A Life* (New York: Basic, 1993).

6

Radical Behaviorism:
Excerpts From a Textbook Treatment

ECKART SCHEERER

PREFACE

The present chapter contains a condensed and partially rewritten English version of some sections of a book on the experimental analysis of behavior that was published, in its original German version, in 1983.[1] It is offered here as an example of the dissemination and reception of Skinner's thought outside of the English-speaking countries. In order to clarify the focus of the book, some comments on my aims and presuppositions in writing it are needed.

I am not a Skinnerian but a cognitive psychologist interested in the systematic foundations and historical background of scientific psychology. In my view, Skinner's conception must be taken seriously by present-day cognitive psychology, as an important corrective to potential pitfalls inherent in the "internalism" that characterizes the cognitive approach to psychology. However, beginning with Chomsky's review of *Verbal Behavior* there has been a tendency among cognitive scientists to misrepresent Skinner's position. In order to correct this situation, I made it my task to describe Skinner's views as accurately as possible and to maintain a charitable interpretation of them even at those points where I disagree with him.

Radical behaviorism is a serious competitor for cognitive psychology, although neobehaviorism is not. When I began to write my book, the differences between radical behaviorism and neobehaviorism were not fully appreciated, at least not in Germany. In this respect, too, my book was intended to correct a number of widespread misinterpretations. However, to a certain extent the book itself was guilty of distorting the historical record. It presented neobehaviorism as a psychological extension or application of logical empiricism. Neobehaviorism had found wide recognition in German psychology, but this happened *after* authors like Kenneth W. Spence and Gustav Bergmann had subjected it to a reformulation along the lines of logical empiricism.[2] In addition, the more recent advances in behaviorism scholarship were not yet available. The present text retains the focus on the confrontation between neobehaviorism and radical behaviorism, though some extreme assertions have been toned down in line with the findings of recent Skinner scholars.[3]

INTRODUCTION

The object of the present chapter is the conception established by Skinner known as "experimental analysis of behavior" (EAB) or "radical behaviorism." The two terms are not synonymous. The first designates the science of behavior and the second the philosophy underlying that science, both as formulated by Skinner.[4] While it is possible to be an experimental behavior analyst without being a radical behaviorist and vice versa, in Skinner's system the two are closely linked. The present treatment will focus mainly on the philosophical aspects of Skinner's thought and thus on radical behaviorism. However, by way of introduction some words on the experimental analysis of behavior as a psychological "school" are needed.

In contrast to other portrayals of psychological theories, the account given here does not construe EAB as one of several variants of neobehaviorism or stimulus-response psychology. Apart from systematic objections, there are also arguments from history and from the sociology of knowledge for its separation from neobehaviorism. With EAB, we cross the boundary between past and present, for it is a psychological school still flourishing today whereas the neobehaviorist systems are chiefly of historical interest. EAB qualifies as a "school" on several counts. It has its own scientific organizations, and certain psychology departments in the United States are firmly in the hands of behavior analysts. They use a jargon so little understood by laypersons and other psychologists that it might be termed a *dialect*. EAB has several journals of its own, which display symptoms of "incest" that are also evident in the publications of Skinner and of other behavior analysts. The "incest" is caused not only by the dialect of EAB but also by its possession of a distinct research methodology that renders it difficult to relate the concepts of EAB to findings obtained by more standard methodologies.[5]

Like Watson, Skinner thought of his approach not as a school within psychology but as *the* "science of behavior." This is no reason, however, for not treating the EAB as a school of psychology. It is quite typical for the founders and members of scientific schools to claim that they have replaced one science with another—indeed, this was always the case with Skinner. In the beginning stages of his scientific career, he stood as a behaviorist in opposition to established psychology and strove to confront psychology with his behaviorism. After neobehaviorism had become established in American psychology in the late 1930s, Skinner's conception was considered part of this paradigm because it did exhibit certain features typical of it. Skinner's intellectual separation from neobehaviorism began in earnest with his 1945 critique of operationism in psychology; it was completed in 1950 at a point when the neobehaviorist systems were about to fall apart because of their anomalies. Likewise, the first efforts to organize behavior analysis took place in the years after World War II and were signaled by the publication of an exclusively behavior-analytic textbook of psychology.[6]

Despite the renewed critique of "psychology" that Skinner gave in his later years,[7] his academic affiliation was always as a psychologist, and behavior analysis became an established part of university psychology in the United States. By this criterion, it is a "school" of psychology, however much of it may be isolated from the mainstream of psychology.

Neobehaviorism: Some Background

The EAB belongs to a larger tradition of psychological theories that deny the existence of a source of knowledge specific to psychology (e.g., introspection or phenomenological description) and restrict the subject matter of psychology to events that can be observed, in fact or at least in principle, from without. The generic term for such events, if displayed by animal or human organisms, is *behavior.* The programmatic statement that psychology ought to be defined as the science of behavior was first made by John B. Watson in 1913. Though Watson expressed it with revolutionary fervor, the idea of an objective psychology had its roots in a long historical development during the second half of the nineteenth century. Watson's own contribution was the claim that the theoretical aim of psychology should be the prediction and control of behavior, not its explanation. He also coined the term *behaviorism,* which was initially considered a "word monster" among native English speakers but is now firmly entrenched in the technical vocabulary of psychology all over the world.

In part because of the personal fate of its founder, Watson's behaviorism was mainly restricted to programmatic statements and tended to fall back on the level of popular science. However, in the twenties behaviorism became a hotly debated issue in American academic psychology, and between 1935 and 1945 it evolved into the leading paradigm of American psychology, now known as *neobehaviorism.* The chief pioneer of the neobehaviorist movement was Edward Chace Tolman, and Clark L. Hull soon became another influential spokesperson.

Watson's concept of behavior had been ambiguous. Programmatically, it was meant to embrace the conduct of the organism as a whole. But when Watson theorized about behavior, he tended to resolve it into single reflexes, which led to the designation of behaviorism as a "muscle-twitch psychology." Tolman's revision of behaviorism, motivated by this ambiguity, involved the introduction of the molar definition of behavior. Analytical units of behavior were defined by virtue of their subordination to (objectively defined) purposes. Single muscle twitches did not fulfill this criterion and consequently fell below the "grain size" relevant for behaviorism. Tolman also initiated two further developments that differentiated neobehaviorism from Watsonian behaviorism. One of these was the transformation of Watson's stimulus-response (S-R) formula into the stimulus-organism-response (S-O-R) formula. That is, the organism was inserted between stimuli and responses as an additional and indispensable determinant of behavior. Organismic mediators between stimulus and response, such as expectancies and motives, were named *intervening variables* by Tolman, a term that originally had a substantive (rather than a merely methodological) meaning. The other development was the search for a philosophical underpinning of behaviorism, which in Watson had arisen from the philosophically naive materialism of the natural scientist. Initially, Tolman and the other neobehaviorists had strong leanings toward American pragmatism (especially as formulated by William James and John Dewey), and the strand of pragmatist thinking has never disappeared from the behaviorist movement. But eventually, neobehaviorism came under the influence of logical empiricism, a movement that had its roots in Central Europe and was exported to the United States as a result of the emigration forced upon its members by the Nazi regime. Logical empiricism (or logical positivism) had brought the sensualist positivism of Ernst Mach into a form congenial to behaviorism. It insisted on a physicalist "observation language" and called for the expulsion of metaphysics from philosophy and a "unified" science modeled after the example of physics. Theoretical concepts were admitted into science, but they had to be tied to observations by "correspondence rules" ensuring that they were not devoid of observational content. In the United States, logical empiricism allied itself with operationism, founded in 1927 by the physicist Percy W. Bridgman, which insisted that scientific concepts be defined "operationally," that is, by means of sets of experimental operations. Under the influence of this doctrine the concept of intervening variables underwent an important change. It now took on a methodological meaning; intervening variables were to be introduced for purely formal reasons, as a means to summarize the functional relations obtaining between sets of independent and dependent variables. As a consequence, intervening variables could no longer be observed directly, though they were still to be "operationalized" through "anchoring" them by the observable variables that entered into their definitions. In the final phase of neobehaviorism, it was recognized that the meaning of organismic mediators between stimulus and response could not be exhausted by defining them in terms of operationally anchored intervening variables. Intervening variables typically had some surplus meaning not covered by their operational definition, and the term *hypothetical construct* was introduced to refer to intervening variables that were interpreted in terms transcending their operational definitions.

The neobehaviorists' urge to work with intervening variables or hypothetical constructs did not come about by mere accident but rather reflected a shift in their research interests. Once the S-R formula had been replaced by the S-O-R formula, the task became to fill in the "O" in the S-O-R formula, that is, to identify and investigate an increasing number of inner processes and states mediating between stimuli and responses. Expressed differently, behavior was no longer an exclusive research topic in its own right but served as an indicator for inner processes. Substantive behaviorism was transformed into methodological behaviorism. This is the common mark of neobehaviorism and also the main difference between it and the experimental analysis of behavior. Methodological behaviorism is the philosophy of neobehaviorism, and radical behaviorism is the philosophy of the experimental analysis of behavior. Although this difference was first explicated by Skinner in 1945,[8] it went largely unnoticed at the time. The final rupture occurred five years later, against the background of developments now to be sketched briefly.

Despite certain commonalities in their philosophical platform, the neobehaviorists diverged widely from one other with respect to the realization of their research programs. In the present context the controversy between Hull and Tolman (and their students) is particularly important. Tolman developed an approach that was oriented strongly toward Gestalt psychology. He considered behavior in terms of its control by cognitive processes, with the result that his point of view became known as cognitive behaviorism. In contrast, Hull strove to develop a formalized "behavior system" relying on a hypothetico-deductive method modeled after Newton's *Mathematical Principles of Natural Philosophy*. Hull tended to fill in the intervening variables of his system with surplus meaning taken from physiology, resulting in a quasi-physiological behaviorism. At its high point (between 1940 and 1950) the participants in the Tolman-Hull controversy believed that it could be resolved by appeal to experiment. One important issue was whether latent learning (i.e., learning without reinforcement) was possible. The issue was never settled but it led to the distinction, typical for neobehaviorism, between learning and performance. Learning was now conceived as an internal process; although not directly observable, it could be inferred from the observable execution of the learned response (performance), which itself depended on a number of additional, mainly motivational, factors.

The controversy about latent learning was only one example of numerous anomalies that beset neobehaviorism and eventually brought about its demise as the leading paradigm of American psychology. For our present purposes, it is not necessary to review all of these anomalies. Suffice it to say that Skinner launched his attack against methodological behaviorism at a time when its limitations had become apparent, even though it remained a vigorous force in American psychology for some time to come. One symptom of its persistence was that significant strides had been made to bring psychoanalysis and social psychology within the domain of neobehaviorism.[9]

WHY DID SKINNER REJECT THEORIES?

The year 1950 saw the appearance of Skinner's controversial essay "Are Theories of Learning Necessary?"[10] Without mentioning their names, Skinner presented a definitive repudiation of such neobehaviorists as Tolman and Hull in the introduction of the article. He did not deal with the contents of their theories, but criticized them from a purely methodological standpoint. The answer to the question posed in the title was a resounding "No."

Skinner's very way of posing the question—"do we need theories of learning?"—was unusual. The problem for him was not the accuracy, completeness, or plausibility of learning theories—in sum, their cognitive value—but rather their utility for the research practice of behavioral science. This utilitarian attitude, which was characteristic of Skinner's philosophy of science, corresponded to his conception of the subject matter of behavioral science as expressed in the empirical law of effect. Because Tolman and Hull also strove to bring their philosophy of science in line with their science of behavior and stressed the utility criterion,[11] the utilitarian attitude did not in itself serve to set Skinner off from neobehaviorism. However, because neobehaviorism gave lip service to the utility of theories, Skinner could attempt to show that its theories failed to meet that standard and thus attempt to defeat neobehaviorism with its own weapons.

Why, in Skinner's view, did behavioral science have no need for learning theories (or, indeed, any theories)? According to Skinner, theories ought to advance research, that is, they ought to direct the search for variables controlling behavior and their more detailed investigation. However, argued Skinner, they in fact produce instead a false sense of security. Theories pretend to give us answers "in place of the answers we might get through further study,"[12] and thus become obstacles to further study. But even if a theory does give rise to research, the research it generates is likely to be wasteful. Research generated by, and immanent to, a particular theory loses its interest once the theory by which it is driven has been discarded (as is the inevitable fate of theories).

The force of Skinner's latter objection can be illustrated through the example of the research generated by neobehaviorist theories and the controversies that raged between them. Consider latent learning, which provided an anomaly for Hull's theory that reinforcement is based on drive reduction. A straightforward index for the topicality of a research problem is the number of publications devoted to it. Krantz[13] has shown that the number of publications on latent learning reached a peak in the years between 1947 and 1954; after that period, there were scarcely any publications on the topic. Secondary reinforcement, a less controversial topic, did not exhibit a similar decline after 1954 but showed a linear growth corresponding to the general increase in psychological publications in the period studied by Krantz (up to 1964). Along with the Hull-Tolman controversy, latent learning had simply become uninteresting as the theories that gave it the status of an issue fell from favor.

If research should not aim at the formulation and validation of theories, what then should be its goals? According to Skinner, all that matters is the discovery of functional relations; in the case of behavioral science, the relations in question are those that obtain between the external conditions of behavior and the behavior as the sum total of an (individual) organism's responses. The former are the independent, the latter the dependent variables with which behavioral science is concerned. The relations between them are expressed in laws of behavior, and systematizations transcending the synthesis of behavioral laws are rejected. As a consequence, the 1957 book by Skinner and Ferster[14] consists of nearly one thousand graphs of functional relations, virtually without any interpretive commentary.

In the language of the logical empiricism that dominated American philosophy of science when Skinner wrote his "antitheory" paper, his approach to behavioral science amounted to the prescription that scientific concepts and propositions should be restricted to the descriptive language level. Accordingly, his approach has often been called descriptive behaviorism. But this name can be misleading unless we take account of some specific ways in which Skinner uses the concepts "law" and "explanation."

(a) The descriptive behaviorist, too, claims to formulate explanations for behavior. In fact, Skinner used the terms *explanation* and *to explain* freely and frequently. Even according to logical empiricism, he would be justified doing so, for according to the deductive-nomological schema, inferring single events from nomological statements and antecedent conditions qualifies as explanation. However, Skinner rejected the hypothetico-deductive methodology in the behavioral sciences. Hypotheses and deductions are necessary only when we are dealing with inaccessible events within the organism that are not directly observable.[15] As long as we stay within the domain of observable events, all that matters is the "demonstration of a functional relationship between behavior and manipulable or controllable variables."[16] To explain behavior means, for Skinner, to know the external conditions (i.e., the causes) of behavior.

(b) Not every observable covariation between an external event and a bit of behavior qualifies as the basis of a behavioral law. The covariation has to be "regular" and "orderly"; plotted as a graph, it ought to display a "smooth course." Ideally, the regularity should reveal itself "before the very eyes" of the scientist[17] rather than being extracted from an initially opaque collection of data. It would be difficult to exaggerate the significance of the regularity criterion for Skinner's approach. It results in the definition of the basic datum of the learning process; it directs the search for units of behavior; it determines Skinner's attitude toward the role of statistics and mathematical modeling in psychology; and last but not least it entails a "tactics of scientific research"[18] that is fundamentally different from the usual procedures in experimental psychology.

(c) According to Skinner, simple and regular relations are obtained only when we study relatively simple organisms with relatively simple histories under relatively simple external conditions. As a result, the formulation of behavioral laws is based on laboratory experimentation with pigeons, rats, and so forth. Nevertheless, Skinner was aware that the simplicity of behavior laws thus obtained may be "to some extent artificial."[19] Also, their universality across species and situations becomes a matter of empirical investigation. Skinner himself mentioned several constraints on universal behavior laws. First of all, we must take into account the fact that the simultaneous effect of several independent and dependent variables may lead to nonadditive phenomena.[20] Second, every animal species including humans is subject to its own evolutionary history, which programs species-specific phylogenetic contingencies.[21] And finally, complex behavior can be studied only in those situations in which it in fact occurs. For this reason, Skinner's monograph on verbal behavior[22] does not contain a single experiment, and he was quite prepared to accept rather casual observations, field research, and clinical observations as material to be analyzed and interpreted in a science of behavior.[23]

In a humorous vein, Skinner claimed to be a Grand Antitheoretician instead of an antitheorist. In fact, he did not advocate the expulsion of every kind of theory from the science of behavior. The interpretation of "familiar facts . . . in the light of scientific analysis" would qualify as theory, as would a "critique of the methods, data, and concepts of a science of behavior."[24] In the 1950 paper, these forms of theory were not yet mentioned, but even there Skinner accepted "theory" in the sense of a "formal representation of the data reduced to a minimal number of terms,"[25] that is, as an economical description of the data. All these uses of "theory" have in common the fact that the theory does not leave the level of observation. Theories that do not meet this criterion are indeed to be rejected. But why? In answering this question, we shall move from methodological to substantive, and even metaphysical, considerations.

A SCIENCE OF BEHAVIOR WITHOUT THEORETICAL CONCEPTS

According to a widely cited definition, Skinner understands by "theory" (of the type rejected by him)

> any explanation of an observed fact which appeals to events taking place somewhere else, at some other level of observation, described in different terms, and measured, if at all, in different dimensions.[26]

At first sight, this definition seems somewhat unusual, but it is not difficult to see that it applies to the notion that theoretical concepts are defined by their surplus meaning. Such meaning accrues to them when intervening variables are "interpreted," first by the mere fact of their linguistic labeling but even moreso by reference to other observations and their embedding into a conceptual network. The crucial point is that the interpretation contains terms that are not covered by the "anchoring" of intervening variables by means of converging operations. Skinner's definition renders more accurate the somewhat vague notion of "surplus meaning"; the latter is objectionable to him because it refers to observations "at some other level" and to measurements "in different dimensions." The concept, implicit here, of levels of observation refers, for instance, to a hierarchy such as society—intact organism—subsystem of an organism—chemical processes. The notion of dimensions of measurement is exemplified by the CGS (centimeter-gram-second) system commonly used in physics.

What kind of observations, then, are open to the objection that they refer to phenomena "at some other level of observation" (i.e., other than behavior) and to measurement "in different dimensions"? With his definition, Skinner presupposes that "behavior" is located at the observational level of the intact organism and is measured in the dimension system of physics. When investigating the functioning of some subsystem of an organism, we use the correct measurement dimensions but we operate at the wrong observational level, namely, at the level of physiological events. On the other hand, if we do introspection in the sense of the classical psychology of consciousness or phenomenological description in the sense of Gestalt psychology, then we are at the correct observational level, but our observations cannot be expressed in the accepted system of physical measurement. These two types of theory (physiological and mentalist) at least rely on observations and measurements that are possible in principle but seemingly not yet feasible owing to the lack of an adequate research methodology. But a third type of theory does not rely on measurements or observations at all. In this case we have, according to Skinner, a theory of the conceptual type. In his 1950 paper, Skinner did not give names. But in other places he acknowledged that the objection to physiologism was directed against Pavlov, the objection of mentalism against Tolman, and the objection of conceptualism against Freud. Hull's system was presumably beset by both conceptualism and physiologism, depending on whether its formal aspects or its substantive interpretation was stressed.

On neobehaviorist principles, Skinner's objections could be taken as an exhortation to drop the interpretation of intervening variables and consequently convert them into hypothetical constructs.[27] But Skinner rejected intervening variables even if taken as purely formal tools.[28] If *one* intervening variable is anchored in more than one class of observations (as in the case of Hullian reaction potential, $_sE_R$, being anchored in amplitude, latency, and resistance to extinction), then this is a justified simplification only when such "indexical variables" all display the same functional relation to those independent variables that constitute the reaction potential through the intermediary of other intervening variables. However, this is not the case, as shown by Skinner and proven by Koch using Hull's own data.[29] Rejecting intervening variables, we are also no longer able to distinguish between learning and performance, even in a purely operational sense. Skinner dealt with performance only; the result of learning was, for him, changed behavior itself rather than some internal state leading to changed behavior. The same was true for those motivational states and processes that had been assigned priority in neobehaviorist research. For instance, in *Science and Human Behavior* Skinner used the expression "drive" only in negative statements: drive was not a stimulus, not a physiological state, not a mental state, not simply a state of response strength. What is called "drive" in folk psychology and most psychological theories is nothing but an inaccurate and misleading mode of referring to the effects of deprivation and satiation on behavior.[30]

Expressions like "satiation" and "deprivation" designate classes of external conditions of behavior and as such serve an abbreviatory function in line with Skinner's Machian principles of economical description. If employed in this capacity only, intervening variables should have been acceptable to Skinner. Nonetheless, he fought against them. This shows that behind the formal argumentation there lurked a concern with the typical subject of intervening variables, namely, processes occurring within the organism and intervening between environment and behavior. In the experimental analysis of behavior, there was to be no place for internal processes, events, or states. This principle has been named the "empty organism" formula,[31] and more than anything else it serves to demarcate radical behaviorism from neobehaviorism. Yet the "empty organism" formula is easily misunderstood. Are we faced with a return to the arch-behaviorist extremism of Watson—the denial of consciousness—made even more extreme now by a "denial of the organism"? Certainly not. Skinner was well aware that behind the observable behavior of the organism there is the work of the central nervous system and other subsystems of the organism. Nor did he have doubts about the reality of what are called conscious processes in folk psychology and in non-Skinnerian scientific psychology. What is at stake is the attempt to explain behavior by appealing to internal processes of a physiological or a mental sort. Depending on whether it is applied to mentalistic or physiological explanations, Skinner's argument takes on a somewhat different form, and thus needs to be described separately for the two points of attack. It should be remembered, though, that the different variants of the argument exhibit a common theme: the rejection of reductionist explanation—of the attempt to explain behavior as a mere epiphenomenon of some more fundamental reality.

BEHAVIOR AND NEURAL PROCESSES

Why is it not possible, for Skinner, to explain behavior by appealing to neural processes, that is, by means of neurophysiological theories? A first reason has to do with the methodological relationship between behavioral science and physiology. Perhaps not surprisingly, in this connection we again encounter the principle of regularity. Already in 1935, Skinner had attacked the widespread belief that physiological processes ought of necessity to be more lawful than behavioral processes.[32] Somewhat later, Skinner added the point that explaining the facts and laws of behavior by means of neurophysiological facts or laws would presuppose that the former are known; an explanation can only be good to the extent that it completely and accurately covers what it pretends to explain. Thus, the potential explanatory value of physiology with respect to behavioral science is constrained by the state of our knowledge concerning behavior.[33] Neurophysiological research never can replace behavior analysis, because it ends at the boundary between organism and environment; in contrast, the interaction between organism and environment is the proper subject matter of behavior analysis.

Thus, we have reached a second point of view: the difference between subject matters. True, like physiology the analysis of behavior is a science of the organism, but it is a science of the organism as a whole in its interaction with the environment. Because the laws of behavior refer to a higher level of integration than the laws of neurophysiology, they are of a different kind and cannot be reduced to the latter. Physiology, insisted Skinner, deals with the "inner workings" of the organism and should pursue its aims with its own "techniques of observation and measurement." Nor will it be helped in its own business by the attempt to infer "inner states" from behavior, for it is extremely unlikely that there will ever be a one-to-one correspondence between inner and outer events.[34]

In the language of present-day philosophy of science,[35] Skinner's approach to the relations between behavior analysis and physiology can be described as nonreductive materialism. That is, while he maintained that behavior and physiological processes are both physical, he did not believe that the laws of behavior could be reduced to physiological laws. Nevertheless, he objected to his approach being called antiphysiological.[36] The task assigned to physiology in experimental analysis is to fill in the temporal gaps in functional analyses and more specifically between the environment and behavior.[37] In current discussions of the reductionism problem, a distinction is usually made between type reduction and token reduction.[38] Type reduction means that *classes* of mental events are reducible to classes of physiological events. In token reduction, such a claim is made only for individual instances of mental events and physiological events. To apply this terminology to the analysis of behavior, the expression "mental event" must be replaced by "behavior event." If this is done, it becomes clear that Skinner accepted token reduction but rejected type reduction. That is, he did not doubt that individual instances of behavioral acts—such as a keypeck occurring at a specified point in time and space—could be explained by appealing to the physiological events taking place between stimulus and response. Behavior analysis, however, deals not with individual behavioral events but with classes of such events, which are defined in terms of their relation to the environment. Because behavior analysis classifies behavior events differently than physiology classifies neural events, it is unlikely that a type-to-type reduction of behavior laws to physiological laws can be realized.[39]

A final objection raised by Skinner against physiological explanations concerned not so much physiology as a whole but one of its subfields, sensory physiology. Though directed against a misleading notion of the workings of the central nervous system, the objection was in fact of an epistemological nature. Consider visual perception, for example. It is common practice to analyze the causal chains underlying it into the following components: object—stimulus—retinal image (and physiological processes in the visual system)—visual perception.[40] The presupposition is that at some place in the causal chain the physiological process is transformed into mental content, the visual percept. This means that (a) the physiological process is conceived as a "copy" of the object and (b) the copy, in turn, is observed by a homunculus, a "little man in the head." In fact, however, we do not look at the retinal image or its central nervous representation, but at objects in the outer world; and seeing is, for Skinner, only a certain way of behaving relative to an object. Apart from the last clause, this argument is not found only in Skinner; he shared it, for instance, with Gestalt psychology and the direct-realist perceptual theory of Gibsonian ecological psychology. Whether or not the argument applies to *all* kinds of sensory physiology, its epistemological import is that the "transformation" of physiological processes into mental contents implies a dualism between matter and mind. We shall now be concerned with this dualism, which was also strongly attacked by Skinner.

Behavior and the Inner Mental World

Ever since John Locke accepted reflection in addition to sensations as a source of "ideas" and assigned the "inner sense" to it, psychology has tended to define itself as the science of inner experience. The definition rests on the opposition between the world of external experience, as the subject matter of physics, and the world of inner experience, as the proper subject matter of psychology. Although the fate of this opposition cannot be traced here, Skinner clearly believed that broad portions of present-day psychology still adhere to it, and he attempted to develop a nonmentalist psychology that would not rely on dualism. However, he subsumed rather different approaches under "mentalism." Though he himself provided an eminently readable presentation of his arguments,[41] for systematic reasons an ordering of arguments is used here that is not found in exactly this form in Skinner.

A first line of argument is directed against that version of mentalism which presupposes the existence of phenomenologically represented contents. In turn, such contents may be considered either with respect to their presumed cognitive function or with respect to their reality status.

If the cognitive function of mental contents is emphasized, then we are confronted with various forms of representational or copy theories of consciousness. As a rule, they are found in the psychology of perception, and we already know Skinner's objections against their physiological version. It is therefore sufficient to add that this type of theory rests on the distinction between the phenomenal world and the physical world. According to *one* variant of the theory, the phenomenal world, being the sum total of percepts, represents the physical world. According to a second variant, the physical world results from the conceptual elaboration of the phenomenal world (and more generally from its secondary reconstruction). Both variants are misleading, according to Skinner. Their basic fault is the presupposition that "seeing implies something seen"[42]—or expressed differently and generalized: that perception must possess some content through which it relates to an object. In fact, Skinner urged, it is exactly the other way around. Seeing is one of the many forms of operant behavior, and like all other forms of operant behavior it comes under stimulus control. What is primary is not what is seen, but seeing itself. If we follow this principle, then the dualism between the (phenomenological) content and the (physical) object of seeing vanishes. Stimulus control is exerted by the events of the one and unitary world in which we exist. All that can be said is that different learning histories may lead to different forms of stimulus control and different forms of behavior. The talk of a physical world and a phenomenological world is a misleading expression of the fact that practical, everyday seeing behavior (the "phenomenological world") and the conceptual-reconstructive activities of the physicist (the "physical world") are maintained by different reinforcement contingencies and come under different kinds of stimulus control.

Thus, mental events do not function as a way station between human and world that mediates our knowledge of the world. Nor do they have a different reality status than the *one* real world by which our behavior is controlled. This illusion arises from a feature of mental events that Skinner calls their privacy. The privacy stems in part from their being controlled by private stimuli, and in part from their consisting of private responses. Because private events occur "under the skin"[43] of the organism, they are difficult or impossible to access from without. A bad tooth, for instance, is a private stimulus for whoever has it. As long as it does not express itself in behavior, the toothache remains a private response. This, however, does not mean that as an event which is in principle unobservable from without, the toothache (a pet example of the philosophical constructions of "inner experience") has a particular status that is different from external reality. The utterance "I have an aching tooth" is a public response shaped and maintained by the social environment, in the same way the utterance "I see a red flower" is controlled by a public stimulus. As Skinner emphasized, the social environment has certain practices for the shaping of responses that are under the control of private events.[44] The contingencies established by such practices between private stimulus, response, and reinforcement are less regular than those involving responses under the control of public stimuli. This explains why the "vocabulary" of the responses under private stimulus control is imprecise and not very reliable. Nothing more is needed to explain "the language of private experience" referred to by mentalist philosophers or the "introspective reports" spoken of by mentalist psychologists.

Skinner's arguments concerning the private stimulus control of public responses also apply to private responses, with the one difference that all private responses first have been public responses (which is of course not true of private stimuli). According to Skinner, public behavior may turn into private behavior for either of two reasons: the private behavior is often more easily executed; and if it is not public, it cannot be subjected to punishing consequences from without.[45] Behavior once turned private may control other private behavior as well as public behavior. If so, it is a particularly efficient means of self-control. But the causes of even this form of behavior—the traditional example of "inner-directed behavior"—"rest ultimately with the environmental variables which generate controlling behavior."[46] As a matter of principle, and without exception, private behavior arises from public behavior under the control of public events.

SKINNER'S ANTIMENTALISM IN RELATION TO OTHER SYSTEMS OF PSYCHOLOGY

With the concept of private behavior we have reached the central—and most controversial—point of Skinner's system. Because Skinner's antimentalist treatment of private events best distinguishes his approach from those of his contemporaries, it also provides a fruitful point of entry for understanding the relation of his system to other systems of psychology. We begin by elaborating on the important differences between Skinner's handling of covert events and their treatment in neobehaviorism.

At first sight it looks as if Skinner meant by private behavior nothing else than what the neobehaviorists called mediating responses. The double function of private behavior (as both a response and a stimulus) and the appeal to "greater ease of execution" for explaining the transformation of public into private behavior[47] could be quoted in support of the neobehaviorist view. Nevertheless, there are two essential differences. For one thing, in contrast to the neobehaviorist approach the roles of explanandum and explanans, of cause and effect, are interchanged. Whereas neobehaviorism used mediating responses for explaining public behavior, Skinner explained private behavior on the basis of public behavior and its consequences. And second, private behavior was for Skinner not merely a passive, intraorganismic link in a chain leading from external stimulation to overt response. As a form of operant behavior, it shared the reality status and causal laws of the latter; more specifically, it was not "elicited," in the sense of mechanical causation, by external stimuli.

If we now take into account the fact that what Skinner called private behavior coincides more or less with introspectively accessible consciousness in the sense of psychological mentalism, then we reach the following conclusion. Far from "negating consciousness," Skinner acknowledged the full and transparent reality of consciousness. "To be conscious" meant to be controlled in one's present (primarily verbal) behavior by one's own earlier behavior. When currently performing controlling functions, earlier behavior is a form of private behavior; it functions as a private stimulus. Behavior that is under private stimulus control is shaped and maintained by the social environment. As a consequence, "conscious" behavior cannot be conceived without a social environment. "Strangely enough," Skinner wrote, "it is the community which teaches the individual to 'know himself'."[48]

Apart from the interjection "strangely enough," this statement could have been made by a representative of the Soviet cultural-historical school. In general, leftist authors have taken a very hostile stance toward Skinner. For instance, he has been chastised for having reduced animal behavior to mere reflexes, for having overlooked the social roots of reinforcement, and in a more general sense for having been an ideologist of bourgeois society.[49] Yet though Skinner was not a Marxist, he shared with Marxism the principle that (social) being determines consciousness, as well as the principle of the inseparable unity of action (Skinner's "operant behavior") and consciousness.

At the same time, Skinner shunned the reification of consciousness (metaphorically or in fact) as a spatially localized mental system, a reification suggested by the noun form "consciousness." If consciousness were conceived in such terms, then Skinner did indeed negate it. This brings us to a third variant of mentalistic approaches, which operates with mental structures or powers that are not necessarily phenomenologically given—the "conceptual" theories mentioned in Skinner's 1950 paper. With respect to them, Skinner's arguments were less sophisticated than those directed against theories of mental contents. He criticized them for filling out explanatory gaps by using "animistic" concepts such as the "vital force" of premechanist physiology or the *vis dormitiva* by which a doctor in a Molière comedy "explained" the effect of opium. More serious than this parallel is the consequence seen by Skinner of a preoccupation with "inner powers," "inner conflicts," and the like, a preoccupation that results in the neglect of actual behavior and the conditions by which it is determined. A prominent example of a theory open to this objection is psychoanalysis.

Skinner's position on psychoanalysis was rather subtle and did not amount to outright rejection. According to Skinner, a great merit of Freud lay in his destruction of the belief that mental contents are directly observable, and in this sense Freud was even said to be a pioneer of behavioral science.[50] In addition, Skinner had a high opinion of Freud as the founder of a strictly deterministic approach to human behavior.[51] Two points testify to the strictness of Freud's determinism. First, Freud was concerned with seemingly accidental aspects of behavior, and second, he traced behavior back to its original determinants in life history. In this context, the psychoanalytical doctrine of defense mechanisms was especially valuable if conceived as an account of functional relations between responses and controlling variables.[52] Freud's doctrine of the unconscious was important not only because of its negative stand on the direct observability of mental events, but also because of Freud's insight that the subject's ability to verbalize his or her own behavior and to identify important causal variables is not a necessary precondition for behavior to occur or for its causes to have an effect.[53]

However, psychoanalysis went astray, according to Skinner, when it divided the mind into regions and conceived mental processes in terms of energy.[54] Expressed in the language of psychoanalytical metapsychology, Skinner thus attacked the "structural" and "economical" models. Provided that they were interpreted in terms of actual behavior rather than in terms of inner conflicts and developmental sequences, he was more favorably disposed toward the dynamical model and the overall genetic approach of psychoanalysis, much more so than would be expected on the basis of the popular stereotype of an unavoidable opposition between psychoanalysis and behavior analysis. In this context, it is instructive to compare Skinner's attitude toward psychoanalysis with that of John Dollard and Neal E. Miller,[55] who were followers of Hull. While leaving intact the conceptual apparatus of psychoanalysis, they attempted to provide it with an empirical data base acceptable to neobehaviorism. Skinner, on the other hand, rejected the conceptual structure of psychoanalysis but took much more seriously the functional relations discovered by it.

Psychoanalysis, though, could be taken seriously only with the provision that the substitution of inner (fictitious) relations for outer (factual) relations was avoided. Quite characteristically, Skinner criticized Freud for relying on the early childhood memories of his patients without independently checking the evidence for their early experiences, and for arguing that "what the patient remembered was more important than what actually happened or whether anything happened at all."[56] As a result, Freud had stopped at a mental way station without noticing that this way station was only one aspect of his patients' behavior. He had then used this single aspect of their behavior to "explain" other kinds of behavior, all along misconstruing the memories or fantasies as mental events rather than as actual behavior.

In Skinner's view, the substitution of mental way stations for actual behavior was also characteristic of another type of psychological mentalism: "Something similar is done when behavior exhibited in taking a mental test is said to explain behavior exhibited elsewhere."[57] This seemingly remote parallel between psychoanalysis and mental testing contains the essential point of Skinner's attitude toward mentalistic explanations by means of dispositional concepts. Such concepts are primarily encountered in personality research, in the form of properties or personality traits, and serve to "explain" actual behaviors when we are concerned with the interindividual variability and intraindividual constancy of behavior.

Skinner did not object to the study of individual behavior—quite the contrary, in fact. The discovery of behavior laws for individual organisms may even be seen as one of the defining features of behavior analysis. Skinner believed, though, that research centered on individuals could not reach its goals when it was done under the auspices of property concepts.[58] The quantitative assessment of personality traits by means of mental tests was suspect because in mental testing such traits could be defined only by reference to a population of individuals. For Skinner, there was only one acceptable definition of "property," and this was the enumeration of the responses of an individual and the (coarse) assessment of their frequency. However, such a definition would be no more than a first step toward a functional analysis. It would establish an individual behavior repertoire, but the emergence of such a repertoire was itself in need of explanation. Putting the elements of a repertoire into groups (e.g., by means of factor analysis) and attempting to predict the occurrence of elements on the basis of their inclusion in one of the resulting groups would not solve the problem, for we would then be predicting responses from responses and more generally effects from effects. For Skinner, this would be impossible, however; prediction always goes from cause to effect. Consequently, we would be forced to show for every single member of a class of behaviors that it was controlled by the same external conditions as all other members of the class. If this could indeed be shown, then the general concept "property" would still be redundant, because the proof for its validity would have to be repeated for every new instance of behavior. If the proof failed, then the property concept was misleading because its application had rested on a wrong presupposition. In sum, we do not gain anything by postulating properties, but we risk losing what is most important, for "we do not change behavior by manipulating a trait."[59]

Having now reviewed Skinner's arguments against four variants of mentalism (mental contents as copies and as subjective reality; mental structures and powers; and mental dispositions), we are in a position to characterize his Weltanschauung in a more comprehensive fashion. In addition to having been a nonreductive materialist, Skinner combined monism and determinism. He was a monist because he rejected all forms of reality doubling; and he was a determinist because he attempted to bring the entire reality, without exceptions, under the reign of cause and effect, although the causality he envisaged did allow for probabilistic effects.[60]

One might be tempted to argue—and Skinner himself would have argued this way—that he did not offer a particular Weltanschauung or metaphysics, but simply took the point of view of natural science as applied to animal and human behavior. This, however, is not the case. In fact, there are several unique points in Skinner's thought that allow us to speak of "Skinnerian metaphysics."[61] For one thing, an antireductionist stance is usually coupled with ontological (mind-matter) dualism—the irreducibility of the mental is taken as proof that it is a separate, nonphysical domain of reality. Skinner circumvented this option by replacing the mental with his concept of private behavior. Second, "virtually every materialistic monist in psychology . . . has been a physiological reductionist."[62] The viability of a Skinner-type "behavioral materialism" hinges on the existence of molar behavior laws—a position that Skinner was able to defend but which is by no means universally accepted by philosophers of science.[63] Third, contrary to the impression conveyed by Skinner, determinism and the acknowledgment of an "inner world" are by no means incompatible with each other. In fact, most scientific psychologists have been determinists, and indeed many of them introduced an "inner world" precisely in order to maintain a thoroughgoing determinism. Approaches as diverse as psychoanalysis, neobehaviorism, and the Marxist "reflectory theory of the mental" all share the principle of mediated determination, brought by Sergei L. Rubinstein under the formula that "external causes act through inner conditions." Skinner rejected this formula. With his "direct determinism" he took a stand against an overwhelming majority; and this, in the final analysis, is what rendered him a radical.

EPILOGUE

A textbook is not the place for putting forth a novel point of view or defending some arresting thesis. My treatment of Skinner's thought was meant to be middle-of-the-road and did not aim at spectacular effects. But it was intended to be reasonably complete, and because the present excerpts cover only about 15 percent of my book, I wish to give a brief conspectus of some additional sections that deal with philosophical, historical, and systematic issues and thus might be of interest to Skinner scholars. In a section on the research paradigm of behavior analysis, I attempted to show that Skinner's metaphysics entails some characteristic features of the research methodology of behavior analysis, such as the rejection of statistics and mathematical modeling and the almost exclusive focus on single-subject research. These precepts follow from Skinner's concern with maintaining a strictly deterministic account of individual behavior.

Concerning the intellectual background of behavior analysis, its philosophical as well as scientific antecedents are discussed. Skinner is seen as a latter-day Francis Bacon, sharing with the lord chancellor a utilitarian approach to science, an urge to destroy "idols" and "illusions" that impede effective action by preventing knowledge of true causes, and a peculiar combination of empiricism and utopian thought. As a loyal follower of Ernst Mach, Skinner resisted the transformation of positivism *tout court* into logical positivism, except for the requirement of a physicalist data language. His attitude toward operationism was ambivalent. On the one hand, he used operational definitions extensively. On the other hand, he charged that excessive reliance on the operational method by his fellow behaviorists had given the appearance of scientific respectability to mind-matter dualism and had transformed substantive behaviorism into a puerile methodological behaviorism.

A section of the book on applied behavior analysis focuses on the obliteration of the boundary between "pure" and "applied" research as demanded by the premises of behavior analysis. Behavior technology is seen as being part and parcel of behavior analysis rather than a mere adjunct to it. Some presumed misuses of behavior technology can and ought to be criticized from the point of view of behavior analysis itself and therefore do not constitute evidence against its application, provided that the criticisms originating from behavior analysis are heeded.

Skinner's utopian efforts are dealt with under the heading "programmatic behavior analysis." His precepts for the design of a culture may be viable for small-scale communal living but not for complex, industrialized societies depending on massive division of labor and characterized by conflict among social classes and not only among individuals. His analyses of "freedom" and "dignity" are seen in part as a merely linguistic exercise aimed at the "translation" of traditional concepts into behavioral terminology. An ironic contradiction is found in Skinner's resort to persuasion in spite of his own principle that behavior can be changed only by changing the contingencies controlling it. He is also criticized for failing to see that the experience of freedom, even if brought about by remote and subtle contingencies, constitutes a potent determiner of behavior.

My critique of behavior analysis as a science elaborates a theme introduced in respect to his behavioral utopia. Its main thrust is that behavior analysis needs "inner processes" if it wants to realize its own program, that is, the functional analysis of behavior aimed at prediction and control. I accept Skinner's basic premise that private behavior, of both a conscious (i.e., rule-based) and an unconscious (i.e., contingency-shaped) nature, arises as the result of differential reinforcement by the verbal community. Once acquired, however, private "mental" processes take on a degree of autonomy that qualifies them as causes of behavior. Skinner's basic fault consists in conflating the (correct) thesis that inner processes are ultimately derived from overt behavior and interaction with the environment with the (incorrect) thesis that they do not play any causal role whatsoever. If behavior analysis is to survive at all, then it *must* turn cognitive.

NOTES

William Woodward suggested the inclusion of the material in the introduction, from my *Die Verhaltensanalyse,* and kindly provided me with a translation of his own, which I have used extensively. The section "Neobehaviorism: Some Background" is an abridged translation of *Verhaltensanalyse,* pp. 13–18; it contains well-known material for which extended documentation is not necessary. Apart from the epilogue, the remaining sections of the chapter are translated from *Verhaltensanalyse,* pp. 23–36.

1. Eckart Scheerer, *Die Verhaltensanalyse* (Berlin: Springer-Verlag, 1983).

2. The *locus classicus* for the final assimilation of neobehaviorism to logical empiricism is Kenneth W. Spence, "The Postulates and Methods of 'Behaviorism'," *Psychological Review 52* (1950): 67–78. In 1953, Gustav Bergmann ("Theoretical Psychology," *Annual Review of Psychology* 4 [1953]: 435–58) could present it as a consensus in (American) psychology.

3. See, for example, Laurence D. Smith, *Behaviorism and Logical Positivism: A Reassessment of the Alliance* (Stanford, Calif.: Stanford University Press, 1986); and Gerald E. Zuriff, *Behaviorism: A Conceptual Reconstruction* (New York: Columbia University Press, 1985). Like the book from which it is derived, the present chapter is chiefly concerned with systematic rather than historical issues. On the other hand, it is based on Skinner's own writings, and an attempt was made to trace his main concepts back to their first appearance in print. As a result, the treatment may be termed *semihistorical.* Though I cannot pretend to be a Skinner scholar, in producing the English version I profited immensely from the advice of Laurence Smith, Stephen Coleman, and William Woodward, who all have a right to that title. In addition, I was able to draw on an additional decade of Skinner scholarship that has accumulated since I wrote the book. Un-

fortunately, it proved impracticable to accommodate all of its results without rewriting the entire book and thus giving a wrong impression of its original contents; but references to more recent works on Skinner are given at appropriate places in the footnotes.

4. To my knowledge, the term *experimental analysis of behavior* first appeared in print in Skinner, "The Experimental Analysis of Behavior," *American Scientist* 4 (1957): 343–71. *Radical behaviorism* was first used by Skinner in 1945 ("The Operational Analysis of Psychological Terms," *Psychological Review* 52 [1945]: 270–77, 291–94), but its widespread use is of more recent origin. For a useful discussion of the meanings attached to the term *radical behaviorism,* see Willard F. Day, Jr. "Radical Behaviorism," in *B. F. Skinner: Consensus and Controversy,* ed. Sohan Modgil and Celia Modgil (New York: Falmer Press, 1987).

5. On the language of EAB as a "dialect," see Philip N. Hineline, "The Language of Behavior Analysis: Its Community, Its Functions, and Its Limitations," *Behaviorism* 9 (1980): 67–86. The EAB journals are: the *Journal of the Experimental Analysis of Behavior* (since 1958), the *Journal of Applied Behavior Analysis* (since 1968), and *Behavior Analyst* (since 1978). The journal *Behaviorism* (since 1972; now titled *Behavior and Philosophy*) is devoted to a discussion of the philosophical problems of behaviorism. The "incest" is evidenced by the fact that behavior analysts rarely cite works by other psychologists and vice versa. See David L. Krantz, "The Separate Worlds of Operant and Nonoperant Psychology," *Journal of Applied Behavior Analysis* 4 (1971): 61–70; and Krantz, "Schools and Systems: The Mutual Isolation of Operant and Non-operant Psychology as a Case Study," *Journal of the History of the Behavioral Sciences* 8 (1972): 86–102.

6. Fred S. Keller and William N. Schoenfeld, *Principles of Psychology* (New York: Appleton-Century-Crofts, 1950).

7. More specifically, the criticism was directed against *cognitive* psychology, which may be said to constitute the current mainstream of scientific psychology. See Skinner, "Why I Am Not a Cognitive Psychologist," *Behaviorism* 5 (1977): 1–10.

8. Skinner, "Operational Analysis."

9. On social psychology, see Neal E. Miller and John Dollard, *Social Learning and Imitation* (New Haven: Yale University Press, 1941). On psychoanalysis, see John Dollard and Neal E. Miller, *Personality and Psychotherapy* (New York: McGraw-Hill, 1950).

10. Skinner, "Are Theories of Learning Necessary?" *Psychological Review* 57 (1950): 193–216. Page references are to the reprint in Skinner, *Cumulative Record,* 3d ed. (New York: Appleton-Century-Crofts, 1972).

11. In the original version, I portrayed the continuity between behavior science and philosophy of science as a distinguishing mark of Skinner's thought alone. I am indebted to Smith, *Behaviorism and Logical Positivism,* for a perspective that does justice to Hull's and Tolman's efforts in the same direction. Skinner's reliance on the utility criterion for the evaluation of scientific knowledge has been stressed by Mark Burton, "Determinism, Relativism and the Behavior of Scientists," *Behaviorism* 8 (1980): 113–22.

12. Skinner, "Theories of Learning," p. 71.

13. David L. Krantz, "Research Activity in 'Normal' and Anomalous Areas," *Journal of the History of the Behavioral Sciences* 1 (1965): 39–42.

14. Charles B. Ferster and Skinner, *Schedules of Reinforcement* (Englewood Cliffs, N.J.: Prentice-Hall, 1957).

15. Skinner, *Contingencies of Reinforcement* (New York: Appleton-Century-Crofts, 1969), preface.

16. Comments of Professor Skinner in T. W. Wann, ed., *Behaviorism and Phenomenology* (Chicago: University of Chicago Press, 1964), p. 102.

17. Skinner, "Reinforcement Today," *American Psychologist* 13 (1958): 94–99, quoted after Skinner, *Cumulative Record,* p. 167.

18. Murray Sidman, *Tactics of Experimental Research* (New York: Basic, 1960).

19. Skinner, *Science and Human Behavior* (New York: Macmillan, 1953), p. 204.

20. Ibid., chap. 14.

21. Skinner, "The Phylogeny and Ontogeny of Behavior," *Science* 153 (1966): 1205–13.

22. Skinner, *Verbal Behavior* (New York: Appleton-Century-Crofts, 1957).

23. Skinner, *Science and Human Behavior,* p. 37.

24. Skinner, *Contingencies of Reinforcement,* preface.

25. Skinner, "Theories of Learning," p. 100. The equation of theory with economical description goes back to Ernst Mach. The paramount importance of theoretical parsimony in radical behaviorism has been recognized by authors who think that Skinner's other criticisms of theoretical concepts are unfounded. See Ben A. Williams, "On the Role of Theory in Behavior Analysis," *Behaviorism* 14 (1986): 111–23.

26. Skinner, "Theories of Learning," p. 69.

27. Such a move was suggested by Howard H. Kendler, "'What Is Learned'— A Theoretical Blind Alley," *Psychological Review* 59 (1952): 269–77.

28. It must be conceded, though, that in his early work (e.g., "The Concept of Reflex in the Description of Behavior," *Journal of General Psychology* 5 [1931]: 427–58), Skinner used intervening variables as formal tools. See William S. Verplanck, "Burrhus F. Skinner," in *Modern Learning Theory,* ed. William K. Estes et al. (New York: Appleton-Century-Crofts, 1954).

29. Sigmund Koch, "Clark L. Hull," in *Modern Learning Theory.*

30. Skinner, *Science and Human Behavior,* chap. 9. Again, it should be noted that in Skinner's earlier work (e.g., *The Behavior of Organisms* [New York: Appleton-Century, 1938]) "drive" was defined in terms of reflex strength and thus would be subject to Skinner's own later criticism.

31. According to Skinner (*Behavior of Organisms,* p. 443), the expression was invented by Edwin G. Boring. It was rarely used by Skinner himself, probably because it was meant to be derogatory.

32. Skinner, "The Generic Nature of the Concepts of Stimulus and Response," *Journal of General Psychology* 12 (1935): 40–65.

33. Skinner, *Behavior of Organisms,* p. 423; Skinner, *Contingencies of Reinforcement,* p. 282.

34. Skinner, *Cumulative Record,* p. 269.

35. For instance, Paul M. Churchland, *Matter and Consciousness,* rev. ed. (Cambridge: MIT Press, 1988).

36. Skinner, *Reflections on Behaviorism and Society* (Englewood Cliffs, N.J.: Prentice-Hall, 1978), p. 123.

37. Skinner, *About Behaviorism* (New York: Knopf, 1974), p. 215.

38. Daniel C. Dennett, *Brainstorms* (Cambridge: MIT Press, 1978), preface.

39. It is interesting to note that the rationale for rejecting type reduction, as spelled out here, coincides with the arguments typically given in favor of the

computational theory of mind. See, for example, Zenon W. Pylyshyn, *Computation and Cognition* (Cambridge: MIT Press, 1984), chap. 1, although Pylyshyn employs the rationale *against* behaviorism.

40. Skinner, *Contingencies of Reinforcement*, p. 249.

41. Skinner, "Behaviorism at Fifty," in *Behaviorism and Phenomenology*, pp. 79–97.

42. Ibid., p. 89.

43. Strictly speaking, the dividing line between "public" and "private" is not the skin, as this boundary can be overcome by instrumental means. Rather, the boundary is determined by the accessibility or nonaccessibility of events to differential reinforcement by the verbal community. See Skinner's comments in *Behaviorism and Phenomenology*, p. 107.

44. Skinner, *Verbal Behavior*, pp. 131–34.

45. Ibid., p. 141.

46. Skinner, *Science and Human Behavior*, p. 254.

47. For the viewpoint in question, expressed by a chief propagandist for mediating responses, see Charles E. Osgood, *Method and Theory in Experimental Psychology* (New York: Oxford University Press, 1953), pp. 397–98.

48. Skinner, *Science and Human Behavior*, p. 261.

49. On Skinner as a reflex theoretician, see Klaus J. Bruder, "Über Skinners 'Radical Behaviorism'" (On Skinner's "radical behaviorism"), *Psychologie und Gesellschaftskritik* 2 (1978): 37–57; on his neglecting social roots of reinforcement, Michail Jaroschewski, *Psychologie im 20. Jahrhundert* (Psychology in the twentieth century) (Berlin: Volk und Wissen, 1975), p. 242; on Skinner as ideologist, Anonymous, *Psychologie—eine Form bürgerlicher Ideologie* (Psychology—a form of bourgeois ideology) (Plankstadt, Germany: Sendler, 1975). For a serious and knowledgeable criticism of behavior analysis from a Marxist viewpoint, see Steinar Kvale, "Skinners radikaler Behaviorismus und operante Verhaltenstherapie—Umriss einer phänomenologischen und marxistischen Kritik" (Skinner's radical behaviorism and operant behavior therapy—Sketch of a phenomenological and Marxist critique), *Psychologie und Gesellschaftskritik* 2 (1978): 7–36.

50. Skinner, "Behaviorism at Fifty," in *Behaviorism and Phenomenology*, p. 82.

51. Skinner, "A Critique of Psychoanalytic Concepts and Theories," *Scientific Monthly* 79 (1954): 300–305; reprinted in Skinner, *Cumulative Record*, pp. 239–48. Skinner's surprisingly sympathetic treatment of Freud is discussed in Marc N. Richelle, *B. F. Skinner: A Reappraisal* (Hillsdale, N.J.: Erlbaum, 1993), chap. 5.

52. Skinner, *Science and Human Behavior*, pp. 376–94; Skinner, "Critique of Psychoanalytic Concepts," p. 246.

53. Skinner, "Critique of Psychoanalytic Concepts," p. 247.

54. Skinner, *Science and Human Behavior*, p. 375.

55. Dollard and Miller, *Personality and Psychotherapy*.

56. Skinner, *Contingencies of Reinforcement*, p. 254.

57. Ibid.

58. Skinner, *Science and Human Behavior*, pp. 194–203.

59. Ibid., p. 203.

60. The probabilistic theme could not be elaborated in this brief sketch. Suffice it to say that the basic unit of behavior analysis, the operant, was defined in terms of response rate, and thus of probability, rather than in terms of absolute necessity. Nevertheless, Skinner's determinism, which evolved early in his career, for a long time prevented him from acknowledging the probabilistic causality involved in

the operant. See Judith L. Scharff, "Skinner's Concept of the Operant: From Necessitarian to Probabilistic Causality," *Behaviorism* 10 (1982): 45–54.

61. I take this phrase, and some of the arguments to follow, from Owen J. Flanagan, Jr., "Skinnerian Metaphysics and the Problem of Operationism," *Behaviorism* 8 (1980): 1–14.

62. Ibid., p. 11.

63. For instance, Richard F. Kitchener ("Are There Molar Psychological Laws?" *Philosophy of the Social Sciences* 6 [1976]: 143–54) denies the existence of Skinnerian molar behavioral laws because they lack the universality and evidential support that is required of physical laws. He then suggests that Skinnerian psychology is basically a technology and that its "laws" are merely rules of thumb for changing behavior. Skinner might well have gone along with this suggestion but then he would have been mistaking technology for science—a confusion lying at the root of behaviorism itself, as conceived by Watson. For a discussion, see Laurence D. Smith, "Knowledge as Power: The Baconian Roots of Skinner's Social Meliorism," this volume.

Part 3
Skinner's Personal World

7

The Personal Culture of Yvonne Blue Skinner

RHONDA K. BJORK

ON 1 November 1936, Yvonne Blue, age twenty-five, married Burrhus Frederic Skinner, a recently appointed thirty-two-year-old instructor of psychology at the University of Minnesota. The ceremony took place at the bride's home, a yellow stucco house in the affluent Chicago suburb of Flossmoor. Grace and William Skinner, the bridegroom's parents, had just arrived by train from Scranton, Pennsylvania, and had met the bride's parents over lunch at the University Club. Mr. and Mrs. Skinner were delighted that their son had finally "done the right thing" and were sure Yvonne would "make a fine sensible wife." The bride's parents, Harriet and Robert Blue, were still reeling from the hasty wedding preparations, having learned of the couple's plan to wed less than twenty-four hours before. Mrs. Blue had called all the guests and made all the arrangements, which included reception cakes decorated in black and orange, the only ones available on such short notice the day after Halloween. As the minister pronounced them "man and wife" and intoned a prayer for their future happiness, Yvonne and Fred held hands making "signalled messages back and forth." Six hours later Yvonne's old friends, Lou and Ken Mulligan, put them on a train for Minneapolis where the couple would live in a hotel until finding an apartment.[1]

The Skinners' wedding dramatized Yvonne's partiality toward the unconventional: "It was a funny wedding. . . . I had to wear a dress of my sister's" and its odd reception cakes "made the party gay." And yet the ceremony confirmed a conventional sentiment. "While we were married I felt incredibly solemn."[2] This juxtaposition of the unconventional and conventional in Yvonne would become an ongoing tension in her personal culture.

Yvonne Blue was an attractive, articulate, sophisticated young woman;

179

she was a graduate of the University of Chicago and had traveled to Europe. As will be shown in this chapter, Yvonne rebelled against the values of her parents and established her own personal culture, an intellectually inclined and liberal style of life, but one essentially individual-oriented.[3] This personal culture evolved from Yvonne's upbringing in a well-to-do family in Chicago at a historical moment in the 1920s and 1930s when American youth, abandoning the ethical and social codes of past generations, discovered that "the alternative to civilization was the self."[4] The aim of this essay is to situate Yvonne Blue's life in the American culture of her time, and in doing so to reveal something both about the shifts that culture was undergoing and about the differences between her own and Fred Skinner's responses to those changes.

Yvonne's fascination with the sights and sounds of her day (movies, plays, urban architecture, radio, and jazz), her extensive reading, and her desire to cultivate image and personality put her firmly in step with others of her generation. The liberalizing influence of the University of Chicago in the early 1930s also contributed to Yvonne's personal culture, exposing her not only to a broad liberal arts education but to ideas and people questioning the status quo and conservatism of the older generation. Culture was no longer viewed as the composite of the best of human knowledge and attainments but rather as "a matter of living a cultured life, informed, influenced and inspired by meanings and values which make interest in knowledge, truth, [and] the enjoyment of beauty . . . vital in one's own life."[5] Whereas Fred Skinner would become a public advocate of an engineered return to the small-town ideals of character-formation, Yvonne belonged to a newer American tradition, a personal tradition of cultivating the self.[6]

FASHIONING A SELF

Born in Chicago on 9 May 1911, Yvonne was the oldest of three daughters born to Robert Blue and Harriet Read Blue, the daughter of Opie Read, famed Chautauqua lecturer and humorous novelist. By the time of his death, Read had written fifty-two books, one of which *The Jucklins* (1895), had sold over a million copies. Before she married, Harriet Blue had been an amateur photographer with an interest in interior decorating, an interest that she retained throughout her life and that was clearly evidenced in her attractive residences. Her husband's income provided her with a well-furnished home and domestic help, which freed her for socializing and involvement in charitable causes and community organizations. As Thorstein Veblen had observed, leisured women of the upper middle class were often themselves symbols of their husband's wealth and status by virtue of their increasing power to purchase and display.[7] Yvonne was close to her mother, but would have ambivalent feelings toward her.

Yvonne's father, Robert Blue, a native of Belle Plaine, Iowa, was a successful ophthalmologist with degrees from Cornell College (Mt. Vernon, Iowa) and Northwestern University Medical School. He was a well-known Chicago physician and had served as president of the Chicago Ophthalmological Society; he was chief of staff at Wesley Memorial Hospital and a member of the faculty at Northwestern University Medical School.[8] Although Dr. Blue said grace at the table, Yvonne's parents did not stress a religious upbringing for their daughters. They did, however, subscribe to the conventional middle-class ethos which emphasized material prosperity and proper standards of conduct. Urging their daughter to be a good girl and to obey all the rules, they instilled in her an awareness of social position, the importance of money, and personal accomplishment.[9] Acculturated in prosperity and material comfort, Yvonne was spared domestic duties and responsibilities, and was free to indulge in reading and personal attainments. Letters from Yvonne's parents give no indication that they imbued her with noblesse oblige, an ethic which would have obligated her to render some degree of social service and self-sacrifice to the larger society.

Parental insistence on correct behavior was relaxed at the home of Yvonne's maternal grandparents, the Reads. Here she found a loving and affirming grandmother who "was always my friend . . . [and] championed me," and a grandfather who told her wonderful stories and provided access to his extensive library. To Yvonne, her grandfather was "my idol." Inspired by his stories and success as an author and equipped with her own vivid imagination, Yvonne developed an early literary interest.[10]

Her formal education began at the age of four when she entered a private school run by two maiden ladies, the Misses Martyns. Although Yvonne suspected she was enrolled to keep her from under her mother's feet, she did learn to read and write. At six, she began public school in the First Grade, but not for long. "I stayed in First Grade a day and Second Grade a day and they put me in Third Grade where I belonged. . . . I was two years ahead of myself all the way through school." She was a voracious reader, reporting at age thirteen a private library of 100 books, including works of Charlotte Brontë, Washington Irving, Alexander Dumas, Jules Verne, Louisa May Alcott, and Rudyard Kipling. By 1925, she reported a personal library of 176 books. Such acquisitions not only testified to her intellectual curiosity, but bespoke the family affluence.[11]

At thirteen, Yvonne recorded her career ambitions:

I am going to start as a newspaper reporter and work up. Maybe I'll get a
position as book reviewer or movie reviewer. Then I'll be on the editorial staff
of a magazine, like the American, and maybe I'll give lectures on the side. I
might be a reporter, on the American, and interview interesting people. And
maybe someday, I'll write books!!![12]

Such ambition reflected not only her literary aspirations and her wide
reading, but also a firm sense of her cultural references and a desire to
meet "interesting people."

In the early decades of the twentieth century American cities were
increasingly perceived as centers of culture. Burgeoning urban centers
often self-consciously paraded American popular culture. Confident of
its position as the midwestern cultural center, a booming Chicago proudly
displayed its unique style, and Yvonne Blue delighted in the Windy City,
its art, and its architecture.

Chicago! There could never be another city like it. It is the modern Baghdad,
the Arabian Night City where anything can happen . . . brilliant theatre lobbies,
the Bohemian restaurants, the motley crowds reek of adventure. . . . But most
of all I love it because it is life and adventure!![13]

Describing herself as a "museum nut," she "knew the Art Institute of
Chicago like the back of my hand."[14] The modern architecture of Chicago
aesthetically thrilled her.

I visited that masterpiece of modern art, Tribune Tower. . . . I was about to
leave when I remembered the promenade and flying buttresses on the twenty-
fifth floor. . . . Beauty has come to mean so much to me. . . . Beauty[,] real
beauty[,] is like the Holy Grail for it is elusive, intangible—no one unworthy
can see it . . . and no one, no *one* can ever possess it.[15]

Her parents' strict code of morality, her grandparents' literary encouragement, and urban Chicago's splendor and achievements generated
Yvonne's personal culture. Her own imagination, spurred by reading and
participation in mass culture (radio, books, movies, and consumerism),
also contributed. Her style of life—encompassing good breeding, art appreciation, and intellectual knowledge—accentuated the cult of personality, the importance of image and posturing. The emergence of these
qualities can be clearly discerned as she entered her teenage years.

With her two best friends, Valerie Von Noé and Virginia Garcia,
Yvonne established a literary-adventure club called the Mystery Seekers'
Band. "The name includes everything of a mysterious nature, such as,
pirates, the mysteries of Lot and Hindu magic, mysteries of India and
Ancient Egypt." After swearing eternal allegiance, the members inun-

dated themselves with literature, plays, and various rituals of Oriental culture. "We pulled down the shades and closed the door. We lit two candles on the bureau. . . . We all dressed up in something red and sat like Budhas [*sic*] with crossed legs, hands in lap, and downcast eyes around an incense burner filled with rose incense." After seeing a Sanskrit play at the Ida Noyes Theatre at the University of Chicago, Yvonne and Valerie vowed to some day visit India together.[16]

Adolescence awakened Yvonne to the opposite sex. And for the Mystery Seekers' Band, fascination with boys took the living form of Lorence O'Hara, a dark, moody, silent boy the girls found eccentric. "He must have something wonderful in him to inspire interest so." To be interesting was to have personality, to be *somebody*. O'Hara would provide hours of endless speculation for the club members and would personify for Yvonne the ideal of a masculine type "that has always . . . attracted me—tall and lean, with dark ruffled hair . . . brilliant and slightly cynical."[17]

Adolescence also brought acute self-awareness. The Mystery Seekers' Band confided to one another their faults and attributes. Yvonne vowed to "revolutionize my character. I shall walk as if I owned the world, talk slightly condescendingly, be extremely self-possessed, spout scintillating sophistication . . . and develop subtlety." These traits were not so much characteristic of character-building as of personality and posing. Detesting those who were too proper, or too perfect, or refused to use slang (precisely the type her parents found admirable), Yvonne admired those who flaunted conventionality and were clever. At fifteen she enumerated the ten qualities she sought most to exhibit: "self possession and control; superiority; cynicism; will power; silence; differentness; subtlety; immense range of knowledge; supreme indifference; and great independence." Yvonne embraced these ideals at a personal time of insecurity—adolescence—when self-help and improvement guides of the 1920s stressed the dangers of feeling inferior and the necessity for self-confidence and personal success. It was also a historical period of self-centeredness amid insecurity. America was between the world wars, a time when the cultural shift from emphasis on character to emphasis on personality helped many Americans face a transformed social environment and a mass society in the new machine age.[18]

Yvonne managed to incorporate many of these cultural emphases into her life. The cultivation of self-possession and independence would enable her to marry an aspiring young scientist, without losing herself in his identity. Her broad knowledge, subtlety, and air of superiority made her attractive to a social circle of individuals sharing similar values. Her willpower and indifference allowed her to maintain a marital relationship both responsive to, and yet insouciant to, her husband's scientific and public orbit. And her silence and cynicism were buffers against personal disappointment as well as means for distancing herself from individuals she found uninteresting. What is strikingly lacking in this culture for self-improvement and self-defense is the larger social dimension. None of the ten traits emphasizes social responsibility to others or a desire to enrich human civilization. Yvonne's quest for cultural expression, unlike Fred Skinner's, would remain self-oriented.

COLLEGE LIFE AND THE BOHEMIAN COLONY

Adolescent insecurities increased when Yvonne's parents moved to Flossmoor, in the spring of 1927. The move was prompted by Dr. Blue's recurring bouts of tuberculosis which made living in the city difficult for him. It also reflected the conventional middle-class need for social mobility and desire to escape urban crime and corruption. Initially Yvonne fretted about her social isolation and the daily train ride to Chicago that was necessary in order for her to continue her education at University High School. She found Flossmoor "horrid. . . . There are no stores or flats . . . it's just *dead.*"[19] But a bedroom that was "perfection itself" and the later addition of a clay tennis court served as appeasements. And during her college years, she would find that having her family tucked away in this quiet suburb provided her with additional freedom to explore her life-style without constant vigilance from her parents.[20]

Shortly after moving to Flossmoor, Yvonne graduated from high school. Later that summer she learned, "I have recently been accepted to the University of Chicago, despite the fact that my application was more than four months too late." At sixteen she was exceptionally well-read and knowledgeable about art. She was easily bored and much interested in eccentric people. About to major in English and minor in art, she was beset with social and personal anxieties. Many of these trepidations were the usual ones of an entering college freshman and were perhaps heightened by her young age; others were self-doubts relating to her ability to realize a literary career.[21]

In the fall of 1927, Yvonne entered the University of Chicago. Founded in 1892, primarily by gifts from John D. Rockefeller, the university had a liberating atmosphere. Enveloping herself in this free academic environment, Yvonne reported: "In class one is treated as a human being—the instructors swear like hell and they're all atheists. I inhale and smoke in public."[22] Professors were not strict about attendance and there was a temptation to cut class. She adopted dress appropriate to the new circumstances, consisting of "severe black clothes, thick make-up, sleek hair" and a baby seal fur. And she posed as a "sophisticated bored blaise [*sic*]" type.[23]

Yvonne's first year in college had mixed results. Her sophistication made her new friends; but her parents were not pleased. They disapproved of her smoking and though her academic marks were mostly A's and B's, she failed two successive quarters of gym for cutting classes. Suspended from the university for one quarter and unable to find a college in the area on the quarter system, Yvonne spent her sophomore year at Beloit College in southern rural Wisconsin. There she would experience her own "Dark Year."[24]

Her pose, so well received at the University of Chicago, made little impression on the more practical students at Beloit. Yvonne remembered the year as hateful and dismal. Her roommate was a "'nice girl,' . . . the type that grows up into a good woman." Exiled and out of her cultural element, the year was brightened by weekend forays and vacation visits to Illinois; but she detested her classes and the rural environment. At the end of the year, with five B's to her credit and the prospect of reviving old friendships, Yvonne returned to Chicago and reentered the university there in 1929.[25]

Highlighting Yvonne's post-Beloit education were two courses she took from Thorton Wilder, the American playwright and novelist whose book, *The Bridge of San Luis Rey* (1927), had brought him international fame. His course "Classics in Translation" introduced Yvonne to Greek drama and stimulated her interest in Greece and eventually in the theater. Other professors recognized her "intelligence and appreciation . . . a nice combination," and encouraged her to develop her writing talent.[26]

Yvonne's university education had introduced her to a liberal intellectual tradition, one standing in stark contrast to the conservatism of her parents. Yet the liberalism she finally embraced as her own remained conventionally middle class and highly individualistic. Visiting with a friend who attended the Lewis Institute, Yvonne encountered poor whites, blacks, Jews, and Asians, recording that the place was peopled with "queer-types." "I enjoyed it but it was as if I were 'slumming.'—I can't imagine really going there." Later when she danced "with two negroes at a speakeasy" it was rather daring, in defiance of her parents' ethics but unrelated to egalitarian concerns.[27]

Straddling the fine line between her parents' idea of respectability and exploring her own independence created considerable tension; Yvonne used the pretense of a chic cultural style to cover up normal adolescent worries and insecurities. Her election as president of the Sunday Evening Club, a religious youth organization in Flossmoor was slightly ironic. Her interest lay not in its religious emphasis but rather in the club's opportunities for socializing with other affluent young people. Yvonne also discovered a way to express her interest in drama and play-acting when she and her Flossmoor friend Martha Vaughan organized the Sunday Evening Club performance of three plays. In addition to these activities, her parents' recent membership in the prestigious Olympia Fields Country Club provided her with opportunities for dances and bridge games.[28] Nonetheless, Flossmoor's staidness grated on Yvonne. She grew convinced that a suburban life-style was not for her. Furthermore, her parents' disapproval of her personal habits served to alienate her even more from their conventional opinions.

Yvonne spent July and August of 1930 touring England and Europe—a gift from her father, who perhaps hoped a change of environment would bring Yvonne back to a conventional life-style. But Yvonne found Europe "different from anything I have ever known before." There she encountered another culture which reified her estrangement. Like other affluent young Americans who came to Europe in the 1920s—some of whom had become members of the "lost generation"—Yvonne felt this was the culture to which she truly belonged.[29] Returning to America, full of the sights and sounds of another cultural alternative, Yvonne designed a new personal image: "Now I have a permanent and I wear my hair off my forehead and behind my ears and I don't use much make-up and my clothes are smart but not sophisticated in the old sense and I act natural instead of posing. . . . I get on much better with people and have more friends and don't feel secretly inferior."[30] But a new image did not solve the problem of an occupation.

Troubled about her future she worried "because I can't teach or do anything else and I simply can't believe that anything I can ever do will conceivably be worth money to someone."[31] Furthermore, her European trip did nothing to ameliorate her attitude to her parents' values and may, in fact, have encouraged her to sample the local Bohemian life. Through college friends she learned about Saturday night parties at the Colony. The Colony was Chicago's equivalent of New York's Greenwich Village, an area of studios and flats occupied by artists and writers of every ilk. Originally constructed as stores and restaurants for the World Columbian Exposition in 1893, these buildings now provided cheap housing for artists and freethinkers. Saturday night parties were occasionally so riotous that the police were called to quell disturbances. Here was a "new morality" and ample opportunity to participate in "the greatest American sport." Despite Prohibition, alcohol was served amid the exciting sounds of jazz. It was at the Colony that Yvonne first met her lifelong friend, Louise Mulligan, and her husband Kenneth—bohemians in their own right.[32] Yvonne recalled:

I was interested in seeing real Bohemian life . . . it was the exact opposite from the thoroughly nice and refined country club dance. . . . The hell of it is

I enjoyed both. If I only knew which I enjoyed most, I'd know which sort of person I really am, but I'm such an odd mixture that I can't tell.[33]

One cultural historian has used the metaphor "the Age of Alfred Adler" to describe the period 1929–38—an era that accentuated personal shame and fear. The individual's problem was not one of strengthening the ego but rather "to find some way for individual adjustment, for overcoming shame and fear, Adler's 'inferiority complex,' by adopting a life-style that enabled one to 'fit in,' to belong, to identify."[34] The "odd mixture" Yvonne felt herself to be was typical. She worried about her activities at the Colony and yet delighted in meeting "people who have a gay reckless-ness, a rebel courage and a sweet and utterly mad love of living." She dreaded "dead, stifling, conventional Flossmoor," but there she could engage in swimming, tennis, golf, and bridge parties.[35] "Fitting in" be-came problematic, and its pursuit produced considerable unease in Yvonne and in other young Americans caught between conflicting styles of life.

Faced with two seemingly contradictory value systems, Yvonne re-sorted to a regimen of personal enhancement. "I've been trying always to look my best lately. I take a cold shower every morning and do exer-cises and keep absolutely immaculate and it really has an enormous psy-chological effect on one's whole attitude." Reading *Technique of the Love Affair* and scoffing at its obvious, heavy-handed techniques for snaring a husband by feminine trickery and posture, Yvonne noted four qualities to make men take notice: "Poise, meaning doing everything beautifully, being lively without being obstreperous; Lightheartedness, requiring cheerfulness and no hint of dejection; Neatness of Apparel, stressing good grooming without distinctive originality; and Flattery, requiring close attention to a man's conversation without appearing overly en-grossed." The final bit of wisdom gleaned from this book was, "Be as dependent materially as you are independent spiritually."[36]

Before graduating from the University of Chicago in March 1932, Yvonne reported, "I've been neglecting my school work and instead have spent hours in the psychology library soaking myself in case histories of the abnormal and neurotic type."[37] It may have been at this time that she read Morton Prince's *Dissociation of Personality* as well as some Freud and Adler. Yvonne's fascination with clinical psychology was once again indicative of the larger culture's increasing interest in probing unique personalities rather than studying the moral and social achievements of a culture of character.[38] Her interest in psychopathology may also have been fueled by the growing self-awareness of her own neurosis as she tried to bridge two distinct life-styles before settling on elements of both as her own.

A year after graduating from college Yvonne was adrift. She acknowledged that "My education has been a complete washout. It is a pleasant
cultural background—nothing more." Most of her friends were married or
had satisfying jobs or both. She worried that she would not find something
rewarding to do with her life: "I used to think I would fall into something,
somehow." But now she suffered from being "vague, lazy, impractical,
too easily discouraged—too timid and inert."[39] Realizing the inadequacy
of her education, she had enrolled at a suburban business school where
she took typing and shorthand. Later she would enroll in night courses
at Northwestern University where she took composition, newspaper reporting and writing, and introductory psychology.[40]

The years 1932–36 were characterized by her inability to find stimulating employment suited to her personal culture. For a time she volunteered
at the Institute for Juvenile Research. She found "the whole psychiatric
atmosphere" fascinating, but when pressed to take social work courses
and to "dig for the facts" in clinical cases, she discovered "I had no
feeling for the work." For a month she worked as a stenographer for a
graphologist. One temporary job at the Oriental Institute of the University
of Chicago, where she arranged field trips, was comparatively satisfying.
But most of the jobs she had were secretarial. She complained: "I want
to travel, to live abroad, to write, to meet interesting people. I don't want
to be stuck in an office."[41]

COURTSHIP AND MARRIAGE

In 1935 Yvonne's friend, Martha Vaughan Smith, who had married an
instructor at Harvard's Business School, told her about a friend of her
husband's, a recent Ph.D. in psychology who was now a Harvard Junior
Fellow. Yvonne learned about "his clavichord, his sound-proof box, his
paintings and love affairs." Later she read his article "Has Gertrude Stein
a Secret?"[42]

She accepted her friend's invitation to visit Cambridge and in late July
1936, met Fred Skinner who joined the group for dinner. She found that
the young psychologist met her masculine ideal and knew he was "the
best person I've ever met, and I knew it the first five minutes I spent with
him." Skinner was pleased that Yvonne was able to "get my allusions" as
well as impressed that she was the granddaughter of Opie Read and had
taken courses from Thorton Wilder.[43] They seemed to share similar values, backgrounds, and experiences.

Skinner had just accepted a position at the University of Minnesota
and promised to visit Yvonne in Flossmoor as he drove to Minneapolis.
He was uneasy about his first teaching position in an unfamiliar place;

and during his visit in Flossmoor, he and Yvonne decided to get married during the Christmas holidays.[44]

Minneapolis was congenial and Fred soon found friends among the faculty as well as freedom to pursue his research. In October 1936, Yvonne visited him. It was an awkward experience. Minneapolis seemed provincial and the faculty and their wives were not as interesting as her friends in Chicago. She further suspected that Fred was less keen on getting married and challenged her ability to be a faculty wife. Two weeks after returning from Minneapolis, she broke their engagement. After Fred's insistent pleas for an explanation she finally explained her reasons in a letter. Among other things, she recalled writing, "If you are an example of an intellectual, I'm going to marry into the Jukes family."[45]

After receiving Yvonne's letter, Fred asked to meet her in a Chicago hotel. She agreed.

> He said, "Let's don't argue. Let's just get married today." I don't remember much more. I said no a lot and then yes, and he read parts of the . . . letter and we laughed. We decided to wait till the next day and tell our families. We bought a license and a ring. . . . He called his family long distance and they got on a train . . . to be in Chicago by the next day. . . . I remembered the announcement in the paper that we would be married at Christmas time and how I'd told everyone it was off, and how tomorrow would only be November 1, and how odd it would look to my family.[46]

Marriage seemed to be the fulfillment of a prophecy. While still in college a friend had predicted for Yvonne "that some very nice man will one day want to marry me and make me mistress of his house," and another friend imagined her "in a beautifully appointed home chatting and laughing with a group of young men."[47] For the first year their marriage seemed idyllic. Fred found his new wife "a perfect foil for an old scientific crank who likes his own way altogether too well." And Yvonne wrote: "I would rather be married to Fred than anything in the world. I'm so happy with him that I'm afraid, and I guard every moment so that I can enjoy happiness in the present instead of in retrospect only, as one usually does." Fred adjusted to Yvonne's lack of domesticity, teaching her to cook and hiring cleaning ladies even though they lived in a one-room apartment. Together they played chess and saw movies. They discussed and agreed on politics and religion. And throughout their marriage they read the same books which they regularly discussed.[48]

But their marital adjustment soon reflected a clash of two different cultural ideals. One was an older ideal—Puritan-republican, producer-entrepreneur, Christian and agrarian in nature, stressing a world of scarcity, hard work, self-denial, sacrifice, and character. It stood in contrast to a newer ideal—one of abundance, leisure, and consumption, self-indulgent in nature, stressing personality, self-realization, and gratification of personal needs and interests.[49]

The question of whether to have children was an early indication of their marital adjustment. Although Yvonne had agreed to have "two children fairly pronto," she had never felt comfortable with infants nor had she been particularly fond of her younger sisters as children. When she did have children, she acknowledged becoming comfortable with them only "when they started getting personalities" as they underwent verbal development.[50] In her role as mother she worried over their sicknesses, falls, and scrapes and delighted in their growth and achievements. But Yvonne preferred keeping long evening hours and was a late riser. As a consequence, most of the baby-tending and child-rearing responsibility rested on Fred. Julie, their older daughter, surmised that this role reversal was less a matter of her mother's disinclination to care for children than a result of her father's "take charge" attitude toward immediate care of needs. Thus, she recalled that it was her father who "put us to bed always, read stories at night, [and] got us off to school in the morning."[51]

With the birth of their second daughter, Deborah, in 1944, Yvonne agreed to raise the baby in her husband's invention, a crib-size, temperature-controlled living space with sound-absorbing walls and a large picture window—a device that the Skinners called a "baby-tender" and that was later sold as the Aircrib.[52]

Another marital adjustment was Yvonne's general unhappiness in Minnesota. She did not learn to like being a faculty wife, nor did she find Fred's colleagues interesting. She found it difficult to fit in. Interesting friends were few and she was house-bound as a mother. Fred was acutely aware of her unhappiness. Partially inspired by Yvonne's predicament, he explored in *Walden Two* a different design for living. To his dismay, however, he found that "In general women detest Walden Two. The curious thing is that I wrote it in an effort to solve some of their problems, to give them a genuine equality and to free them from the traditional slavery implied by the role of women in Western culture. Little thanks did I get!" Yvonne agreed. "We had tremendous arguments about Walden Two. I wouldn't like it; I just like change and privacy." When asked why he did not join the experimental community of Twin Oaks, based on *Walden Two,* Fred replied: "I'd had to get a divorce. . . . My wife doesn't believe in community." He hypothesized that the negative female reaction to *Walden Two* was based on the "horrible thought" that "if you free women of the responsibility of cooking, cleaning and bearing and taking care of children, they can see no reason why they should be loved."[53] Later, however, Yvonne did experience a communal living arrangement of sorts, but with cultural dimensions more satisfying to her.

The one bright star for Yvonne on the otherwise bleak Minnesota horizon was her association with Mrs. Gretchen Pillsbury, a wealthy social leader in Minneapolis. Mrs. Pillsbury, originally from Boston and then in her seventies, was an avid theater-goer who regularly attended plays in New York City; but failing eyesight prohibited her from reading. Yvonne agreed to read plays and books on art to her. These weekly outings provided her with an aesthetically pleasing social setting, complete with gourmet luncheons, and fulfilled her own interests in art and theater.[54]

Despite her dissatisfaction, Yvonne was reluctant to leave Minneapolis when Fred became chair of the Psychology Department at Indiana University in 1945. Bloomington, a village compared to Minneapolis, was a further "comedown" from the sophistication and interesting friends of Chicago.[55] The change in location did, however, offer her the opportunity to change her name from Yvonne (which she had always disliked) to Eve.

The two and a half years at Bloomington were not satisfying ones for Eve. Further differences in styles of life between her and Fred emerged. She enjoyed dancing, having put on exhibitions of the tango and other popular dances at the Colony; Fred "was a serious man" and "never a good dancer." He enjoyed symphonies and classical music, an interest which left Eve bored, though she had enjoyed operas in Chicago before her marriage.[56] And once again, their socializing centered exclusively around faculty members. But one faculty associate, William Verplanck, a colleague of Fred's in the Psychology Department, provided Eve with some social diversion. He would take Eve dancing and often visited the Skinner residence, staying up all night talking and gossiping with Eve while Fred went to bed early.[57]

Nonetheless, social occasions consisted mostly of endless cocktail parties with faculty and luncheons for faculty wives. Eve remembered that for women there were "no careers in Indiana. . . . Once they married they were stuck with the dishpan." She did not look to the university to further her interest in art and theater nor to volunteer in community organizations. She found little in Bloomington to praise. The place seemed culturally impoverished, and even the farms surrounding the community lacked the prosperity and abundance of the Iowa farms she had visited in her childhood.[58] Consequently, when Harvard offered Fred a full professorship in 1947, Eve was elated.

RETURN TO CULTURE

For Eve, moving to the Boston area meant returning to a cultural center, and to all the diversity it had to offer. Moreover, she had close friends there from her Chicago days. One of these was Lou Mulligan, who with her husband and three daughters lived in Wakefield, Massachusetts. At

Lou's suggestion the Skinners moved into their home for about six weeks. Here Eve and Lou divided domestic chores. Although hardly a *Walden Two*, the living arrangement suited Eve well. She "lived [Lou's] social life," the children got along splendidly, the four adults were compatible and enjoyed frequent games of bridge, and there was "never a cross word." This living design could have gone on indefinitely, but the inconvenience of getting Fred to Harvard and Julie to school necessitated finding living quarters in Cambridge.[59]

Once in Cambridge, the Skinners joined a play-reading group begun by Babs Spiegel and Katherine Wilder (sister-in-law of Thornton). The Mulligans also joined. Monthly performances were held, hosted by two couples who selected a play and edited and cast it. Sunday evening performances were preceded by cocktails with dinner served after the reading. The plays ranged from Greek dramas and Shakespeare to burlesque and modern drama. Both Eve and Fred enjoyed the creativity and sociability provided by these activities. Fred later observed that Eve "used the skills acquired at the play-readings" for her eventual role as lecturer at the Boston Museum of Fine Arts, and a friend recalled "the wit and gaiety" Eve brought to the readings.[60]

On their fourteenth anniversary, 1 November 1950, the Skinners moved into their newly built home in the Larchmont section of Cambridge, a mile and a half from Harvard. By now the divergence in their interests had evolved into distinct styles of living. Eve enjoyed social gatherings, long lunches with her friends at fine restaurants, and attending cultural exhibitions. Fred, finding his work rewarding and absorbing, required less frequent social entertainment. Eve never shared an interest in her husband's science. "He doesn't tell me much about his work because one, I'm not a psychologist and wouldn't understand, and two, I'm not terribly interested." Fred complained that Eve "never got the slightest satisfaction out of anything I did, so that I just stopped telling her of the honors I received." Throughout the 1950s and 1960s, but especially after the publication of *Beyond Freedom and Dignity* (1971), Fred received increased professional recognition. Yet Eve remained surprised that "when we go somewhere people know who Fred is." She continued to keep late hours and it was not unusual for her to spend the day reading two or three novels.[61] During the 1950s and 1960s, she traveled abroad extensively, sometimes with Fred and her daughters, but sometimes alone. Foreign travel enhanced her appreciation of history and culture and provided the joys of seeing new places.[62]

In the mid-1970s Eve began weekly readings for the Braille Press. She read "mainly books which students requested to have put on tape for their courses." Some of these books were psychology texts. "I'd always look up Fred in the index and see what they said about him and if it wasn't nice I would not read it!"[63] The Braille readings were, however, abandoned for a new opportunity which finally launched her on a satisfying avocation.

In 1972, through her friend Nancy Homans, Eve learned of volunteer work with the Education Department at the Boston Museum of Fine Arts. The work required undergoing a rigorous interview and called for "a commitment to give at least two talks a week, . . . to take courses [and] to pass them with very good grades." For the next several years Eve took art history courses, specializing in the classical period, and used her writing skills on course requirements, finally qualifying as a gallery instructor.[64] Work at the museum provided her with the perfect cultural milieu. Here she could incorporate her liberal education, her interests, her travel experiences, and her talents in a satisfying and rewarding activity outside her husband's domain. Here Fred, on one occasion, was introduced as the husband of Eve Skinner.[65] By 1978 Eve was deeply involved in her new role, as Fred attested. "Eve is completely caught up in her work at the Museum and is taking more and more time."[66] The museum association provided her with an opportunity for self-realization, for expressing her values and personality. It was an endeavor she found individually rewarding; and a friend recalled that once Eve found an outlet for her interests, she was visibly happier.[67]

A CONTRAST OF CULTURES

Given the Skinners' differing cultural ideals, the emergence of some tension between them was to be expected. Eve admitted "we went through some bad patches," and Fred reported "we've thought at times of breaking up, but I don't think Eve ever wanted to."[68] As Carolyn G. Heilbrun has noted, "the happiest marriages are not always the best behaved," and midlife marriages often undergo redefinition and reinvention.[69] The Skinners' marriage, too, underwent redefinition. In later years, they maintained separate living areas—Fred working and sleeping in his basement study, Eve remaining upstairs. This was necessitated by Fred's messiness: his study provided a place for his books, papers, files, equipment, and music. Separate sleeping arrangements resulted from Fred's practice of retiring early while Eve stayed up reading or watching television. Fred was something of a workaholic, and found reinforcement from his work; Eve found other interests reinforcing. Their joy in literature provided a bond, and elements of equality, friendship, and loyalty persisted in their relationship. They were solicitous of one another. When Fred suffered symptoms of angina, Eve insisted on a therapeutic regimen, and Fred maintained that he always tried to provide Eve with a pleasant environment.[70] Each made accommodations to the other. Still, their marriage illustrated the clash of two cultures. Fred's was a "Baconian search for cultural universals" grounded in particular biological, psychological or historical processes.[71] Eve's culture was an "anthropological relativism that saw dignity" in popular culture as well as in high culture.[72]

Both Fred and Eve needed stimulation and change, requiring interesting people and invigorating escapes. But Eve did not share Fred's social vision, his sense of social responsibility, his mission to design a culture. She was, in fact, more at home with the culture that had shaped her. That culture both repelled and attracted her and this ambivalence did more to define her life-style than anything else.

NOTES

1. Grace Burrhus Skinner to B. F. Skinner, n.d., Skinner personal papers at residence. "Half-Hour Before Class Notes," [1 November 1937], manuscript in the Yvonne Blue Skinner Collection (hereafter referred to as YBSC), Arthur and Elizabeth Schlesinger Library on the History of Women in America, Radcliffe College, Cambridge, Mass. B. F. Skinner, *The Shaping of a Behaviorist* (New York: New York University Press, 1984), p. 194.

2. "Half-Hour Before Class Notes," [1 November 1937], YBSC.

3. Gerda Lerner has argued that to find "the actual *experience* of women in the past," the historian is led "to the use of women's letters, diaries, autobiographies, and oral history sources" (Lerner, "Placing Women in History: Definitions and Challenges," in *The Majority Finds Its Past: Placing Women in History,* ed. Lerner [New York: Oxford University Press, 1979], pp. 145–59, on p. 153). This reconstruction of Yvonne Blue Skinner's life has utilized such sources. Yet as Daniel Aaron has observed, "writing about one's contemporaries can be as painful as it is challenging. It is bad enough to probe into a person's political or private life. . . . But the [historian] may also be troubled by the very abundance of alleged 'facts' that don't reveal as much as they obscure" (Aaron, "The Treachery of Recollection: The Inner and the Outer History," in *Essays in History and Literature,* ed. Robert H. Bremmer [Columbus: Ohio State University Press, 1966], pp. 3–27, on p. 14).

4. Loren Baritz, "The Culture of the Twenties," in *The Development of an American Culture,* ed. Stanley Coben and Lorman Ratner (Englewood Cliffs, N.J.: Prentice-Hall, 1970), pp. 150–78, on p. 172.

5. F. R. Cowell, *Culture in Private and Public Life* (New York: Praeger, 1959), p. 29.

6. On the personal tradition of self-cultivation, see Warren I. Susman, "The Thirties," in *The Development of an American Culture,* ed. Stanley Coben and Lorman Ratner (Englewood Cliffs, N.J.: Prentice-Hall, 1970), pp. 179–218, on pp. 214–15. Despite the seeming novelty of Fred Skinner's application of science to the design of society, a number of observers have noted that he actually stood in opposition to the cultural shift away from character toward personality. As Krishan Kumar has stated: "If Skinner has any overall view of the good life, it seems to derive primarily from his small town, middle-class Protestant background. . . . What we get [from *Walden Two*] is a view of behavior, and its moral

significance, that brings Skinner strangely close to traditional ethical and Christian concepts of the development of *character*" (Kumar, *Utopia and Anti-Utopia in Modern Times* [Oxford, England: Basil Blackwell, 1987], pp. 350, 357). On Skinner's affinity for the traditionalists in American history rather than the liberators, see Daniel W. Bjork, *B. F. Skinner: A Life* (New York: Basic, 1993); and Bjork, "B. F. Skinner and the American Tradition: The Scientist as Social Inventor," this volume.

7. Obituary notice of Opie Read in Skinner personal scrapbooks at residence. Memorial Service for Harriet Read Blue, 9 June 1972, YBSC. Gerda Lerner, "Just a Housewife," in *The Majority Finds Its Past: Placing Women in History,* ed. Lerner (New York: Oxford University Press, 1979), pp. 129–44.

8. *Chicago Heights Star,* 10 August 1937. Skinner personal papers at residence.

9. Letters from Robert Blue to Yvonne Blue, n.d., YBSC.

10. On her grandmother, Diary of Yvonne Blue 1926–37, 21 July [1928], YBSC; on her grandfather, Yvonne Blue to Margaret [Artman], n.d., YBSC. Yvonne recalls her grandfather reading Shakespeare to her (Yvonne Blue Skinner, "The Prose of Yvonne Blue," YBSC).

11. Interview with Yvonne Blue Skinner, transcribed by Rhonda K. Bjork, 6 July 1989. Diary of Yvonne Blue, January-June 1925, 7 February [1925], YBSC. Yvonne reports reading George Eliot, H. L. Mencken, Oscar Wilde, and Thomas Babington Macauley and was familiar with the Stoic authors and Renaissance literature.

12. Diary of Yvonne Blue, January-June 1925, 1 March [1925], YBSC.

13. For a discussion of the growing perception of cities as cultural centers, see Reuel Denney, "The Discovery of the Popular Culture," in *American Perspectives: The National Self-Image in the Twentieth Century,* ed. Robert E. Spiller and Eric Larrabee (Cambridge: Harvard University Press, 1961), pp. 154–77. Diary of Yvonne Blue 1926–37, 7 November [1926], YBSC. Yvonne further acknowledged: "I could never be happy away from Chicago—it is in my blood," YBSC.

14. Interview with Yvonne Blue Skinner, transcribed by William R. Woodward, 19 December 1988.

15. Yvonne Blue to Margaret [Artman], n.d. [22 June 1927], YBSC.

16. Diary of Yvonne Blue for 1924, 7 October [1924], 6 December [1924], YBSC. Diary of Yvonne Blue, January-June 1925, 16 January [1925], YBSC.

17. Diary of Yvonne Blue 1926–37, 15 December [1926] and 18 December [1931], YBSC.

18. Ibid., 10 October [1926], YBSC. Warren I. Susman, *Culture as History: The Transformation of American Society in the Twentieth Century* (New York: Pantheon, 1984), p. 278.

19. Diary of Yvonne Blue, July-December 1925, 3 September [1925], YBSC. Interview with Yvonne Blue Skinner, 6 July 1989.

20. Diary of Yvonne Blue 1926–37, 12 August [1927] and 21 July [1928], YBSC.

21. Ibid., 20 June [1927], and 4 November [1926], YBSC.

22. Ibid., 5 November [1927]. "Diary," paper written for Advanced Composition, 20 November 1933, YBSC.

23. Diary of Yvonne Blue 1926–37, 19 December [1927] and 15 March [1928], YBSC.

24. Diary of Yvonne Blue 1926–37, 21 July [1928], YBSC. Interview with Yvonne Blue Skinner, 6 July 1989.

25. Ibid., 12 September [1929], YBSC.

26. Interview with Yvonne Blue Skinner and Julie S. Vargas, transcribed by Rhonda K. Bjork, 5 March 1990. Diary of Yvonne Blue 1926–37, 23 February [1931] and 20 April [1931], YBSC.

27. Diary of Yvonne Blue 1926–37, 27 November [1930] and 21 March [1932], YBSC.

28. Ibid, 31 December [1930], 28 March [1931], and 16 November [1931], YBSC.

29. Ibid., 24 February [1931] and 30 August [1930]. Also "MY TRIP ABROAD," diary of 1930 European trip, YBSC. On the infatuation young Americans had with post-World War I Europe, see Malcolm Cowley, *Exile's Return: A Literary Odyssey of the 1920s* (New York: Viking, 1951).

30. Diary of Yvonne Blue 1926–37, 26 October [1930], YBSC.

31. Ibid., 6 November [1931] and 4 April [1933], YBSC.

32. Ibid., 6 December [1931] and 4 April [1933], YSBC. Interview with Yvonne Blue Skinner, 6 July 1989.

33. Ibid., 6 December [1931], YBSC.

34. Susman, *Culture as History,* pp. 200, 284.

35. Diary of Yvonne Blue 1926–37, 2 June [1932] and 21 March [1932], YBSC.

36. Ibid., 1 February [1931] and 26 February [1931], YBSC.

37. Ibid., 19 January [1932], YBSC.

38. Interview with Yvonne Blue Skinner and Julie S. Vargas, 5 March 1990. Susman, *Culture as History,* p. 276.

39. Diary of Yvonne Blue 1926–37, 29 April [1931] and 17 February [1933], YBSC.

40. Ibid., 21 March [1932] and 19 November [1933], YBSC.

41. Ibid., 16 February [1933], 17 December [1933], and 29 April [1931], YBSC. Interview with Yvonne Blue Skinner, 6 July 1989.

42. Diary of Yvonne Blue 1926–37, 24 March 1937, YBSC.

43. Ibid., YBSC. Interview with B. F. Skinner, transcribed by Rhonda K. Bjork, 10 July 1989.

44. Interview with B. F. Skinner, 10 July 1989.

45. "Half-Hour Before Class Notes," [1 November 1937], YBSC. Arthur H. Estabrook's *The Jukes in 1915* (Washington, D.C.: Carnegie Institution, 1916) chronicled genetic feeblemindedness, which cost the state considerable sums of money for incarceration and rehabilitation. See Daniel Boorstin, *The Americans, The Democratic Experience* (New York: Random, 1973), pp. 222–23. Interview with Yvonne Blue Skinner, 6 July 1989. Eve used the term "the Jukes family" to mean "illiterates."

46. "Half-Hour Before Class Notes," [1 November 1937], YBSC.

47. Diary of Yvonne Blue 1926–37, 24 February [1931], YBSC.

48. Skinner, *Shaping of a Behaviorist,* p. 199. Diary of Yvonne Blue 1926–37, 24 March 1937, YBSC. Interview with Yvonne Blue Skinner, 6 July 1989; Yvonne Blue Skinner to Rhonda Bjork, 12 June 1990, author's possession.

49. Susman, *Culture as History,* pp. xxii, xxiv, 112.

50. Interview with Yvonne Blue Skinner, 6 July 1989, and interview with Yvonne Blue Skinner and Julie S. Vargas, 5 March 1990.

51. Yvonne Blue Skinner to Rhonda Bjork, 12 June 1990, author's possession. Interview with B. F. Skinner and Julie S. Vargas, transcribed by Daniel W. Bjork, 12 December 1989.

52. Skinner, *Shaping of a Behaviorist,* pp. 275–76.

53. B. F. Skinner to Wade Van Dore, 21 April 1969; "Skinner's Utopia," *Time,* 20 September 1971, pp. 47–53 (Eve's comments on *Walden Two,* p. 53); *Miami Herald,* 27 January 1979. B. F. Skinner Papers (hereafter referred to as BFSP), Harvard University Archives, Cambridge, Mass.

54. Interview with Yvonne Blue Skinner, 6 July 1989.

55. Ibid.

56. Ibid. "Evening in Athens," unpublished manuscript by Yvonne Blue Skinner.

57. Interview with Yvonne Blue Skinner, 6 July 1989.

58. Interview with Yvonne Blue Skinner and Julie S. Vargas, 5 March 1990.

59. Interview with Yvonne Blue Skinner, 6 July 1989, and interview with Yvonne Blue Skinner and Julie S. Vargas, 5 March 1990.

60. Ibid. Interview with B. F. Skinner and Julie S. Vargas, 12 December 1989. For the origin of the Cambridge Playreaders, see B. F. Skinner, *A Matter of Consequences* (New York: New York University Press, 1984), p. 122; Elena Levin to Rhonda K. Bjork, 12 June 1990, author's possession.

61. *Cosmopolitan,* 1971 August, p. 80, BFSP. Interview with B. F. Skinner and Julie S. Vargas, 12 December 1989. Interview with Yvonne Blue Skinner, 6 July 1989.

62. Interview with Yvonne Blue Skinner, 6 July 1989. Although not a complete compilation of her foreign travels, the following list does give an idea of the many trips she made abroad during the 1950s and 1960s:

Norway, Sweden—1951
Europe, Egypt—1954
Mexico—1956
Greece, Sicily—1959
Russia—1961
Egypt—1964
Portugal—1964
India, Japan—1966
England, Ireland—1967
Greek Islands—1969

Eve never considered publishing her travel experiences.

63. B. F. Skinner to H. C. Seabrook, 21 January 1976, BFSP. Eve continued taping for the Braille Press until 1976. Praised for her clear, distinctive reading, she made several tapes for national distribution. Interview with Yvonne Blue Skinner, 6 July 1989.

64. Interview with Yvonne Blue Skinner, 19 December 1988. Skinner, *Matter of Consequences,* p. 373.

65. Interview with B. F. Skinner and Julie S. Vargas, 12 December 1989.

66. B. F. Skinner to Mathilda Elliott, 17 February 1978, BFSP.

67. Elena Levin to Rhonda K. Bjork, 12 June 1990, author's possession. Lerner in *The Majority Finds Its Past,* pp. 160–67, discusses how women find autonomy by defining themselves and their values in terms of institutional arrangements that serve their needs (p. 161). On the societal value of volunteer museum work, see Karl E. Meyer, *The Art Museum: Power, Money, Ethics* (New York: Morrow, 1979), pp. 227–31; and Anne Firor Scott, "Part III. Voluntary Associations," in *Making the Invisible Woman Visible* (Champaign: University of Illinois Press, 1984), pp. 259–94. Scott draws on Robert Merton's essay "Insiders and Outsiders" (*American Journal of Sociology* 78 [1972]: 9–47) to illuminate the insights a volunteer brings to a profession. On the institution of voluntarism as a reflection of

sexism, see Doris B. Gold, "Women and Voluntarism," in *Woman in Sexist Society: Studies in Power and Powerlessness,* ed. Vivian Gornick and Barbara K. Moran (New York: New American Library, 1971), pp. 384–400.

68. Interview with Yvonne Blue Skinner, 6 July 1989. Interview with B. F. Skinner and Julie S. Vargas, December 12, 1989.

69. Carolyn G. Heilbrun, *Writing a Woman's Life* (New York: Norton, 1988), pp. 93–95.

70. Skinner, *Matter of Consequences,* pp. 330–31. Interview with B. F. Skinner and Julie S. Vargas, 12 December 1989.

71. Clifford Geertz, "The Impact of the Concept of Culture on the Concept of Man," in *New Views of the Nature of Man,* ed. John R. Platt (Chicago: University of Chicago Press, 1965), pp. 93–118, on pp. 102–3.

72. Denney, "Discovery of the Popular Culture," in *American Perspectives,* p. 175.

8

Freedom and the Control of Children: The Skinners' Approach to Parenting

Elizabeth A. Jordan

By 1944, B. F. Skinner was an unqualified intellectual success. His list of publications included over thirty articles as well as his first book, *The Behavior of Organisms*. Skinner's scientific work had been recognized by his peers, and he had been awarded the Howard Crosby Warren Medal by the Society of Experimental Psychologists in 1942 and a Guggenheim Fellowship in 1943.[1] Yet this year Skinner was faced with a fresh and unparalleled intellectual challenge: how could he simplify the care of a baby?[2] After some difficulty conceiving a second child, Skinner's wife Eve was now expecting their second child. Upon hearing Eve's complaints about the difficulties involved in caring for an infant, Skinner decided to try to make the care of their second baby easier for her. His solution was an enclosed "crib-sized living space" that he dubbed the "baby-tender."[3]

The baby-tender (also known as the Aircrib) was designed for the comfort of the infant as well as for the convenience of the mother. It was enclosed in order to allow the temperature and humidity inside the crib to be regulated. Controlling the crib temperature eliminated the need for clothing and bed covers that might bind the infant. The walls of the baby-tender were insulated, thus protecting the baby from loud noises. In addition, a shade could be drawn over the Plexiglas front of the baby-tender so that the infant would not be disturbed by lights while sleeping. To help the mother, the baby-tender was higher than a conventional crib, which eliminated the need for the mother to bend over to care for the infant. It was also equipped with a length of sheeting that was stretched across the canvas mattress and fitted over a roller. This sheeting could be easily moved if it became wet or soiled.[4]

Skinner's invention was evidently effective. His daughter Deborah spent time in the baby-tender from the first day she came home from the hospital and she "enjoyed its advantages."[5] Eve found that it did simplify her tasks, especially when she needed to change Deborah's diaper.[6] Because he was so pleased with the baby-tender, Skinner sent an article describing the apparatus to the *Ladies' Home Journal*. The *Journal* editors were hesitant to publish the article, having reservations and questions about this new mode of child care. But after Skinner answered their questions and sent them photographs of Deborah in and out of the baby-tender, they eventually published the article in October of 1945 under the title "Baby in a Box."[7]

Skinner's article caught the attention of many readers as well as the media. The Skinners and the baby-tender were featured in numerous newspapers, on the radio, and on a Pathé News reel.[8] This press coverage of the baby-tender evoked a mixture of responses. One individual wrote to Skinner to accuse him of being a "crack-pot" scientist who could not care properly for his children.[9] Many others, including Edward L. Thorndike and the British Committee on Domestic Engineering, responded more positively and wrote to request instructions for building their own baby-tenders.[10] Skinner was also approached by several companies who were interested in manufacturing a commercial model of the baby-tender, but these attempts to mass-produce the baby-tender never succeeded, primarily due to the relatively high projected cost of a commercially produced model.[11]

With the exception of the coverage of the baby-tender by the popular press and news media, very little is known about Skinner's approach to child-rearing. Most people who learned about Skinner in his role as a parent did so through exposure to these brief news features on the baby-tender. Studies of the psychology of rumor indicate that the proliferation of rumor relies on a lack of information as well as anxiety regarding the details that are available.[12] The news reports of the baby-tender gave only a small piece of information about Skinner's parenting. Yet this bit of information provided a vague frame onto which individuals could project their concerns about behaviorism and other issues. Given these conditions the news of Skinner's baby-tender was perfect grist for the rumor mill. In fact, a number of rumors about Skinner's child-rearing were circulated as a result of misinterpretations of the news stories. The use of the word "box" in the title of the *Ladies' Home Journal* article led to the fallacious belief that Skinner raised his children in a Skinner Box as if they were pigeons. In the absence of information about the actual effects of the baby-tender on the child, rumors evolved to include details of Deborah's fate after having been "experimented on" during her childhood; the most sensational of them was that she had become mentally ill and committed suicide.[13]

In fact, Deborah did neither. Yet the continued presence of these rumors[14] not only indicates the persistence of misinformation regarding the Skinners' family life, but also suggests something of the fascination and suspicion with which the American public regards behaviorism. In order to counter the misinformation about the Skinners' family life, the following section describes their conduct as parents. Ironically, we shall see that the Skinners' approach to child-rearing was a generally permissive one, far removed from the image of the rigid, authoritarian style of the strict behaviorist. But if the Skinners' parenting style failed to fit an authoritarian stereotype, it nonetheless did conform both to child-rearing trends of the postwar era and to Skinner's avowed views about human behavior. Thus, the subsequent sections of this chapter are devoted to situating the Skinners' parenting style in its social and intellectual contexts by examining it from the perspectives of cultural trends in child-rearing and of Skinner's beliefs about the control of human behavior.

THE SKINNERS AS PARENTS

The Skinners raised two daughters, Julie who was born in 1938 and Deborah who was born in 1944. Fred and Eve began the adventure of parenting with a mixture of fear and excitement. They were also somewhat unprepared.[15] When Eve was pregnant with Julie she did not believe that she would live through the pregnancy, and she thus neglected to buy the necessary baby care items.[16] After Julie was born, Fred went shopping to buy what they would need when Julie and Eve were sent home from the hospital.[17] Because neither of the Skinners had any experience with babies, they hired a nurse to help them take care of Julie for a few days. This did little to relax Eve who was still very uneasy around her newborn. Alone with Julie for the first time, Eve panicked and called the doctor when Julie cried.[18] Eventually the Skinners' apprehensiveness waned since Julie proved to be an easy baby. Although Julie experienced two serious bouts of tonsillitis before the age of two, she presented no other unusual problems for the Skinners.[19]

The Skinners described themselves as fairly permissive yet reasonably strict parents. In fact, they believed themselves to have been more permissive than other parents at the time.[20] For example, the girls had no household chores to perform. The Skinners employed housekeepers, and this kept the family chores to a minimum. Although Eve liked to have a neat house, she soon learned that her daughters were not going to be neat, so she allowed them to be messy in their own rooms.[21] The household was not governed by a rigid set of rules and schedules. There were prescribed times for bed and the girls were forbidden to handle certain objects in the house, but they were not strictly supervised. The children were often left to their own devices to play as they wished in their rooms or in the neighborhood. When they reached school age, most afternoons the girls played in the neighborhood. The only restriction was that they return in time for dinner, which the family tried to eat together every night.[22]

From a relatively young age, the girls were given considerable freedom as well as responsibility. The family often vacationed on Monhegan Island in Maine. Julie loved to sail and was allowed to take the boat out by herself from the time she was ten years old. Sometimes she would take the dog for companionship. The only rule was that she return by sundown.[23] The Skinners also let their children explore the island as much as they wished, and the girls would hike through the woods and scramble around the rocky headlands of the island.

Because the Skinners did not provide a great deal of direction for their children's activities, the girls were required to be relatively self-controlled and to initiate their own activities. They could choose how they wanted to spend their time. Reflecting on that now, Julie says that she was treated "like a boy."[24] Not being confined to the home or restricted to any stereotyped role, she was given opportunities that perhaps only boys typically had at that time. She was free to roam and explore and to try new experiences if she wished. The girls were allowed to keep a variety of pets, including some unusual ones such as snakes and a sparrow hawk.[25] Julie reports that she was encouraged to do whatever she felt she could do, whether that was pursuing her interest in music or sailing alone for an afternoon.[26] Because the Skinners had had unpleasant experiences with religious education when they were young, they imposed no formal religious training on their daughters; yet when Julie became interested in religion they did not prevent her from exploring that as well. As a young girl, she went to Sunday school with a couple of friends to satisfy her curiosity.[27] Deborah was also free to pursue her own interests. She chose to develop her artistic talent, a decision that eventually took her to different schools in the United States and Europe.[28] In sum, the Skinners' permissiveness gave their children the freedom and autonomy to develop their own interests and to develop self-reliance.

In terms of schooling, the Skinners preferred a less structured environment for their children. After moving to Cambridge, they enrolled Julie and Deborah in the Shady Hill School, a private school with a good reputation. However, Fred and Eve soon became dissatisfied with the school because they believed it was too strict and too highly structured compared to the environment in which their daughters were raised.[29] One day Julie refused to taste her squash at lunch and as a result was confined to her seat for a whole afternoon.[30] The school also organized many competitive games for the children, and both Julie and her parents were unhappy about her forced participation in these activities.[31]

The Skinners' permissiveness was coupled with a tolerance of their daughters' developmental conflicts. Both girls went through brief periods of rebellion as teenagers. Eve described these periods as times when the girls seemed to lack direction and had difficulty deciding what they wanted to do.[32] Eve and Fred talked about these problems and discussed them with their daughters. Sometimes there were quarrels. However, the Skinners as parents did not do much besides talk and worry, and eventually the difficulties passed.[33] Deborah was more rebellious than Julie, and this caused her parents to be "depressed" because they saw that their daughter was unhappy.[34] Nevertheless, they remained reluctant to be more directive with their daughter. For example, when Deborah was in college the Skinners called her and casually recommended that she flush her marijuana down the toilet because they had heard about some college students who had become ill after smoking marijuana that had been contaminated with some toxic substance.[35]

The Skinners' permissiveness and tolerance were in no way an indication that they were uncaring or uninterested in their daughters. The family was close-knit, spending time together for meals, holidays, and vacations. Eve did not work outside the home until after the girls were grown, and she spent time with the girls whenever they were home. Fred was a very involved father, perhaps more so than other fathers at that time.[36] He played, read, and worked with both of his daughters. He spent hours teaching Julie how to throw a ball skillfully, and he also helped her with her school reading assignments. He regularly took his daughters to his office and laboratory at Harvard, where he taught them how to shape a pigeon's behavior and to wire simple circuits. He also gave them opportunities to tinker and invent on their own. At Monhegan Island, Fred set up a work bench for Julie where she had her own tools.[37] From an early age Deborah demonstrated considerable artistic ability, and the Skinners provided her with paper, pens, and pencils for drawing.[38] Clearly, the Skinners took an active interest in their children's development.

As the girls became old enough to participate in family decision-making, child-rearing became a cooperative venture in the Skinner household. The Skinners were quite attentive, and the girls had a voice in how they were raised. A very early example of this occurred when Julie was about five years old. About that time, the Skinners were struggling with the issue of punishment, and they had spanked Julie occasionally. One day Julie announced that they should not spank her because it only made her mad.[39] After that they never spanked her again. The Skinners tried, whenever possible, to share with their daughters the responsibility for certain decisions involving them. The girls attended private boarding

schools, and both participated in the process of selecting their schools.[40]
When Julie and Eve went to Mexico together when Julie was a teenager,
Eve divided the spending money evenly at the beginning of the trip.[41]

The Skinners by no means gave their daughters carte blanche. There
were some rules and expectations. Julie recalls that she always felt that
she was "expected to behave in a certain way and uphold certain rules
of conduct. But they were never really specified to me as rules."[42] Perhaps
these expectations were not seen as rules because the Skinners used
reasoning whenever possible in dealing with their daughters. They talked
about problems and tried to negotiate solutions. Discipline was not arbitrary, and they always explained their reasons for a decision. As the girls
got older, they temporarily rebelled against this approach and accused
their parents of "using psychology on them."[43] In other words, they were
objecting to their parents' use of reasons and explanations as a way to
manipulate them.

In the language of child experts, the Skinners were using an authoritative, rather than authoritarian, child-rearing style.[44] That is to say, they
were permissive in allowing their children a fair amount of freedom to
express themselves and to act on their own impulses, yet they were mildly
restrictive in setting up rules and enforcing them. They were firm, but
without making the children powerless, and they were consistently child-
centered, attending carefully to their children's needs. They explained
rules to the girls, considered their opinions, and provided them with numerous kinds of enriching experiences. The girls were encouraged to be
independent, but they were also nurtured and protected. This description
of the Skinners as authoritative parents affords a much more complete
and accurate picture of their parental behavior than does a simple description of the baby-tender, which was but one small part of their parenting.
It also shows the myths associated with the baby-tender's use in the
Skinner household to be curiously hyperbolic.

CONTEXTS OF PARENTING

The authoritative approach to parenting that the Skinners used can be
understood in at least two contexts. First, it can be interpreted as a
reflection of a particular social and cultural milieu. The Skinners had their
first daughter in 1938 and their second in 1944. Set in the context of the
late 1930s, 1940s, and 1950s, their style of child-rearing can be compared
to contemporaneous modes of child-rearing and attitudes about children.
Second, their manner of parenting can be understood in relation to Skinner's behaviorism, particularly his ideas about the control of behavior.
Because parenting involves, among other things, controlling children's

behavior, Skinner's well-known philosophy of freedom and control could scarcely fail to be relevant to a discussion of his behavior as a parent.

Cultural Context: The Rising Tide of Permissiveness

The Skinners became parents during the early wave of a movement toward more permissive parenting. During the 1920s and early 1930s, a relatively rigid approach was the norm for child-rearing.[45] Parents believed that children's impulses were unhealthy and that children should be tightly controlled to stave off the ill effects of these impulses. This attitude was embodied in a government pamphlet titled *Infant Care*.[46] Editions of the pamphlet issued in 1914 and throughout the 1920s recommended the use of physical restraints to prevent less desirable child behaviors such as thumbsucking.[47] At this time, John B. Watson was the leading expert on children and child care,[48] and Watsonian ideas about parental detachment and regimentation of the child's routine were evident in the government publications available at the time.[49]

By the late 1930s, attitudes about children were changing rapidly. Advances in the study of child development were producing increased understanding of children's needs and abilities. Greater interest in children's mental health also led to a shift toward concern for the psychological impact of the treatment of children.[50] In particular, the potential consequences of corporal punishment were beginning to receive some attention.[51] Parents were moving toward modes of response that involved greater tolerance of the child's desires. Discipline involved an increasing reliance on "psychological" methods, such as reasoning and appeals to guilt.[52]

Seen more as individuals different from adults, children were now understood to have needs that were distinct from those of adults. One particular need was that for self-expression.[53] As a result, the spontaneity and free activity of the child became more highly valued. As children's impulses became viewed as more benign, parents were advised to relax and to be more "natural" with children.[54] They were instructed to let children be children, not to force them to adhere to the harsh, rigid, artificial schedules advocated by Watson. They were told to accept and respond to what children do naturally. By 1940, the research and writing of the developmental psychologist Arnold Gesell had dramatically changed child-rearing theory. This new theory focused more on the social and emotional development of the child and recognized the child's need for trust and love.[55] The mother could build the infant's trust by responding promptly and appropriately to the child's needs. Gesell's developmental approach to child-rearing required full participation of the mother in the child's mental life.[56] The ideal mother "aims first of all to be perceptive of and sensitive to the child's behavior. Thus she becomes a true complement to him, alertly responsive to his needs."[57]

Gesell's ideas set the stage for Benjamin Spock, who published his first child care book, *The Common Sense Book of Baby and Child Care,* in 1946.[58] With this book, Spock became the leader of the movement away from strict parenting. His child care books became the standard references for generations of parents who wished to raise their children properly yet at the same time be more easygoing in their parental style. Spock's first advice to parents was to "Trust yourself."[59] According to Spock, child-rearing involved a combination of the mother's watchfulness and the child's expression of impulses, resulting in a balanced mother-child relationship. It was best, of course, if all of this could occur in a nurturing, loving family environment.[60] Spock advocated a democratic style of child-rearing. The parent must be responsive to the child. At the same time, the parent was to be a firm yet warm authority, and the child was to be given the opportunity to participate in the child-rearing process.[61]

This attitude and style of child-rearing continued to gain popularity during the time when the Skinners were raising their daughters. The Skinners' style of child-rearing appears to have fit this trend toward more tolerant, permissive parenting. Although Eve in particular was reluctant to trust her own instincts, she soon grew more comfortable with her daughters and became adept at responding to their signals. She remembers vividly that when Julie was learning to talk she paid very close attention to Julie's speech, following her through every moment of language development. She thought it was "wonderful" and "fascinating" to observe that development and to be a part of it.[62] The Skinners were indeed permissive in letting their daughters discover and pursue their own interests and in allowing them to select their own activities. However, the girls knew that there were limits and rules. These standards were set by their parents in such a gentle but firm way that the girls did not even see them as explicit rules. Rather they were felt as "vague expectations" that were understood "exactly."[63] The Skinners' willingness to give their children the power to contribute to the family's decisions also made the treatment of their children democratic. In all of these ways, the style of child-rearing used by the Skinners was highly similar to that advocated by Gesell, Spock, and their followers in the 1940s and 1950s.

In spite of this close fit between the Skinners' practices and the child-rearing advice of Gesell and Spock, there is no reason to conclude that they were directly influenced by such advice. Fred read Spock, but did not think it was a good resource for parents.[64] Eve does not recall the books, if any, that she read. It is possible that their parenting style was largely a reaction against the ways in which their own parents raised them. Eve believed that her parents were too strict, causing her to "disobey them constantly."[65] Although she did not know much about children, she never asked her parents for advice because she thought she knew more than they did.[66] Fred did not seem to share this blatant desire to rebel against his own parents. It is most likely that a number of factors influenced the particular style of parenting that the Skinners adopted. They may have sensed the cultural trend toward permissiveness and responded to it, perhaps doing so in ways that were shaped by their own childhood experiences. But whatever the cultural and familial determinants of the Skinners' parenting style may have been, it is also quite likely that Fred Skinner's strong beliefs about behavioral control had a definite influence on their behavior as parents.

Skinner's Philosophy of Freedom and Control

Viewed in light of Skinner's beliefs about the control of human behavior, the Skinners' parental behavior takes on a new dimension. Skinner was long concerned with how behavior is controlled and the degree to which individuals are free to determine their own behavior. He believed that people are free only in the sense that they are relatively free from aversive control.[67] For Skinner, the ultimate source of control is the environment, but people can have "self-control" by controlling their environments. In other words, people can determine their own behavior by managing the environmental circumstances that control that behavior. Skinner also believed, of course, that we can and should take part in the design of our culture, that we must construct an environment in which the enactment of valued behaviors is effortless.[68] According to Skinner, a science of behavior is essential for the design of a culture in which people are "happy, informed, skillful, well behaved, and productive."[69]

As parents, the Skinners provided an environment in which their children could acquire those valued characteristics. Permissiveness gave the girls the opportunity to manipulate and control their environments. Through operating on their environments, they discovered how to control them and how to gain self-control. The Skinners resisted controlling the children by imposing too much structure on their environments. In his notebooks, Skinner discussed the importance of letting a child struggle by himself or herself to complete a task. It is through this independent effort that the child will experience meaningful learning and acquire finely skilled behaviors.[70]

The Skinners routinely put their children in situations where they could become "informed." They read to them, sent them to private schools, and conversed with them often. They planned for them such cultural activities as going to the theater and to museums. They traveled with them, including trips to Europe.[71] When Julie was older, her father often talked with her at length about the papers or books he was writing.[72] In addition, the Skinners provided their children with opportunities to become "skillful." The girls learned various skills in Skinner's lab and workshop, such as wiring circuits, building equipment, and training pigeons and other pets.[73] The Skinners seemed particularly adept at noticing their children's talents and encouraging their development, as when they supplied Julie with a workbench and tools because she was skilled with her hands. The Skinners encouraged their children to be productive and instrumental in order to gain mastery over their surroundings.

To get the children to be "well behaved," the Skinners used milder forms of control. They relied heavily on appeals to reason. They explained any rules in order to help the girls understand why it made sense to obey them. For example, it was important to have dinner together because the family members might not see much of each other during the day. For that reason, it was important to return home in time for dinner.[74] These appeals to reason were less aversive than threats of punishment, and they seemed to be readily accepted by the girls.[75]

Thus, it appears that the Skinners' method of raising their children fitted closely with Skinner's beliefs about control. He did not believe his daughters had direct control of their behavior, but there were ways to control their behavior that involved acting on the environment. Both Fred and Eve acted on the environment to produce certain results from their children, and they also encouraged their children to actively create environments for themselves that would make them happy. In other words, the Skinners tried to provide an environment in which their daughters could discover or develop environments that would evoke the desired responses.

THE PARADOX OF FREEDOM AND CONTROL

The child-rearing practices arising out of Spock's permissiveness and Skinner's philosophical orientation share an interesting paradox: the coexistence of freedom and control. Spock said that children must be free to express themselves, but that parents must always provide leadership and guidance. For Spock, permissive parenting did not involve a loss of parental authority; rather the parent's control would become somewhat disguised. As Spock put it, the parent must "stay in control as a friendly leader."[76] Although the parent maintains control of the child, the control appears more benign because it is now combined with warmth and empathy. The parent is giving more freedom to the child, and that freedom may serve only to give the child the illusion of control. One function of this illusion of control may be to keep the child well behaved by internalizing discipline. Discipline becomes internalized because acquiring freedom also involves taking responsibility. As the historian William Graebner has argued, if that freedom is granted to an individual within a group such as a family, then the ensuing responsibility is not only for the individual's own actions but also for the welfare of the group.[77] In this way, freedom increases one's willingness to abide by the group's standards, because discipline becomes internalized rather than being imposed from an outside force. Through these very subtle means, the authority maintains control and the individual maintains the illusion of freedom and self-control. At the social level, this approach to parenting may have placated a society that was particularly distrustful of authorities following World War II. It is not surprising that parents who were eager to avoid any semblance of authoritarianism would readily embrace an approach to child-rearing that was touted as permissive and democratic.

Skinner also saw the paradox of the coexistence of freedom and control, and he concluded that *freedom* was a relative term.[78] Freedom was simply another form of control—it just happened to be a much more palatable kind of control for people in Western societies. Skinner fully acknowledged the value of the feeling of freedom, and saw that children in particular may benefit from the illusion of control.[79] Thus, Skinner's style of parenting, like Spock's, involved disguising the true source of control. The Skinner children were led to believe that they had complete freedom of choice and that they were independent. The rules became internalized as expectations, and the desire to meet these expectations was increased as the number of shared responsibilities increased. This situation is reflected in Julie's statement that in spite of the lack of direct commands from her parents she had a clear understanding of what to do, and that this understanding was coupled with a strong desire to please her parents.[80] The Skinners had succeeded in internalizing discipline in their children by giving them the freedom to act on, and react to, their environments, both physical and familial.

Evidently these illusions of freedom can serve a parent well, particularly when they function to increase obedience. But illusions of freedom and personal control are not without positive benefits for the children as well. As researchers have recently shown, positive illusions regarding the self can increased one's sense of autonomy and competence.[81] Julie's accounts of her childhood seem to indicate that she developed a positive self-concept as a result of the freedom she was given.[82] These illusions of control and freedom are not necessarily detrimental to the child because they are false beliefs.

Although labeled "permissive," the child-rearing styles of Skinner and Spock involved careful manipulations of control to serve the needs of the child and the family. The goal of these parenting styles was to internalize control. Once self-discipline was achieved, less discipline would be required from the parent. In effect, the goal of self-discipline was realized by fostering false beliefs about who and what controls behavior. Children were given freedom in order to encourage them to believe that they controlled their own behavior. Ironically, the child's illusion of self-control functioned to increase the effectiveness of the parent's control of the child. The Skinners succeeded as parents not because they effectively controlled their children's behavior but because the Skinners convinced their children that they themselves were in control.

NOTES

1. B. F. Skinner, *The Shaping of a Behaviorist* (New York: New York University Press, 1984), pp. 257, 258.

2. Ibid., p. 275. Interview with Yvonne Blue Skinner, 30 November 1988, transcribed by Elizabeth Jordan. Skinner, of course, had long been interested in gadgetry and labor-saving devices. He would later liken his proposals for large-scale social engineering to the invention of domestic machines to "spare the laundress on the river's bank struggling against fearful odds to achieve cleanliness" (Skinner, "Freedom and the Control of Men," in *Cumulative Record*, enl. ed. [New York: Appleton-Century-Crofts, 1961], pp. 3–18, on p. 16). On the history of the home efficiency movement that swept America during the first two decades of this century, see Barbara Ehrenreich and Deirdre English, *For Her Own Good: 150 Years of Experts' Advice to Women* (Garden City, N.Y.: Anchor Press, 1978), chap. 5. Skinner's domestic inventions included a mechanical toilet-training device that reinforced micturation by playing a tune when it detected the first drops of urine entering the potty; see Skinner, *Shaping*, p. 288.

3. Skinner, *Shaping*, p. 275.

4. Ibid., pp. 275–76. Skinner, "Baby in a Box," *Ladies' Home Journal*, October 1945, pp. 30–31, 135–36, 138.

5. Skinner, *Shaping*, pp. 276, 293.

6. Interview with Yvonne Blue Skinner, 30 November 1988.

7. Skinner, *Shaping*, p. 303.

8. Ibid., p. 304.

9. Ibid., p. 305.

10. Ibid., pp. 304, 309.

11. Ibid., pp. 308–10, 313–17, 332–33. Skinner was given an estimate of $420 per crib from J. J. Weste and over $200 from Dan Caldemeyer. For a more detailed account of the efforts to market the baby-tender, see Daniel W. Bjork, *B. F. Skinner: A Life* (New York: Basic, 1993), pp. 128–42.

12. Gordon W. Allport and Leo J. Postman, "Psychology of Rumor," in *Social Psychology: Experimentation, Theory, and Research*, ed. William S. Sahakian (Scranton, Pa.: Intext Educational Publishers, 1972), pp. 489–504.

13. Lois Wingerson, "Sure, She Spent Time in a Box, Says Deborah Skinner, But B. F.'s Daughter Was Never His Guinea Pig," *People Weekly*, 11 June 1979.

See the discussion in Marc N. Richelle, *B. F. Skinner: A Reappraisal* (Hillsdale, N.J.: Erlbaum, 1993), pp. 21–22. For an instructive inventory of other myths and misconceptions about behaviorism, see James T. Todd and Edward K. Morris, "Misconception and Miseducation: Presentations of Radical Behaviorism in Psychology Textbooks," *Behavior Analyst* 6 (1983): 153–60; and the further analysis in James T. Todd and Edward K. Morris, "Case Histories in the Great Power of Steady Misrepresentation," *American Psychologist* 47 (1992): 1441–53. Rumors of Deborah's suicide may have stemmed in part from a confusion of Skinner with the behaviorist John B. Watson, whose son William did kill himself in the early 1960s; see Kerry W. Buckley, *Mechanical Man: John B. Watson and the Origins of Behaviorism* (New York: Guilford, 1989), chap. 10.

Although Skinner did not use the baby-tender to experiment on Deborah, Skinnerian theory and methods were later applied to research on children. For reviews, see Jacob L. Gewirtz and Martha Pelaez-Nogueras, "B. F. Skinner's Legacy to Human Infant Behavior and Development," *American Psychologist* 47 (1992): 1411–22; and Henry D. Schlesinger, Jr., "Theory in Behavior Analysis: An Application to Child Development," *American Psychologist* 47 (1992): 1396–1410.

14. An informal survey conducted by the author in a section of Introduction to Psychology in the fall of 1989 revealed that 41 percent of the students had heard that Skinner raised his children in a Skinner box. Skinner himself was aware of such rumors. He reported, for example, that he was once awakened by a phone call at night from a caller who inquired, "Professor Skinner, is it true that you kept one of your children in a cage?" He also reported that "a well-known psychiatrist told Eunice Shriver that the child we 'raised in the box' became psychotic," and admitted that the rumors about Deborah may have made him oversolicitous of her. See Skinner, *A Matter of Consequences* (New York: Knopf, 1983), p. 386. Skinner's experiences with Eunice and Sargent Shriver are recounted in ibid., pp. 271–72.

15. Interview with Yvonne Blue Skinner, 30 November 1988.

16. Ibid.

17. Skinner, *Shaping*, p. 217. Interview with Yvonne Blue Skinner, 30 November 1988.

18. Ibid.

19. Interview with Yvonne Blue Skinner, 30 November 1988.

20. Ibid.

21. Interview with Julie Skinner Vargas, 19 December 1988, transcribed by Elizabeth Jordan. Interview with Yvonne Blue Skinner, 30 November 1988.

22. Interview with Yvonne Blue Skinner, 30 November 1988.

23. Interview with Julie Skinner Vargas, 19 December 1988.

24. Ibid.

25. Interview with Yvonne Blue Skinner, 30 November 1988.

26. Interview with Julie Skinner Vargas, 19 December 1988. Interview with Yvonne Blue Skinner, 30 November 1988.

27. Skinner, *Shaping*, p. 278.

28. Interview with Yvonne Blue Skinner, 30 November 1988.

29. Ibid.

30. Ibid.

31. Ibid. Skinner also once protested Shady Hill's practice of assigning two hours' worth of homework per night to ninth-graders, feeling that the time was excessive for that grade level (Skinner, *Matter of Consequences*, p. 64).

32. Interview with Yvonne Blue Skinner, 30 November 1988.

33. Ibid.

34. Ibid.

35. Ibid. For a different version of the story, see Skinner, *Matter of Consequences,* pp. 290–91, where Fred and Eve's own experiences with marijuana are amusingly recounted.

36. Interview with Yvonne Blue Skinner, 30 November 1988. A reading of Skinner's autobiographical works, where Julie and Deborah figure prominently, tends to confirm this impression. For example, Fred spent a sabbatical at Putney, Vermont, to be near his daughters who were in boarding school there while Eve spent the term touring Europe and North Africa (Skinner, *Matter of Consequences,* p. 78). For a suggestion that Fred was all along more interested than Eve in having children, see Rhonda K. Bjork, "The Personal Culture of Yvonne Blue Skinner," this volume. Skinner also appears to have shown considerable interest in his two granddaughters; see Julie S. Vargas, "B. F. Skinner: Father, Grandfather, Behavior Modifier," *Human Behavior* 1 (1971): 19–23.

37. Interview with Julie Skinner Vargas, 19 December 1988.

38. Interview with Yvonne Blue Skinner, 30 November 1988.

39. Ibid. Cf. Skinner, *Shaping,* p. 279.

40. Interview with Yvonne Blue Skinner, 30 November 1988.

41. Interview with Julie Skinner Vargas, 19 December 1988.

42. Ibid. The use of implicit control over individuals' behavior by means of face-to-face sanctions, rather than by explicit rules or laws, was explicitly advocated by Skinner in *Walden Two* and elsewhere. For a critique of this approach to social control as misplaced nostalgia for small-town rural values, see Richard Sennett, review of *Beyond Freedom and Dignity,* by Skinner, in *New York Times Book Review,* 24 October 1971.

43. Interview with Yvonne Blue Skinner, 30 November 1988. Cf. Skinner, *Matter of Consequences,* p. 221, where Skinner records "Don't try psychology on me!" as an actual or likely response to his efforts to talk with Julie about personal relationships.

44. The important distinction between authoritative and authoritarian parents was first expounded by Diane Baumrind in "Child Care Practices Anteceding Three Patterns of Preschool Behavior," *Genetic Psychology Monographs* 75 (1967): 43–88. For recent summaries of research on these parenting styles and on their effects on children, see Kenneth O. McGraw, *Developmental Psychology* (San Diego, Calif.: Harcourt, 1987), pp. 641–45; and Eleanor E. Maccoby and John A. Martin, "Socialization in the Context of the Family: Parent-Child Interaction," in *Handbook of Child Psychology, vol. 4, Socialization, Personality, and Social Development,* ed. E. M. Hetherington (New York: Wiley, 1983), pp. 1–101.

45. Steven Mintz and Susan Kellogg, *Domestic Revolutions: A Social History of American Family Life* (New York: Free Press, 1988).

46. Nancy Pottesdam Weiss, "Mother, the Invention of Necessity: Dr. Benjamin Spock's *Baby and Child Care,*" *American Quarterly* 29 (winter 1977): 318–46; Elizabeth M. R. Lomax, Jerome Kagan, and Barbara G. Rosenkrantz, *Science and Patterns of Child Care* (San Francisco: Freeman, 1978), especially pp. 129–40.

47. Mary Wolfenstein, "The Emergence of Fun Morality," *Journal of Social Issues* 4 (1951): 15–25.

48. For a review of Watson's popular writing and an analysis of the social context that influenced him, see Ben Harris, "'Give Me a Dozen Healthy Infants . . .': John B. Watson's Popular Advice on Childrearing, Women, and the

Family," in *In the Shadow of the Past: Psychology Portrays the Sexes,* ed. Miriam Lewin (New York: Columbia University Press, 1984), pp. 126–54.

49. Fred Matthews, "The Utopia of Human Relations: The Conflict-Free Family in American Social Thought, 1930–1960," *Journal of the History of the Behavioral Sciences* 24 (1988): 343–62. Unfortunately, Watson appears to have put his ideas about regimentation and detachment into practice with his own children; see Buckley, *Mechanical Man,* chap. 10.

50. W. F. Ogburn and Michael F. Nimkoff, *Technology and the Changing Family* (Boston: Houghton, 1955).

51. Ibid.

52. Urie Bronfenbrenner, "The Changing American Child: A Speculative Analysis," *Journal of Social Issues* 17 (February 1961): 6–18.

53. Lawrence K. Frank, *Childhood and Youth: Recent Social Trends* (New York: McGraw-Hill, 1933), p. 751.

54. Weiss, "Mother, the Invention of Necessity."

55. Arnold Gesell and Frank L. Ilg, *Infant and Child Care in the Culture Today* (New York: Harper, 1943), pp. 56–57.

56. Margaret P. Ryan, *Womanhood in America: From Colonial Times to the Present* (New York: New Viewpoints, 1975), p. 351.

57. Gesell and Ilg, *Infant and Child Care Today,* p. 56.

58. Spock, *The Common Sense Book of Baby and Child Care* (New York: Duell, Sloan and Pearce, 1946).

59. Benjamin Spock, *Baby and Child Care* (New York: Meredith, 1968), p. 3.

60. William Graebner, "The Unstable World of Benjamin Spock: Social Engineering in a Democratic Culture, 1917–1950," *Journal of American History* 67 (December 1980): 612–29; Weiss, "Mother, the Invention of Necessity"; Michael Zuckerman, "Dr. Spock: The Confidence Man," in *The Family in History,* ed. Charles E. Rosenberg (Philadelphia: University of Pennsylvania Press, 1975), pp. 179–207.

61. Graebner, "Unstable World of Spock."

62. Interview with Yvonne Blue Skinner, 30 November 1988.

63. Interview with Julie Skinner Vargas, 19 December 1988.

64. Skinner to Elizabeth Keyser, 18 April 1968, B. F. Skinner Papers, Harvard University Archives, Cambridge, Mass.

65. Interview with Yvonne Blue Skinner, 30 November 1988.

66. Ibid.

67. Skinner, *Beyond Freedom and Dignity* (New York: Knopf, 1971).

68. Skinner, "Freedom and the Control of Men," in *Skinner for the Classroom,* ed. Robert Epstein (Champaign, Ill.: Research Press, 1982), pp. 135–51.

69. Ibid., p. 142.

70. Skinner, *Notebooks,* ed. Robert Epstein (Englewood Cliffs, N.J.: Prentice-Hall, 1980), pp. 12, 63–64. Skinner repeatedly cited Jean-Jacques Rousseau and John Dewey as important advocates of education through hands-on learning and direct manipulation of environments; see, for example, Skinner, *The Technology of Teaching* (New York: Appleton-Century-Crofts, 1968), pp. 85, 153. On Skinner's admiration of Rousseau, see also n. 79.

71. Interview with Yvonne Blue Skinner, 30 November 1988.

72. Interview with Julie Skinner Vargas, 19 December 1988.

73. Skinner, *Matter of Consequences,* p. 103.

74. Interview with Yvonne Blue Skinner, 30 November 1988.

75. Ibid.

76. Spock, *Baby and Child Care*, p. 272.

77. Graebner, "Unstable World of Spock," pp. 623–25.

78. Skinner, *Beyond Freedom and Dignity*, p. 38.

79. Ibid., p. 37. See also Skinner's remark, "I am all for *feelings* of causal adequacy as I am for feelings of freedom and dignity" (Skinner, "Some Consequences of Selection," *Behavioral and Brain Sciences* 7 [1984]: 502–10, on p. 507). Noting Skinner's "affinity for Jean-Jacques Rousseau," one astute commentator has written: "In *Emile* Rousseau proposes that a teacher's student will be happiest if the student feels free, but is kept under the teacher's subtle control. Skinner's *Walden II* is a Rousseauian Utopia. Control is benign and hidden, so feelings of freedom and dignity remain, even though they have no referents beyond those feelings" (Thomas H. Leahey, *A History of Psychology: Main Currents in Psychological Thought*, 2d ed. [Englewood Cliffs, N.J.: Prentice-Hall, 1987], p. 462). Skinner, in fact, often discussed Rousseau in his writing, and even considered giving the title *The New Émile* to his book *The Technology of Teaching* (see Skinner, *Matter of Consequences*, pp. 295–96).

80. Interview with Julie Skinner Vargas, 19 December 1988.

81. Shelley E. Taylor, *Positive Illusions: Creative Self-Deception and the Healthy Mind* (New York: Basic, 1989).

82. Interview with Julie Skinner Vargas, 19 December 1988.

9

Skinner at Harvard: Intellectual or Mandarin?

JOHN J. CERULLO

MUCH has been written about B. F. Skinner's views of human social relations. Yet surprisingly little has been written about his own relationships. This chapter, an inquiry into the way in which Skinner conducted himself socially at Harvard University, represents a preliminary probe into that subject.

Skinner earned his doctorate at Harvard and later spent many productive years there as a faculty member. It was Harvard that provided his introduction to the institutionalized practice of psychology. For that reason, his social conduct in the intellectual environs of Harvard can suggest something of his orientation toward his own profession and, perhaps obliquely, toward the larger social order within which that profession was embedded.

In surveying Skinner's relationships at Harvard, the present essay aims not only to portray his social world there but also to advance a thesis concerning the manner in which he constructed that world. Although the essay is broadly gauged, and its conclusions are necessarily provisional, it indicates how a better understanding of Skinner the social actor can enhance our understanding of Skinner the psychological thinker and cultural critic. As we shall see, the former understanding has much to contribute to the latter.

SKINNER AND THE SOCIOLOGY OF INTELLECTUALS

Sociologists who investigate intellectual life have provided useful analytical categories for a study of this sort. The sociology of intellectuals assesses the historical evolution and social function of intellectuals as a definable social group. This literature proceeds from the assumption that relàtions between intellectuals and society are mutually consequential, and far from unproblematic.

In this literature, one finds a pronounced strain of disrespect for practitioners in those fields we call the social and behavioral sciences, precisely because their relations with their host society are deemed more comfortable than they should be. Indeed, practitioners of the social sciences are sometimes described as renegade or even pseudo-intellectuals, uncommitted to, or even unaware of, the mission undertaken by real intellectuals ever since the inception of civilization itself.

The historical mission of intellectuals, argue many sociologists, has been the construction and defense of cultural systems that "specify what in some sense *should* be done . . . rather than either describing what is in fact done or predicting what will be."[1] Building and sustaining culture, they argue, is an enterprise quite distinct from the mere maintenance of that ongoing network of structured role-relations that make up day-to-day societal life. The latter—the "social order"—is the domain of law, economics, and politics. But the defense of culture has properly been exalted over any sort of involvement in those mundane, structural societal arrangements from the beginning.[2] It is the framers and defenders of culture who demand that such arrangements be held accountable to higher notions of the true and the good, without which the normal structures of society lack purpose and honor, and life itself becomes meaningless.[3]

In modern times, the argument goes, this has unfortunately proven to be beyond the epistemological and moral strength of certain sectors of the intellectual classes. Those engaged in social and behavioral science have succumbed to the call of positive knowledge wafting from the precincts of natural science, abandoned its higher normative calling, and struck a sort of devil's bargain with the economic and political elite; institutional support and other social benefits will be devolved upon such scientists in exchange for their delivery of usable technologies of social control. Economists, sociologists, psychologists, and political scientists have become social technocrats—in reality, minions of money and power—augmenting the efficiency of various societal arrangements rather than challenging the basic values underlying them.[4] Indeed, by this reckoning social scientists are not really intellectuals at all. They are a successor group, mere "mandarins."[5]

It is in the modern university that the bargain is struck. This is where the normative function that properly belongs to intellectuals, and the dissent it so often catalyzes, can be managed, contained, and eventually all but deprogrammed for those willing to serve new masters. The university is the crucial site of socialization into those professions that serve from within, rather than judging from without, the various sovereigns of

society.[6] It is the place where professionalized representatives of the social sciences stand waiting to transform students from defenders of cultural imperatives into functionaries of the social elite. Once a specific
technological skill or product is traded for access to a pre-existing network of personally advantageous social relations, a career in social science is established—and another mandarin is at hand.

Prominently situated within that mandarinate would be the proponents,
in various guises, of Skinnerian behaviorism, that supremely efficient
device for the production of socially prescribed behavior. Heirs of the
"Frankfurt School" of critical social theory, for example, have found in
behaviorism the great heresies of social-behavioral science writ large.
These include the epistemological imperialism of scientism, as well as
the subsequent alignment of social thought with the allegedly universal
principles of biological nature rather than with humanly constructed
moral visions.[7] On the face of it, this seems to be a fair characterization
of behaviorism as a school of thought, especially given its long-standing
concern with social control. But Skinner himself presents a complex case.
For all his advocacy of scientific method, biological determinism, and
social control, the picture of Skinner as a career-oriented, technocratic
mandarin is not one that accords readily with what can be learned of his
conduct at Harvard.

The Calling of B. F. Skinner: "Higher and Wider Truth"

The existing accounts of Skinner's life, from his earliest articulations
of intellectual interest onward, suggest that even prior to his arrival at
Harvard he was a young man struggling with a very unconventional calling—a genuine *intellectual's calling,* by any reasonable definition of the
term. Scholars who have inquired into Skinner's pre-Harvard intellectual
life have found not an internally consistent body of ideas but rather a
deeply held set of general concerns and commitments. They note Skinner's adolescent and college-age drift toward an amorphous sort of bohemianism, and his restless dissatisfaction with the small-town pieties,
commercial Philistinism, and above all the restrictive and sometimes
hypocritical moral codes of his early environments of Susquehanna and
Scranton, Pennsylvania.[8] Even these scant details of his early life begin
to suggest the aptness, as a description of Skinner, of one sociologist's
typological delineation of intellectuals as

> those who exhibit in their activities a pronounced concern with the core values
> of society . . . the men who seek to provide moral standards and to maintain

meaningful symbols. Intellectuals are men who never seem satisfied with things as they are, with appeals to custom and usage. They question the truths of the moment in terms of higher and wider truths.[9]

It is tempting, in fact, to say that Skinner held the quest for that "higher and wider truth" sacred. Certainly, he felt through much of his life that those effectively engaged in that quest merited social leadership and access to such resources as they might require. In 1935, responding to a request from Hamilton College for suggestions on the improvement of undergraduate education, Skinner campaigned for a redirection of college resources so as to favor the serious intellectual ("the really good man") over his inferiors by allowing him virtually limitless freedom. "At present the better student is held at the level of the mediocre," he complained. "The man who is taking college as he would military school needs all the paternalism he can get; the man who is capable of it needs freedom."[10] More strikingly, in 1937 he based his opposition to nationalism and totalitarian government not on the then-customary humanitarian or democratic grounds, but on the grounds that those political forms dethroned the natural aristocracy of intelligence. His views regarding the proper status of "the top-crust of intellect" were vividly expressed in a letter of that year.

> Personal resistance to strong society gathers strength from the fact that regimentation levels the achievements of men. Germany and Russia lift the unintelligent into a higher plane of life, but they apparently pull down the intelligent. . . . A society ultimately depends on its top-crust of intellect. . . . If nationalism prevails, human society will have adopted the principle of the ant-hill and the bee-hive. Intelligence must protest and can hardly fail to triumph.[11]

Clearly, the B. F. Skinner who could write in this manner conceptualized intellectuals in general as natural leaders of society, not as hired agents of other, more common social elements. Just as clearly, by the time he was ready to enter Harvard he conceptualized himself more as an intellectual with a leadership task to perform than as a budding psychologist with an institutionalized profession to enter and a career to advance. From the beginning, Skinner aspired to help fashion a more authentic and sustainable culture.

In the years immediately prior to Harvard, however, he had been uncertain about the means by which to attain that end. After graduating from Hamilton College, he had dedicated two years to an unsuccessful pursuit of a literary career.[12] Disenchanted, he had turned to science. This transition from a literary to a scientific career track, however, represented no intellectual disjunction for Skinner. Intrigued by Wells, then Pavlov, then more deeply by Russell and Watson, he had simply begun conceptualizing a science of behavior as the medium wherein the "higher and wider truths" he sought about human beings could be most definitively captured, and quite appropriately abandoned literature for it.

Skinner was not a full-fledged behaviorist on the eve of his admission to Harvard's graduate program in psychology in 1928.[13] During his first year or so there, however, his readings of Poincaré and especially Mach crystallized his thinking and his agenda. By 1929, with his full conversion to Machian positivism, the epistemological foundation for a science of behavior became clear to him.[14] With the zealotry of the converted, he began expunging "mentalisms" from his own thought and speech ("catching myself as I started to say 'mind' or 'think' like an atheist who finds himself saying 'Thank God'"[15]). By then, of course, the question was no longer whether a science of behavior was feasible. It was whether psychology could contain it.

At and shortly through the threshold of his Harvard experience, Skinner thought of himself not as an aspiring psychologist at all, but rather as an intellectual whose attachment to psychology (or to any profession) was wholly contingent on its ability to afford him the information and other resources his own preformed and personal agenda required. "I had come to Harvard," he announced blithely in his autobiography, "not because I was a convert to psychology, but because I was escaping from an intolerable alternative."[16] That agenda—the construction and dissemination of a science of behavior—undoubtedly represented the driving force of Skinner's life at Harvard. What held primacy for Skinner was not the securing of proper professional credentials; not the establishment of a conventionally successful career in the psychological profession; not training for service to whatever forces that profession might bid him serve; but the project of building and promoting a science of behavior.

That project represented an intellectual's calling, not a mandarin's career. And the salience of that project, not a mandarin's career calculations, is what Skinner's social relationships reflected more than anything else.

SKINNER AT HARVARD: REJECTING THE MAINSTREAM

In the Skinner collection of the Harvard University Archives, there is an undated, vividly written note titled "Extract from a student's notebook in elementary psychology laboratory." The title suggests that Skinner wrote it rather early in his graduate-school days. But the substance of it was something to which he would return throughout graduate school and afterward. That substance is disdain for the conventional work of the conventional psychologists he found at Harvard—rejection, in a word, of the mainstream of the profession he was about to enter.

The ostensible subject of the note is the Bogardus Social Distance Test, which was intended to measure social prejudice. The note is a string of fulminations, directed in part at the "unreasoned national bigotry," the "personal warp and jaundiced intolerance," that the test was intended to document. Skinner considered himself above such primitive sentiments ("nationality as affecting personal relationships rarely enters my mind, and difference in race but little"). But he also knew full well that that viewpoint was a minority one. The test itself, he felt, "but threw into relief a consuming popular prejudice already a matter of common knowledge among persons with some claim to intelligence." Oddly, the harshest invective in the note is reserved for the work of his fellow psychologists. He expressed "gnawing disgust at the inane artificiality of current social measurement tests, of which the Bogardus is a typical example," and finally lapsed into a denunciation of a profession that could fritter away its energies in meaningless testing projects of this sort.

> What [the tests'] purpose is other than furnishing little intricacies for the satisfaction of pedagogues far enough removed from reality to be immune from thought-provoking situations, I must confess to be ignorant of. They do provide for the manufacture of nominal measurement, enough at least to clutter up scattered psychological laboratories maintained for those misfits and future pedagogues entangled in the red tape of university and state requirements.

Even if the note were less acerbic in tone, it is remarkable for its expressed disaffection from testing, an important element of the psychological profession as Skinner found it. Indeed, reading the note leaves the impression that Skinner's real impatience came from his sense of the massive gap between the genuine function of psychology (guiding a culture beyond the "unreasoned national bigotry" so obvious to "persons with some claim to intelligence") and the fecklessness of the responses to it by professional psychologists ("those misfits and future pedagogues entangled in the red tape of university and state requirements"). This would not be the only way in which Skinner would reveal, while at Harvard, a pronounced lack of respect for mainstream elements of the profession within which he might have been mandarinized.

Perhaps Skinner's most significant show of disrespect was through his dealings with the chairperson of his department, E. G. Boring. Boring, an intellectual descendant of E. B. Titchener, was one of the most articulate and self-conscious representatives of the psychological mainstream. He saw himself above all as a centrist, as a moderator of controversies. That self-ascribed function was based firmly on his understanding of the history of science generally, and that of psychology particularly. As an historian, Boring felt that the progress of science was poorly served when the adherents of divergent schools of thought (scholastics, as he called them) were allowed to compete among themselves for leadership of any discipline. His view was that controversies among schools were, after a certain point, scientifically unproductive because their proponents grew less interested in the advancement of knowledge than in the establishment of personal power and prestige. That is, politics all too easily replaced science, and in the struggle for power good and useful scientific work was invariably obliterated because it was politically inconvenient for one side or another.[17] Boring was ever-vigilant to incursions of "scholasticism" into psychology. Among the early warning signs were attempts to claim original credit for ideas that were, in fact, historically precedented, which was why the historical record had to be kept scrupulously accurate. His own vision for psychology prescribed a middle course between the twin perils of "philosophical" speculation on the one hand and "technocratic" labors on the other. He stewarded his department accordingly.

In Skinner's view, Boring's four systematic courses "clearly established the central position of the department," and it was not one he found intellectually congenial.[18] By 1930 he had begun drafting a doctoral dissertation explicitly designed to advance the behaviorist cause. Serious conflict with the antischolastic Boring was perhaps inevitable.

At issue was the historical portion of the dissertation, wherein Skinner examined the history of theorizing on the reflex.[19] Skinner undertook that exploration because he "wanted to define the concept of the reflex so it is workable."[20] That is, he wanted a definition of use to behaviorists. Boring, however, objected to the results ("Skinner's school of reflexism," he called it), which he felt were mistakenly presented as innovative ("it's only a matter of terminology, there's nothing new."[21]) More generally, in Boring's eyes Skinner was reading an historical record selectively rather than accurately. This, Boring felt, represented precisely the sort of distortion of history in the interests of some "scholastic" design that could not be countenanced. "What's the use?" he wrote in a five-page critique of Skinner's reconceptualization of the reflex. "To wrench the word from its well-entrenched meaning you need more than a paper; you need propaganda and a school."[22] Boring doubtless intended this suggestion that Skinner was moving toward scholasticism as a withering criticism. Skinner, however, saw that the shoe fit, and wore it proudly. "I accept the challenge," he wrote in the margin of Boring's critique, noting later "I want to define a science, the discipline, behavior (*does it include psychology? I have no idea!*)."[23]

Whatever the merits of their positions, in social terms the conflict between Boring and Skinner was hardly a struggle between equals. It pitted a powerful, well-known department chair against an ambitious fledgling.

It would have made sense, had Skinner been committed primarily to success in the profession of psychology, for the younger man to accommodate the older. Yet at no point did Skinner give an inch. Indeed, what is most striking about his conduct throughout the entire affair is his apparent indifference to the very real career perils he faced. Those were perils that stemmed, in fact, not only from this specific incident but from a long record of opposition to departmental orthodoxy. "I am coming up for my degree this month," he wrote Percy Saunders. "There may be a good deal of trouble about it, as I have taken a very active role in opposing the department on several systematic issues. . . . But the degree seems less and less important anyway."[24]

What seems most significant about the incident is the cavalier orientation Skinner expressed toward Boring and, necessarily, toward what Boring so publicly strove to represent: middle-ground, mainstream psychology. That was all, in a sense, tangential to Skinner's real interests. Boring, who voluntarily withdrew from Skinner's committee, understood this full well. On the occasion of Skinner's application for a National Research Council (NRC) Fellowship, Boring dryly observed of Skinner that "his interest in psychology is rather limited to the problem of behavior," an acknowledgment that the psychological profession per se held little attraction for Skinner.[25] Indeed, Skinner's overall comportment at Harvard must have confirmed all of Boring's fears, for Skinner conducted himself socially in a fashion that can only be described as highly "scholastic" indeed. It was the behaviorist cause that drove him. To promote it he developed a firm awareness of what was needed for making behaviorism a scientific force, and himself a leader of it.

Skinner had the politician's appreciation of public image: he denied his parents the opportunity to publicize his accomplishments with articles in their hometown newspapers, not from modesty but because it "might hurt me considerably if it happened to be picked up by the clipping bureaus and sent back to . . . Harvard." He had the politician's feel for long-run strategy: while an NRC Fellow, he mapped out an explicit and detailed "Plan of the Campaign for the Years 30–60." He had the politician's grasp of short-run tactics: he requested the opportunity to review Boring's *History of Experimental Psychology* for the *Saturday Review of Literature,* "mainly to help Boring out on selling the book," since that "will help me in the Department's political situation also."[26] But this was political behavior of a special sort. It was motivated not by conventional career concerns but by commitment to the truth as he had grasped it. He was, in fact, less the politician than the crusader, with the crusader's sense of mission.

Boring, always keen in his observations of Skinner, understood that crusading zeal very well. In 1946 he would tell Skinner:

The differences between you and me were always, I think, that you had a very strong cathexis for your ideas, seeming a fanatic to me, and that you were definitely aware of differences from yourself and constantly directing your invective against them, whereas I did not feel those differences mattered very greatly and thought they probably lay within the Spielraum of human fallibility anyhow.[27]

BUILDING THE MOVEMENT: FRIENDS

At Harvard, Skinner had a wide circle of friends, drawn from a variety of fields. Of special interest here, however, are his relations with people of major professional consequence to him. Harvard could have represented to Skinner (as it can to any of its students) access to a pre-existing web of advantageous professional contacts, the activation and deployment of which could usher students into the highest levels of professional life. But Skinner did not so activate or deploy them. Rather than forming and conducting his professional relationships on the basis of the orthodox career goals of the upwardly mobile professional, Skinner organized a set of relationships around the greater imperative of building and promoting the behaviorist movement. He did not simply enter into the existing institutional world of American psychology through Harvard's special portals. Instead, he seems to have built a professional world of his own—in effect, an alternative to Boring's department—constructed of individuals selected not for their standing in American psychology but for the utility of their work to the evolving science of behavior. He would, of course, eventually ascend to the upper echelons of his own profession. But he would do it on his own terms, as leader of a behaviorist movement he had spent much of his time and energy at Harvard building, not as the hireling of some range of "interests" originating within the social order.

We should not be surprised, then, to see Skinner moving outside the psychology department completely for some of his most rewarding personal and professional associations. Among these were the associations he formed with the physiologist W. J. Crozier and members of Crozier's Laboratory of General Physiology (where Skinner conducted the research on the reflex that he eventually molded into his dissertation). Crozier had purposefully gathered together a group of young researchers, often "borrowing" them from other departments, who were committed to intense experimentation in diverse areas. The social atmosphere seems to have been a rather free-wheeling one.[28] But for Skinner, professional relations always *followed* intellectual utility. As a behaviorist, he was delighted by the fact that Crozier "talked about animal behavior without mentioning the nervous system and with surprising success." Crozier had "cancelled out the physiological theorizing of Pavlov and Sherrington and thus clarified what remained of the work of these men as the beginnings of an independent science of behavior."[29] So deep was Skinner's involvement with Crozier's laboratory that Boring described Skinner's work to the NRC as "on the borderline between the Psychological Laboratory and the Laboratory of General Physiology. . . . His experiments could probably be presented to either department for the degree."[30] This was the sort of extradisciplinary association from which a movement might be constructed; it was not the sort to elicit enthusiasm from Skinner's own department chair.

Within the psychology department itself, Skinner's most integral relationship was certainly with Fred Keller. Like Skinner, Keller had arrived at Harvard with clear behaviorist sympathies, and from the beginning Skinner found him "expert in both the technical details and the sophistry of Behaviorism."[31] Not surprisingly, their intellectual affinity provided the basis for Skinner's strongest association while at Harvard. "It was largely because of Fred," he wrote, "that I resisted the mentalistic predispositions of the department and remained a behaviorist."[32] Skinner described their relationship as fellow graduate students in words that effectively convey both its personal warmth and its "scholastic" utility.

> Fred and I were only graduate students, but we had kept our position steadily at the center of attention in Emerson Hall. Possibly we had done so not only because our cause was just, but because we worked well together.[33]

That the two men could work well together in an alliance against the powers that resisted behaviorism is actually rather remarkable. For one thing, they brought very different styles to the conceptual work they had undertaken. In fact, Keller seems to have failed, at first, to see in Skinner the qualities necessary for a leader of the behaviorist school. "Burrhus was a solitary worker . . . and a very cautious one," he noted. "He was not the kind to discuss his hopes or plans or half-analyzed data around the laboratory coffee-pot. . . . Such prudence may win respect, but is unlikely to initiate joint enterprise."[34] More surprisingly, throughout their graduate-school days Keller was unaware of just what Skinner was doing (as Skinner impishly noted, so was everyone else "until I handed in some kind of flimsy report").[35]

Yet, despite all the apparent impediments to "joint enterprise," the relationship was both strong and professionally fruitful. Keller and Skinner evolved a highly effective division of labor on behalf of their common goal of advancing behaviorism. Keller described their preferences for different tacks within the general behaviorist course while in graduate school.

Burrhus Skinner was primarily a systematist, even then, and I was essentially a teacher. While he was doing the spade-work for his paper on the reflex, I was translating mentalistic terms into stimulus-response and peddling the result to college undergraduates as a kind of ready-to-wear behaviorism. . . . He was a producer of systems; I was a promoter, and he had nothing yet ready for promotion.[36]

By the publication of the *Behavior of Organisms* in 1938, of course, Skinner had readied something very substantial. Keller was at Columbia then, and his promotional activities there would include the initiation of an entire course based on the book, as well as an introductory textbook (with his colleague William Schoenfeld) explicitly designed to substitute behaviorist principles for more traditional fare.[37] The alliance that had begun at Harvard served as the opening wedge of a surge in operant behaviorism.

NONALLIES AND ESTRANGEMENTS

The degree to which Skinner elevated intellectual affinity above all else in fashioning his professional relationships at Harvard is also indicated by those relationships that never fully ripened, or that even evinced a degree of estrangement. The simple fact seems to have been that, whatever the level of interpersonal compatibility Skinner felt with a colleague, his modus operandus was to subordinate that to the mandates of behaviorist solidarity—that is, to the furtherance of the "higher and wider truth" he had come to pursue.

The case of Walter Hunter is illustrative. Hunter taught a weekly seminar in animal behavior that deliberately avoided any reference to recent Gestalt work in that area in favor of earlier research. He defined himself as a behaviorist, skeptical of mentalistic inferences and sensitive to the careless use of behavioral terms.[38] But at least some of his work was directed toward comparative investigations of "symbolic processes" in animals and humans, an investigative framework the young Skinner appears to have questioned. In actuality, Hunter was an animal psychologist with a behaviorist bent; but Skinner's variety of behaviorism, even in the late 1920s, was purer. He was interested in establishing behavior as the fundamental unit of psychological analysis. In fact, the publication of the *Behavior of Organisms* would fully distinguish the field of "the experimental analysis of behavior" from "the animal psychology of Watson, Hunter, and Lashley, and in particular the work of Hull and his students at Yale."[39] Hence, his insistence on maintaining some distance from the less single-minded Walter Hunter.

In late 1933, Skinner was admitted to one of Harvard's most intriguing inner circles, the Society of Fellows. The society was chaired by L. J. Henderson, a young professor of physiology whom Skinner knew from his work in Crozier's laboratory. Entrance into the society promised both a stipend and companionship with "like minds," for at least the next three years.

Henderson himself was a compelling lecturer and a strong personality who often drew people together in a shared enterprise. In 1932 he had begun a series of seminars on the works of the sociologist Vilfredo Pareto. The Pareto Circle attracted a large number of present and future luminaries (Henry Murray, Robert Merton, and George Homans), and Skinner might plausibly have been expected to join them. After all, since his youth he had been interested in issues relating to the interaction between the individual and society, and he had recently moved toward the belief that observed regularities in the behavior of the individual organism could exist on the level of society as well. Yet Skinner's mention of Henderson's interest in the writings of Pareto is succinct and dismissive. "I bought a copy [of Pareto's *Traité de sociologie générale*] soon after I began to audit [Henderson's course in the history of science], but Pareto was not a behaviorist, and I was not quite sure what to do with him."[40] Pareto's work simply did not provide any of the furnishings behaviorism needed at the time, so Skinner had no use for him. It was not a question of intolerance of an alternative viewpoint so much as lack of interest in it, and in those who had immersed themselves in it, such as Henderson. Skinner would eventually write "I did not know until he died many years later how much I liked Henderson," a comment suggesting the degree to which Skinner's professional associations were built on intellectual convergences, not interpersonal affinities.[41]

The period from 1936 to 1945, when Skinner was at Minnesota, witnessed the first flowering of the operant-behaviorist movement, and of Skinner's skill and confidence in leading it. He published some twenty papers there, extending the behaviorist perspective to ever-wider areas of language and knowledge. After a stint as chair of the Department of Psychology at Indiana, his stature was such that a return to Harvard as a faculty member was possible.

Upon Skinner's successful delivery of the William James Lectures in 1947, Boring (still department chair) suggested that he and his colleague S. S. Stevens would support a faculty appointment for Skinner. The appointment confirmed his success—and, perhaps, his manner of conducting his professional relationships, as well. His relationship with Stevens is intriguing in this regard, because it indicates the degree to which relations between Skinner and even his admirers remained distant if serious intellectual divergences persisted.

Stevens was indeed an admirer. He had first encountered Skinner at Harvard in the Society of Fellows, and the esteem he felt for Skinner grew so high over time that by 1969, on the occasion of Skinner's sixty-fifth birthday celebration, Stevens could enthuse, "He is indeed a great man! I have often said that the best thing I ever did for Harvard was set in motion the procedure that succeeded in retrieving him from Indiana and returning him to the local scene."[42] Yet throughout the duration of the relationship, dealings between the two men alternated between the cordial and the strained. The crucial fact was that they (like Boring and Skinner in an earlier period) were on opposite sides of the behaviorist divide, with Skinner promulgating the view that mind and other mentalistic terms are meaningless and Stevens insisting just as firmly on their scientific validity.[43] The issue turned on their distinct views of operationism, a concept introduced in 1927 by the physicist Percy Bridgman. As Bridgman had outlined it, operationism referred to the practice of defining scientific concepts in terms of the procedures used to measure them. In Skinner's view this dictum was well established in behaviorism. Stevens, however, conceived it as a means of admitting mentalist terms into the scientist's vocabulary.[44] The strain grew worse with the often unexpected transfer of graduate students from Stevens's psychophysics laboratory to Skinner's pigeon laboratory. For Skinner, behaviorism's requirement of lab research for acolytes was sufficient justification for such shifts of allegiance, and if, as Stevens complained, it were really true that "psychology had deserted psychophysics," so much the better.[45]

Although Skinner's relationships with Boring and Stevens remained overtly cordial, his philosophical differences with them (and other departmental colleagues) left him with scant grounds for identifying with the department. By the midfifties, his sense of alienation from Harvard psychology had become acute. He wrote that the department was "no longer of interest" to him, doubted whether psychology would be important at Harvard, and even considered a plan to escape the department by moving to Harvard's School of Education.[46]

NONPSYCHOLOGIST ALLIES

In the last analysis, there may be no better indication of the vigor with which Skinner pursued his calling amid the institutional settings provided by Harvard than his ability to attract allies from areas outside psychology. The phenomenon of nonpsychologists at Harvard infusing their own work with behaviorist principles after forming personal relationships with Skinner suggests the force of Skinner's commitment not only to a science of behavior, but to its application across as wide a range of intellectual endeavors as possible. This, finally, represents that brand of cultural leadership that, in the view of sociologists, separates the intellectual from the mandarin: the willingness and ability to promote a vision with general applicability, as opposed to a "theory" or even a "paradigm" that necessarily remains within a specific disciplinary framework.

One of these allies was a sociologist himself, George Homans, whose subsequent work on the social dynamics of small groups would represent one of the most significant beachheads Skinnerian behaviorism would establish in a related field of social science. Homans, a protégé of Henderson, first met Skinner in the Society of Fellows at Harvard in the midthirties. To Homans, Skinner was a standout from the beginning, someone who even then radiated "effortless superiority, which was innate."[47] Actually, Skinner seems to have been working hard to make an impression. Each Junior Fellow was expected to bring a copy of every publication he produced to the attention of the entire society, and the scale of Skinner's output was, to Homans, downright intimidating. "It seemed to me that Fred Skinner, for instance, placed a reprint of some new article on the table at least once a week, snowing under a person like me."[48]

If Skinner's immediate impact on Homans was sharp, his long-term effects proved lasting and powerful. Homans was studying both psychology and social anthropology under Elton Mayo at the Harvard Business School's Department of Industrial Research. Like Skinner, his prime concerns were intellectual and epistemological. As he would later write, his interest in sociology was not in its possibilities

> as agent of change or as a means of understanding my immediate environment, but as a generalizing science. What were the best possibilities for establishing generalizations? What were the main intellectual issues?[49]

By the time he returned to Harvard as a faculty member in the Department of Social Relations, Homans was committed to a version of the "covering-law" model of hypothetico-deductive science, wherein explanation consists of the logical derivation of specific "explicanda" from propositions of ever-higher orders of generality. In explaining the interpersonal dynamics he observed in small groups, it was Skinnerian propositions that Homans employed as the highest and most general of his explanatory principles. In his famous "exchange theory," elemental social behavior became a fairly stark function of its payoffs.[50] He would spend much of his career promoting an explicitly Skinnerian "psychological reductionism," arguing that "the principles of behavioral psychology are the general propositions we use, whether implicitly or explicitly, in explaining all social phenomena," and that failure to accept that approach was attributable largely to mistaken views of the nature of theory.[51]

Perhaps the most illustrious of Skinner's nonpsychologist allies at Harvard was the renowned philosopher Willard Van Orman Quine. Like Homans, Quine met Skinner through the Society of Fellows, where both were Junior Fellows. As Quine would later write, "Fred and I were congenial, sharing an interest in language and a behavioristic bias in psychology. . . . It was particularly in language theory . . . that Fred opened doors for me."[52] The two quickly became "great friends," and appeared to enjoy puncturing the formality of the society's meetings.[53] Quine commented approvingly on Skinner's *Behavior of Organisms* upon its publication in 1938, supported Skinner's extended labors in writing the manuscript that eventually became *Verbal Behavior,* and even encouraged Skinner to found an experimental community based on Walden Two.[54] For his part, Skinner felt that Quine's treatment of logic "came close to what I wanted" in terms of a behavioral analysis of logic; in *Verbal Behavior,* he referred to Quine's early work on logic as "very revealing" and praised him for being "concerned with an empirical analysis of the function of verbal behavior."[55] While at the University of Minnesota, he initiated an (unsuccessful) effort to hire Quine in the Department of Philosophy there.[56] Upon Skinner's return to Harvard in 1948, their personal relationship was renewed, and they remained friends and mutual admirers for life.

Although Quine had already acquired behaviorist sympathies while an undergraduate at Oberlin College,[57] these sympathies were reinforced by the strong interests he shared with Skinner in the behavioral analysis of language and in its implications for ontology and epistemology. Just as Skinner viewed consciousness as a by-product of verbal behavior generated by a language community, Quine adopted "the strategy of looking to speech to escape the mentalistic ontology of thoughts."[58] His behaviorist view of language learning would later form the cornerstone of his controversial positions on meaning, reference, and the indeterminacy of translation. Quine's behaviorism also figured crucially in his famous naturalization of epistemology, according to which epistemology would become a branch of natural science, specifically behavioristic psychology.[59] As in the case of Skinner's own lesser-known behavioral epistemology, the upshot was a striking rejection of traditional representational theories of knowledge, with their dualism of knower and known, and a dethronement of epistemology from its traditional status as a branch of transcendental philosophy.[60] The radical vision shared by Skinner and Quine at Harvard in the mid-1930s issued in an influential new direction in Western culture's understanding of knowledge processes.[61] Despite spending their careers in separate professional spheres, the two proved to be formidable allies in an important kind of cultural leadership.

CONCLUSION

What the foregoing review of Skinner's professional relations at Harvard seems to indicate is that his relationships most often served his intellectual agenda, that they were in fact largely epiphenomenal to his intellectual interests. We find scant evidence of efforts by Skinner to ingratiate himself with individuals or social elements that would promote his career in conventional terms. Instead, we find much to suggest that he fashioned and deployed his personal relationships to promote the behaviorist cause. The difference may seem subtle, but it is significant. It suggests that, in Skinner's own mind, the object of his labors was never simply a successful career in psychology. Behaviorism as he understood it was not intellectual capital to be traded for professional prominence and the proximity to power it would have entailed. In Skinner's case, at least, the "mandarin" scenario fails; behaviorism was his "higher and wider truth," a culture-regenerating—indeed, world-transforming— mission to which other activities were properly subordinated. As early as 1928, he had written Percy Saunders that a career in psychology might entail "making over the entire field to suit myself."[62] That, of course, is exactly what he proceeded to do.[63]

A full awareness of this is useful in attaining a sound understanding of Skinner himself and, perhaps more important, behaviorism as he conceptualized it. For it reminds us that, whatever the merits of the "social technology" interpretation of behaviorism (the interpretation manifest in the "mandarinism" interpretation of behaviorism by some sociologists), Skinner's own vision was richer, more expansive, more radical, in ways we do well to consider. He clearly saw more in it than do those who interpret his movement as mere social technology, and perhaps more than do many practicing behaviorists themselves.[64]

There are many, sociologists and others, who contend that the epistemological norms of positivist science, when embraced by those who investigate society and human behavior, tend to preclude cultural—that is, moral—leadership. These critics tend to see the social and behavioral sciences as so inextricably tied to the objectivist, predictive, and ultimately manipulative agenda of natural science that their once-lively critical function has been lost, and practitioners' sense of their role in the maintenance and reform of culture has been sacrificed. But Skinner embraced those epistemological norms in the most uncompromising and enthusiastic way, and yet his comportment at Harvard was anything but mandarinesque.

What might Skinner have seen in those norms that his critics do not recognize? How could the norms have served, for him, as the basis of a radical, culture-building enterprise, when so many others see in them only echos of the prediction-and-control dynamic of the natural sciences? How did he extract from them the driving force for an intellectual's calling, rather than a mandarin's career? Such questions, though outside the domain of this essay, are pointedly raised by it.

For it was a calling, not a career, that seems to have guided B. F. Skinner socially at Harvard and, for that matter, everywhere else.

NOTES

The author and editors wish to acknowledge the assistance of Sande Webster during the early stages of research for this chapter. Responsibility for its present contents and their interpretation rests, of course, with the author.

1. Talcott Parsons, "The Intellectuals: A Social Role Category," in *On Intellectuals,* ed. Philip Rieff (New York: Doubleday, 1969), pp. 3–24, on p. 3.

2. Historically, the most eloquent articulation of this position may still be Julien Benda, *The Treason of the Intellectuals,* trans. Richard Aldington (New York: Norton, 1969). Sociologically, the position owes much to Karl Mannheim's classic formulation of intellectuals "floating free" of any particular social structure or interest (Mannheim, *Ideology and Utopia* [New York: Harcourt, 1968]). For a valuable exposition, see Lewis Coser, *Men of Ideas: A Sociologist's View* (New York: Free Press, 1965).

3. J. P. Nettl, "Ideas, Intellectuals, and Structures of Dissent," in *On Intellectuals,* pp. 53–122. Edward Shils, "The Intellectuals and the Powers: Some Perspectives From Comparative Analysis," *Comparative Studies in Society and History* 1 (October 1958): 5–22.

4. C. Wright Mills was a particularly influential critic of social technocracy in American society. See his "Social Role of the Intellectual" and "On Knowledge and Power," in *Power, Politics, and People: The Collected Essays of C. Wright Mills,* ed. Irving Louis Horowitz (London: Oxford University Press, 1967). For the application of a similar argument to Skinner himself, see Isaac Prilleltensky, "On the Social Legacy of B. F. Skinner: Rhetoric of Change, Philosophy of Adjustment," *Theory & Psychology* 4 (1994): 125–37.

5. Nettl reminds us that the term came from "what has possibly been the most stable and conservative regime and society in history, the Chinese Empire," and that it essentially co-mingles "the articulate bureaucrat" with "the supportive intellectual" (Nettl, "Structures of Dissent," in *On Intellectuals,* p. 86).

6. For a recent example of this line of thought on academe, see Russell Jacoby, *The Last Intellectuals: American Culture in the Age of Academe* (New York: Basic, 1987).

7. See, for example, Jurgen Habermas, *On the Logic of Social Science,* trans. Sherry Weber Nicholson and Jerry A. Stark (Cambridge: MIT Press, 1988).

8. See, for example, Daniel W. Bjork, *B. F. Skinner: A Life* (New York: Basic,

1993); S.˙R. Coleman, "B. F. Skinner: Systematic Iconoclast," *The Gamut* 6 (1982): 53–75; Coleman, "B. F. Skinner, 1926–1928: From Literature to Psychology," *Behavior Analyst* 8 (spring 1985): 77–92; and Nils Wiklander, "From Hamilton College to Walden Two: An Inquiry into B. F. Skinner's Early Social Philosophy," this volume.

9. Coser, *Men of Ideas*, p. viii.

10. Skinner to W. P. Shepard, 18 April 1935, B. F. Skinner Papers (hereafter referred to as BFSP), Harvard University Archives, Cambridge, Mass.

11. Skinner to Edward M. Freeman, 18 March 1937, BFSP.

12. Coleman, "Literature to Psychology."

13. Ibid.

14. Laurence D. Smith, *Behaviorism and Logical Positivism: A Reassessment of the Alliance* (Stanford, Calif.: Stanford University Press, 1986).

15. Skinner, *The Shaping of a Behaviorist* (New York: Knopf, 1979), p. 80.

16. Ibid., p. 37.

17. John J. Cerullo, "E. G. Boring: Reflections on a Discipline-Builder," *American Journal of Psychology* 101 (winter 1988): 561–75.

18. Skinner, *A Matter of Consequences* (New York: New York University Press, 1984), p. 17.

19. Coleman, "When Historians Disagree: B. F. Skinner and E. G. Boring, 1930," *The Psychological Record* 35 (1985): 301–14. For Skinner's own account of his thinking on this subject at the time, see his "Concept of the Reflex in the Description of Behavior," in *Cumulative Record,* enl. ed. (New York: Appleton-Century-Crofts, 1961), pp. 319–46 (original work published 1931).

20. Marginal notes, Skinner to E. G. Boring, 9 December 1930, BFSP.

21. E. G. Boring to Skinner, 13 October 1930, BFSP.

22. Ibid.

23. Marginal notes, Ibid. (emphasis added).

24. Skinner to Percy Saunders, 6 January 1931, BFSP.

25. E. G. Boring to Frank A. Lillie, NRC, 19 December 1930, BFSP.

26. Skinner, *Shaping,* pp. 49, 65, 115.

27. E. G. Boring to Skinner, 2 December 1946, BFSP.

28. Philip J. Pauly, "General Physiology and the Discipline of Psychology, 1890–1935," in *Physiology in the American Context,* ed. G. L. Seison (Bethesda, Md.: American Physiological Society, 1987), pp. 195–208.

29. Skinner, "A Case History in Scientific Method," in *Cumulative Record,* enl. ed. (New York: Appleton-Century-Crofts, 1961), pp. 76–100, on p. 80.

30. E. G. Boring to Frank A. Lillie, NRC, 19 December 1930, BFSP.

31. Skinner, "Case History," p. 80.

32. Skinner, *Shaping,* p. 14.

33. Ibid., p. 80. For his part, Fred S. Keller regarded Skinner as "not only a comrade in arms, but a leader and a friend"; see Keller, "Burrhus Frederic Skinner (1904–1990)," *Journal of the History of the Behavioral Sciences* 27 (1991): 3–6, on p. 4.

34. Keller, "Psychology at Harvard (1926–1931): A Reminiscence," in *Festschrift for B. F. Skinner,* ed. P. B. Dews (New York: Appleton-Century-Crofts, 1970), pp. 29–36, on pp. 34–35.

35. Ibid., pp. 34–35; Skinner, *Shaping,* p. 35.

36. Keller, "Reminiscence," in *Festschrift for B. F. Skinner,* p. 35.

37. Keller and William N. Schoenfeld, *Principles of Psychology* (New York: Appleton-Century-Crofts, 1950). On the Columbia courses, see Skinner, *Shaping,*

pp. 306–7; and Keller and Schoenfeld, "The Psychology Curriculum at Columbia College," *American Psychologist* 4 (1949): 165–72.

38. Skinner, *Shaping*, pp. 11–12.

39. Skinner, *Matter of Consequences*, p. 138.

40. Skinner, *Shaping*, p. 49.

41. Ibid., p. 131.

42. S. S. Stevens, "Notes for an Autobiography," S. S. Stevens Papers, Harvard University Archives, Cambridge, Mass.

43. Stevens, "Psychology and the Science of Science," *Psychological Bulletin* 36 (1939): 221–63.

44. Ibid., p. 231.

45. Stevens, "Notes," p. 30. For further discussion of the relationship between the two laboratories, see John K. Robinson and William R. Woodward, "Experimental Analysis of Behavior at Harvard: From Cumulative Records to Mathematical Models," this volume.

46. Skinner, *Matter of Consequences*, p. 72.

47. George Homans, *Coming to My Senses: The Autobiography of a Sociologist* (New Brunswick, N.J.: Transaction Books, 1984), p. 126.

48. Ibid.

49. Homans, *Sentiments and Activities: Essays in Social Science* (New York: Free Press, 1962), pp. 9–10.

50. Homans, *Social Behavior: Its Elementary Forms* (New York: Harcourt, 1961).

51. Homans, *Autobiography*, p. 204.

52. W. V. Quine, *The Time of My Life: An Autobiography* (Cambridge: MIT Press, Bradford Books, 1985), p. 110.

53. W. V. Quine to Laurence D. Smith, 8 December 1980 (letter in possession of recipient); Giovanna Borradori, *The American Philosopher: Conversations with Quine, Davidson, Putnam, Nozick, Danto, Rorty, Cavell, MacIntyre, and Kuhn*, trans. Rosanna Crocitto (Chicago: University of Chicago Press, 1994), p. 35; Skinner, *Shaping*, pp. 131, 132.

54. Skinner, *Shaping*, pp. 221–22, 151; Skinner, *Matter of Consequences*, p. 9.

55. Skinner, *Matter of Consequences*, p. 395; Skinner, *Verbal Behavior* (New York: Appleton-Century-Crofts, 1957), p. 342.

56. Skinner, *Shaping*, p. 249.

57. Quine, *Time of My Life*, p. 110; Skinner, *Matter of Consequences*, p. 174. Quine has recorded that he "had already imbibed behaviorism in about 1928 in Raymond Stetson's course at Oberlin, where we were assigned Watson's *Psychology from the Standpoint of a Behaviorist*" (Quine to Smith, 8 December 1980). For an example of the widespread but mistaken impression that Skinner introduced Quine to behaviorism, see Max Hocutt, review of *Enlightened Empiricism: An Examination of W. V. Quine's Theory of Knowledge*, by Roger F. Gibson, Jr., in *Behavior and Philosophy* 18 (1990): 69–72, on p. 69.

58. Quine, "Sellars on Behaviorism, Language and Meaning," *Pacific Philosophical Quarterly* 61 (1980): 26–30, on p. 26. For Skinner's analysis of consciousness, see his "Operational Analysis of Psychological Terms," *Psychological Review* 52 (1945): 270–77, 291–94.

59. On the central role played by Quine's behaviorism in his characteristic philosophical doctrines, see Roger F. Gibson, Jr., *The Philosophy of W. V. Quine: An Expository Essay* (Tampa: University Presses of Florida, 1982); and Gibson,

Enlightened Empiricism: An Examination of W. V. Quine's Theory of Knowledge (Gainesville: University Presses of Florida, 1988).

60. Ibid.; Richard Rorty, *Philosophy and the Mirror of Nature* (Princeton: Princeton University Press, 1979), chap. 4. On Skinner's behavioral epistemology, see Smith, *Behaviorism and Positivism,* chap. 9. The mutual influence of Skinner and Quine on each other's epistemological views is a matter that needs further historical study. Given the eminence that both achieved, the dearth of literature on their intellectual relationship is surprising. For one discussion, see the afterword "Epistemology Skinnerized," in Paul T. Sagal, *Skinner's Philosophy* (Lanham, Md.: University Press of America, 1981), pp. 103–20.

61. Quine is widely considered to be a central player—often *the* central player—in instigating the postpositivist revolution in epistemology. Quine's role, which predates Thomas Kuhn's, began with his classic essay "Two Dogmas of Empiricism," *Philosophical Review* 60 (1951): 20–43. For Kuhn's acknowledgment of Quine's influence, see Kuhn, *The Structure of Scientific Revolutions,* 2d enl. ed. (Chicago: University of Chicago Press, 1970), p. vi. The recent flourishing of naturalized epistemologies attests to Quine's continuing influence; see, for example, Ronald N. Giere, *Explaining Science: A Cognitive Approach* (Chicago: University of Chicago Press, 1988); and Alvin I. Goldman, *Epistemology and Cognition* (Cambridge: Harvard University Press, 1986).

62. Skinner to Percy Saunders, 15 December 1928, BFSP.

63. Skinner's aim to remake the field of psychology has been criticized by Robert W. Proctor and Daniel J. Weeks (*The Goal of B. F. Skinner and Behavior Analysis* [New York: Springer-Verlag, 1990]) as having set the pattern for a single-minded intellectual intolerance among proponents of the operant tradition. Although the analysis of Proctor and Weeks is in some ways congruent with the present account of how Skinner negotiated his social world at Harvard, their conclusion that Skinner's crusading role in advancing the operant viewpoint was more promotional than substantive is clearly at odds with the present thesis about Skinner's larger role in providing intellectual leadership.

64. This is not to deny that behavioral technologies have often been used in ways that serve the vested interests of social powers, or that many behaviorists have followed mandarinesque career paths; rather it underscores that Skinner's own failure to follow such a path may shed light on the radical aspects of his vision for both psychology and society. On Skinner's radicalism, see "Interview With B. F. Skinner," *Behaviorists for Social Action Journal* 2 (1979): 47–52; and Laurence D. Smith, "Situating B. F. Skinner and Behaviorism in American Culture," this volume.

4
The Diversification and Extension
of Behaviorism

10

B. F. Skinner and the Origins of Programmed Instruction

E. A. VARGAS AND JULIE S. VARGAS

BEGINNINGS

THE eleventh of November 1953, in a fourth-grade classroom: Father's Day at Shady Hill School. Milling among those parents watching the mathematics lesson was B. F. Skinner. As he later described the class:

> The students were at their desks solving a problem written on the blackboard. The teacher walked up and down the aisles, looking at their work, pointing to a mistake here and there. A few students soon finished and were impatiently idle. Others, with growing frustration, strained. Eventually the papers were collected to be taken home, graded, and returned the next day.[1]

Having spent eighteen years researching and shaping behavior in the laboratory, it appalled Skinner to watch what was (and probably still is) a normal math class. As he trenchantly put it,

> the teacher was violating two fundamental principles: the students were not being told at once whether their work was right or wrong (a corrected paper seen 24 hours later could not act as a reinforcer), and they were all moving at the same pace regardless of preparation or ability.
>
> But how could a teacher reinforce the behavior of each of 20 or 30 students at the right time and on the material for which he or she was just then ready?[2]

Clearly automation was needed.

Skinner reacted immediately. Richard Herrnstein in a later recollection mentions that he and another graduate student were to meet Skinner that same day for a lecture at the Massachusetts Institute of Technology. Arriving early, they found him sitting in an empty auditorium, busy cut-

237

ting up manila folders. When asked what he was doing, Skinner replied, "I'm making a model of a teaching machine."[3]

A Drill-and-Practice Machine

From the manila folder model, Skinner built his first teaching machine. Though lacking elegant looks, it nevertheless solved the problems of providing feedback and letting students go at their own rates. This first machine provided "drill and practice": students were to have learned how to solve problems before working on the machine. Though not designed to build new behaviors, it would replace the exercises that dismayed Skinner during his visit to the math class.

When ready to work on the machine, a student would bring a pile of cards to it. Inserting a card brought a problem to a window. The student moved metal sliders to set the two digits of his or her answer in a space off to the right of the problem. When the student was ready to check an answer, he or she pressed a button; that action locked the sliders in place and turned on a light. If the student answered correctly, the light showed through a hole in the card, making the answer visible to the student. If the answer was not correct, releasing the locking lever enabled the student to rearrange the sliders and to try again. The student proceeded to the next problem by replacing the card in the machine with another from the pile.

The critical characteristics of the first of Skinner's teaching machines were thus three. It required students to produce answers as opposed to picking one from among a set of alternatives. It provided immediate feedback to students on the correctness of their responses without revealing correct answers in case of error. It permitted each student to progress at his or her own rate. This first machine tested rather than taught.

Revisions appeared quickly. A larger version of the slider teaching machine soon replaced the first model. This larger machine permitted problems with answers of up to nine digits. A second improvement employed paper tape instead of punched cards. The tape provided the opportunity for the instructional designer to sequence problems—and the possibility of *shaping* behavior rather than just providing practice and checking answers.

Earlier Drill-and-Practice Machines

Long before Skinner's first teaching machine, many other "teaching" devices had been invented. The U.S. Patent Office records dozens of patents for teaching devices prior to 1900, beginning with "Mode of

Teaching to Read" in 1809 and continuing into the 1900s.[4] The machines were as varied as the concerns of their inventors. For example, in 1914 Maria Montessori obtained a patent in this country on a device designed to "adapt (children's) mental and muscular system to express itself in the form of writing,"[5] and others offered apparatuses to teach walking, dancing, and boxing. The military also made early use of devices to teach. In 1918, H. B. English utilized a column of liquid to give visual feedback to soldiers on how well they were squeezing rifle triggers. If the column rose smoothly they were squeezing evenly, if it jerked, the pull was uneven.[6] No doubt, other earlier teaching devices of the same sort appeared, that is, ones that primarily employed feedback to enhance practice effects, but without any clear analysis of the functional effect of the postcedent stimulus as reinforcer or punisher or its relation to a schedule of delivery.[7] None made much headway, except for Sidney Pressey's.

In 1923 Pressey, working at Ohio State University, invented "A Simple Apparatus Which Gives Tests and Scores—and Teaches."[8] Pressey's machine presented items with up to four multiple-choice options. It could tally correct answers, and the number of tries for incorrect answers. In writing about his machine, Pressey reported,

> It . . . tells the subject at once when he makes a mistake (there is no waiting several days, until a corrected paper is returned, before he knows where he is right and where wrong). It keeps each question on which he makes an error before him until he finds the right answer; he must get the correct answer to each question before he can go on to the next.[9]

Items mastered could be dropped from those the student encountered on repeated testings, and the machine even included a metal shoot, out of which candy would drop when the subject made a preset number of correct responses.

In the 1920s, Pressey also tried using punchboards that held an answer sheet on top of thick cardboard containing holes for the answer key. When a student pressed a pin or pencil under his choice, it would puncture the paper only if over a correct answer hole, but leave marks for wrong answers.[10] A 1948 variant revealed a red spot through correct holes.[11] In 1931, a student of Pressey's, J. C. Peterson, devised "chemo-sheets," answer sheets that turned blue when the spot for the correct multiple-choice answer was correct, but that turned red if incorrect.[12] Another of Pressey's students, Leslie J. Briggs, worked with the Air Force in designing a "Subject-matter Trainer." This machine, looking like the front half of a pinball machine, presented a panel of twenty windows with a button next to each. A question or name appeared in the window, and the trainee, standing in front of the panel, pushed the button for the matching response.[13]

In all of the devices deriving from Pressey's work, the series of questions and answers could not be called programmed instruction in any sense: the machines simply gave feedback following responses to multiple-choice items presented in random order. The testing format lacked a careful shaping of the answer through, for example, formal and thematic prompting. The only "teaching" occurred when a student who had made an error was shown the answer that should have been selected. When the devices were used for training, students typically made many errors and retook the same sets of problems over and over before reaching mastery.

But in spite of their inability to allow for shaping, these early multiple-choice testing machines, compared to quizzes without feedback, increased scores on final exams. In an overview of relevant studies, Pressey asserted that

> If test materials or simple testing devices could be developed such that, as a student answered each question, that answer was immediately and automatically scored and recorded as right or wrong, then clearly much trouble would be saved. . . .
>
> Additional advantages of self-scoring devices are more important, however. A test in French or mathematics or navigation is of little value if it does not in some way further the student's learning of that subject.[14]

His investigations showed

> *that when the self-instructional tests were used systematically in college courses as an integral part of the teaching method, gains were substantial, and sufficiently generalized to improve understanding of a topic as a whole—even help on related topics.*[15]

As he later wrote in his autobiography,

> Carefully controlled experiments evidenced that class use of this . . . machine [the punchboard] as an instructional aid significantly increased learning as measured by midterm and final examinations.[16]

Other studies of such "test-scoring and drill devices" (a phrase of James Kenneth Little, one of Pressey's students) had given the same results.[17]

Despite the successes, however, the revolution in instructional technology that Pressey hoped for did not transpire. His efforts to change education and to interest business in his self-scoring machines were to no avail. He continued those efforts sporadically, but his disappointment is captured by his 1932 statement: "The writer had found from bitter experience that one person alone can accomplish relatively little and he is regretfully dropping work on these problems."[18]

From Drill-and-Practice to Shaping

Skinner, tinkering in his shop to produce new versions of teaching machines, did not yet know about Pressey's work. On 12 March 1954, just four months after visiting his younger daughter's class, he presented his first paper on teaching machines, "The Science of Learning and the Art of Teaching."[19] The paper described a teaching technology evolving from the experimental analysis of behavior and set forth the basis for that technology. Skinner demonstrated the paper tape version of the teaching machine and listed its important features. They included the constructed response, the go-at-your-own-rate, and the immediate-reinforcement features from earlier machines, but also some additional advantages.

> The device makes it possible to present carefully designed material in which one problem can depend upon the answer to the preceding problem and where, therefore, the most efficient progress to an eventually complex repertoire can be made. Provision has been made for recording the commonest mistakes so that the tapes can be modified as experience dictates. Additional steps can be inserted where pupils tend to have trouble, and ultimately the material will reach a point at which the answers of the average child will almost always be right.[20]

Thus Skinner described three new features: programming (sequencing problems in complexity but with characteristics that shaped the student's response); cybernetic feedback (student behavior providing data to improve just those parts of a sequence that were ineffective); and error-free (as much as possible) progression of the student.[21]

The spring of 1955 found Skinner on sabbatical leave at Putney, Vermont, finishing his analysis of language soon to be published as *Verbal Behavior*.[22] He realized that a number of things he was saying in *Verbal Behavior* applied to the instructional setting. The teaching of the kinds of verbal behaviors that made up a large part of most subject matters involved subtleties of stimulus control like those he was discussing under the headings of prompting, probing, priming, vanishing, and fading. Skinner began to differentiate between simply presenting harder and harder problems and an "entirely new type of educational program" that would use the principles detailed in *Verbal Behavior* to shape new behavior.[23] The first time an answer was to be written it had to be "primed" by providing directions and examples using the student's imitative or direction-following repertoire to guarantee a correct response. After having written the correct response under conditions that essentially gave away the answer, the student would probably still need formal prompting (being given part of the response) or thematic prompting (hints related to the relevant variables controlling the desired response). These supplementary stimuli or aids would be gradually withdrawn by removing parts of text or drawings (called vanishing) or by making them increasingly hard to see by lightening print, decreasing size or contrast, or reducing thematic help (fading). Linear programming, as Skinner's careful sequencing of frames came to be called, was born—gradually.

The earlier "slider" machine could not shape complex responses. Like Pressey's machines, it only presented feedback to selected items. While at Putney, however, Skinner designed a little program about procrastination for his younger daughter Deborah. This program consisted of cards with blanks to fill in—his first nonmachine programmed instruction. By April 1955, Skinner had built a new "disk" machine that enabled students to write or draw answers to frames that appeared through an opening in the top of the machine.

> The material is printed on twelve-inch disks exposed one sector at a time. The pupil writes an answer on an exposed strip of paper, then moves a lever which covers his answer with a transparent mask, and reveals the correct answer. If he is right, he moves the lever in a different direction. This punctures the paper to record his judgment, and moves a detente so that the material does not appear again, or will appear only once again as the disk revolves. [When the lever was moved back in place, a new frame appeared.] After finishing the disk, the student tears out the strip of paper and puts it in a file to record his progress.[24]

Skinner had constructed a machine to handle material that was *programmed,* as well as to provide problems and feedback.

But the distinction between Skinner's programmed instruction machine and earlier "teaching" machines was not well understood. Nothing illustrates this better than an attempted priority claim initiated by H. B. English. In a letter to E. G. Boring in January 1958, English protested against the overlooking of Pressey's role in the development of the teaching machine, fulminated indignantly that Skinner was given credit for its origination, and wondered whether Skinner even knew of Pressey's contribution.[25] In fact, Skinner had written to Pressey, almost three years earlier, in November 1955, and though requesting a paper, he was obviously maintaining a contact already established.

> Dear Professor Pressey:
>   I am still hoping to do a short general article on teaching machines. Now I

find that I have somehow lost a reference to your work dating back to 1915. The earliest paper to which I have a reference is dated 1926, but I am sure I remember an earlier paper. Was it by any chance your thesis? In any case, can you give me the reference?

I am still not getting the kind of support I need to move full steam ahead in this area. I am, however, preparing material in beginning arithmetic, and hope to have some kinds of machines for classroom test next fall.[26]

Boring replied to the letter by English. In his letter, Boring interpreted Skinner's description of his work as "a slight claim toward originality."[27] Boring's letter indicated that he, along with English and others, did not understand Skinner's instructional technology. However, the difference between Skinner's programmed teaching machine and earlier drill-and-practice machines was far from slight.

Skinner pointed to this difference in his article and in his book *Technology of Teaching*,[28] and noted the misunderstanding in his letters. In an earlier letter, he had stated, "My own device was aimed not so much at immediate reinforcement, although the newspapers emphasized that point, as at the programming of the material to be learned."[29] And in a letter to Robert M. Gagne, then technical director of the Armament Systems Personnel Research Laboratory at the Lowry Air Force Base, Skinner wrote:

Following the pioneer work of S. J. Pressey in the field of mechanized education, there has obviously been a broad realization of the need of mechanical devices to simplify and extend the educational process. However all of these seem to me to be based upon rather outmoded theories of learning. . . . I have been impressed by the fact that such machines make it possible to approach the matter of teaching in an entirely new way. . . . What the teaching machine does is to permit the experimenter or teacher to arrange a very much larger number of contingencies for the student than could possibly be the case in personal instruction. And this makes it possible to analyze the nature of the behavior to be taught and to design an entirely new type of educational program.[30]

Furthermore, Skinner's teaching machine did not simply present new items to the student. As he pointed out in distinguishing between his and Pressey's approach, as well as those of others,

Pressey assumed that the student had studied a subject before coming to the testing machine, but some modern versions also present the material on which the student is to be tested. They thus imitate, and could presumably replace, the teacher. But holding a student responsible for assigned material is not teaching, even though it is a large part of modern school and university practice. It is simply a way of inducing the student to learn without being taught.[31]

By applying a new science to the old problem of instruction, the programmed teaching machine produced a discontinuous jump in the evolution of the teaching machine.

The development of programmed instruction and its distinctive feature as a *shaping technique* marks the leap from Skinner's first slider teaching machine to the disk teaching machine. The slider machine, though able to sequence problems, emphasized drill-and-practice and feedback to incorrect and correct answers. It strengthened the topography of a repertoire already in place. The disk machine, however, emphasized the development of a new complex verbal repertoire through a gradual buildup of its "parts," or more accurately, of its operant characteristics. Behavior could be shaped by applying the techniques outlined in *Verbal Behavior.*[32]

Skinner's instructional technology exemplified the move from a transformationist to a selectionist interpretation of behavior. The former is indicated by a stimulus→organism→response formulation, however subtle, in which psychological events in the students or in their minds determine their performance. In the latter, actions are the prime focus of analysis, and changes in well-defined topographies of action are brought about by contingencies designed to increase their frequency, or to evoke them, or to do both in combination. A machine, like the classroom, was only an opportunity to arrange by proper programming those contingencies that could strengthen existing behavior, produce new behavior, or generate novel behavior. In Skinner's technology of teaching, there was no interest in feedback, per se, or in forming connections.[33]

DEVELOPMENT

In the winter of 1956, back from his sabbatical, Skinner submitted a proposal to the Ford Foundation "for the investigation of the use of mechanical teaching aids in elementary college instruction."[34] That spring the Fund for the Advancement of Education awarded the grant for research "directed toward more effective utilization of faculty resources," stating in its cover letter that

> the experiment will involve the building of ten mechanical self-testing devices adapted to college teaching in elementary languages and science, and requiring creative thinking on the part of the student. This will, if successful, free the instructor from routine tasks in basic courses and enable him to spend more time on counseling and guidance. We understand that these will go far beyond present devices and will permit immediate grading of multiple response answers, require the student to compose an answer, thus demanding creative activity rather than mere recognition.[35]

Once the project had started, other agencies also provided support or expressed interest.

> The Army, through its contracting agency, Human Resources Research Office, Washington, D.C., offered us a small contract to be executed concurrently with the Fund Project, and this is being continued through a second year. The Navy Special Devices Center at Port Washington, New York, asked permission to duplicate the improved model of the machine. . . . The Air Force had prepared a review of the work at Harvard on teaching machines; it is now looking for a man to undertake similar research work under its auspices.[36]

Skinner moved the project into an old ramshackle place called Batchelder House. Joining the project were Lloyd Homme, on leave for a year from the University of Pittsburgh, Irving Saltzman on leave from Indiana University, and several graduate students (Susan Meyer [later Markle], Douglas Porter, and Matthew Israel). Terminology evolved. The term *frame* was coined to designate the basic unit of instruction. Providing examples and asking the student to derive rules from examples (induction) was named "egrule" and its opposite process (deduction) labeled "ruleg." "Size of step" referred to how rapidly a program built a repertoire (roughly the inverse of the number of frames required to teach a particular skill), and was tied to "density of errors" (the percent of frames on which mistakes were made by a particular student population). The technique of "branching" was also explored for students who made errors.

With grant support in hand and clear objectives ahead, the team took up the task of writing programs.

> Materials prepared and informally tested during the year include a series of approximately 1500 frames covering areas essential to the beginning physics student, such as trigonometry, coordinate systems, and vectors, as well as substantive work in kinematics. About 1000 frames have been designed for the teaching of beginning French, about 500 frames for beginning English composition, and several hundred frames for a special general education course in psychology (the latter will be incorporated in the program for teaching Natural Sciences 114 next spring.)[37]

Skinner also hired a machinist who produced ten disk machines, one of which was demonstrated at the American Psychological Association conference of 1957, along with a geography program.

James Holland joined the project for its second year (1957–1958), replacing Homme who returned to Pittsburgh. Holland described those early days.

For me it began when I arrived, in the fall of 1957, at a gray clap-board building, Batchelder House. Batchelder House, then in decay, had been a rambling residence just across the street from Harvard's Memorial Hall where the Psychology Department, including Skinner's office and laboratory, was housed. . . . Memories of those days in Batchelder House give me a special verification of humorist Francis Parkinson's claim that active, productive and innovative activities are to be found, not in new buildings which instead house moribund organizations, but in small, converted, understaffed, and unkept buildings.[38]

Holland's task consisted in helping Skinner put his course, Natural Sciences 114, on machine. The thirty wedges they could fit on a disk encouraged brevity and a high density of responding by students. Most frames asked students to fill in a missing word or to supply a technical term, a definition, or example. New instructional principles emerged. Blanks for responses should occur near the end of a sentence to avoid the slight adverseness of going back to write. Only stimuli required for the response should be included in a frame. To find out what part of a frame was critical for correct responding, Holland devised the blackout technique.[39] Portions of a frame were inked out to see how well students could perform with those parts missing. Parts that could be removed without affecting what the student wrote clearly did not contain material critical to responding. When material irrelevant to learning the instructional task efficiently was included, the instruction did not meet the requirements for being programmed.[40]

The next semester, spring 1958, Harvard and Radcliffe students went to the teaching machine room and worked on the disks before attending Skinner's lectures. The course proved to be popular. As Skinner later described it, Natural Sciences 114

has been given for eight years, and the enrollment is usually about 115. . . . At the early meetings of the course the teaching machine was explained, and students were invited to try out certain preliminary disks in the Self-Instruction Room. . . . The prospect of studying by machine was apparently responsible for an increase in enrollment to 187. Sophomores were most heavily represented, although there were many juniors and seniors, and a number of freshman admitted on special petition. The group also included twelve graduate students. . . .

Some disks were available at the beginning of the course and more were available as time passed. The students were asked to complete all the machine work by the end of the first two months. Forty-eight disks were prepared, each usually carrying 29 frames of material. Among the subjects covered were reflexes and Pavlovian conditioning, operant conditioning, discrimination, motivation, emotion, techniques of personal control, and illustrated or demonstrated material, in which the students were required to analyze and comment upon experiments, illustrative episodes, and so on. This was the basic "scientific" part of the course. Lectures and outside readings dealt with broader implications. Although the machine material overlapped the text to some extent there was very little in common between the frames and the lecture.[41]

By the end of a semester each of the 250 students had generated about 3,000 answers, providing Holland and Skinner with precise data on the items most frequently missed, as well as alternative correct answers. There were "wide individual differences among students," and the "typical student completed all 48 disks in about 14.5 hours."[42] Students filled out a questionnaire, adding additional comments if they liked, after they completed their machine work. Their sentiments and comments were overwhelmingly positive. They highly rated the teaching machine instruction on its value and on its ability to motivate them, and indicated their preference for similar instruction in the future. A specific item comparing machine instruction with studying a text such as, "When I read *Science and Human Behavior* after working through relevant material on the machine, I felt that the machine_____", obtained the following results: "1% of the respondents checked 'contributed nothing,' 37% checked 'was of some help,' and 62% checked 'made the text much easier to understand'." Even though the text involved was his own, written to be accessible to a lay audience, Skinner evidently was pleased by such results. For he stated in his report that

> Considering the fact that the student population was highly selected and contained many juniors and seniors of considerable college experience and high caliber it appears to be encouraging that 99% felt that the machine helped them understand the text, and that 70% felt that they learned more from the machine than from the text.[43]

After three cycles of tryout and revision, the program was published in 1961 in book form.[44]

MOTIVES

Skinner's special interest with education in general and instruction in specific was not simply the result of an accident of a father happening to attend his daughter's fourth-grade Open House. Many fathers visit their children's classes. Some are scientists. But by anyone's standard, just because of a classroom visit, it is unusual for a scientist to "suspend" his basic line of research and suddenly devote himself wholeheartedly to the revolutionizing of instructional practices. Skinner's chance visit evoked a primed set of concerns.

Skinner's concerns fitted the utopian themes continually found in his writings. These themes inevitably addressed how a science of behavior could be applied to better the human condition. In particular, he addressed how his basic discoveries could have practical applications. He felt that an acid test of a scientific assertion was the beneficial technologies that would ensue from it. In his very first book, *The Behavior of Organisms,* he raised this issue: "The importance of a science of behavior derives largely from the possibility of an eventual extension to human affairs."[45] Bettering the human condition was a theme he pursued throughout his life, and with particular energy in the area of education.

An excerpt of Skinner's notes from a running diary of daily events gives a flavor of some of his concerns.

6/12/67

A meeting of the Committee on Instruction yesterday. . . . Gerry Holton began to describe the need for new kinds of science teaching. . . . I finally spoke up. No one had asked what the student was to do as the result of having had a course in science. No one had asked what scientists do. No one had discussed the nature of teaching. Science was to be made interesting. But how? In ways which interest what kind of student? Why were so few high school students indicating (upon entrance into Harvard) that they wanted to be physicists and why did so few of them last? Why were we so frightened of teaching already known facts—because we have lost the needed control of the students? Were the "discoveries" students make anything like the discoveries scientists make? Was there really any point in the excited classroom? Doug Porter was then emboldened to ask why we went on with the lecture system. . . . Franklin Ford said that people like George Wald felt they got something out of the response of an audience. I said I was sure *George* did and perhaps it was worth saving the system for (I think they got my point), and I then pointed out some of the bad effects of a responsive audience in shaping a lecture. Afterwards I walked back with Ed Purcell. He said he had never thought of asking what he wanted his students to do.[46]

Skinner's questions made clear that there was an instructional technology in place at the university and that those who practiced it were not only complacent about it, but actually did not recognize that what they practiced was a technology of instruction. Lecturing, to them, was simply the way teaching was done and had always been done.

Skinner was always up-front about the necessity of "needed control" of the students' behavior. Such a recognition was required if teachers and principals were to take responsibility for their students' performances. The entire educational establishment appeared to operate on an "I win, You lose" axiom. If a student did well, teachers and principals congratulated themselves on that student's performance. Brochures announced the fact, and reports provided the statistics of all the exemplary accomplishments. What was not trumpeted were the failures. These failures were attributed to the students. It was their fault if they did not do well. They just did not "have it," or if bright enough, they did not have sufficient "desire to learn." For Skinner, such an easy disavowal of the responsibility of control came dangerously close to blaming victims for their difficulties.

Programmed instruction set the responsibility for teaching and learning where it belonged: in the contingencies that shaped behavior. The machine was only a means by which these contingencies could be delivered. It provided an opportunity to design the proper sequence of contingent instructional events for each individual. If done successfully, the students' own behavior would maintain their learning and continued efforts. No artificial rewards would be necessary. A classroom set another opportunity. After all, the classroom provides a space where people gather to be controlled by the contingencies the teacher puts into place. When those contingencies are designed properly, each student's variability is taken into account. But, as Skinner observed, skillful programming of the proper pace and the proper size of instructional step with respect to each individual repertoire rarely occurs in the typical classroom. With help from machines, however, teachers could provide the individualization necessary. Punishment and its disastrous outcomes could be avoided. If instructed properly, the student would be not only accomplished, but free and happy.[47]

Others saw these possibilities. Perhaps not as clearly, but with Skinner they shared a vision of the schoolhouse in which both successful teacher and student would reside. Skinner received hundreds of letters from anxious parents, from business people, and from professional educators. Each letter, implicitly, voiced a concern and a hope and an ambition. From a businessman:

Dear Dr. Skinner:

. . . I would appreciate it if you could send us any type of literature what so ever that would help us evaluate the advantages and disadvantages of teaching by machine. We have a staff of some twenty-five instructors that cover the entire United States teaching courses relating to life insurance. We are interested in knowing the quality of teaching, the depth of teaching, the retention of learning and the lack of an instructor when a machine is used in place of an instructor. If you have any information that would be helpful to us, we would appreciate knowing about them.

Thank you kindly for your attention to these matters. We are vitally interested, for a decision must be made in the near future.[48]

From a high school teacher:

My dear Professor Skinner,

. . . I have long advocated teaching a similarly "streamlined" shorthand for personal use. . . . However, despite my efforts, it seems impossible to find a spot in the already crowded program of the college-bound student into which shorthand for personal use can be "squeezed."

Having used it extensively in my own college career, I know how valuable to the student a short method of note taking can be, and I am wondering if your "programmed instruction," to be taken at the student's individual pace, would not be the answer. Indeed, the idea of working out such programmed instruction fascinates me.

Could you tell me how to pursue this idea further? Perhaps if you would give me the names of firms which manufacture the "teaching" machines, I could check with them on what has been done and on what the potentialities are for this kind of learning as far as "self-taught" shorthand would be concerned.

I know you are a busy man, but would appreciate what suggestions you may give me.[49]

From a parent in the Bronx:

Dear Dr. Skinner,

. . . . I am extremely interested in your methods due to the fact that my grand-daughter, who has cerebral palsy, has a great deal of difficulty with arithmetic. . . . Please let me know what progress has been made with this device. Is it now commercially available? If not, is it possible that it can be made available to me?

Anything you can do will be appreciated. I anxiously await your reply.[50]

Skinner took these letters seriously and answered every one. The letters raised to a high pitch his efforts to apply his science to education, for they confirmed the necessity of realizing his utopian dream of reforming education. They also, however, made more keen the failure of education to adopt an instructional technology that would be not only more effective but more humane.

CONCLUSION

In the last two sentences of the last paragraph of his last article on education Skinner stated, "Changing our schools will be troublesome. . . . In the long run better schools will . . . make the future of the world much brighter."[51] It was typical Skinner: recognizing the difficulties, yet being optimistic in spite of them.

Both the hardheaded worry and the idealistic faith were warranted. It typically takes a long time for a new technology to make its way when the successful execution of that technology demands a radical change in how a culture views events that the technology impacts. Only then are the fiscal and organizational changes made that make the technology feasible. But a preliminary and profound step is first demanded—the understanding and accepting of the science from which the technology ensued. The understanding and accepting of the science Skinner founded has been slow, and therefore the technologies based on that science are often misunderstood or rejected. The difficulty with successfully using a new instructional technology, and thus with teaching, lies in the general ignorance of the science dealing with its subject matter—behavior, especially human behavior. Not until this century could there be said to be a science of much merit. The science yet tells us little on how to handle many complex human problems, but it tells us enough to improve education dramatically. As the science that Skinner founded becomes more accepted by the educational establishment, the instructional technology he devised three decades ago will be given the attention it deserves, and his hope that schools could be designed so that students learn enthusiastically and effectively will be realized.

NOTES

Portions of this article were previously published in E. A. Vargas and Julie S. Vargas, "Programmed Instruction and Teaching Machines," in *Designs for Excellence in Education: The Legacy of B. F. Skinner,* ed. Richard P. West and L. A. Hamerlynck (Longmont, Colo.: Sopris West: 1992), pp. 33–64.

1. B. F. Skinner, *A Matter of Consequences* (New York: Knopf, 1983), p. 64.
2. Ibid.
3. Richard J. Herrnstein, "Remarks at Skinner's Eightieth Birthday Celebration," March 1984, B. F. Skinner Foundation Archives, Cambridge, Mass.
4. Ibert Mellan, "Teaching and Educational Inventions," in *Teaching Machines and Programmed Learning: A Source Book,* ed. A. A. Lumsdaine and Robert Glaser (Washington, D.C.: Department of Audio-Visual Instruction, National Education Association, 1960), pp. 265–74.
5. Maria Montessori, "Educational Device," 1914, Patent Number 1,103,369, U.S. Patent Office, Washington, D.C.
6. Cited in Douglas Porter, "A Critical Review of a Portion of the Literature on Teaching Devices," in *Teaching Machines and Programmed Learning: A Source Book,* pp. 114–32, on p. 122.
7. For a more detailed description of some of these early efforts to teach by machine, see Ludy T. Benjamin, Jr., "A History of Teaching Machines," *American Psychologist* 43 (1988): 703–12.
8. Sidney L. Pressey, "A Simple Apparatus Which Gives Tests and Scores—and Teaches," *School and Society* 23 (March 1926): 373–76. This and the 1950 article cited in n. 10 are reprinted in *Teaching Machines and Programmed Learning,* pp. 35–41, 69–88.
9. Pressey, "Simple Apparatus," p. 375.

10. Pressey, "Development and Appraisal of Devices Providing Immediate Automatic Scoring of Objective Tests and Concomitant Self-Instruction," *Journal of Psychology* 29 (1950): 412–47.

11. George W. Angell and Maurice E. Troyer, "A New Self-Scoring Test Device for Improving Instruction," in *Teaching Machines and Programmed Learning*, pp. 66–68.

12. Ibid., p. 66.

13. A. A. Lumsdaine, "Teaching Machines: An Introductory Overview," in ibid., pp. 5–22.

14. Pressey, "Development and Appraisal," p. 417.

15. Ibid., p. 445 (Pressey's emphasis).

16. Pressey, "Sidney Leavitt Pressey," in *A History of Psychology in Autobiography*, vol. 5, ed. Edwin G. Boring and Gardner Lindzey (New York: Appleton-Century-Crofts, 1967), pp. 311–39, on p. 322.

17. See, for example, James Kenneth Little, "An Investigation by Means of Special Test-Scoring and Drill Devices of the Effect of Certain Instructional Procedures on Learning in Educational Psychology," *Abstracts of Doctors' Dissertations*, No. 16 (Columbus: Ohio State University Press, 1935), pp. 113–23; Barry T. Jensen, "An Independent-Study Laboratory Using Self-Scoring Tests," *Journal of Educational Research* 43 (October 1949): 134–37; and Avery Livingston Stephens, "Certain Special Factors Involved in the Law of Effect," *Abstracts of Doctors' Dissertations*, no. 64 (Columbus: Ohio State University Press, 1953), pp. 505–11. These studies reference other efforts that obtained similar results.

18. Pressey, "A Third and Fourth Contribution Toward the Coming 'Industrial Revolution' in Education," in *Teaching Machines and Programmed Learning*, pp. 47–51, on p. 51 n. 5.

19. Skinner, "The Science of Learning and the Art of Teaching," *Harvard Educational Review* 24 (1954): 86–97; also published in *Current Trends in Psychology and the Behavioral Sciences*, ed. John T. Wilson (Pittsburgh: University of Pittsburgh Press, 1954); and in Skinner, *The Technology of Teaching* (New York: Appleton-Century-Crofts, 1968), pp. 9–28.

20. Skinner, *Technology of Teaching*, p. 24.

21. "Cybernetic feedback" means feedback not to the student, but to the teacher in order to revise the program according to the instructional goals designated for it.

22. Skinner, *Verbal Behavior* (New York: Appleton-Century-Crofts, 1957).

23. Skinner, *Matter of Consequences*, p. 95.

24. Ibid., p. 97.

25. Horace B. English to Edwin G. Boring, 30 January 1958, B. F. Skinner Papers (hereafter referred to as BFSP), HUG (FP) 60.25, Teaching Machine Correspondence ca. 1953–69, Harvard University Archives, Cambridge, Mass. To get an idea of the tone of the letter, see Benjamin, "History of Teaching Machines." In his letter to Boring, English added a postscript saying, "In the main the damned thing works to help 'form connections'." For a further discussion of the distinction between the selection and transformation paradigms in the analysis and explanation of behavior, see E. A. Vargas, "Behaviorology: Its Paradigm," in *Human Behavior in Today's World*, ed. Waris Ishaq (New York: Praeger, 1991), pp. 137–47; Vargas, "A Science of Our Own Making" *Behaviorology* 1 (1993): 13–22; and Vargas "The Construction of a Science Community" *Behaviorology* 1 (1993): 9–18.

26. Skinner to Pressey, 28 November 1955, BFSP, HUG (FP) 60.25, Teaching Machine Correspondence ca. 1953–69.

27. Edwin G. Boring to Horace B. English, 3 February 1958, BFSP, Teaching Machine Correspondence ca. 1953–69.

28. Skinner, *Technology of Teaching*.

29. Skinner to Richard S. Neville, 2 December 1954, BFSP, Teaching Machine Correspondence ca. 1953–69.

30. Skinner to Robert M. Gagne, 27 June 1955, BFSP, Teaching Machine Correspondence ca. 1953–69.

31. Skinner, *Technology of Teaching*, p. 60.

32. Skinner, *Verbal Behavior,* especially chap. 10.

33. For a more detailed and technical discussion of programmed instruction, especially in relation to Skinner's analysis of verbal behavior and to the science of behaviorology, see E. A. Vargas and Julie S. Vargas, "Programmed Instruction: What It Is and How to Do It," *Journal of Behavioral Education* 1 (1991): 235–51.

34. Skinner to Ford Foundation, 7 February 1956, BFSP, Teaching Machine Correspondence ca. 1953–69.

35. G. Clarence Faust to Nathan M. Pusey, 9 April 1956, BFSP, Teaching Machine Correspondence ca. 1953–69.

36. Skinner, "Final Report of a Project at Harvard University Sponsored by the Fund for the Advancement of Education, 1956–57," summer 1957, BFSP, Teaching Machine Correspondence ca. 1953–69.

37. Ibid.

38. James G. Holland, "Reflections on the Beginnings of Behavior Analysis in Education," in *Behavior Research and Technology in Higher Education,* ed. Lawrence E. Fraley and E. A. Vargas (Reedsville, W.Va.: Society for the Behavioral Analysis of Culture, 1976), pp. 323–33.

39. James G. Holland, "A Quantitative Measure for Programmed Instruction," *American Educational Research Journal* 4 (1967): 87–101.

40. James G. Holland and F. D. Kemp, "A Measure of Programming in Teaching Machine Material," *Journal of Educational Psychology* 56 (1965): 264–69.

41. Skinner, "Part IV: Use of the Machines in Teaching a General Education Course in Human Behavior: Spring Term, 1958," BFSP.

42. Ibid.

43. Ibid.

44. Holland and Skinner, *The Analysis of Behavior: A Program for Self-Instruction* (New York: McGraw-Hill, 1961).

45. Skinner, *The Behavior of Organisms: An Experimental Analysis* (New York: Appleton-Century, 1938), p. 441.

46. Skinner, Unpublished Notes, Volume marked 1965, pp. 27–28, B. F. Skinner Foundation Archives, Cambridge, Mass.

47. Skinner, "The Free and Happy Student," *New York University Education Quarterly* 122 (winter 1973): 1–3.

48. John T. Childs to Skinner, 10 March 1961, BFSP, Teaching Machine Correspondence. Childs worked for the Equitable Life Assurance Society.

49. Virginia P. Altieri to Skinner, 8 March 1961, BFSP, Teaching Machine Correspondence. Altieri taught at Newton High School, Newton, Mass.

50. Anna L. November to Skinner, 24 November 1956, BFSP, Teaching Machine Correspondence.

51. Skinner, *Recent Issues in the Analysis of Behavior* (Columbus, Ohio: Merrill), p. 96.

11

Experimental Analysis of Behavior at Harvard: From Cumulative Records to Mathematical Models

JOHN K. ROBINSON AND WILLIAM R. WOODWARD

PERCEPTIONS of behaviorism are badly in need of revision. The lay public is familiar with B. F. Skinner through his contributions to behavioral science and social philosophy. But much of this reception has a critical tone. By contrast, the scientific public has uncritically voted Skinner to the rank of most eminent psychologist.[1] Yet behavioral psychologists comprise only a small minority among psychologists, such that a given academic department seldom has more than one.

Despite the widespread respect among psychologists for Skinner himself, scientific psychology has paradoxically not yet granted the same kind of status and recognition to the tradition of laboratory work he initiated. The operant laboratory of the 1950s led to applications in education, mental health, and organizational behavior. However, the public, both lay and scientific, remain largely unaware of the more recent extensions of the laboratory science that Skinner initiated.

In fact, Skinner's radical behaviorism first attracted a scientific following beyond his immediate circle in the 1950s.[2] Graduate students, a professional journal, annual meetings, and extensive applications have all appeared since then. While psychology continues to represent Skinner's work as "operant conditioning" or "instrumental conditioning" in introductory textbooks, the laboratory science called the experimental analysis of behavior (EAB) has moved far beyond the single-key pigeon chamber and the cumulative record. Whereas recent developments in other fields of psychology have received considerable attention, the shift in EAB to mathematical modeling and testing of these models in naturalistic environments has largely been overlooked.[3]

The purpose of this chapter is to document how one laboratory initiated a proliferating research program.[4] This program has the characteristics of a scientific specialty. Persons trained in operant laboratories, and even those who have learned its methods secondhand, publish in a wide variety of journals and find employment in different kinds of institutional settings.[5] But they also bring extrabehavioral techniques and interests to their work on animal and human behavior. Thus, Skinner's "experimental analysis of behavior" has evolved beyond the simple methodology portrayed in textbooks into an approach disseminated in many disciplines.

THE TWO COMMUNITIES OF OPERANT PSYCHOLOGY

Sociometric Characterization of the Field of Behavior Analysis

In an extensive study, Martha Chappell Dean documented the growth of the experimental analysis of behavior from 1958 to 1979.[6] She conducted cocitation analyses (a technique commonly used in the information sciences) to reveal the most popular or dominant research areas. "Dominance" is defined quantitatively by citation in new publications. Dominant documents have had the most impact of all those published during a certain period, and they can be clustered together around a theme to reveal thriving subspecialties.

The results of her analysis are striking. Compare two of her figures, representing cocitation cluster analyses for 1961–62 and 1979, respectively. The height of the "bumps" on these three-dimensional graphs represent frequency of citation for documents clustered by theme for the specified years. Figure 1 shows that work in 1961–62 was centered in the area of schedule effects and otherwise spread fairly evenly in six secondary categories.[7] Figure 2, on the other hand, reveals a much-reduced peak for schedule effects.[8] Rising to prominence instead are two other areas called biological constraints on learning and quantitative law of effect. The lower part of each figure shows the thematic proximity of the most highly cocited documents. Comparing figure 1 with figure 2 again, it is clear that the centers of interest of 1979 are much more similar in frequency of cocitation than the diffuse centers of 1961–62. In sum, Dean's work demonstrates the magnitude of change in the experimental analysis of behavior from 1960 to 1980, especially in the incorporation of mathematical modeling and theory.

One possible interpretation of these changes in the experimental analysis of behavior is that the community has remained homogeneous, gradually and continuously moving into new subject matters.[9] Although this

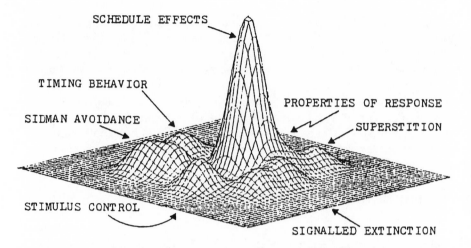

Figure 1. Dean's cocitation plot for the early 1960s. The bulk of the research activity is on schedules of reinforcement, following up the original work pioneered by Skinner in the thirties. From Martha Chappell Dean, "The Evolution of Experimental Operant Psychology" (Ph.D. diss., Syracuse University, 1981); reproduced by permission of the author.

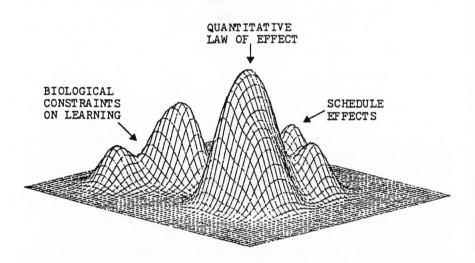

Figure 2. Dean's cocitation plot for 1979, showing the shift of research interests toward quantitative models and biological factors. Source as for Figure 1.

interpretation is plausible, we will argue here that Dean's data instead show that the research scientists of the EAB diverged roughly twenty-five years ago into two relatively distinct fields with polarized defining characteristics, and that one of these groups has come to dominate the norms of EAB's scientific practice.[10] We begin the discussion of this development by delineating the defining characteristics of both groups and then proceed to discuss the broader implications of the separation.

Characteristics of the EAB Community

The "classical" operant group first emerged in the 1930s with B. F. Skinner and the publication of *The Behavior of Organisms: An Experimental Analysis* in 1938.[11] Although Skinner's approach was slow to win converts in psychology at large in the 1930s and 1940s, it did retain the allegiance of several colleagues and students, including Fred S. Keller, William N. Schoenfeld, and William Estes. During the 1950s, these researchers in turn trained a number of graduate students and worked primarily in the psychology departments at Columbia, Harvard, and Minnesota. As these students graduated and scattered to academic and applied positions throughout the country, the amount of research produced by this community became large enough to demand its own publication outlet in the form of the *Journal of the Experimental Analysis of Behavior* (*JEAB*) in 1957.[12] Charles Ferster, a Columbia Ph.D., worked with Skinner in the early 1950s at Harvard, and the mutual product of their labor, *Schedules of Reinforcement* (*SOR*), became the research bible of this generation of researchers.[13]

The journal and the model of research practice provided "exemplars," enabling others to enter the field of experimental operant research. The style of research and theory in early issues of *JEAB* and in *SOR* may be described as follows: First, its authors specified their experimental variables in molecular (microscopic) terms. Second, they measured behavior in absolute terms and primarily presented qualitative data. Finally, they considered an explanation of behavior complete if it included the determination of controlling variables. We will explore each of these in turn.

Molecular variables. In several papers of the 1930s Skinner, simultaneously with, but independently of, two Polish researchers, distinguished a conditioning paradigm distinct from that of Pavlov. Skinner showed that contingent consequences of a response could influence the future occurrence of that behavior.[14] When the stimulus context of this event is taken into account, a simple model emerged by the 1950s, called the "three-term contingency":

$$S^D: R \rightarrow S^R$$

Here R represents the response, and S^R is the reinforcer, and S^D the discriminative stimulus that signals the contingency between response and reinforcer. In the classic example, a rat in an operant chamber received a food reinforcer following a lever press when a chamber light was illuminated, but not when it was off. In this situation, the light acts as a S^D.

Skinner saw this relationship between response and reinforcer as one of *contiguity*. As in classical associationism, events that are similar and in close proximity in time and space (contiguous) become associated.[15] A rat's lever press produced reinforcement "contiguously," whereupon it became more probable in the future.

Absolute measures and qualitative data. While developing this conceptual system, Skinner also pioneered a novel experimental technology. Besides the well-known "Skinner box," he constructed a novel data-recording apparatus called the "cumulative recorder."[16] This simple device consisted of a roller that moved paper slowly but steadily along and a pen that moved a small distance laterally across the paper with each operant response. Reinforcer deliveries deflected the pen downward, creating hash marks. The pen reset automatically to the near edge of the paper when the far edge was reached. Typical cumulative records are shown in figure 3. Importantly, these cumulative records of responding and reinforcement constituted the primary data of the experimental analysis of behavior from the 1930s through the 1950s. Since hundreds of feet of paper could be used in recording the behavior of a single animal, the experimenters selected a few "representative" records (as few as several feet) for publication. They assumed that these selected records reflected the essence of the animal's performance under those conditions and produced the greatest generality, and that no further analysis was necessary. They discussed these data in terms of the shape of the tracing, as slopes, curves, plateaus, and scallops. In sum, these descriptions represented absolute measures of responding, described in qualitative terms.

Classical explanation of behavior. Implicit in Skinner's style of observing behavior was a deep respect for the experimental method inspired by Pavlov.[17] Skinner stated that he adopted Pavlov's maxim of "control your conditions and you will see order." When translated by his followers, especially W. N. Schoenfeld, this directive became the Machian philosophy of empirical description that guided the early operant research.[18]

Skinner sought to avoid the need for theoretical reduction, either to underlying physiology or to animal behavior observed outside the laboratory. This empirical methodology consisted of the specification and systematic manipulation of external, observable independent variables under the control of the experimenter.[19] Skinnerian experimenters then observed and recorded change in observable behavioral dependent variables. They manipulated other independent variables in additional experiments, making no appeal to internal mediating or motivational

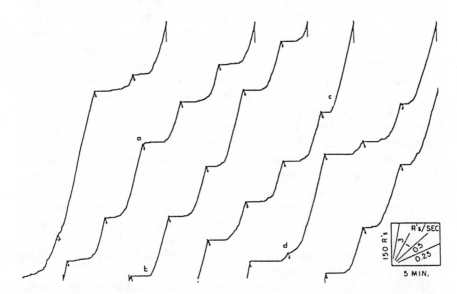

Figure 3. Cumulative records from Ferster and Skinner's *Schedules of Reinforcement* **([New York: Appleton-Century-Crofts, 1957], p. 159) exemplifying the use of absolute measures and molecular variables that was characteristic of the original EAB community. The records have been rotated 90 degrees so that time is on the horizontal axis and cumulative responses are on the vertical axis.**

processes and not attempting to relate laboratory behavior to behavior in the wild. For example, they translated an unobservable motivational state traditionally called hunger into an observable deprivation process (e.g., by varying the animal's body weight), and they measured its influence by changes in the rate of lever-pressing for food, an observable behavior.

The important point here is that these were "functional" relationships between observable independent and dependent variables. The relationship that they specified between two sets of numbers in graphical coordinates constituted a *complete* explanation of the behavior. One had no need to go beyond these "proximate" controlling variables to understand the function of the behavior in terms of other environmental consequences.

Characteristics of the Quantitative Analysis of Behavior (QAB) Community

In the late 1950s a distinct community of the experimental analysis of behavior began to emerge within Skinner's own operant laboratory at

Harvard University. Skinner's collaborator was his postdoctoral research associate, Charles Ferster. Donald Blough and Richard J. Herrnstein were graduate students from 1953 to 1955.[20] The psychophysicist S. Smith "Smitty" Stevens had considerable influence in these years, for he taught the departmental proseminar for one semester in the first year, as well as a course on psychophysical measurement.[21] Herrnstein worked with him in his first summer as a graduate student in 1953, the summer in which Stevens developed the psychophysical power-law analysis for which he is best known. There was tremendous excitement in the psychophysics laboratory, and Stevens decided not to go to Princeton on sabbatical because he had so much work to do. Joseph Stevens, a close friend of Herrnstein since their mutual graduate student days, did stay with S. S. Stevens and continued his work in psychophysics.

During three years of military research at the Walter Reed Research Center following graduation, Herrnstein continued to run three pigeons. Returning to Harvard as assistant professor in 1958, he brought two of those three pigeons with him. Skinner, meanwhile, had turned his attention away from experimental research to writing.[22]

Herrnstein, like other graduate students, had been drawn to Harvard because of "Smitty" Stevens in psychophysics. He then learned to apply psychophysical measurement to animal behavior. From Skinner he accepted the three-term contingency of discriminative stimulus, response, and reinforcing stimulus. From Stevens, he developed an interest in mathematical modeling.[23] With this hybrid perspective, Herrnstein gained a following among a new generation of graduate students. Among them were William Baum, Shin-Ho Chung, Philip Hineline, Edmund Fantino, Laurel Furumoto, Peter Killeen, Allen Neuringer, Howard Rachlin, Bruce Schneider, Richard Schuster, and John Staddon. Neuringer retained a more Skinnerian approach, and Furumoto went into the history of psychology. In this group of scientists a unique approach to theory and research emerged that eventually set it apart from Skinner's traditional experimental analysis of behavior. In general, three clusters of characteristics contrast directly with those of the classical operant community. First, the data were quantitative and were presented as relative measures. Second, these researchers specified molar (or macroscopic) variables for both behavior and reinforcement. Finally, they expanded their theory to incorporate "ultimate" causes of behavior. We will consider each of these in turn.

Quantitative, relative measures. In 1961, Herrnstein finally published the results of experiments begun at Walter Reed and continued on his return to Harvard in 1958. He had offered pigeons two keys instead of one to peck[24]; the birds received food following responding for some average period of time (a concurrent variable-interval, variable-interval schedule of reinforcement, or conc VI–VI).[25] What was very different about Herrnstein's concurrent schedule study was not his procedure, but his analysis. Both Findley[26] and Ferster and Skinner, consistent with the classical operant procedures just discussed, presented qualitative and absolute measures in the form of cumulative records. By contrast, Herrnstein gathered quantitative data collected on digital recorders and computed relative rates of responding and reinforcement. From this analysis he proposed an equation to describe the relationship between these rates:

$$\frac{B_1}{B_1 + B_2} = \frac{R_1}{R_1 + R_2} \tag{1}$$

Here B_1 and B_2 represent responses to alternatives 1 and 2, and R_1 and R_2 represent reinforcers obtained at each alternative. Thus, Herrnstein suggested that the relative response rate would match the relative rate of reinforcement.[27] This equation in several forms has come to be called the matching law, and it has been shown through later work to be quite general.[28]

The distinctive feature of this equation is that all the terms could be measured directly. It was an empirical law, much like those derived from psychophysical scaling. It took seven years of plotting relations between strength of reinforcement and response for Herrnstein to recognize a pattern in his data that could be fitted by an equation. He described performance on a single simple schedule of reinforcement (e.g., those that were common in Skinner's work) as

$$B = \frac{kR_1}{R_1 + R_e} \tag{2}$$

where B_1 and R_1 are as previously indicated and k is a constant representing the maximum rate of responding. The term R_e, which reflects reinforcement available from unmeasured sources, will be discussed later.

Molar controlling variables. One extension of this quantitative and relativistic change involved the independent variables that were of interest to the experimenter. During the 1960s, two important conceptual shifts occurred, as seen in figures 4 and 5. First, in both data sets, the relative rate of reinforcement is the independent variable. Both dependent variables are relative rates of responding. Herrnstein measured responding in keypecks, and Baum and Rachlin measured it as the amount of *time* allocated by the animal to responding on one side or the other of a special chamber.[29] The experiment presented food at two feeders on opposite

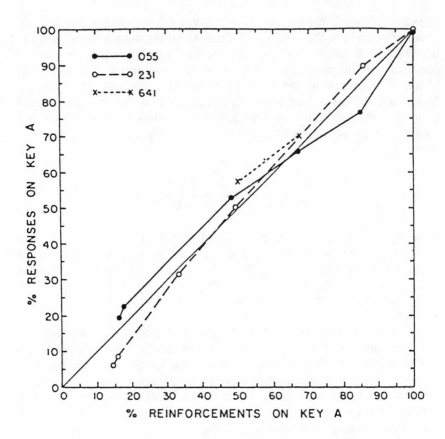

Figure 4. Graph from Herrnstein's seminal 1961 paper on relative response rates, showing the molar dependency of the rates on relative reinforcement rates. R. J. Herrnstein, "Relative and Absolute Rates of Response as a Function of Frequency of Reinforcement," *Journal of the Experimental Analysis of Behavior* **4 (1961): 267–72. Copyright by the Society for the Experimental Analysis of Behavior.**

sides of the chamber; the feeders were activated intermittently when the bird stood on a panel and behaved on a concurrent interval schedule. This is a very different conceptualization of the action of reinforcement from Skinner's. Recall that Skinner saw reinforcement and responses as discrete events encountering each other contiguously.

The molar specification of controlling variables and behavior was not just a convenience in data analysis; rather, it embodied a new theory of contingency between response and consequence. An animal's behavior did not reflect the action of local response-reinforcer encounters. Instead, it was sensitive to the long-term payoff (in reinforcers) of long-term patterns of responding.[30]

QAB explanation of behavior. A corollary of this molar view of behavior and reinforcement produced another conceptual change. It is best illustrated in another form of the matching equation, although it was already implied in Equation 2:[31]

$$\frac{B_1}{B_1 + B_i} = \frac{R_1}{R_1 + R_i} \tag{3}$$

where B_1 and R_1 are defined as before. B_i and R_i represent behavior and reinforcers, respectively, arising from sources other than the primary sources (i.e., the explicitly arranged VI/VI alternatives). In the extreme, these secondary sources include behavior and reinforcement *not* measured by the experimenter.

What this approach suggests is that a complete explanation of behavior must incorporate the influence of reinforcers from sources not programmed by the experimenter on behavior not specified (or perhaps even identified) by the researcher. Assumed by this approach is that the animal is always behaving in some way or another. If it is not doing one thing (e.g., responding on the key), it must be doing another (e.g., sleeping, scratching, walking, or staring). These "extraneous" influences are no longer seen as just nuisance variables to be controlled. Instead, they become important factors contributing to the behavior patterns observed in the experimental situation. Crucially, the activities in question might include those species-typical or "instinctive" behaviors, such as would occur in the wild, that arise from nonproximate evolutionary sources. Herrnstein's inclusion of alternate, unspecified sources of reinforcement thus gave the QAB community a way of quantifying the constraints placed by an animal's inherent behavioral tendencies on theoretical generalizations about learning derived from laboratory settings.

Implications and Later Developments

The implications of the bifurcation of the experimental analysis of behavior into two communities are twofold. First, the revised approach of QAB is not the version of the experimental analysis of behavior presented to psychology undergraduates, nor is it the approach that most behavioral scientists understand operant psychology to be. Second, the bifurcation

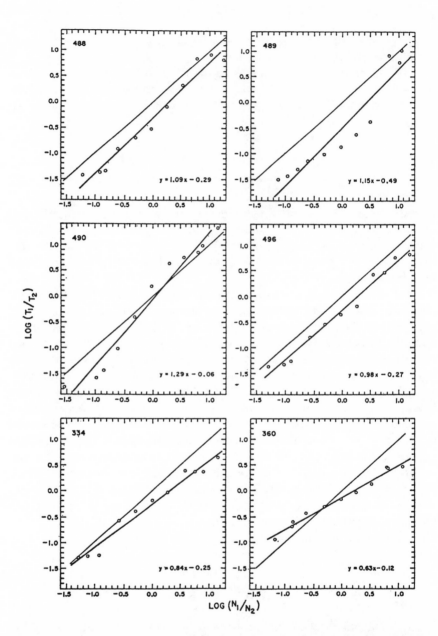

Figure 5. Graph from Baum and Rachlin's 1969 paper on temporal matching. The relative time spent engaging in two activities matches the relative rate of reinforcement for the alternatives. The matching law proved to be general across different responses and laboratory species. William M. Baum and Howard C. Rachlin, "Choice as Time Allocation," *Journal of the Experimental Analysis of Behavior* 12 (1969): 861-874. Copyright by the Society for the Experimental Analysis of Behavior.

has provided opportunities for the QAB community to extend contacts to other fields.

The Popular Context of EAB

Every scientific discipline attempts to make contact with nonspecialists through a limited number of communication channels. It is important for each subgroup to present a coherent image to the general public and to scientists in other specialties. This public relations activity is part of the legitimization of the expert knowledge that scientists are assumed to possess.[32]

One important public communication channel is through introductory psychology courses and their textbooks. Few who take Psychology 101 end up as research psychologists. The textbook or introductory lecture is the one chance a subspecialty may have to form a lifetime impression in the introductory student. Yet virtually every introductory textbook presents the experimental analysis of behavior as possessing only the characteristics of classical operant psychology.[33] Textbook treatments include depictions of rats or pigeons in single-response chambers, examples of cumulative records, and acts of "misbehavior" that show animals engaging in species-typical behaviors that fail to conform to reinforcement theory. Completely absent from the introductory psychology image of operant psychology are the mathematical models, complex schedules, and alternative apparatuses of the post-Skinnerian quantitative analysis of behavior. One consequence of this situation may well be that to many undergraduates (and possibly instructors as well), operant learning appears to be included in texts and lectures for historical interest only.

The Applied Audiences of the Classical Operant Community

Sociologists of science have emphasized how scientific practice can be understood in terms of social context, especially the audience to which information is directed.[34] They have underscored the different outlets and uses of scientific information, the primary product of the scientific endeavor. For example, a particular style of research may generate information that gains scientific respect and perhaps even influences research practice in other fields, but that offers little in terms of practical application. The opposite may also occur. Some groups of scientists produce information destined for immediate practical application, with little emphasis on more general theoretical or methodological issues. The sociological terminology of "exchange theory" serves to describe the production and dissemination of scientific information in the two periods of behavior analysis described here.[35] Scientists produce a product through their activities, and that product is information disseminated in exchange for recognition. For this information to be successfully transferred, though, it must be understandable and relevant to the audience. It follows that different kinds of information would be relevant to different audiences. These two sorts of orientations, toward practical application and toward scientific status-improvement, are not necessarily incompatible, but they are probably difficult to execute simultaneously. It is possible to use the economic metaphor of information as an exchangeable commodity to interpret the process of change within the EAB.

David Krantz, a historian of psychology writing in the 1970s, considered behavior analysis a prototypical example of an isolated subdiscipline, temporarily surviving in its own journals and distinct society, but showing little development as time passes.[36] In a subsequent textbook, Thomas Leahey argued that Skinner developed more than an isolated school or "ghetto community."[37] We agree, and we have herein documented the relevant change in research practices. In fact, Skinner went to extraordinary lengths to make his work practically useful, especially after he left the laboratory in the early 1960s, as evidenced by the immense volume of correspondence he devoted to the implementation of the teaching machine.[38]

In marketing Skinner's invention of a behavioral technology to a spectrum of consumers inside and outside the discipline, psychologists of the classical operant community put the three characteristics described earlier to good use. Molecular variables such as immediate praise were appropriate to fields such as behavior modification, education, social change, organizational behavior, and behavioral medicine. Qualitative data on increases or decreases in response rate were easily collected on individual human subjects. And proximate causes such as discrete reinforcers were easy to manipulate by behavior technologists of all stripes.

The product that Skinner's consumers demanded was effective behavioral control. His laboratory-inspired ideas—precisely because they were molecular, qualitative, and proximate—offered usable techniques of control that would meet the demands of socially important markets. In education, for example, consumers needed to establish control over the classroom and to acquire more efficient methods of teaching. In business, employers sought to increase productivity. In medicine, physicians required an effective means of enabling patients to reduce stress and addictive behaviors.

The Social Context of the Quantitative Analysis of Behavior

On the other hand, post-Skinnerian laboratory research maintained its legitimacy as scientific practice before a very different social group.[39] Although this research since the 1960s has seen relatively little practical application, it has adopted investigative practices that put the field in a better position to export and import research findings to and from other sciences.

The QAB was much better prepared for interdisciplinary interaction for reasons involving the three characteristics outlined here. The use of mathematical modeling, for example, opened up the opportunity to incorporate molar concepts such as maximizing and optimization[40]—ideas are central to conceptualizing and investigating behavior from the standpoints of both economics and behavioral ecology. As a consequence, behavior analysts began to collaborate with economists and ecologists, building interdisciplinary bridges. Quantitative data, of course, are essential to the testing of any mathematical model. Complex schedules with more than one response alternative allowed animal foraging behavior to be interpreted with models of decision processes, that is, as choices of where to feed and what to feed on. This was the basic approach of the behavioral ecologists.[41] Incorporating choice allowed reinforcers to be understood not only in Skinner's original sense as events strengthening behavior, but also economically as commodities with different values and with nonadditive properties.[42]

The most significant conceptual shift to occur with the advent of QAB was the inclusion of the influence of evolutionary, ultimate causes directly into theory. Recall R_e of Equation 3. Though Skinner frequently wrote about evolution, he made no specific practical contributions to its inclusion into operant theory. To fully integrate proximate and ultimate causal variables into a single conceptual framework would represent the achievement of a goal that has eluded students of animal behavior since Darwin.

CONCLUSION

We have seen that a modern field of science had its origin in a specific social organization with certain cognitive interests: the quantitative analysis of behavior at Harvard was a program of research in which psychophysics and animal behavior were the leading sources for investigative work. The shift to digital recorders was one important feature of the method of this school; the resort to mathematical models of behavior was another. The behavior of the subject in at least a concurrent response environment, and at most a naturalistic habitat, reflected the loosening of the constraints of Skinner's box. Moreover, the presence of S. S. Stevens in the department, and his ability to attract students with mathematical ability, served to bring talented graduate students into proximity with Skinner. In more than one case, students came because of the reputations of Stevens in psychophysics or Skinner in learning and ended up combining the two approaches in a quantitative project in experimental analysis of behavior under Herrnstein.

A new approach to the experimental analysis of operant behavior took hold, and gradually achieved hegemony over EAB. The modified Skinner box; the talented direction of Skinner's younger associates such as Ferster, Charles Catania, and Herrnstein; and the arrival of mathematically talented students provided a combination of circumstances that promoted a particular kind of social organization. Loosely directed projects, lively debate about alternative approaches, and eventually the ability of these students to obtain professional positions in universities gave life to a fledgling specialty in experimental psychology.

NOTES

The authors would like to thank the many people who generously gave of their time by providing comments on earlier drafts of the manuscript or by allowing us to interview them: William Baum, Charles Catania, Stephen Coleman, Michael Commons, Edmund Fantino, Laurel Furumoto, Richard Herrnstein, Peter Killeen, Edward Morris, John A. Nevin, Howard Rachlin, B. F. Skinner, Laurence Smith, John Staddon, Sande Webster, and Ben Williams.

1. On the public reception, see Terry J. Knapp, "The Verbal Legacy of B. F. Skinner: An Essay on the Secondary Literature," this volume; and Rae Goodell, *The Visible Scientists* (Boston: Little, Brown, 1977). On Skinner's eminence, see Leonard Zusne, *Biographical Dictionary of Psychology* (Westport, Conn.: Greenwood, 1984); and Albert R. Gilgen, *American Psychology Since World War II: A Profile of the Discipline* (Westport, Conn.: Greenwood, 1982).

2. R. J. Herrnstein, "The Evolution of Behaviorism," *American Psychologist* 32 (1977): 593–603. On membership figures, see the *Directory of the American Psychological Association* (Washington, D.C.: APA, 1989); and the *Directory of the Association for Behavior Analysis* (Milwaukee, Wis.: ABA, 1988).

3. See, for instance, Rita L. Atkinson, Richard C. Atkinson, and Ernest R. Hilgard, *Introduction to Psychology,* 8th ed. (New York: Harcourt, 1983), pp. 200–210; and Henry Gleitman, *Psychology* (New York: Norton, 1981), pp. 77–90.

4. The concept of "research program" is anchored in the two lines of secondary literature on the nature of scientific change. On the philosophy of research pro-

grams, see Imre Lakatos, *The Methodology of Scientific Research Programs* (Cambridge: Cambridge University Press, 1978); and in the psychology of science, see Ryan D. Tweney, "Programmatic Research in Experimental Psychology: E. B. Titchener's Laboratory Investigations, 1891–1927," in *Psychology in Twentieth-Century Thought and Society,* ed. Mitchell G. Ash and William R. Woodward (New York: Cambridge University Press, 1987), pp. 35–57.

5. Radical behaviorism is represented by the Association for Behavior Analysis, an organization of about 2,000 members founded in 1974. Its organ is *The Behavior Analyst.* Introductory textbooks, as well as history and systems textbooks, sometimes describe behaviorism as one of the five major psychological schools, along with functionalism, structuralism, Gestalt, psychoanalysis, and humanistic psychology.

6. Martha Chappell Dean, "The Evolution of Experimental Operant Psychology" (Ph.D. diss., Syracuse University, 1981). University Microfilms Order No. 8123895.

7. Ibid., p. 99, figure 5.4, and discussion pp. 89–93.

8. Ibid., p. 117, figure 5.22, and discussion p. 140.

9. One could understand it through a gradualistic theory of scientific change, for example, Larry Laudan, *Progress and Its Problems: Towards a Theory of Scientific Growth* (Berkeley: University of California Press, 1977).

10. Compatible with our interpretation is a more discontinuous theory of scientific change such as Thomas S. Kuhn, *The Structure of Scientific Revolutions,* 2d ed. (Chicago: University of Chicago Press, 1970).

11. Skinner, *The Behavior of Organisms: An Experimental Analysis* (New York: Appleton-Century, 1938).

12. The journal was founded by a group who met informally and circulated a newsletter. At the time of the founding, E. G. Boring argued that the journal would serve to marginalize the behavioral movement instead of integrating it with mainstream psychology. The relative merits of this course remain uncertain. In any case, Skinner himself continually strove to keep behaviorism within psychology.

13. Charles B. Ferster and Skinner, *Schedules of Reinforcement* (New York: Appleton-Century-Crofts, 1957).

14. Skinner, "Two Types of Conditioned Reflex and a Pseudo Type," *Journal of General Psychology* 12 (1935): 66–77. Cf. Skinner, "Two Types of Conditioned Reflex: A Reply to Konorski and Miller," *Journal of General Psychology* 16 (1937): 272–79. S. Miller and J. Konorski, "Sur une forme particulière des réflexes conditionnels," *Contes rendus des séances de la société polonaise de biologie* 49 (1928): 1155–57 [English translation: "On a Particular Form of Conditioned Reflex," *Journal of the Experimental Analysis of Behavior* 12 (1969): 187–189]. See also J. Konorski and S. Miller, "On Two Types of Conditioned Reflex," *Journal of General Psychology* 16 (1937): 264–72.

15. On the law of association, see L. S. Hearnshaw, *A Short History of British Psychology, 1840–1940* (New York: Barnes & Noble, 1964). Cf. Deborah F. Johnson, "The Utilitarian-Associationist Tradition and the Development of British Psychology, 1855–1903" (Ph.D. diss., University of New Hampshire, 1988). It is important to note that the role assigned to contiguity in learning differed among behaviorist theorists. Clark L. Hull saw contiguity as one factor, along with practice and reinforcement, that jointly yielded conditioning; see Hull, *Principles of Behavior: An Introduction to Behavior Theory* (New York: Appleton-Century, 1943); Hull, *A Behavior System* (New Haven: Yale University Press, 1952). Edwin

R. Guthrie saw contiguity as the necessary and sufficient condition for conditioning to occur; see Guthrie, *The Psychology of Learning*, rev. ed. (New York: Harper, 1952).

16. On Skinner's novel experimental technology, see S. R. Coleman, "Quantitative Order in B. F. Skinner's Early Research Program, 1928–1931," *Behavior Analyst* 10 (1987): 47–65; see also Skinner, *Shaping of a Behaviorist* (New York: Knopf, 1979); and Skinner, *A Matter of Consequences* (New York: Knopf, 1983). Skinner's fondness for the cumulative recorder was such that he later published a lament over its decreasing use by operant psychologists. See Skinner, "Farewell, My LOVELY!" *Journal of the Experimental Analysis of Behavior* 25 (1976): 218.

17. Skinner, "Pavlov's Influence on Psychology in America," *Journal of the History of the Behavioral Sciences* 17 (1981): 242–45. Cf. I. P. Pavlov, *Conditioned Reflexes* (Oxford, England: Clarendon Press, 1927). On the transition from Pavlovian conditioning to the operant, see Coleman, "Historical Context and Systematic Functions of the Concept of the Operant," *Behaviorism* 9 (1981): 207–26.

18. Laurence D. Smith, *Behaviorism and Logical Positivism: A Reassessment of the Alliance* (Stanford, Calif.: Stanford University Press, 1986). Willard F. Day, Jr., "The Historical Antecedents of Contemporary Behaviorism," in *Psychology: Theoretical-Historical Perspectives*, ed. Robert W. Rieber and Kurt Salzinger (New York: Academic Press, 1980), pp. 203–62. For Skinner's statement of the Pavlovian maxim, see Skinner, "A Case History in Scientific Method," in *Cumulative Record*, enl. ed. (New York: Appleton-Century-Crofts, 1961), pp. 76–100, on p. 80.

19. G. E. Zuriff, *Behaviorism: A Conceptual Reconstruction* (New York: Columbia University Press, 1985); Murray Sidman, *Tactics of Scientific Research* (New York: Basic, 1960).

20. Ferster and Skinner, *Schedules of Reinforcement*. Herrnstein ("Reminiscences Already?" *Journal of the Experimental Analysis of Behavior* 48 [1987]: 448–53) reports that Ferster

had migrated from Columbia University to Harvard as Skinner's "research associate" in 1950, Harvard's designation for a soft-money, postdoctoral research appointment made at the convenience of a member of the regular faculty. Ferster's job was to run Skinner's operant laboratory, which he more than did. He not only ran it, he refashioned it. He rebuilt and greatly enlarged the "pigeon lab." He was an indefatigable, enthusiastic researcher, an 80-hour-a-week-man, and an unselfish, natural leader for graduate students eager to dig into a subject. . . . Ferster set and enforced exacting technical standards for research, which remained Harvard's standard even after Ferster left in 1955 for the Yerkes Laboratories. (pp. 448–49).

21. Interviews with Edmund Fantino, 12 January 1988; Laurel Furumoto, 13 April 1990; William Baum, 7 June 1990; and Peter Killeen, 8 June 1990.

22. Herrnstein, "Reminiscences," p. 453. Others on the staff were Geraldine "Didi" Stone [Stevens], who managed the department, and Antoinette Papp, who ran the pigeon laboratory. In some respects it was a competitive environment. Richard Schuster's dissertation was rejected and he had to redo it, costing years of work. Those who retained Skinner's perspective felt like outsiders; the insider track was with Herrnstein in those years. Personal communications with Baum, Fantino, Furumoto, Herrnstein, and Killeen.

23. Personal communication, R. J. Herrnstein to John K. Robinson and William R. Woodward, April 1988. Evidence of the climate in the laboratory was Herrnstein's remark that behaviorism is "an acquired taste" (Furumoto to au-

thors, 13 April 1990). Cf. Bruno Latour and Steve Woolgar, *Laboratory Life: The Construction of Scientific Facts* (Princeton: Princeton University Press, 1979).

24. Herrnstein was not the first to study these concurrent schedules of reinforcement. Ferster and Skinner reported concurrent work in *Schedules of Reinforcement,* and J. D. Findley published a thorough study of concurrent VI–VI schedules in 1958. Findley included various concurrent or successive presentations of more than one simple reinforcement schedule, either with or without signaling stimuli to indicate which was in effect. Still, studies of complex schedules were infrequent before the early 1960s.

25. R. J. Herrnstein, "Relative and Absolute Rates of Response as a Function of Frequency of Reinforcement," *Journal of the Experimental Analysis of Behavior* 4 (1961): 267–72.

26. J. D. Findley, "Preference and Switching under Concurrent Scheduling," *Journal of the Experimental Analysis of Behavior* 1 (1958): 123–44.

27. See, for example, R. J. Herrnstein, "Some Factors Influencing Behavior in a Two-Response Situation," *Transactions of the New York Academy of Sciences* 21 (1958): 35–45. This paper marks the beginning of an important departure from Skinner's design.

28. Herrnstein, "On the Law of Effect," *Journal of the Experimental Analysis of Behavior* 13 (1970): 243–66. In personal communications of April 1988 and 9 June 1990 with the authors, Herrnstein emphasized the excitement of his discovery of this law (Equation 2) on 10 December 1965. On the crucial role of Herrnstein's discovery of the matching law in transforming the operant tradition, see Charles P. Shimp, "Timing, Learning, and Forgetting," in *Timing and Time Perception,* ed. John Gibbon and Lorraine Allan (New York: New York Academy of Sciences, 1984), pp. 346–60. Shimp calls the discovery a "critical historical event," and describes the law as "beautiful in its simplicity and perfect as an object of theoretical speculation" (p. 353).

29. William M. Baum and Howard C. Rachlin, "Choice as Time Allocation," *Journal of the Experimental Analysis of Behavior* 12 (1969): 861–74.

30. J.E.R. Staddon and V. L. Simmelhag, "The 'Superstition' Experiment: A Reexamination of Its Implications for the Principle of Adaptive Behavior," *Psychological Review* 78 (1971): 3–43. See also Staddon, "Attention and Temporal Discrimination: Factors Controlling Responding Under a Cyclic-Interval Schedule," *Journal of the Experimental Analysis of Behavior* 10 (1967): 349–59; and Staddon, "The Effect of Informative Feedback on Temporal Tracking in the Pigeon," *Journal of the Experimental Analysis of Behavior* 12 (1969): 27–38.

31. For a detailed discussion, see Michael Davison and Dianne McCarthy, *The Matching Law: A Research Review* (Hillsdale, N.J.: Erlbaum, 1988).

32. See, for example, Joseph Rouse, *Knowledge and Power: Toward a Political Philosophy of Science* (Ithaca, N.Y.: Cornell University Press, 1987). Our experience in conducting interviews for this chapter made us aware of the public relations aspect of scientific subspecialties. The participants in this historical episode were eager to see it recorded and agreed that it represented a crucial decade. Cf. Derek J. de Solla Price, *Little Science, Big Science* (New York: Columbia University Press, 1963), pp. 110–15.

33. Missing from all areas of psychology is familiarity with the research in the experimental and quantitative analysis of behavior; instead, one finds merely applications of the classical operant paradigm. See, for example, Robert C. Carson, James N. Butcher, and James Coleman, *Abnormal Psychology and Modern Life* (Glenview, Ill.: Scott, Foresman, 1988), pp. 69–73. More sympathetic to op-

erant work, but still neglecting research, is David L. Rosenhan and Martin E. P. Seligman, *Abnormal Psychology*, 2d ed. (New York: Norton, 1989), pp. 112–18.

34. For a review, see Karin D. Knorr-Cetina and Michael Mulkay, eds., *Science Observed: Perspectives on the Social Study of Science* (Beverly Hills, Calif.: Sage, 1983), especially pp. 9–14 on the linguistic turn and discourse.

35. Cf. Warren O. Hagstrom, *The Scientific Community* (New York: Basic, 1965); Diana Crane, *Invisible Colleges* (Chicago: University of Chicago Press, 1972); and Everett Mendelsohn, Peter Weingart, and Richard Whitley, eds., *The Social Production of Scientific Knowledge* (Dordrecht, The Netherlands: D. Reidel, 1977).

36. David L. Krantz, "Schools and Systems: The Mutual Isolation of Operant and Non-Operant Psychology as a Case Study," *Journal of the History of the Behavioral Sciences* 8 (1972): 86–108. For an updated version of Krantz's argument, see Robert W. Proctor and Daniel J. Weeks, *The Goal of B. F. Skinner and Behavior Analysis* (New York: Springer-Verlag, 1990).

37. Thomas H. Leahey, *A History of Psychology*, 2d ed. (Englewood Cliffs, N.J.: Prentice-Hall, 1986), pp. 461–64.

38. Harvard University Archives (Cambridge, Mass.) contains about 30 boxes of letters to and from Skinner from 1928 to 1977, organized alphabetically and chronologically. A large proportion of this correspondence is devoted to the Aircrib, teaching machines, and recording equipment. The call numbers are HUG (FP) 60.10, 60.15, and 60.20.

39. This group continues as the Society for the Quantitative Analysis of Behavior. Led for many years by Michael Commons (a Columbia Ph.D. in signal detection under John A. Nevin) and an informal "board" that included Richard Herrnstein, the group has convened annual conferences since 1978, and their papers are reviewed and published in the series *Quantitative Analyses of Behavior*, vols. 1–4 (Cambridge, Mass.: Ballinger); vols. 5–11 (Hillsdale, N.J.: Erlbaum). One branch of this school is described in John K. Robinson and William R. Woodward, "The Convergence of Behavioral Biology and Operant Psychology: Toward an Interlevel and Interfield Science," *Behavior Analyst* 12 (1989): 131–41.

40. Howard C. Rachlin et al., "Maximization Theory in Behavioral Psychology," *Behavioral and Brain Sciences* 4 (1981): 371–417.

41. Staddon, "Optimality Analyses of Operant Behavior and Their Relation to Optimal Foraging," in *Limits to Action: The Allocation of Individual Behavior*, ed. Staddon (New York: Academic, 1980), pp. 101–141. Cf. Sara J. Shettleworth, "Foraging as Operant Behavior and Operant Behavior as Foraging," in *The Psychology of Learning and Motivation: Advances in Research and Theory*, vol. 22, ed. Gordon Bower (New York: Academic, 1988).

42. Steven R. Hursh, "Economic Concepts for the Analysis of Behavior," *Journal of the Experimental Analysis of Behavior* 34 (1980): 219–38.

12

The Verbal Legacy of B. F. Skinner: An Essay on the Secondary Literature

Terry J. Knapp

During the past sixty years, reactions to B. F. Skinner's professional and scientific publications have produced a voluminous mass of books, articles, reviews, dissertations, popular magazine and newspaper accounts, artwork, video and audio productions, and even an occasional song and poem. In excess of nine hundred articles, gathered from library periodical, newspaper, and review indexes, as well as from Skinner's own collection, have been abstracted as a part of a larger project intended to provide a reference guide to works by and about Skinner.[1] This chapter surveys the secondary literature thus far reviewed, beginning with the 1930s up through the early 1990s. It is intended to give a feel for the terrain that must be covered in coming to grips with Skinner's influence on American culture, not so much in terms of his ideas or concepts, but in the simpler sense of the verbal artifacts that remain as a consequence of his having spoken and written about the science of behavior and the philosophy of radical behaviorism for the better part of this century. The first portion of the chapter analyzes the growth of the secondary literature on Skinner and the patterns evident in the citing of his works; the second part surveys the range of material available; and the final section summarizes some themes that emerge in attempting to broadly categorize the professional and popular literature about Skinner.

GROWTH OF THE SKINNER LITERATURE

A cumulative plot of the publications about Skinner contained in the data base just described is presented in figure 1, where a number of conspicuous changes in rate are noticeable. There is a slow steady rise of publications beginning in the late 1930s following the publication of

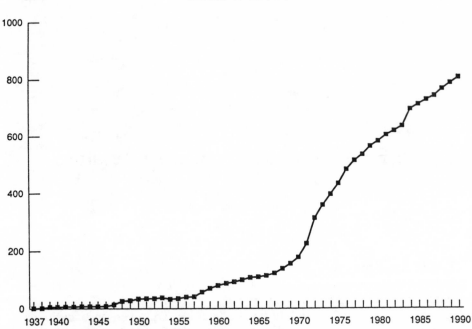

Figure 1. **Cumulative number of periodical and journal articles, doctoral disserta-tions, and books about B. F. Skinner from 1937 to 1990.**

The Behavior of Organisms, the book that began Skinner's professional career and that led to his recognition among academic psychologists concerned with learning. But it is *Beyond Freedom and Dignity* that appears to have established Skinner's lasting place in intellectual and popular culture. The most conspicuous and significant change in rate of secondary publications occurs during the 1971–72 period, shortly after its publication. Without this particular book, a good deal less would have been said about Skinner, and his influence outside the field of behavior analysis and psychology would undoubtedly have been less extensive.

Many persons have written *about* Skinner, and many more have cited his works. One way to gauge the influence of Skinner is to compare his citation rate to that of a prominent psychological contemporary. Figure 2 displays the citation of Skinner's work relative to that of Carl Rogers, as cataloged by the *Social Science Citation Index.* The plot shows a declining rate for Rogers and a growing difference between the two in cumulative citations during the past several decades, despite the fact that their rates were nearly equal at the beginning of the 1970s.

The citation of Skinner's works has been most frequent in the broad field of the social sciences, with relatively little citation in arts and human-

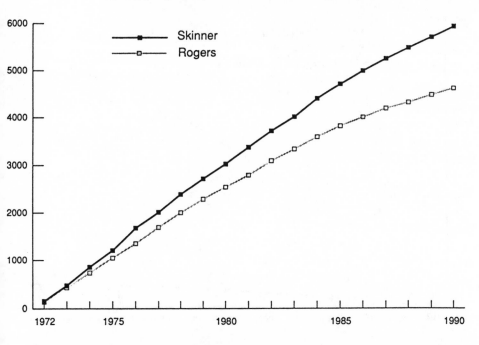

Figure 2. A comparison of the citation rates of B. F. Skinner and Carl R. Rogers based on the *Science Citation Index, Social Science Citation Index,* and *Arts and Humanities Citation Index*.

ities journals. A plot of the cumulative number of citations of Skinner's works during the past ten years for three indexes—the *Science,* the *Social Science,* and the *Arts and Humanities* citation indexes (see fig. 3)—supports such a conclusion, as do other data. For example, Skinner was not among the sixty most cited authors in a 1980 survey of the *Arts and Humanities Index,* although three twentieth-century psychologists were: Freud, Jung, and Piaget. (Freud ranked second overall, exceeded only by Lenin.[2]) However, among a list of the most frequently cited social scientists, Skinner ranked twelfth. Again, Freud was first, followed by Piaget.[3] Skinner has taken his place among "what every American needs to know" with his inclusion in the *Dictionary of Cultural Literacy,*[4] where Freud, James, and Jung also find a place.

Outside of the social sciences, the largest number of publications about Skinner in recent years has appeared in the philosophy journals. A cumulative plot of articles indexed under "Skinner, B. F.," from 1970 to 1989 (see fig. 4), shows totals of 191 for philosophy (*Philosopher's Index*), 50 for popular culture (*Reader's Guide to Periodical Literature*), and only 38 for journals in education (*Education Index*). In fact, the rate of General

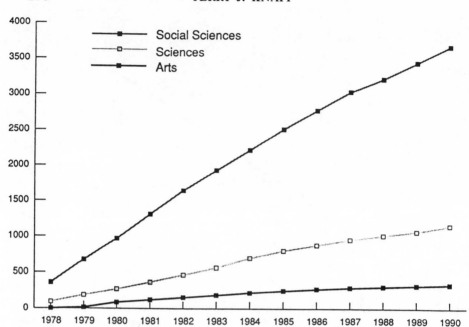

Figure 3. The citation rate of works by B. F. Skinner in three indexes: *Science Citation, Social Science Citation,* and *Arts and Humanities Citation.*

and Educational literature was nearly flat after 1984. The contrasting growth in the philosophical literature is in large measure attributable to the appearance in 1972 of the journal *Behaviorism,* where over half of the philosophy publications relating to Skinner have appeared, and which Skinner assisted in establishing.

In gauging Skinner's influence on psychological literature, one is handicapped by the plethora of terms that make reference to some aspect of his work. *Operant,* a term he chose to describe behavior controlled by its consequences, is perhaps the most widely used among all the expressions of his system. The *Psychological Abstracts* began to categorize publications under *conditioning, operant* in 1940, and later in 1973, under *operant conditioning.* Figure 5 displays the cumulative frequency of operant articles from 1940 to until 1990. A high rate in the early 1960s and a still higher rate in the 1970s are especially evident. Many of the studies indexed under this term only employ the operant-conditioning procedures developed by Skinner, and thus do not necessarily represent a commitment to his views; however, the rate at which operant studies appear may

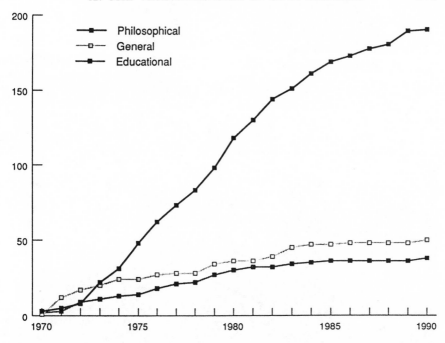

Figure 4. Cumulative number of articles about B. F. Skinner in three periodical indexes: the *Reader's Guide to Periodical Literature, Education Index,* **and** *Philosopher's Index.*

be the best single measure of Skinner's lasting influence on American psychology.

VARIETIES OF SECONDARY LITERATURE

Skinner's laboratory methods have resulted in a significant research program, reflected in the number of studies indexed under "operant conditioning"; but his worldview, his radical behaviorism, has been less than influential if the attention paid to it in humanities journals is taken as the measure. He offered many interpretations of cultural phenomena based on his analysis of behavior, but the following survey of the secondary literature suggests that little of this interpretive *practice* is in evidence outside the radical behaviorists' house journals. It is not possible to provide a thorough or even a systematic review of the literature. The attempt made here is merely suggestive of the variety of categories and of the quantity and quality of the available materials in each.

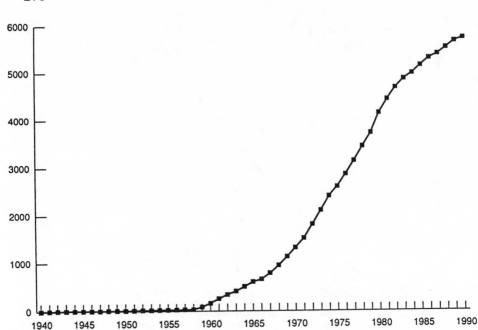

Figure 5. Cumulative number of publications indexed under "operant conditioning" in the *Psychological Abstracts* from 1940 to 1990.

There are nearly two dozen books about B. F. Skinner. If one were to include books on operant psychology, the count would increase considerably. Books on Skinner date from 1968 when R. I. Evans published his extended interview with Skinner as *B. F. Skinner: The Man and His Ideas*. The works that followed vary enormously in quality, and fall into several categories: religious tracts, reactions to *Walden Two* or *Beyond Freedom and Dignity,* surveys contrasting Skinner with other noted psychologists, and scholarly works.

In 1968, Daniel B. Stevick, while acknowledging the tensions between Skinner's views and those of Christianity, offered a noncaustic treatment of Skinner. This is not true of books that followed the publication of *Beyond Freedom and Dignity* in 1971. For example, *Back to Freedom and Dignity* by Francis A. Schaeffer claimed that "Skinner's war is not simply against Christians, it is against anyone who thinks that there is such a thing as a mind and anyone who writes concerning the freedom and dignity of man." A volume in the Rosemead Psychology Series concluded with a chapter on "Behaviorism in the Light of Scripture," wherein Christians were told that "biblical revelation" is compatible with the basic research data of Skinner's behaviorism, but not with his determinism and ethical system.[5]

Among the authors who have surveyed Skinner's work, Robert D. Nye contrasted Skinner's views with the psychological perspectives of Sigmund Freud and Carl Rogers, and also wrote a brief survey titled *What Is B. F. Skinner Really Saying?*[6] James A. Schellenberg compared Skinner's analysis of social topics with those of Freud, Kurt Lewin, and George Herbert Mead. And Frank Milhollan and Bill E. Forisha contrasted Skinner with Carl Rogers on matters of education.[7]

Among the more exotic books is *The Pseudo-Science of B. F. Skinner* by Tibor R. Machan,[8] who wrote from a libertarian perspective having been greatly influenced by Nathaniel Branden, an associate of Ayn Rand (who herself devoted a chapter to Skinner).[9] Several philosophy professors have authored short monographs.[10] The first doctoral dissertation on Skinner's work has become a book.[11] In one of the few works that is not a polemic, Finely Carpenter in *The Skinner Primer* described meanings of freedom that Skinner neglected, and gave a fair, if not sympathetic, appraisal of *Beyond Freedom and Dignity*.[12] An edited volume by Harvey Wheeler contains numerous professional reactions to *BFD*, including an essay by the noted historian Arnold Toynbee.[13]

There are aids for the reading of *Walden Two*, one by Monarch Notes, another by Cliff Notes.[14] Both were written by English professors, and attest to the wide use of *Walden Two* in college courses. There is also a volume in the literary Twayne World Leaders Series devoted to Skinner.[15] In the late 1980s, two broad professionally based volumes appeared: *B. F. Skinner: Consensus and Controversy,* one of a series that includes books on Chomsky, Piaget, Hans Eysenck, and A. R. Jensen among others; and *The Selection of Behavior: The Operant Behaviorism of B. F. Skinner: Comments and Consequences,* a collection of Skinner's papers and associated commentaries that originally appeared in the journal *Behavioral and Brain Sciences.* The 1990s saw the appearance of a biography by Daniel W. Bjork (*B. F. Skinner: A Life*) and Marc N. Richelle's *B. F. Skinner: A Reappraisal.* The *American Psychologist* devoted a lengthy issue to Skinner in 1992.[16] Even schoolchildren are an audience for books about Skinner. Elizabeth Hall's *From Pigeons to People: A Look at Behavioral Shaping* is an introduction to the ideas of Skinner for grade levels four to five.[17]

The content of doctoral dissertations is another gauge of intellectual influence. Judged by such a standard the conceptual work of Skinner has made its mark. Figure 6 displays a cumulative plot of doctoral dissertations in which Skinner's work is the central focus (as reported in *Dissertation Abstracts,* with experimental studies excluded). As early as 1964 Skinner's ideas began to attract doctoral candidates, primarily because

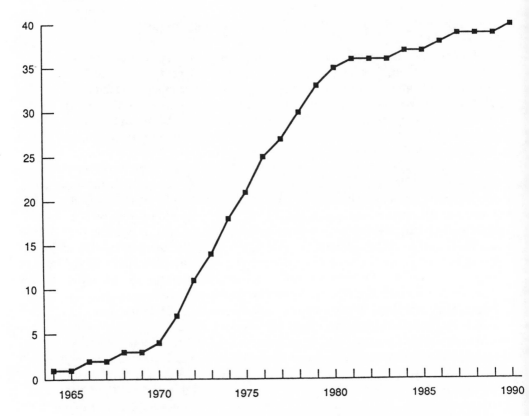

Figure 6. Cumulative number of nonexperimental doctoral dissertations on the work of B. F. Skinner, based on *Dissertation Abstracts*.

of his political views. Subsequent dissertations were written at a relatively low rate, until the publication of *Beyond Freedom and Dignity*. The dissertations have usually drawn contrasts and comparisons between Skinner and some other significant figure in the social sciences, or have critically explicated some aspect of Skinner's radical behaviorism.

Two dissertations may be of special interest to historians. Kristjan Gudmundsson focused on the early experimental work of Skinner in "The Emergence of B. F. Skinner's Theory of Operant Behavior: A Case Study in the History and Philosophy of Science."[18] A history of the writing, publishing, and reception of *Walden Two* constitutes a good portion of Richard D. Ramsey's "Morning Star: The Value Communication of Skinner's *Walden Two*."[19] Although the master's thesis literature is not easily accessed through routine indexing,[20] several adventitious discoveries have occurred. The earliest is "Toward an Operational Definition of Freedom" by Maynard Yasmer at the University of Nevada, Reno, in 1962.

There are more than a thousand periodical articles of greatly varying length concerning Skinner as a person or some aspect of his work. This excludes the extensive "operant psychology" literature of animal and human research studies. In terms of the latter literature, Skinner's early publications were cited in the experimental psychology literature shortly after their appearance, but it was not until the late 1930s that Skinner's *theoretical position* became the focus of publications. Early examples include Konorski and Miller's critical analysis of Skinner's distinction between operant and respondent conditioning, D. G. Ellson's unfavorable review of Skinner's concept of the "reflex reserve," and R. B. Louck's criticism of Skinner's alleged rejection of physiological psychology.[21] Aside from the reviews of *The Behavior of Organisms,* these are the earliest papers to take a position on Skinner's emerging system of behavior. The content of their criticisms addressed the adequacy of Skinner's approach for explaining the phenomena of animal learning.

A second set of papers began appearing in the mid-1950s and took the conceptual and intellectual views of Skinner as their object of analysis and criticism. These are the views that Skinner began publishing in the mid-1940s with a paper on the operational analysis of psychological terms, followed by *Walden Two* in 1948 and *Science and Human Behavior* in 1953. In these works Skinner greatly expanded the range of matters that he had committed himself to in print, as well as extending the audiences he was addressing, and by the mid-1950s, these audiences began to respond. Hacker in the *Journal of Politics* likened Skinner's political proposals to the "conditioned" societies of the former Soviet Union, Nazi Germany, and Marxist China. In 1955 Hamburg argued against Skinner's "scientific" ethics of survival, and in 1956 the philosopher of science Michael Scriven wrote a broadly conceived critique of Skinner's views.[22] These articles form a kind of bench mark in the growing influence of Skinner. His views were now being discussed by academics outside the field of psychology, and not merely in brief book review notices or in circumscribed papers on animal behavior, but rather in extended commentaries of political and philosophical discourse. The context of criticism had moved from animal learning to social theory and philosophy of science.

In any survey of the secondary literature on Skinner, no paper deserves more comment than Noam Chomsky's 1959 review of *Verbal Behavior.*[23] It is the most frequently cited article in the secondary literature, and continues to exert an influence despite several attempts by radical behaviorists to moderate its impact.[24] The review is cited once for every two citations of *Verbal Behavior,* as shown in figure 7. Chomsky wrote an

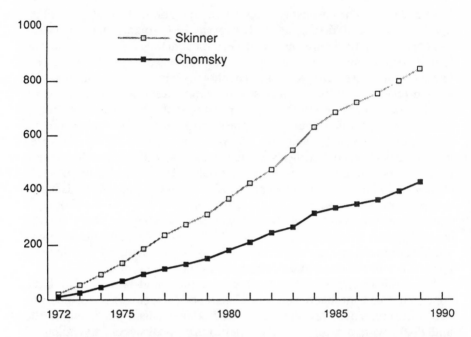

Figure 7. Cumulative number of citations of B. F. Skinner's book *Verbal Behavior* and Noam Chomsky's review of the book, based on the *Science Citation Index* and *Arts and Humanities Citation Index*.

equally vitriolic essay review of *Beyond Freedom and Dignity* in the *New York Review of Books,* where he titled his essay, "The Case Against B. F. Skinner."[25] In each instance Chomsky's thesis was the same: if behaviorism is taken literally, its claims are obviously false, and if taken metaphorically, the claims show no advantages over other views, and in fact obscure valuable distinctions. Any final assessment of Skinner's radical behaviorism will require a careful analysis of the role of Chomsky's criticism, and of Chomsky's contribution to moving mainstream psychology back toward a cognitive perspective.

Skinner's admission to popular magazines came very early in his career. This includes not only his own 1934 publication on Gertrude Stein in the *Atlantic Monthly,* but secondary accounts as well. As early as 1937, *Life* magazine featured two pages of photographs and a brief description of a rat named Pliny that Skinner had trained to place marbles in a hole; Pliny was described by *Life* as a "smart" rat that "works a slot machine for a living." *Life* would return to the work of Skinner in 1947 with a "boxes for babies" article. *Look,* its competitor, presented photographs in 1952 of a dog that Skinner had trained when challenged to demonstrate the principles of operant psychology. *Life* was also the source of an un-signed review of *Walden Two* in which the book was characterized as a "slur upon a name, a corruption of an impulse."[26] The *New Yorker,* often a source of learned pieces on Freud and other intellectuals, has never devoted a lengthy article to the work of Skinner, although his name ap-peared from very early on, for example, in a two-page article devoted to the Aircrib in 1947.[27] *Time* magazine put Skinner on its cover in 1971 in connection with the publication of *Beyond Freedom and Dignity,* but its first reference to Skinner's work was probably a two-page article in 1950 on Skinner's having switched from rats to pigeons as subjects; two pi-geons were shown playing Ping-Pong.[28]

Skinner's writings have not escaped the attention of politicians. In a speech before the Farm Bureau, former Vice President Spiro Agnew at-tacked *Beyond Freedom and Dignity* as a "new kind of despotism," and on the floor of Congress Rep. Cornelius E. Gallagher requested oversight of the funds that Skinner had received from the National Institutes of Mental Health. Like Agnew, Gallagher regarded *Beyond Freedom and Dignity* as inimical to American society.[29] Nor has Skinner escaped treat-ment by poets—at least three poems about him have been published.[30] There is no lack of discussion of Skinner's personal motives either. These range from explaining Skinner's "dark year," to examining the influence of his Presbyterian upbringing, to suggesting that his entire philosophy of radical behaviorism is a personal defense against contact with people.[31]

There are several dozen published interviews with Skinner, the greatest number of which appeared in connection with the promotion of *Beyond Freedom and Dignity.* The best known is the previously mentioned inter-view by R. I. Evans, which forms one in a series of filmed interviews completed in the mid-1960s with the world's most eminent psychologists. Among the more obscure are an interview in *Family Circle* in the late 1960s and another in a little-known journal titled *Practical Psychology for Physicians.*[32] Several introductory psychology textbooks have in-cluded their own interviews with Skinner. Despite the wide-ranging per-sonages featured in *Playboy* interviews, Skinner was never among them, though in 1972 a long portrait piece on him appeared under the title "God Is a Variable Interval."[33]

Supplementary interviews with Skinner's daughters are also available, each with interesting titles. *People* magazine said, "Sure She Spent Time in a Box . . . but B. F.'s Daughter Was Never His Guinea Pig," and the *Los Angeles Times* led with "Developer of 'Air Crib' Defended by Daughter."[34] There are apparently no published interviews with Eve Skin-ner about her husband's life work, though she has been quoted as saying she knew he was a genius from the time she first met him.[35]

From the inception of his professional career, in fact even before, Skinner came to the attention of the daily print media. The *New York Times* chronicled many of Skinner's activities, beginning on 27 December 1946 with an announcement of his appointment as William James Lecturer.[36] What makes the material from daily print media useful is the unusual items one encounters: for example, an account of Skinner's first visit to Disneyland as covered by the *Los Angeles Times,* or the extensive account of his "Growing Up in Susquehanna" in the Sunday supplement of the *Press and Sun Bulletin.* In the latter case, the authors took much of their material from the first volume of Skinner's autobiography, but original photographs of his childhood home, grammar school, and other local sites were included.[37] A great number of editorials have been written about Skinner, most of them as a consequence of *Beyond Freedom and Dignity.* For example, the *Atlanta Constitution* in "Of Mice and Men" claimed that Skinner could find no significant difference between the two.[38] The *Des Moines Register* marked Skinner's passing with an editorial.[39] Letters to the editor are another source of opinion about Skinner. The most extensive set appeared after the 1971 *Time* magazine cover story,[40] but many others can be located.

One large body of secondary source material consists of the treatment afforded Skinner in psychology textbooks. Ernest R. Hilgard's *Theories of Learning* may be the first textbook to have devoted a chapter to explicating operant conditioning, relying almost exclusively upon *The Behavior of Organism,* of which Hilgard was one of the original reviewers.[41] In a recent sample of introductory psychology textbooks, Knapp found that Skinner ranked second in rate of citation, following Freud and tied with Piaget.[42] A more systematic analysis of which of Skinner's ideas are included in introductory textbooks would be helpful, particularly in identifying those aspects of his work that have been ignored. A partial step in this direction is the cataloging of errors in the presentation of radical behaviorism contained in a variety of textbooks in the subfields of psychology.[43] It seems that only in the fields of perception and cognition has Skinner failed to gain the attention of textbook writers.[44]

The second edition of the *Random House Dictionary* includes three items under the "Skinner": an entry for Skinner himself, as well as entries for the "Skinner box" and "Skinnerian." In some dictionaries, the entries reveal as much about the editors as they do about Skinner. For example, in the *Baker's Encyclopedia of Psychology,* one learns that "Skinner espouses materialistic humanism," which has "shape[d] his scientific conclusions," and led to his "anti-Christian philosophy." Upon consulting the preface, one learns that the encyclopedia "was born out of an awareness of the need for a comprehensive treatment of psychology from a Christian point of view."[45] At the other end of the spectrum is an encyclopedia of psychology jointly dedicated to Skinner and Rogers.[46]

Verbal artifacts that are unpublished and have limited circulation are sometimes the gems for which biographers search. There are many such items in connection with the career of Skinner. The various advertisements that appeared for *The Behavior of Organisms,* and Skinner's own concern over them, have been described elsewhere.[47] The effusive blurb printed on the dust jacket of the original edition of *Walden Two* does not reflect the ordinarily subdued writing of Skinner, suggesting that Macmillan's publicists were the source of such remarks as: "Ever get tired of hustling and worrying? Completely satisfied with your lot? Yeasty ideas crown this novel about an ideal society. Men are not stretched to fit this society, it is stretched to fit them." An advance announcement from Macmillan stated that *Walden Two* "is the story of two young veterans who don't want to go back to the old way of living, and who find a new way in an experimental community in the Middle West. In the daily life of this community, Walden Two, new and exciting psychological and economic theories are put to the test."

Some of the most interesting things that people have had to say about B. F. Skinner have been said not with words, but with various works of art. On the cover of *Time* Skinner appeared as a rat. Elsewhere he has been cast as a pigeon, or as a boxer with a bird rather than a chip on his shoulder.[48] The illustrations produced in connection with Skinner often use strong images, of the sort more likely used for a political figure than for an academic psychologist.

Skinner and his work have been the subject of many television programs, educational films, slide shows, and audiotape productions. The PBS science series *Nova* has featured programs on only two psychologists: Skinner was first, Freud second. Skinner's appearances on network television shows—beginning with CBS, and including William Buckley's *Firing Line,* the *Dick Cavett Show,* morning network shows, and a variety of productions of limited circulation—reflect a cultural influence that has been afforded few other academic psychologists.[49] One notable item in the category of documentaries is *Together,* a film of Skinner and Fred Keller reminiscing about their careers; Prentice-Hall has withdrawn the film, and it is obtained only with difficulty.[50]

Among the sound filmstrips that have been produced, one "summarizes the elements of Skinner's Utopia and reviews the critical reaction to it."[51] Audiotape recordings run the gamut from the full-length dialogue between Carl Rogers and Skinner (not to be confused with their 1956 debate held at the American Psychological Association), which took place over two days at the University of Minnesota at Duluth in June of 1962, to cassettes that offer students of psychology a thirty-minute introduction to, and summary of, Skinner's science of behavior.[52] The American Psychological Association has made available tape recordings of eight of Skinner's addresses of recent years, as well as a video recording of his remarks upon receiving the Lifetime Scientific Contribution Award.[53]

THEMES AND PROSPECTS

An informal inspection of the materials just surveyed suggests six thematic groupings in the secondary literature on Skinner. The first involves political philosophy. The works of few other psychologists have prompted discussions among political theorists, and none has produced a reaction to match that accorded Skinner. It was Skinner's analysis of political systems in *Walden Two* that first attracted the attention of critics outside of psychology. With few exceptions the criticism has been fairly civil, which is remarkable given the arguments against democracy that Skinner advanced in *Walden Two*. Americans may not vote in record numbers, but American ideology still holds the process to be a sacred one. A careful examination of the exchanges between Skinner and his political commentators may be worthwhile for reasons beyond that of understanding Skinner's influence. American culture has tolerated few "antidemocratic" critics, especially during the McCarthy era. How did Skinner's ideas survive? There is also the interesting possibility that Skinner's political analysis shares more in common with the critic Noam Chomsky than one would suspect. Both the American political right and the American left have at times found Skinner a useful target. Yet, despite the number of papers and dissertations written on Skinner's analysis of government and political matters, there has been a remarkable dearth of studies connecting the ideas of *Walden Two* to the greater political and cultural scene of midtwentieth-century America.[54]

A second theme is religion, especially as defended against Skinner by Christian fundamentalists. It is perhaps strange that fundamentalists should have singled out Skinner as a special focus of their dialogues. Their efforts did not begin with the publication of *Beyond Freedom and Dignity,* though Skinner's analysis of values in chapter 6 did much to stimulate their opposition, as did his signature on the Humanist Manifesto II and his selection in 1972 as Humanist of the Year by the American Humanist Association.[55] The literature on Skinner and religion may prove to be especially useful because it embodies one of the few contemporary confrontations between religion and psychological science. In the opinion of many fundamentalists, religious values have not been so clearly threatened by a psychologist since Freud. The problems created by Skinner's views for these critics stem not only from his overarching commitment to science, but also from his explicit, and generally unfavorable, discussions of religion in *Walden Two* and *Science and Human Behavior*. Much of the literature by religious commentators is found in periodicals of limited circulation, but is accessible through the *Index to Religious Literature*. Paradoxically, serious students of theology have described Skinner as a secularized Puritan whose psychology bears resemblance to the theological beliefs of Jonathan Edwards.[56]

A third theme to emerge from the secondary literature on Skinner involves his relation to humanism and humanistic psychology. If asked to identify Skinner's chief critics, many persons in academic psychology would respond with "the humanistic psychologists." There is the famous Rogers-Skinner debate, and the general issue of freedom and control on which it turned. The rise of humanistic psychology in America largely paralleled Skinner's own rise to national prominence. Skinner was widely known among academic psychologists by the 1940s. But it was only in the fifties and sixties that his work received attention in the popular media and among a wider academic audience. It was during the same period that Carl Rogers, Abraham Maslow, Rollo May, and Fritz Perls achieved prominence. The parallel in their development does not end with their shared criticism of mainstream academic psychology: for example, both perspectives formed their own organizations and journals, and continued to function in isolation from mainstream academic psychology, despite the fact that in another sense the names Maslow, Rogers, and Skinner are as about mainstream as one could find in American psychology. An inspection of the secondary literature since the mid-1980s suggests that the dialogue between radical behaviorism and humanistic psychology has played itself out. Because both perspectives are still well represented in contemporary psychology, historians may wish to determine the reasons for their disengagement.

A fourth theme from the secondary literature is best described as ethical and epistemological. Here one finds not merely critics, but advocates: those who regard Skinner as having made a fundamental contribution to philosophy, one that has for the most part gone unrecognized. The writings on Skinner's analysis of values and ethics form a small bibliography in their own right, and a fair number of commentators have favorably reviewed Skinner's analysis and even taken up his call for a naturalistic ethics. One has even suggested that *Beyond Freedom and Dignity* may be among the "most important" moral works of Western civilization.[57] Other philosophers have raised the possibility that Skinner's analysis of teleological behavior has provided a "serious alternative to commonsense mentalism."[58] Skinner's call for a behavioral epistemology is one still awaiting an answer, but his views are no longer rejected outright. It has even been argued that Skinner's epistemological work anticipated crucial aspects of the recent turn toward naturalized, psychologistic epistemologies.[59]

A fifth theme is the ongoing tension between behaviorism and cognitivism. The most vitriolic of Skinner's critics have been the cognitivists. Chomsky's 1959 review of *Verbal Behavior* in many ways marks the beginning of the exchanges between the cognitivists and Skinnerians, which ultimately led to Skinner's explaining "why he was not a cognitive psychologist." Though cognitive psychology textbooks have generally neglected what Skinner had to say on topics related to cognition, some positive exchanges began occurring in the 1980s,[60] along with a series of hostile exchanges.[61] In general, it may be said that cognitive psychology has taken as its enemy a broader view of behaviorism than Skinner's experimental analysis of behavior. Although there is a clear literature exhibiting this theme, mutual isolation is a better description of the general relationship between Skinner's work and the recently emerged cognitive psychology.[62]

A final, and narrower, theme concerns the status of private events in psychology. The inclusion of an analysis of private events in the science of behavior is a major point used by both Skinner and his commentators to differentiate radical behaviorism from methodological behaviorism.[63] The dialogue is a continuing one, largely conducted within the radical behaviorist community. In recent years it has appeared in basic research journals as Skinnerians explore the private experiences of pigeons.[64] The recently published commentaries on Skinner's operational analysis of psychological terms thoroughly discuss the status of private events.[65]

CONCLUSION

No aspect of American culture is untouched by Skinner's works. Anyone seeking to chronicle all of the material produced in reaction to Skinner is thus faced with an enormous task. The passage of time will likely provide a perspective from which selection among an otherwise vast array of materials will be possible. But there is a sense in which the real extent of an individual's influence is revealed only by a careful inspection of the remnants remaining in the smallest nooks and cracks of a culture. In reviewing Skinner's *Reflections on Behaviorism and Society,* one critic asserted that in the future Skinner's work will be reduced to a mere footnote. If that is true, it will at least be a very long footnote.

NOTES

1. Robert Epstein and Terry J. Knapp, *B. F. Skinner: A Guide to the Primary and Secondary Works* (Boston: G. K. Hall, forthcoming).
2. Eugene Garfield, "Is Information Retrieval in the Arts and Humanities

Inherently Different from the Sciences? The Effect that ISI's Citation Index for the Arts and Humanities Is Expected to Have on Future Scholarship," *Library Journal* 50 (1980): 51–53.

3. Perhaps surprisingly, the following psychologists ranked above Skinner: Hans J. Eysenck (5th), Albert Bandura (8th), Raymond B. Cattell (9th), and Ben J. Winer, a statistician-psychologist (6th).

4. Eric D. Hirsch, Joseph F. Kett, and James Trefil, *The Dictionary of Cultural Literacy: What Every American Needs to Know* (Boston: Houghton, 1988), p. 409.

5. Daniel B. Stevick, *B. F. Skinner's Walden Two: Introduction and Commentary* (New York: Seabury Press, 1968); Francis A. Schaeffer, *Back to Freedom and Dignity* (Downers Grove, Ill: Inter-Varsity Press, 1972), p. 44; Mark P. Cosgrove, *B. F. Skinner's Behaviorism: An Analysis* (Grand Rapids, Mich.: Zondervan, 1982), pp. 116–17.

6. Robert D. Nye, *What Is B. F. Skinner Really Saying?* (Englewood Cliffs, N.J.: Prentice-Hall, 1979).

7. Robert D. Nye, *Three Psychologies: Perspectives from Freud, Skinner, and Rogers,* 2d ed. (Monterey, Calif.: Brooks/Cole, 1975/1981); James A. Schellenberg, *Masters of Social Psychology* (New York: Oxford University Press, 1978); Frank Milhollan and Bill E. Forisha, *From Skinner to Rogers: Contrasting Approaches to Education* (Lincoln, Nebr.: Professional Educators, 1972).

8. Tibor R. Machan, *The Pseudo-Psychology of B. F. Skinner* (New Rochelle, N.Y.: Arlington House, 1974).

9. Ayn Rand, "The Stimulus and the Response," in *Philosophy: Who Needs It?* (Indianapolis: Bobbs, 1972), pp. 166–96. There are a small number of anti-Skinnerian papers written from a libertarian perspective.

10. Ramakrishna Puligandla, *Fact and Fiction in B. F. Skinner's Science and Utopia* (St. Louis, Mo.: Warren H. Green, 1974); Paul T. Sagal, *Skinner's Philosophy* (Lanham, Md.: University Press of America, 1981); Ilham Dilman, *Mind, Brain, and Behavior: Discussions of B. F. Skinner and J. R. Searle* (London: Routledge, 1988).

11. Anne E. Freedman, *The Planned Society: An Analysis of Skinner's Proposals* (Kalamazoo, Mich.: Behavioradelia, 1972).

12. Finely Carpenter, *The Skinner Primer: Behind Freedom and Dignity* (New York: Free Press, 1974).

13. Harvey Wheeler, ed., *Beyond the Punitive Society* (San Francisco: Freeman, 1973).

14. Peter Ruppert, *B. F. Skinner's Walden Two: A Critical Commentary* (New York: Simon & Schuster, 1976); Cynthia C. McGowan and James L. Roberts, *Walden Two: Notes* (Lincoln, Nebr.: Cliff Notes, 1979).

15. John A. Weigel, *B. F. Skinner* (Boston: G. K. Hall, 1977).

16. Sohan Modgil and Celia Modgil, eds., *B. F. Skinner: Consensus and Controversy* (East Sussex, England: Falmer, 1987); A. C. Catania and Steven Harnad, eds., *The Selection of Behavior: The Operant Behaviorism of B. F. Skinner: Comments and Consequences* (Cambridge: Cambridge University Press, 1988). Daniel W. Bjork, *B. F. Skinner: A Life* (New York: Basic, 1993); Marc N. Richelle, *B. F. Skinner: A Reappraisal* (Hillsdale, N.J.: Erlbaum, 1993); Kennon A. Lattal, ed., "Reflections on B. F. Skinner and Psychology," *American Psychologist* 47 (1992): 1265–1560.

17. Elizabeth Hall, *From Pigeons to People: A Look at Behavior Shaping* (Boston: Houghton, 1975). Though written at a higher grade level, *The Psychology*

Primer, ed. Linda Wood (New York: Dell, 1975) contains a section on Skinner and a depiction of him on the cover where he is seen holding a pigeon.

18. Kristjan Gudmundsson, "The Emergence of B. F. Skinner's Theory of Operant Behavior: A Case Study in the History and Philosophy of Science" (Ph.D. diss., University of Western Ontario, 1983), *Dissertation Abstracts International, 444,* 3086.

19. Richard D. Ramsey, "Morning Star: The Value Communication of Skinner's *Walden Two*" (Ph.D. diss., Rensselaer Polytechnic Institute, 1979), *Dissertation Abstracts International, 408,* 5465.

20. An index is available for education: Herbert M. Silvey, ed., *Master's Theses in Education* (Cedar Falls, Iowa: Research Publications, 1962-to date).

21. These were the three longest pieces to appear until the chapter by Ernest Hilgard in *Theories of Learning* (New York: Appleton-Century-Crofts, 1948); and later William S. Verplanck, "Burrhus F. Skinner," in *Modern Learning Theory,* ed. William K. Estes et al. (New York: Appleton-Century-Crofts, 1954), pp. 267–316. A sense of the growth of Skinner's influence from pre-1940 (but post-1938) to the late 1940s can be gained by comparing *Theories of Learning* with the earlier Ernest R. Hilgard and Donald Marquis, *Conditioning and Learning* (New York: Appleton-Century, 1940).

22. Andrew Hacker, "Dostoevsky's Disciples: Man and Sheep in Political Theory," *Journal of Politics* 17 (1955): 590–613; Carl Hamburg, "Skinner's 'Scientific' Ethics of Survival," *Tulane Studies in Philosophy* 4 (1955): 49–60; Michael Scriven, "A Study of Radical Behaviorism" in *Minnesota Studies in the Philosophy of Science,* vol. 1, ed. Herbert Feigl and Michael Scriven (Minneapolis: University of Minnesota Press, 1956), pp. 88–130.

23. Noam Chomsky, review of *Verbal Behavior,* by Skinner, *Language* 35 (1959): 26–59.

24. For example, Kenneth MacCorquodale, "On Chomsky's Review of Skinner's *Verbal Behavior,*" *Journal of the Experimental Analysis of Behavior* 13 (1970): 83–99; and Evalyn Segal, "Chomsky's Anguish," 1972, unpublished manuscript submitted to the *New York Review of Books.* With attention directed to Chomsky's review, the more than two dozen other reviews of *Verbal Behavior* have been neglected; see Terry J. Knapp, "*Verbal Behavior:* The Other Reviews," *Analysis of Verbal Behavior* 10 (1992): 87–95.

25. Chomsky, "The Case Against B. F. Skinner," *New York Review of Books,* 27 December 1971, pp. 18–24.

26. *Life,* 31 May 1937, pp. 80–81; *Life,* 3 November 1947, pp. 73–74; [John K. Jessup], "The Newest Utopia Is a Slander on Some Old Notions of the Good Life," *Life,* 28 June 1948, p. 38. Many other relevant articles have appeared in *Life.*

27. *New Yorker,* 19 July 1947, pp. 19–20.

28. *Time,* 19 June 1950, pp. 72–73; *Time,* 20 September 1971, pp. 47–53. *Newsweek* was slower in providing coverage, but ran essentially the same story as the first *Time* piece on 7 May 1951, p. 56. Skinner was photographed in his laboratory, and quoted as saying that he could build a better gambling device, but for ethical reasons would not tell how. Skinner's intimation that behaviorism is in possession of powerful knowledge was a frequently used rhetorical device. For other popular press accounts appearing about the same time, see *Popular Science,* July 1950, pp. 116–18; *New York Times,* 14 June 1950, pp. 38:7; and 18 June 1950, 9:6; and *Science Newsletter,* 17 June 1950, pp. 371–72.

29. "Agnew's Blast at Behaviorism," *Psychology Today,* January 1972, pp. 4, 84, 87. For Skinner's reaction to Agnew, see Elizabeth Hall, "Will Success Spoil

B. F. Skinner?" *Psychology Today,* November 1972, pp. 65–72, 130. Cornelius E. Gallagher, "Federal Funds of $238,000 to Harvard Psychologist B. F. Skinner to Write *Beyond Freedom and Dignity,*" *Congressional Record* 117:36 (15 December 1971): 47187, 92nd Congr., 1st sess. (an appendix summarizes the funds by year and identifies their purpose and outcome). The *New Republic* came to Skinner's defense on 28 January 1972, p. 14.

30. For example, Robert Epstein, "Behaviorist at Fifty," *Division 25 Recorder* 16 (Spring 1981): 18; and Steve Harrison, "B. F. Skinner," *Southern Humanities Review* 14 (1980): 222–23.

31. Alan C. Elms, "Skinner's Dark Year and *Walden Two,*" *American Psychologist* 36 (1981): 470–79; Daniel B. Shea, Jr., "B. F. Skinner: The Puritan Within," *Virginia Quarterly Review* 50 (1974): 416–37.

32. Maria Wilhelm, "An Interview with Behavioral Psychologist B. F. Skinner," *Family Circle,* October 1975, pp. 8, 179, 181–84; "An Interview with B. F. Skinner," *Practical Psychology for Physicians* 1 (November/December 1974): 23–25, 29–30.

33. Donn Pearce, "God Is a Variable Interval," *Playboy,* August 1972, pp. 81–86, 172–74, 176.

34. Lois Wingerson, "Sure She Spent Time in a Box, Says Deborah Skinner, But B. F.'s Daughter Was Never His Guinea Pig," *People Weekly,* 11 June 1979, pp. 73–74; "Developer of 'Air Crib' Defended by Daughter," *Los Angeles Times,* 4 July 1972, 1-B, 4:1, 3:1. However, for the best piece by a family member see Julie S. Vargas, "B. F. Skinner, Father, Grandfather, Behavior Modifier," *Human Behavior* 1 (1971): 19–23, reprinted in *About Human Nature: Journeys in Psychological Thought,* ed. Terry J. Knapp and Charles R. Rasmussen (Dubuque, Iowa: Kendall/Hunt, 1987), pp. 52–63; see also Vargas, "B. F. Skinner—The Last Few Days," *Journal of Applied Behavior Analysis* 23 (1990): 409–10.

35. See Rhonda K. Bjork, "The Personal Culture of Yvonne Blue Skinner," this volume; and Elizabeth A. Jordan, "Freedom and the Control of Children: The Skinners' Approach to Parenting," this volume.

36. Although this is the first item indexed by the *New York Times Index,* it is possible that earlier articles appeared.

37. Jay Horowitz, "B. F. Skinner in Utopia: A Reinforcing Place," *Los Angeles Times,* 21 February 1979; Steve Hambalek, *The Press & Sun Bulletin,* 29 August 1976. Newspaper accounts are an excellent source of original photographs; for example, in the *Indiana Daily Student* (5 April 1973) Skinner is shown hanged in effigy complete with a rat's feet and tail.

38. "Of Mice and Men," *Atlanta Constitution,* 12 January 1972.

39. *Des Moines Register,* 25 August 1990.

40. *Time,* 11 October 1971, p. 4; and 18 October 1971, p. 6.

41. Ernest R. Hilgard, *Theories of Learning* (New York: Appleton-Century-Crofts, 1948). The subsequent editions, through the 5th (with Gordon Bower as the first author), provide an interesting serial appraisal of Skinner's theories. For example, *The Behavior of Organism* is described in the 4th edition as "a historically significant book" (1975, p. 207). Hilgard's review has recently been reprinted in the *Journal of the Experimental Analysis of Behavior* 50 (1988): 283–86; it originally appeared in the *Psychological Bulletin* 36 (1939): 121–25.

42. Terry J. Knapp, "Who's Who in American Introductory Psychology Textbooks: A Citation Study," *Teaching of Psychology* 12 (1985): 15–17.

43. James T. Todd and Edward K. Morris, "Misconceptions and Miseducation: Presentations of Radical Behaviorism in Psychology Textbooks," *Behavior Ana-*

lyst 6 (1983): 153–60. Cf. the remarks by John K. Robinson and William R. Woodward ("Experimental Analysis of Behavior at Harvard: From Cumulative Records to Mathematical Models," this volume) regarding the omission by textbook writers of post-1960 developments in the experimental analysis of behavior.

44. See Knapp, "Perception and Action," in *Consensus and Controversy*, pp. 283–94.

45. David G. Benner, ed., *Baker Encyclopedia of Psychology* (Grand Rapids, Mich.: Baker Publishers, 1985).

46. Raymond Corsini, ed., *Concise Encyclopedia of Psychology* (New York: Wiley, 1987). Paradoxically the coverage of Skinner is brief, even though Skinner himself is the author of a two-page section on operant conditioning. Skinner was a frequent contributor to encyclopedias: see, for example, the entry in the *World Book of Knowledge* for E. L. Thorndike.

47. Knapp, "The Natural History of *The Behavior of Organisms*," in *Modern Perspectives on Classical and Contemporary Behaviorism*, ed. James T. Todd and Edward K. Morris (Westport, Conn.: Greenwood, 1995), pp. 7–23.

48. Bruce Bower, "Skinner Boxing," *Science News*, 8 February 1986, pp. 92–94.

49. PBS, *Nova*, 1979, "A World of Difference: B. F. Skinner and the Good Life"; PBS, *Firing Line*, 17 October 1971, "Case against Freedom." Skinner's appearance on the *Dick Cavett Show* is recounted in his *Matter of Consequences* (New York: Knopf, 1983), p. 299. During his brief segment on the program (for which Cavett's other guests were Ella Fitgerald and the comedians Bob and Ray), discussion was sidetracked to the topic of Sigmund Freud and the question of what psychologists could do to prevent murder; he later canceled a second scheduled appearance on the show upon realizing that Cavett's substitute host, the comedian Zero Mostel, would provide even fewer opportunities for serious discussion of his views (ibid., pp. 327–28). Skinner reported being little more satisfied with his appearance on Buckley's *Firing Line*, during which his fellow guest, the British physicist Donald McKay, "spent much of the hour explaining God's plan for the world" (ibid., p. 319).

50. Several universities (e.g., West Virginia University) acquired the film, but it is apparently no longer available for purchase. Several years ago it took some insistence on my part to persuade Prentice-Hall to loan me a copy.

51. Titled *Walden II: B. F. Skinner's Utopia*, it is available from Social Studies School Service, Culver City, Calif.

52. Robert S. Stone, "Listen & Learn: B. F. Skinner," Box 2124, Reseda, Calif., 91335. The 19-page booklet accompanying the Skinner-Rogers dialogue provides a brief description of the informal interactions between the two during their two days together in Duluth; see Gerald A. Gladstein, *A Dialogue on Education and the Control of Human Behavior* (New York: Jeffrey Norton, 1976).

53. Available from the American Psychological Association, Order Department, 750 First Street, NE, Washington, D.C. 20002.

54. For a discussion, see Daniel W. Bjork, "B. F. Skinner and the American Tradition: The Scientist as Social Inventor," this volume; and Laurence D. Smith, "Situating B. F. Skinner and Behaviorism in American Culture," this volume.

55. There were "humanists" who objected as well; see "Is B. F. Skinner a Humanist?" *Humanist* 32 (November/December 1972): 43.

56. David R. Williams, "Horses, Pigeons, and the Therapy of Conversion: A Psychological Reading of Jonathan Edwards's Theology," *Harvard Theological Review* 74 (1981): 337–52.

57. Because of the analysis of values contained in chapter 6; see William A. Rottschaefer, "Skinner's Science of Values," *Behaviorism* 8 (1980): 99–122.

58. Jon D. Ringen, "Explanation, Teleology, and Operant Behaviorism: A Study of the Experimental Analysis of Purposive Behavior," *Philosophy of Science* 43 (1976): 223–53. Ringen treats Skinner's radical behaviorism as a serious and significant piece of philosophy.

59. Smith, *Behaviorism and Logical Positivism: A Reassessment of the Alliance* (Stanford, Calif.: Stanford University Press, 1986), chaps. 9 and 10. For examples of recent psychologistic epistemologies, see Ronald N. Giere, *Understanding Science: A Cognitive Approach* (Chicago: University of Chicago Press, 1988); and Barry Gholson et al., eds., *Psychology of Science: Contributions to Metascience* (New York: Cambridge University Press, 1989).

60. The exception is Michael G. Wessell, *Cognitive Psychology* (New York: Harper, 1982).

61. For examples of both see Terry J. Knapp and Lynn C. Robertson, eds., *Approaches to Cognition* (Hillsdale, N.J.: Erlbaum, 1986), and especially these chapters: Donald Riley, Michael F. Brown, and Sonja I. Yoerg, "Understanding Animal Cognition," pp. 111–136, and Roger Schnaitter, "A Coordination of Differences: Behaviorism, Mentalism, and the Foundations of Psychology," pp. 291–315.

62. See, for example, Knapp, "The Emergence of Cognitive Psychology in the Latter Half of the Twentieth Century," in *Approaches to Cognition,* pp. 13–35.

63. For a review of references, see Knapp, "Private Events, Private Experiences, and Secrets" (paper presented at the annual meeting of the Association for Behavior Analysis, Milwaukee, Wis., May 1983).

64. David Lubinski and Travis Thompson, "An Animal Model of the Interpersonal Communication of Interoceptive (Private) States," *Journal of the Experimental Analysis of Behavior* 48 (1987): 1–15.

65. Catania and Harnad, eds., *Selection of Behavior,* chaps. 3, 5.

Conclusion
Situating B. F. Skinner and Behaviorism in American Culture

LAURENCE D. SMITH

MORE than any other American psychologist of the twentieth century, B. F. Skinner became something of a cultural icon. The preceding chapters have documented Skinner's rise from the boy tinkerer of small-town Pennsylvania, to the self-styled enfant terrible of Harvard psychology during the 1930s, to the controversial polemicist of the 1970s. By the midseventies, he had been featured on the cover of *Time* magazine, had appeared on television talk shows, and had been publicly attacked by an American vice president. His *Beyond Freedom and Dignity* had survived on the New York Times best-seller list for twenty weeks, and *Walden Two* had sold a million copies. A 1975 study showed him to be the most widely known American scientist among college students, outranking the likes of Margaret Mead, Jonas Salk, Linus Pauling, and James D. Watson.[1] It was a remarkable fate for a psychologist who began his career running rats in handmade apparatuses on the fourth floor of Emerson Hall. Though his public exposure peaked during the 1970s, Skinner never shied away from controversy. In his last public appearance only days before his death in 1990 at the age of eighty-six, he delivered a sharp critique of cognitive psychology to an audience of several thousand psychologists.[2]

Skinner's transition from rat-runner to social philosopher was accompanied by waves of both adulation and notoriety.[3] He was, of course, the founder and revered leader of the operant movement in psychology, and the gurulike chief architect of its multifarious applications in education, medicine, mental health, forensics, and industry.[4] And despite the isolation of operant psychology from mainstream American psychology, Skinner was widely admired by American psychologists.[5] To those who formed communities modeled after Walden Two, he was a savior figure, the visionary prophet of a practicable behavioral technology for salvaging culture from its wrong-headed path. But he was also reviled by many. To scholars in the humanities, he became a bête noire who represented the worst trends in the technocratic dehumanizing of culture and a dangerous perversion of Enlightenment ideals. He was attacked by leftist groups as a "leading light of fascist behaviorism" and as a perpetrator of "Nazi medicine."[6] The left-wing linguist Noam Chomsky, who had earlier established himself as the foremost critic of Skinner's *Verbal Behavior,* portrayed Skinner's views on cultural design as leading to a totalitarian state with "gas ovens smoking in the distance." A 1971 speech by Spiro Agnew depicted Skinner as a dangerous radical bent on undermining the American family and such cherished precepts as the individual and human freedom. Among Skinner's detractors was the noted philosopher Karl Popper, who described him as "an enemy of freedom and of democracy" and a "megalomaniac behaviorist who defends a behaviorist dictatorship."[7]

Under attack from scholars, politicians, and laypersons—and from both ends of the political spectrum—Skinner clearly stood at the intersection of powerful cultural currents that somehow elevated him to a bigger-than-life stature. Yet for all his notoriety, Skinner himself was widely perceived as a gentle and unassuming person. He frequently managed to charm even his opponents, more than one of whom found themselves disarmed by his friendly demeanor, humor, and modesty. The humanist psychologist Carl R. Rogers admitted during the course of his extended debates with Skinner that he had come to "prize" Skinner, and Skinner's own daughter was once startled by his congenial interaction with his arch-opponent Chomsky.[8] In a book sharply critical of behaviorism, the English writer Edmund Ions confessed his surprise at having found Skinner to be "a modest, witty, urbane and unpretentious scholar," rather than the "anti-humanistic dogmatist" he had expected.[9]

At a personal level, Skinner was no John B. Watson—by all accounts the latter had actually lived up to his behaviorist image as an emotionally cold individual and a crass entrepreneur.[10] Skinner, in contrast, was cultured and literate. He was, among other things, a published poet and a competent classical pianist. He wrote pieces on literature for the *Saturday Review* and the *Atlantic Monthly,* and enjoyed personal encounters with such literati as Robert Frost, Robert Penn Warren, Clifford Odets, and John Dos Passos.[11] His psychological writings contained references to Erasmus, Descartes, Diderot, and La Rochefoucauld, as well as to Darwin, Pavlov, and Thorndike; titles for his own writings were self-consciously derived from those of Shakespeare, Nietzsche, Freud, and E. B. White.[12] For recreation he listened to opera and read plays with a group of friends in Cambridge. His larger circle of friends included such figures as James Agee, Ivor Richards, and Zero Mostel.

If Skinner was a cultured behaviorist, he was also a product of the larger American culture—a creation of his own environment, as he himself insisted—even as he assumed the mantle of cultural iconoclast. Skinner's place in American culture depends crucially on the fact that he simultaneously personified long-standing trends in the culture *and* radical criticism of it. The very duality of Skinner's public image—as hero and villain, savior and fascist—suggests the conflict of ideologies in the culture that produced him. To understand these paradoxical aspects of his stature calls for an examination of the ways in which he was both a product and a provocateur of American culture.

Skinner as Cultural Product

In broadest purview, the significance of Skinner's work for American culture lay in his insistence that behaviorist technology be applied to the remaking of humans through the redesign of culture. Social reform, technology, and the reshaping of humans are themes that have pervaded this volume. Yet the point bears stressing that these are also, in many respects, typically American themes. The American experience from the Puritans on down has been a story of building new forms of society in a new world.[13] The possibilities for constructing society anew, unencumbered by the rigidity of the old world order, naturally gave rise to strong currents of social meliorism and utopianism in American history. As the historian of technology Howard P. Segal has observed:

> Since its discovery and first settlement by Europeans, America had been the object of utopian hopes abroad and those hopes fed America's own. What made America a potential utopia was its status as a blank slate on which a new society could be written and its possession of enough natural resources to provide material plenty for all.[14]

The notions of progress and utopia were European in origin, but once transported to America they took on a less intellectual and more pragmatic bent. In a land where the taming of a raw environment was viewed as essential to progress, it was technology, not theory, that became the key to realizing the new order. Thomas P. Hughes has remarked that America's "most notable and character-forming achievement for nearly three centuries has been to transform a wilderness into a building site,"[15] and the conquest of nature and its transformation into an artifactual world is the essence of technology. As a consequence, invention—as epitomized in the figure of Benjamin Franklin—was destined to become a crucial component of the "American genesis" and of the remaking of the "world as artifact."[16] To the considerable extent that Americans saw themselves as products of their environment, the Lockean themes of human malleability and self-improvement became closely intertwined with those of remaking and improving the environment.

All of these well-entrenched characteristics of American culture—the utopian optimism, the favoring of praxis over theory, the love of invention, the belief in human malleability—are also Skinnerian characteristics. But Skinner's rootedness in the early phases of American culture also lies in unexpected directions. Alongside the traditionally cherished notions of political liberty and individual self-determination, there has been a strong countercurrent of religiously inspired determinism dating from colonial times. According to the influential Calvinist determinism of Jonathan Edwards, freedom of will is a prideful illusion, and the experience of freedom is nothing more than having the liberty to follow one's prior inclinations. But such inclinations are themselves products of past habits, built up by "a kind of reflex" according to Edwards.[17] Moreover, these habits do not depend crucially on consciousness, which "feels" the habits as they run their course, but neither creates nor controls them. More than one scholar has pointed out the marked similarity of Edwards's and Skinner's thinking on such matters, and Skinner himself admitted, "much of my scientific position seems to have begun as Presbyterian theology, not too far removed from the Congregational of Jonathan Edwards."[18]

The growth of the Industrial Revolution in America during the nineteenth century spawned new versions of the drive for cultural reform. With the growing ability to create new wealth (rather than to just exploit existing resources) and the decline of the original Puritan millenarianism, proposals for the reform of society became increasingly secular and more tied to both technological innovation and the demands of industrial production.[19] Though the first technological utopias were written before the Civil War, the genre blossomed during the late nineteenth century, a period in which the country was undergoing rapid urbanization. The sudden growth of cities and the need for new means of social control to replace the traditional social controls of small-town rural America were crucial factors in the rise of progressivism at the turn of the century and eventually the Technocracy movement in the 1930s.

Urging social reform through control, order, and efficiency, progressivists such as John Dewey and Walter Lippman conceived the essential role that social scientists would play in society.[20] The requisite order and control called not only for the discovery and development of physical technology at the hands of experts in the natural sciences, but also for the devising of social technologies for enhancing efficiency, adjusting individuals to new social structures, and designing psychosocial conditions that would promote further technological progress. These tasks would be carried out by a new elite of experts—the social engineers or "architects of adjustment"—drawn largely from the ranks of psychologists.[21] For their part, the proponents of the New Psychology—the much-heralded Wundtian experimental psychology, now supplemented with strains of native Jamesian pragmatism—proved more than eager to justify the new discipline of scientific psychology in terms of its social utility.[22]

In a related development, the scientific management movement initiated by Frederick W. Taylor underwent a brief but intense surge in the 1910s and 1920s. Having begun with Taylor's crude measurements of the physical operations of the workplace, scientific management expanded into a popular movement and a nationwide "efficiency craze," encompassing not only the work environment but also applications in government, education, and a widespread home efficiency movement.[23] Efficiency became an end in itself, but was by no means limited to the enhancement of profits; rather efficiency was typically understood as a moral crusade that fitted such enduring American values as the elimination of waste (in both human and material resources) and the promotion of a spirit of cooperation. The use of science for rational planning in the interests of efficiency was likewise a theme of the Technocracy movement of the 1930s.[24] Originally proposed as a panacea for the Great Depression, the Technocracy movement viewed the efficient production and use of energy as the key to human progress, and promised to replace an era of scarcity with one of permanent abundance by introducing strictly scientific decision-making into the social machinery of the industrialized world. By virtue of its promise of expanding wealth for all and its avoidance of explicit political ideology, Technocracy appealed to both workers and management during its brief heyday in the 1930s.

As a number of scholars have shown, behaviorism emerged out of the nurturing matrix of progressivist thought alongside its sibling movements of scientific management and Technocracy.[25] Behaviorism was, as Watson himself stressed, a uniquely American movement, concerned with prediction, control, practical application, and social reform. Although thinly wrapped in the terminology of Pavlovian conditioning, behaviorism was from the outset a largely practical, atheoretical set of techniques for controlling behavior; as the psychologist E. B. Titchener observed as early as 1914, psychologists were being asked to trade their science for a technology.[26] But it was a technology with a difference. The mental testing movement had supplied a technology for the screening of employees and immigrants, but behaviorism promised something more powerful—a direct, hands-on means of changing behavior. As a technology of controlled change, behaviorism was destined to appeal not only to the progressivists who had originally formulated a social role for it—indeed Dewey enthusiastically welcomed its advent—but also to an American population that had long looked to technology for solutions and felt an affinity for behaviorism's anti-intellectual practicality, for its concrete methods of self-improvement, and for the egalitarian implications of its antihereditarianism.[27] In the wake of World War I, social engineers had been cast in the role of saviors, and Watson—the first pop psychologist of the new urban middle class—had little difficulty selling himself in that role.[28] In an oft-quoted review of Watson's 1924 popular exposition of behaviorism, Stuart Chase wrote that the book was perhaps "the most important book ever written. One stands for an instant blinded with a great hope."[29]

Progressivism, scientific management, and the Technocracy movement were also crucial components of the American cultural milieu that nourished technological utopianism.[30] Skinner's *Walden Two* may be the best-known psycho-technological utopia today, but, as Jill Morawski has documented, more than a few psychologists who saw the implications of their work for social engineering preceded Skinner in writing psychologically based utopias. In the case of G. Stanley Hall—one of the founders of the New Psychology in America—this utopian vision prefigured Walden Two's blend of Baconian ideals and Darwinian notions of cultural evolution. Moreover, Watson himself authored a brief utopian work that anticipated many of the central features of Walden Two: small-scale communities, an emphasis on efficiency, absence of political and religious institutions, rule by a scientific elite, and the raising of children by the group in accord with scientific principles.[31]

If Walden Two was radical in its implications, it was nonetheless well within the centuries-old American tradition of reconstructing society on the basis of the latest technological advances. The historian Gordon Wood has commented that the temporal coincidence of the American Revolution with the early stages of the Industrial Revolution

> had momentous consequences for the way Americans came to identify technological progress with the promise of their own history. Political and physical science seemed to be providentially linked, and technology became as important as virtue in achieving America's realization of itself as a moral republic.[32]

With the emergence of psychological science during the progressivist era, the American habit of equating technological progress with social progress was readily extended to the realm of psycho-technology. The reformers of the late nineteenth century had drawn the blueprint for such a development and behaviorism answered the call; the social engineers had arrived at the building site.

SKINNER AS PROVOCATEUR

In the words of Watson's biographer Kerry W. Buckley, Watsonian behaviorism provided "the tools with which psychologists would become social engineers."[33] Watson's tools were crude ones, however, relying on a simplistic conditioned-reflex model of behavior and a smattering of laboratory findings. With Skinner's formulation of the concept of the operant in the 1930s, the expansion of laboratory research, and the dramatic demonstration of precise control in Project Pigeon in the 1940s, the tools of behavioral engineering underwent major refinement. The success of subsequent applications of operant methods in a variety of fields reinforced the point that the tools of behaviorism had become powerful and their applications realizable. The larger implications of the technology could no longer be ignored. As Skinner put it,

> Pigeons were behaving in more complex ways than ever before in the history of the species simply because they had been exposed to more complex contingencies than ever before. What might human beings do if we could build a more favorable environment for them?[34]

For Skinner himself, issues of whether and how behavioral engineering should be applied to society at large had become unavoidable. And the American public, long enamored of technology and steeped in the gospel of progress, proved willing to hear him out despite the clash of his message with other long-cherished beliefs.

At one level, Skinner's critique of social institutions consisted largely of the traditional progressivist charge of inefficiency. In the early 1950s, he launched his decades-long attack on the American system of education, counterposing the inefficiency of traditional educational techniques based on commonsense methods of aversive control with the efficacy of programmed instruction based on a scientific analysis of positive reinforcement. As the operant movement grew through the fifties, similar critiques and reformist interventions were applied to practices in such fields as industry, mental health, and prison reform. As one otherwise sympathetic critic wrote during the 1960s, Skinner's "final passion is for smooth operations; his greatest regret is our present inefficiency."[35]

Yet the Skinnerian drive for efficiency was not a narrowly pragmatic one, nor was it geared to maximizing profits in any simple pecuniary sense. Whereas Watson had explicitly urged that the progress of individuals be measured as the growth curve of their personal incomes, Skinner's complaint about inefficiency was that it weakens culture by constraining individuals' opportunities for full expression of their genetic and environmental endowments, and hence limits their contributions to the culture. Because the function of all social institutions—whether political, legal, economic, or religious—is to control human behavior, all could be viewed as behavioral technologies in their own right.[36] But, Skinner argued, being outmoded prescientific technologies, the existing social institutions embodied contingencies that were failing to produce effective behavior consonant with larger cultural ends. For Skinner, social institutions, like operant behavior itself, were to be known and evaluated by their consequences.[37] In his analysis, a capitalist system that tolerated unemployment and a skewed distribution of wealth not tied to actual contributions to the system was not merely inefficient in its use of human resources; it also failed to contribute to the overall strength of the society. Political systems that arranged contingencies for the personal aggrandizement of power and wealth were not operating for the benefit of the group. Religious institutions offered reasonable codes of ethics but, in their focus on consequences in an afterlife, lacked efficient means of producing behavior that would conform to those codes.[38] In sum, the major traditional institutions of social control had been tried and were failing.

In Skinner's view, the institution of science was different. Although not wholly immune from the trappings of individual aggrandizement, it offered a means of studying and controlling nature (physical *and* human) that was largely independent of the scientist's self-interest. According to Skinner, the same contingencies in science that set it apart as a uniquely cumulative enterprise would also ensure a healthy disinterest on the part of the scientist.[39] Frazier, the scientist-founder of Walden Two, derived no monetary benefit from the community, arranged for his own quiet abdication as its leader, and even designed the same fate for the elite Planners of the community.[40]

The very scope of Skinner's faith in the beneficence of science and his scientistic critique of existing societal practices were enough to make him a provocateur of culture, and his utopianism made him something of a visionary. But, in these respects at least, his views were perhaps not so far off the path of progressivism as to qualify him as a radical. The cultural alterations proposed by technological utopians have been described as being, in actuality, "conservative extrapolations from trends in existing society"—a generalization that fits Skinner to a considerable degree.[41] But to leave it at that would be to neglect the ways in which Skinner's views *were* radical, and even deeply so.

As noted earlier, the Lockean notion that people are products of their environments has long been widely accepted in American culture, a fact that no doubt helps account for Americans' general willingness to entertain behavioristic ideas. Skinner's uncompromising insistence on the wholesale application of determinism to human beings, however, was another matter. In his attacks on the literature of freedom and dignity, Skinner attributed all control of human action to the environment—free will was an illusion stemming from simple ignorance of the real causes of action. The demise of "autonomous man" at the hands of science meant that no human action could be either blameworthy or praiseworthy; there could be no villains or heroes, only bad and good environments. By arranging salutary environments that automatically produce virtuous inhabitants, Skinner said, we can eliminate the need for saintly sacrifice and heroic action. "We may mourn the passing of heroes but not the conditions which make for heroism."[42] In their world of conditioned virtue, the residents of Walden Two eschewed the practice of saying "thank you" as an unneeded relic of prescientific modes of attributing responsibility for action, and they were depicted as genuinely nonplussed by expressions of gratitude from outsiders.

The available evidence suggests that Skinner was sincere in his denial of moral autonomy. In discussing his childhood immersion in Calvinistic determinism, he commented that "it has never bothered me in the least to accept myself as a completely determined system."[43] He repeatedly denied personal credit for his own works, viewing them as the products of his past and present environmental conditions.

> My analysis of the role of the individual in *Beyond Freedom and Dignity* was so convincing that by the time I finished the book I actually did not feel that I had written it. I do not mean that I attributed it to some mystical "other one." There was no divine afflatus. My book was the inevitable consequence of what had happened to me and of what I had read.[44]

Like his characters in *Walden Two,* Skinner was disturbed and embarrassed by expressions of gratitude and public awards and honors, especially those that focused more on personal achievement than on the positions he was advocating.

In Skinner's Darwinian ontology, the organism can be no more than a product of causal forces, of genetic and environmental contingencies of selection. While working in Crozier's physiology laboratory at Harvard in the late twenties, Skinner encountered Jacques Loeb's concept of the tropism—the automatic movement of an organism in a field of forces. Despite Skinner's replacement of Loeb's mechanism of tropism with that of the operant, the basic conception stuck. For Skinner, the organism, however complex, would remain a "locus of variables," a unique spatio-temporal site of converging forces.[45] Just as Hume's radical positivism had left no enduring soul beneath the flux of experience, Skinner's Machian positivism left no agent or self behind the behavior. The resulting annihilation of the self, curiously enough, was tantamount to a form of Buddhism. Skinner's philosophical idol Ernst Mach had become a Buddhist in his later years, and Skinner himself recognized his own affinity with Eastern thought. The denial of the self, he wrote,

> is, of course, a strong theme in Eastern mysticism. It will no doubt strike many people as strange that it should be, as I think it is, the central theme of a behavioral science.[46]

In the final pages of his autobiography, Skinner alluded to "the problems raised by the cult of the individual," and recorded the following comment: "If I am right about human behavior, I have written the autobiography of a nonperson. I have collected alms for oblivion. . . . An individual is only the way in which a species and a culture produce more of species and culture."[47] Viewed from this perspective, the seeming "selflessness" of Frazier's abdication of rule in Walden Two had its ontological as well as its ethical significance.[48]

In the course of castigating Skinner for his failure as a utopian to offer a new image of the improved human, George Kateb posed the rhetorical question: "Could it not be said, though in caricature, that Skinner is more concerned to improve functions than to improve men?"[49] The demurral about caricature was, of course, needless. In Skinner's worldview, the human being *is* its functions, or, more precisely, its functional relations with the social and natural environment; there are no persons to be improved, only loci of variables to be reworked for the long-term benefit of the culture. But if commentators on Skinner have not always grasped the philosophical depths of his rejection of the autonomous individual, they have at least understood its radical implications for American culture. Spiro Agnew's speech writers displayed perspicuity as well as political rhetoric when they depicted Skinner as a dangerous radical and asserted that "our traditional concept of the individual would disappear completely if it were left up to the behaviorists."[50] Indeed, the Skinnerian denial of the self struck at the root of American values of individualism, including entrepreneurial initiative, the free choice of leaders, and personal autonomy in moral and legal matters. In doing so, it triggered consternation and debate, making Skinner a lightning rod for criticisms of the encroachment of social science into other hallowed realms of discourse. The ongoing concern over this encroachment—as suggested by the titles of such recent works as *American Freedom and the Social Sciences* and *Psychology and Law: Can Justice Survive the Social Sciences?*[51]—extends to the continuing nationwide debates over funding for the social sciences. In the terminology of the philosopher Larry Laudan, such debates are the surface skirmishes of deeper "worldview conflicts" between well-entrenched traditions of discourse—conflicts that weaken the claims of both traditions to the rational allegiance of those who live under their sway.[52]

In diminishing the ontological status of the individual, Skinner was simultaneously placing a quasi-Darwinian emphasis on the collective as the unit of selection, whether in the form of the culture or of the entire species. The old tension between the "liberator" tradition of individualism and the "traditionalist" orientation of collectivism was transformed by Skinner into an issue of whether to subject the individual to the collective spirit of science and, with it, the supposedly benign rule of scientists. The incursion of science into politics that had formed a large part of the progressivist agenda reappeared in exaggerated form in Walden Two's elevation of scientists into the ruling Planners. In effect, Skinner's writings confronted Americans with a test of entrenched faiths, posing a disjunction between their faith in science and their faith in electoral government.

As Skinner himself realized, his call for the submission of the individual and culture to the rule of science linked him to the Enlightenment and to its ideal of a rationally planned society. A number of scholars have noted this connection. According to the philosopher Paul T. Sagal,

> Skinner is in many ways a man of the enlightenment—a throwback to that age dominated by faith in science and the perfectability of man. . . . Skinner might well say that the only thing wrong with the faith of the enlightenment was that it was premature, especially in respect to its knowledge of, and hopes for, man.[53]

However premature the application of behavioral psychology may yet seem with respect to the planning of a rational society, the parallels between Skinner's proposals and those of the Enlightenment are not hard to discern. The thinkers of the Enlightenment—notably Condorcet, with his "social mathematics"—shared what Crane Brinton has called a "sturdy faith in 'cultural engineering'" and in "the possibility of changing all human beings for the good by changing their environment, and in particular their education, from infancy on."[54] The irony, of course, is that in the hands of behaviorists the same education that eighteenth-century figures saw as the critical basis of self-rule by an enlightened population had become a deterministic process of conditioning to be arranged by scientific managers. If the Enlightenment architects of democracy never quite reconciled their beliefs about political liberty with their depiction of humans as a part of the naturalistic world-machine, Skinner's eighteenth-century sympathies would not prevent his resolution of the tension in favor of the latter.[55] The "natural salvation" promised by the Enlightenment could still be had, in Skinner's view, but only at the expense of freedom and dignity, as traditionally conceived.

SKINNER AND BEHAVIORISM IN POSTMODERN PERSPECTIVE

The linkage of scientific and technological progress with social progress that has long seemed providential to Americans thus constituted the portentous first premise of Skinner's social philosophy, and it enabled him to urge the sacrifice of certain political ideals to the progressive, perhaps inevitable, march of science. Yet recent decades have witnessed a serious challenge from various quarters to cardinal assumptions about the inevitability of such a linkage. Indeed, the very concept of progress that underlay the Enlightenment ideal has come to be questioned in unprecedented fashion. In philosophy, the attack on the possibility of foundations for knowledge has been accompanied by death notices for the "grand narrative" view of Western history—for those grand historical schemes of human betterment, whether in the form advocated by Condorcet or Comte, Hegel or Marx.[56] Postpositivist philosophers of science have challenged the traditional claims that science yields a cumulative growth of knowledge and that it does so in a value-free fashion; many depict science as but one form of cultural discourse among others, as a discourse no more privileged than the discourses of law, art, or literature, and no less subject to interpretation in terms of self-interested communities of specialists. On the level of the wider culture, there is talk of a postmodern fragmentation of culture into a kaleidoscopic array of self-referential discourses, and a concomitant waning of the once widely accepted cultural values commonly associated with the Enlightenment. In particular, the progressivist ideal of a rational coordination of natural, human, and industrial resources into a smoothly functioning social organism is dismissed as a quaint relic of a now-crumbling faith in science and in the Enlightenment dream of natural salvation.

Although some scholars have argued that technological knowledge grows in a cumulative fashion even if theoretical science does not, technology itself has not escaped the postmodernist critique. Indeed, in the words of one historian of technology, "technological pessimism has become an integral part of the emerging culture of postmodernism," and this pessimism extends to "a growing disenchantment with . . . all forms of social and political engineering."[57] Another historian of technology, George Basalla, has analyzed the notion of technological progress by delineating six traditional assumptions about technology and its effects, *all* of which have been come under strong attack in recent years.

First, technological innovation invariably brings about a marked improvement in the artifact undergoing change; second, advances in technology directly contribute to the betterment of our material, social, cultural and spiritual lives, thereby accelerating the growth of civilization; third, the progress made in technology, and hence in civilization, can be unambiguously gauged by reference to speed, efficiency, power, or some other quantitative measure; fourth, the origins, direction, and influence of technological change are under complete human control; fifth, technology has conquered nature and forced it to serve human goals; and sixth, technology and civilization reached their highest forms in the Western industrialized nations.[58]

The conclusion drawn by Basalla from his careful analysis is that the customary association between technological and social progress must be abandoned, or, as he puts it, that "the advancement of technology must be disengaged from social, economic, or cultural progress."[59] Moreover, historical and philosophical analyses such as Basalla's have been supplemented by sociological data suggesting a nonexistent or even negative relationship between technological developments and human happiness.[60]

Part of the critique of technology, of course, draws on its currently well-publicized potential to produce unforeseen damaging effects. In America, where the national agenda has been more closely tied to a growing technological mastery over the environment than in any other nation in history, this disconcerting unruliness of technological innovation has provoked something like a spiritual as well as environmental crisis. If the prospects for salvation through physical technology now seem dimmed to many, the prospects for technological utopias and for salvation from relatively new *behavioral* technologies cannot seem bright. Reflecting on Skinner's proposals for large-scale reform, one religious scholar has written that

> the images and symbols of science no longer sound salvific. God has died (it is said), the individual has died (Skinner says), but science, too, has died; it has lost its purity and its credibility. What the church is to Christianity, technology is to science, and by their fruits both have been judged harshly. The appeal that the cure for *bad* design is *good* design is on a homiletic par with the claim that "the only thing wrong with Christianity is that men have never tried it."[61]

In a postmodern context, schemes for salvation—whether secular or religious—are likely to be dismissed as further attempts to revive the grand narrative, and the refractoriness of a postmodern fragmented society to large-scale planned interventions can only seem daunting to all but the boldest of reform-minded thinkers.

Yet, in their proclamations and proposals, behaviorists have been nothing if not bold. However quaint the drive for intervention in the name of efficiency may appear to the postmodern sensibility, it is well to remember that behavioral technologies *have* become well-engrained in American cultural practices during the eighty years since behaviorism's inception, and not without demonstrable benefits.[62] Moreover, the bold Skinnerian substitution of the ontology of the collective for the ontology of the individual begins to seem oddly germane once again. The tragedy of the commons, after all, is a tragedy of interacting individuals pursuing their self-interest, not one of collective planning.[63] In a world of overpopulation, diminishing resources, and ecological damage, the American tradition of treating efficiency as a moral crusade takes on new and wider meaning, and the Darwinian ontology of the group may yet find a way to assert itself against the tradition of the individual. The need for self-control and for a renewed stress on collective effort likewise seems relevant in the face of economic challenges from countries that forgo the trappings of Western individualism in favor of corporate cohesion.

Adaptation to changing conditions in the face of necessity is not a new theme in American culture—and it has long been a central motif in the theories and urgings of behaviorists. If, as some commentators have sensed, the American nation is on the cusp of a momentous tilting toward a more collectivist ethic, that change may well be effected with the aid of behavioral technologies that have long permeated many aspects of American life. As an ongoing tradition of investigation, operant behaviorism has already made an important niche for itself in the emerging field of environmental psychology, for example by designing programs of contingency management for helping people achieve self-control over their wasteful and environmentally destructive behaviors.[64] But such "appropriate technologies" for self-management, however useful, still fall far short of integrated cultural design of the sort envisioned by Skinner. It remains to be seen what role behaviorism's larger vision for remaking society might yet play in bringing about the shift to an ecologically grounded collectivism.

Against the grain of postmodern pessimism, some commentators have argued that limited forms of utopianism can survive the postmodern fragmentation of science and politics.[65] If so, the simple fact of behaviorism's enduring and adaptable role in American culture—as well as what one critic has called its "unsuspected dialectical resources"[66]—suggests that it cannot be dismissed out of hand as a source of cultural reform. Among behaviorism's "unsuspected" resources is its long-standing, and now timely, insistence that the human individual is a deeply enmeshed part of the social and natural world. As one operant behaviorist has put it:

> According to Skinner's behavioral philosophy, individual action derives from genetics and environment, and the private life of thinking and feeling is continuous with the public life of speaking and acting. The private individual is therefore continuous with the natural world, and just as aspects of the world affect behavior, so behavior in turn affects the world. . . . This is essentially a holistic, ecological vision of interaction between organism and environment.

Shorn of its dubious public image as a mechanistic and dehumanizing ideology, the passage continues, behaviorism's view of human nature "may actually be welcomed by the ethically and spiritually inspired movement for survival and wellbeing."[67]

Whatever the merits of individual autonomy as traditionally construed in the discourses of political philosophy, the embeddedness of humans in the natural order—an embeddedness posited by behaviorism and confirmed by ecological science—carries the message that we are creatures constrained in multiple ways by our earthly existence. Our growing awareness of being stationed in a web, not just of human culture but also of the larger biological culture that makes up an ecosystem, has its implications for the behaviorist image of human nature that so many have found distasteful. One is to lend new moral and ontological credence to some old behaviorist questions about the limits of humans' freedom of action. Another may be to weaken traditional criticisms of behaviorism for its likening of humans to other animals; the postmodern shift from anthropocentrism to biocentrism as a guiding precept somehow makes such comparisons both more germane and less unflattering than they once appeared.[68]

As noted by Daniel W. Bjork in his writings here and elsewhere,[69] the abiding preoccupations of American history have been the relation between individual and environment and the tension between freedom and restraint. If, as it has been recently urged, "technological pessimism can and often does represent a progressive shift in worldview," the behaviorism that Skinner bequeathed to American culture does not lack viable means, conceptual and practical, for contributing to that new worldview by adding its voice once again to the process of recasting our notions of individual and environment, freedom and restraint.[70]

Commenting some years ago on the tangled implications of science and technology for the fate of humans, the historian of science Gerald Holton wrote:

> To this day, we see all around us the Promethean drive to *omnipotence through technology* and to *omniscience through science*. [But] with the motivating imperative of society continuing to be the very different one of its physical and spiritual survival, it is now far less obvious than it was in Francis Bacon's world how to bring the three imperatives into harmony.[71]

B. F. Skinner proposed one way of bringing such a harmony about. Although his proposal has not had the reception he had hoped for it, he put himself squarely at the convergence of major cultural issues, and thus personified the deepest of cultural tensions. Whether or not Holton's three imperatives are ever reconciled, those who shape and reshape these enduring issues are to be counted among the signal contributors to culture. And whatever else he was, Skinner—as product and provocateur—was a contributor to his culture.

NOTES

1. Rae Goodell, *The Visible Scientists* (Boston: Little, Brown, 1977).
2. Published posthumously as B. F. Skinner, "Can Psychology Be a Science of Mind?" *American Psychologist* 45 (1990): 1206–10.

3. Skinner's shift from laboratory scientist to social philosopher has been documented in S. R. Coleman, "B. F. Skinner: Systematic Iconoclast," *The Gamut* (spring/summer 1982): 53–75. Coleman's analysis of Skinner's publications from 1928 to 1978 reveals that Skinner's lab-based research reports outnumbered his philosophical publications by a ratio of 20 to 1 during the first two decades of this period, whereas the philosophical works outnumbered the research reports by about 3 to 1 during the last two decades of the period. A similar impression is conveyed by the analysis of Skinner's publications presented in Robert W. Proctor and Daniel J. Weeks, *The Goal of B. F. Skinner and Behavior Analysis* (New York: Springer-Verlag, 1990), pp. 124–27.

4. Aspects of the history of applied operant psychology are treated in Alan E. Kazdin, *History of Behavior Modification: Experimental Foundations of Contemporary Research* (Baltimore, Md.: University Park Press, 1978); Leonard Krasner, "The Future and the Past in the Behaviorism-Humanism Dialogue," *American Psychologist* 33 (1978): 799–804; and Leonard P. Ullman, "Behavior Therapy as a Social Movement," in *Behavior Therapy: Appraisal and Status,* ed. Cyril M. Franks (New York: McGraw-Hill, 1969), pp. 495–523. For an interpretation of operant psychologists as a dogmatic, even pseudoscientific cult, see Proctor and Weeks, *Goal of Skinner and Behavior Analysis.*

5. On the isolation of operant psychology from mainstream psychology, see David L. Krantz, "Schools and Systems: The Mutual Isolation of Operant and Non-Operant Psychology as a Case Study," *Journal of the History of the Behavioral Sciences* 8 (1972): 86–102; S. R. Coleman and S. E. Mehlman, "An Empirical Update (1969–1989) of D. L. Krantz's Thesis that the Experimental Analysis of Behavior Is Isolated," *Behavior Analyst* 15 (1992): 43–49; and Proctor and Weeks, *Goal of Skinner and Behavior Analysis,* especially chap. 4. On Skinner's standing among American psychologists, see George D. Wright, "A Further Note on Ranking the Important Psychologists," *American Psychologist* 25 (1970): 650–51; and James H. Korn, Roger Davis, and Stephen F. Davis, "Historians' and Chairpersons' Judgments of Eminence Among Psychologists," *American Psychologist* 46 (1991): 789–92. The sociologist of science Ian Mitroff has found evidence among physical scientists that those scientists who are most extreme in their views and most committed to them tend to be rated the most outstanding by their peers, a finding that may help to account for the esteem bestowed on Skinner by psychologists. See Mitroff's "Norms and Counter-Norms in a Select Group of Apollo Moon Scientists: A Case Study of the Ambivalence of Scientists," *American Sociological Review* 39 (1974): 579–95.

6. Recounted in Skinner, *A Matter of Consequences* (New York: Knopf, 1983), pp. 351–52. Other allegations of Nazism are cited in Marc N. Richelle, *B. F. Skinner: A Reappraisal* (Hillsdale, N.J.: Erlbaum, 1993), p. 4; and James A. Dinsmoor, "Setting the Record Straight: The Social Views of B. F. Skinner," *American Psychologist* 47 (1992): 1454–63, on pp. 1456, 1457. Dinsmoor's essay also offers a reflective analysis of why the reactions to Skinner's social proposals have been so vehement.

7. Noam Chomsky, "Psychology and Ideology," in *For Reasons of State* (New York: Pantheon, 1973), pp. 318–69, on p. 344; the text of Agnew's speech is reprinted in "Agnew's Blast at Behaviorism," *Psychology Today,* January 1972, pp. 4, 84, 87; Popper's remarks were published in *Free Inquiry* and are quoted in Skinner, *Matter of Consequences,* pp. 391–92. For the opposing view of Skinner as a defender of traditional liberal values, see Dinsmoor, "Setting the Record Straight."

8. Carl R. Rogers and Skinner, "Some Issues Concerning the Control of Human Behavior: A Symposium," in *The Technological Threat*, ed. Jack D. Douglas (Englewood Cliffs, N.J.: Prentice-Hall, 1971), pp. 122–49, on p. 137; Skinner, *Matter of Consequences*, p. 297.

9. Edmund Ions, *Against Behaviouralism: A Critique of Behavioural Science* (Totowa, N.J.: Rowman and Littlefield, 1977), p. 133.

10. See Kerry W. Buckley, *Mechanical Man: John Broadus Watson and the Beginnings of Behaviorism* (New York: Guilford, 1989), especially chap. 10.

11. Skinner, "On 'Having' a Poem," *Saturday Review*, July 1972; Skinner, "Has Gertrude Stein a Secret?" *Atlantic Monthly*, January 1934, pp. 50–57; Skinner, *Particulars of My Life* (New York: Knopf, 1976), pp. 227–28, 248–49 (on Frost); Skinner, *The Shaping of a Behaviorist* (New York: Knopf, 1979), p. 297 (on Warren); Skinner, *Matter of Consequences*, p. 122 (on Odets), pp. 287–88 (on Dos Passos).

12. The title *Particulars of My Life* was taken from a line in Shakespeare's *Henry IV; Beyond Freedom and Dignity* drew on Nietzsche's *Beyond Good and Evil* and Freud's *Beyond the Pleasure Principle;* and Skinner's "Farewell, My LOVELY!" (*Journal of the Experimental Analysis of Behavior* 25 [1976]: 218) was taken from E. B. White's well-known essay on the Model T Ford.

13. See, for example, Kenneth M. Roemer, ed., *America as Utopia: Collected Essays* (New York: Burt Franklin, 1981); and Ernest L. Tuveson, *Redeemer Nation: The Idea of America's Millenial Role* (Chicago: University of Chicago Press, 1968).

14. Howard P. Segal, *Technological Utopianism in American Culture* (Chicago: University of Chicago Press, 1985), p. 75. Segal's statement reflects a common cultural self-perception, even though the America that greeted European settlers was neither devoid of pre-existing civilizations nor unlimited in natural resources. See Segal's "American Ideology of Technological Progress: Historical Perspectives," in *Future Imperfect: The Mixed Blessings of Technology in America* (Amherst: University of Massachusetts Press, 1994), pp. 1–9, on pp. 4–6.

15. Thomas P. Hughes, *American Genesis: A Century of Invention and Technological Enthusiasm, 1870–1970* (New York: Viking, 1989), p. 1.

16. Ibid.

17. Quoted in David R. Williams, "Horses, Pigeons, and the Therapy of Conversion: A Psychological Reading of Jonathan Edwards's Theology," *Harvard Theological Review* 74 (1981): 337–52, on p. 344.

18. Skinner, *Matter of Consequences*, p. 403. For discussions of Skinner and Edwards, see Williams, "Edwards's Theology"; Daniel B. Shea, "B. F. Skinner: The Puritan Within," *Virginia Quarterly Review* 50 (1974): 416–37; and James W. Woefel, "Listening to B. F. Skinner," *Christian Century*, 30 November 1977. See also John Passmore's remark on the "interesting similarity between Skinner and the powerful Christian tradition that God's grace, not individual effort, should be given the credit for what we normally describe as 'our' achievements" (Passmore, *Science and Its Critics* [New Brunswick, N.J.: Rutgers University Press, 1978], p. 15).

19. Segal, *Technological Utopianism*, chap. 5.

20. John C. Burnham, *Paths Into American Culture: Psychology, Medicine, and Morals* (Philadelphia: Temple University Press, 1988); Sidney Kaplan, "Social Engineers as Saviors: Effects of World War I on Some American Liberals," *Journal of the History of Ideas* 17 (1956): 347–69; Thomas H. Leahey, *A History of*

Psychology: Main Currents in Psychological Thought, 2d ed. (Englewood Cliffs, N.J.: Prentice-Hall, 1987), chaps. 10 and 12.

21. Donald S. Napoli, *The Architects of Adjustment: The History of the Psychological Profession in the United States* (Port Washington, N.Y.: Kennikat Press, 1980).

22. See John M. O'Donnell, *The Origins of Behaviorism: American Psychology, 1870–1920* (New York: New York University Press, 1985).

23. Samuel Haber, *Efficiency and Uplift: Scientific Management in the Progressive Era, 1890–1920* (Chicago: University of Chicago Press, 1964); Daniel Nelson, *Frederick W. Taylor and the Rise of Scientific Management* (Madison: University of Wisconsin Press, 1980).

24. William E. Akin, *Technocracy and the American Dream: The Technocrat Movement, 1900–1941* (Berkeley: University of California Press, 1977); Henry Elsner, Jr., *The Technocrats: Prophets of Automation* (Syracuse, N.Y.: Syracuse University Press, 1967).

25. Buckley, *Mechanical Man;* Burnham, *Paths Into Culture,* chaps. 3, 5, and 12; O'Donnell, *Origins of Behaviorism.*

26. Edward B. Titchener, "On 'Psychology as the Behaviorist Views It'," *Proceedings of the American Philosophical Society* 53 (1914): 1–17, on p. 14. For a treatment of behaviorism as an outgrowth of the "engineering ideal" in biology, see Philip J. Pauly, *Controlling Life: Jacques Loeb and the Engineering Ideal in Biology* (New York: Oxford University Press, 1987), chap. 8.

27. For John Dewey's endorsement of behaviorism, see Dewey, "Psychological Doctrine and Philosophical Teaching," *Journal of Philosophy, Psychology and Scientific Methods* 11 (1914): 508–11. Further analysis of behaviorism's appeal in America, including its anti–intellectualism, is in Bernard J. Baars, *The Cognitive Revolution in Psychology* (New York: Guilford, 1986), pp. 44–48.

28. Buckley, *Mechanical Man,* chap. 8.

29. Quoted in ibid., p. 173.

30. See Segal, *Technological Utopianism,* chap. 6.

31. J. G. Morawski, "Assessing Psychology's Moral Heritage Through Our Neglected Utopias," *American Psychologist* 37 (1982): 1082–95; G. Stanley Hall, "The Fall of Atlantis," in *Recreations of a Psychologist* (New York: Appleton, 1920); John B. Watson, "Should a Child Have More than One Mother?" *Liberty Magazine,* 29 June 1929, pp. 31–35.

32. Gordon S. Wood, "Republican Technology," in *The Rising Glory of America, 1760–1820,* ed. Gordon S. Wood (New York: Braziller, 1971), pp. 237–52, on p. 237. On the earlier, and more general, temporal coincidence of the beginnings of utopianism with the emergence of modern science, see J. C. Davis, "Science and Utopia: The History of a Dilemma," in *Nineteen Eighty-Four: Science Between Utopia and Dystopia,* ed. Everett Mendelsohn and Helga Nowotny (Dordrecht, The Netherlands: D. Reidel, 1984), pp. 21–48.

33. Buckley, *Mechanical Man,* p. 77.

34. Skinner, *Matter of Consequences,* p. 47.

35. George Kateb, *Utopia and Its Enemies* (New York: Free Press, 1963), p. 215. Skinner's fascination with efficiency and ethical self-control is evinced in his sharply ambivalent reflections on German culture (see Skinner, *Matter of Consequences,* pp. 292–93).

36. Skinner's argument to this effect is presented in his "Design of Cultures," in *Cumulative Record,* enl. ed. (New York: Appleton-Century-Crofts, 1961), pp. 36.01–36.12, on p. 36.09. The argument that all means of social control are

technologies played an important rhetorical role for Skinner in defusing the complaint that his proposals for cultural design comprise artificial technologies whereas the existing means of social control are somehow natural and benign.

37. Skinner's notion of operants as responses that are defined and known by their consequences can be viewed as a behavioral translation of the pragmatist notion that the meaning and value of ideas lies in their consequences for practical action. Although Skinner himself acknowledged no particular debt to the pragmatists, it seems clear that the emphasis of operant conditioning on the practical consequences of behavior made his version of behaviorism especially well-suited to application in an American culture already infused with pragmatist thought and widespread belief in the need for control over the environment.

38. Skinner, *Science and Human Behavior* (New York: Free Press, 1953), chap. 23; Skinner, *Matter of Consequences,* p. 246.

39. See, for example, Skinner, "Design of Cultures," p. 36.10.

40. One of Skinner's chief critics, Joseph Wood Krutch, noted that Frazier might well have turned out to be a power-hungry despot rather than the generally benevolent character he seemed to be. Skinner replied that such a possible outcome would be corrected for in the long run because "it is unlikely that a government can survive which does not govern in the best interests of everyone"; this reply loses much of its effectiveness, however, because of its appeal to the same long-run processes of cultural selection that cultural design is said to supersede in terms of efficiency. See Krutch, *The Measure of Man* (Indianapolis, Ind.: Bobbs, 1953); and Skinner, "The Control of Human Behavior," in *Cumulative Record,* enl. ed. (New York: Appleton-Century-Crofts, 1961), pp. 18–23, on pp. 22–23.

41. Quote from Segal, *Technological Utopianism,* p. 102. Christopher Lasch has depicted Skinner's social views as being so rooted in the dogma of traditional progressivism that they amount to little more than a rehashing of progressivist clichés (review of *The Shaping of a Behaviorist,* by Skinner, *New Republic,* 4–11 August 1979, pp. 36–38). See also Kateb's comment that "Skinner's descriptions are not premonitory of some new image of man: they are, in fact, too close to reality: they correct reality in ways that one would have guessed only too easily" (Kateb, *Utopia and Its Enemies,* p. 216).

42. Skinner, "Freedom and the Control of Men," in *Cumulative Record,* enl. ed. (New York: Appleton-Century-Crofts, 1961), pp. 3–18, on p. 16. Cf. William James's classic treatment of this issue in "The Moral Equivalent of War," in *Pragmatism and Other Essays* (New York: Washington Square Press, Pocket Books, 1963), pp. 289–301 (original work published 1910).

43. "Interview With B. F. Skinner," *Behaviorists for Social Action Journal* 2 (1979): 47–52, on p. 47.

44. Skinner, *Matter of Consequences,* p. 409.

45. Skinner, "Current Trends in Experimental Psychology," in *Cumulative Record,* pp. 223–41, on p. 236; Skinner, *Verbal Behavior* (New York: Appleton-Century-Crofts, 1957), p. 313.

46. Skinner, *Matter of Consequences,* p. 408. For a further discussion of the relation of Skinner's thought to Eastern mysticism, see John L. Williams, "The Behavioral and the Mystical: Reflections on Behaviorism and Eastern Thought," *Behavior Analyst* 9 (1986): 167–73; and Michael Novak, "Is He Really a Grand Inquisitor?" in *Beyond the Punitive Society,* ed. Harvey Wheeler (San Francisco: Freeman, 1973), pp. 230–46, on p. 234. More generally, the link between Zen

Buddhism and utopianism is noted by Thomas Steven Molnar, *Utopia: The Perennial Heresy* (London: Tom Stacey, 1971), p. 150.

47. Skinner, *Matter of Consequences,* pp. 412–13.

48. Skinner came to view Walden Two as an anarchistic community. He argued that although the Planners and Managers designed and implemented contingencies, the control of behavior was exerted by the environment (including the social environment) and no *person* was in control. The controlling functions usually assigned to government were carried out by the inhabitants through face-to-face contact. See Skinner, *Matter of Consequences,* pp. 426–27; and Evalyn F. Segal, "Walden Two: The Morality of Anarchy," *Behavior Analyst* 10 (1987): 147–60.

49. Kateb, *Utopia and Its Enemies,* p. 215. For a recent version of the argument that Skinner's social philosophy offers inadequate grounds for value choices, see Isaac Prilleltensky, "On the Social Legacy of B. F. Skinner: Rhetoric of Change, Philosophy of Adjustment," *Theory & Psychology* 4 (1994): 125–37; and Prilleltensky, *The Morals and Politics of Psychology: Psychological Discourse and the Status Quo* (Albany: SUNY Press, 1994).

50. "Agnew's Blast at Behaviorism," *Psychology Today,* January 1972, p. 4.

51. James Deese, *American Freedom and the Social Sciences* (New York: Columbia University Press, 1985); Daniel N. Robinson, *Psychology and Law: Can Justice Survive the Social Sciences?* (New York: Oxford University Press, 1980).

52. Larry Laudan, *Progress and Its Problems: Towards a Theory of Scientific Growth* (Berkeley: University of California Press, 1977), pp. 61–64, 101–3. Laudan's claim is that conflicts between worldviews weaken both worldviews only until the conflict is resolved in favor of one or the other; in the case of psychological determinism versus legal and political conceptions of free will, however, it seems unlikely that any resolution will soon emerge.

53. Paul T. Sagal, *Skinner's Philosophy* (Lanham, Md.: University Press of America, 1981), p. 1.

54. *Encyclopedia of Philosophy,* s.v. "Enlightenment," by Crane Brinton.

55. See the discussion of this tension in Deese, *American Freedom,* and Novak, "Grand Inquisitor," p. 231.

56. See Jean-Francois Lyotard, *The Postmodern Condition: A Report on Knowledge* (Manchester, England: Manchester University Press, 1984); and the discussion in Madan Sarup, *An Introductory Guide to Post-structuralism and Postmodernism* (Athens: University of Georgia Press, 1989), chap. 5. On the postmodern turn in the social sciences, see Pauline Marie Rosenau, *Post-Modernism and the Social Sciences: Insights, Inroads, and Intrusions* (Princeton: Princeton University Press, 1992).

57. Howard P. Segal, introduction to *Technology, Pessimism, and Postmodernism,* ed. Yaron Ezrahi, Everett Mendelsohn, and Howard P. Segal (Dordrecht, The Netherlands: Kluwer, 1994), pp. 1–10, on p. 3.

58. George Basalla, *The Evolution of Technology* (Cambridge: Cambridge University Press, 1988), p. 211.

59. Ibid., p. 216. For telling philosophical analyses of the concept of progress and detailed case studies of the problematic relation of technology to social progress, see Steven L. Goldman, ed., *Science, Technology, and Social Progress* (Bethlehem, Pa.: Lehigh University Press, 1989).

60. See, for example, Nicholas Rescher, "Technological Progress and Human Happiness," in *Unpopular Essays on Technological Progress* (Pittsburgh, Pa.: University of Pittsburgh Press, 1980), pp. 3–22.

61. Novak, "Grand Inquisitor," p. 241.

62. These benefits are as numerous and as complex in their ramifications as they are undeniable. In his *Governing the Soul* (London: Routledge, 1990), Nikolas Rose has cogently argued that, by placing effective means of self-improvement in people's hands, behavioral technologies have succeeded in their "liberatory and democratic aspirations" of helping individuals with the "profoundly emancipatory project of learning to be a self" (p. 238). "Behaviour modification . . . thus becomes consonant with the liberating theologies of self-assertion" (p. 237). Rose argues further that critics who focus on the uses of behavioral technology for manipulating behavior toward institutional conformity have missed the technology's larger effect of bolstering the culture's popular philosophy of individual self-fulfillment. But, of course, such self-assertion is likely to manifest itself as consumerism and other forms of individualism that Skinner would have decried. If Rose's analysis is right, even in general outline, then it would appear that Skinner's broad social aim of applying behavioral technology to the design of a sustainable culture that fosters individual self-restraint may be undercut by the very technologies he helped to create. The migration of technologies in directions inimical to their originators' intent is, of course, a phenomenon not unknown in the history of technology.

63. See Garrett Hardin, "The Tragedy of the Commons," *Science* 162 (1968): 1243–48; and Dennis R. Fox, "Psychology, Ideology, Utopia, and the Commons," *American Psychologist* 40 (1985): 48–58. The tragedy of the commons is discussed in relation to the ethics of Walden Two in Segal, "Morality of Anarchy."

64. See, for example, E. Scott Geller, "Applied Behavior Analysis and Social Marketing: An Integration for Environmental Preservation," *Journal of Social Issues* 45 (1989): 17–36; and John D. Cone and Steven C. Hayes, *Environmental Problems/Behavioral Solutions* (New York: Cambridge University Press, 1984).

65. For example, Yaron Ezrahi, "Science and Utopia in Late 20th Century Pluralist Democracy," in *Nineteen Eighty-Four: Science Between Utopia and Dystopia*, ed. Everett Mendelsohn and Helga Nowotny (Dordrecht, The Netherlands: D. Reidel, 1984), pp. 273–90. The difficulties posed by postmodern information technologies for the implementation of Skinner's social vision are discussed in Richard F. Rakos, "Achieving the Just Society in the 21st Century: What Can Skinner Contribute?" *American Psychologist* 47 (1992): 1499–1506.

66. *Encyclopedia of Philosophy*, s.v. "Behaviorism," by Arnold S. Kaufman.

67. John A. Nevin, "B. F. Skinner: On Behalf of the Future," *Behavior and Social Issues* 2 (spring/summer 1992): 83–88, on p. 87. For a further discussion of the holistic aspects of Skinner's Darwinian ontology, see Edward K. Morris, "Contextualism: The World View of Behavior Analysis," *Journal of Experimental Child Psychology* 46 (1988): 289–323; and Steven C. Hayes, "Contextualism and the Next Wave of Behavioral Psychology," *Behavior Analysis* 23 (1988): 7–22.

68. It is perhaps ironic that many who would view animal models of psychological processes as epistemologically irrelevant to human psychology are eager to see in every species threatened with extinction a potential model of the fate of humans.

69. Daniel W. Bjork, "B. F. Skinner and the American Tradition: The Scientist as Social Inventor," this volume; Bjork, *B. F. Skinner: A Life* (New York: Basic, 1993).

70. In assessing the "cognitive revolution" in psychology and its role in displacing behaviorism from the forefront of American psychology, one critic of behaviorism has acknowledged the likelihood that "a minority of psychologists will continue to be behaviorists," adding that "this is probably healthy for the

future of psychology." The same can no doubt be said for behaviorism's continuing voice in the wider realm of cultural criticism. See Bernard J. Baars, *The Cognitive Revolution in Psychology* (New York: Guilford, 1986), p. 398. The ongoing viability of behaviorism as a theoretical tradition is nicely evidenced by such recent works as Peter R. Killeen, "Mathematical Principles of Reinforcement," *Behavioral and Brain Sciences* 17 (1994): 105–72; and J. E. R. Staddon, *Behaviorism: Mind, Mechanism and Society* (London: Duckworth, 1993).

71. Gerald Holton, "Science, Technology, and the Fourth Discontinuity," in *Information Technology and Psychology: Prospects for the Future,* ed. Richard A. Kasschau, Roy Lachman, and Kenneth R. Laughery (New York: Praeger, 1982), pp. 1–19, on p. 5 (Holton's emphasis).

Appendix
The Papers of B. F. Skinner and His Harvard Colleagues: Documenting an Academic Community in Psychology

Clark A. Elliott

THE history of science, as a field of study, has been characterized in the past by a number of foci. These have included biographies of the great personages who contributed to scientific thought, the historical development of ideas within particular disciplines, and studies in intellectual history on a broader front and with varying sweeps of time. Histories also have been written on particular institutions—frequently as part of an anniversary celebration. Other historical endeavors have traced the relations of science to literature or religion, while the organization of science and its mutual relations to society, politics, and economics also are studied. Often the economic consequences of science are seen from the view of the relations between science and technology, or even through a confusion of science and technology. The extremes of historiographical practice have been labeled by historians as internalist and externalist history of science—internalist being a more or less pure form of intellectual history, externalist being concerned with the social dimensions of science. These still are valuable reference points for understanding the emphases of historians of science, but the trend is toward an approach that sees the intellectual and social dimensions as part of a whole. The scientist is seen as part of a community involved in the construction of knowledge, and that community as part of a larger social or political entity.

This essay has as its purpose the promotion of the history of psychology through a consideration of the historical sources available in the Harvard University Archives for the study of B. F. Skinner, his colleagues, and related topics. Although the larger purpose is to illuminate the history of science through its various approaches, the emphasis here is on using the perspective of scientific and social community as an organizing and evaluative principle. Granting that Harvard University is a small world, as place and as immediate community, it was nonetheless Professor Skinner's environment for a large part of his adult life. His personal development and activities, interactions with colleagues, the actions and interests of these colleagues, conflict and resolution in psychological approach, and the multifaceted relations of the university with the extramural environment, all are part of the story to be documented and studied.

The Harvard University Archives has as its primary mission to document the history of the university in all of its aspects—administrative, curricular, social, intellectual, and personal. This inevitably has to be done with a certain degree of selectivity, simply because we could not possibly save all the paper and other forms of documentation that a large university produces every day. Even if we could, it would not serve the needs of historians. It would only transfer to them the burden of selection. To preserve an adequate and usable body of historical records that will meet the needs of historians with varying interests or emphases is a difficult task.

The idea of the university as community—or as middle and mediating ground between its component persons and the surrounding political and social structure—is a useful means to help make decisions on what an institutional archives should contain. The communal concept, therefore, is relevant to the interests of both scholars and archivists. In this essay, I begin with a couple of documentary issues that are especially relevant to a consideration of the relations of individuals to their institutional settings, and then draw a general picture of what the Harvard University Archives contains. The institutional history of psychology and related areas at Harvard is then briefly sketched, followed by a discussion of the various collections there for the historians of psychology. For all of this the idea of community will serve, at least implicitly, as a backdrop.

SOME ISSUES OF DOCUMENTATION

There is a quandary for archivists these days, and that is a consideration of the proper balance of person and institution in the historiography of science. There is a feeling about modern science—and particularly in the age of Big Science (post-World War II science)—that biography is a dying art.[1] To a certain extent, of course, this represents the degree to which physics has come to stand as a surrogate for all science. In an age of large laboratories, large budgets, and a characteristically multiauthored scientific literature, the part of the individual is obscured if not diminished. What is featured is the team, the institution, the incremental and collaborative nature of scientific knowledge. There is truth to this and perhaps truth that calls for a re-evaluation of the role of the individual in all of the sciences. Financial records and reports on grants are examples of records that illustrate something of the modern character of science. In certain important respects, the dependence of university researchers on federal and other outside grant sources overrides the individuality of research in the sciences and inevitably makes it less of a private or personal enterprise than it might have been in an earlier period of ad hoc, less centralized funding. From a documentary point of view, the administration of research moneys and facilities is one of the ways in which science is woven into the administration—and therefore the communal fiber—of the institution. An interesting question always is the degree to which any one field of study, or any individual, is part of this kind of intermeshed social construction.

Another feature that has come to characterize academia in the last century or so, as compared to the older American college, is a sense of the academic community outside the particular institution. This is an attractive force that counteracts the place of the researcher within the local institution. There is, in fact, a tension between intramural activity and professional or emotional attachment to the institution, and a concurrent external orientation to the superordinate discipline with its subject matter and its own string of journals, societies, and other centers of activity and attention. No university can document its own history if it neglects to connect itself also to the life of the larger disciplines or to the other extramural activities of its faculty and staff. This realization came early, such that the collecting of personal and professional papers of tenured faculty members has become an integral part of the ongoing activities of the Harvard Archives, as it is with many others.

A hypothetical examination of faculty files can illustrate the complexity of relations between institutional, disciplinary, and political or other interests and activities. Faculty collections are valuable as a source for university history in the narrower sense. For example, the only complete record of a university committee may be in the papers of the professor who chaired it. Some groups of faculty papers may relate entirely to outside activities, such as cases where the faculty member served as president of a professional society. Other file series document simultaneously both local and external matters. Secretaries cannot and do not always differentiate, when filing, between what is a personal outside activity and what is a local function of the same person as chair of the department. Even a single letter or exchange of letters can dwell on several matters—paragraph one is in response to a request for evaluative information that aids in placing a graduate student in a first teaching position, the second paragraph reports or comments on a meeting of a professional society's committee, the third outlines a section of a paper on which the correspondents are collaborating, and the closing words are greetings from one family to another, friends since the correspondents were junior faculty members together twenty years before. One point to keep in mind from this illustration is that the life of any person is composed of overlapping constituencies or communities, some immediate, others more remote or occasional.

HARVARD UNIVERSITY ARCHIVES

The core of the Harvard University Archives consists of the official records of the university generated by the governing boards (i.e., the Harvard Corporation and Board of Overseers) and the correspondence and other records of the Office of the President. Minutes of meetings of the Corporation go back to the earliest years of Harvard College in the seventeenth century and continue up to the present. In the second quarter of the nineteenth century, historical interest was generated through the 1836 celebration of the university's two-hundredth anniversary and by the two-volume history of Harvard published in 1840 by Pres. Josiah Quincy. One of the outcomes of Quincy's project was the midcentury gathering of many valuable documents, which were arranged, bound, and preserved to form the basis of an archives. Through subsequent years, the library also preserved a number of items of historical interest. By the time the university observed its three-hundredth year in 1936 further historical interest was promoted and in 1939 the corporation officially established the archives as a department of the University Library.

Over the years, and through the systematic collection of Harvard-related materials, the holdings of the archives have reached somewhere near 50,000 linear feet—that is, about nine shelf-miles of paper. The official life of the university still stands at the center of the archives' mission, and an active records management program operated out of the archives attends to the systematic selection and preservation of currently produced records that are presumed to have long-term historical value. In addition to files for the presidents and vice presidents, the archives includes correspondence and other records from the offices of the deans, of various administrative units in the graduate professional schools, the academic departments in the Faculty of Arts and Sciences, laboratories, research centers, and the libraries. Also included are holdings of routine but significant records such as student folders, and financial ledgers and journals.

As just indicated, the personal and professional papers of tenured mem-

bers of the faculty constitute a very significant part of the ongoing collecting activities. The Harvard University Archives also preserve curricular
material. The student and teacher lecture notes, examinations, course
papers, syllabi, and other materials that constitute the curricular collection date from the colonial period to the present. Also among the holdings
are printed and manuscript materials for hundreds of student organizations, some of them of an ephemeral character representing a short-lived
cohort of students, others organizations that have survived two centuries.
Supplementing these materials are student diaries and letters that give a
special perspective on student life over the years. The archives, however,
does not collect the papers of alumni, except as they relate directly to
the student experience. The University Archives is one of about fifty
libraries at Harvard that collect manuscript material, and sometimes
alumni papers can be referred to one of these other repositories. The archives has a very useful biographical clippings file of some 80,000–90,000
folders for former students, faculty, and staff. An attempt is made to
collect a copy of all university publications—a goal never to be achieved
entirely—and also clippings, pamphlets, or books about the university,
its various departments or constituent institutions, and faculty members.
The archives is a very busy research facility with some 10,000 visitor
requests for use of material per year, and the recipient of about 1,200
letters annually inquiring about every imaginable topic where Harvard
or its personnel may have been involved.

HISTORY OF PSYCHOLOGY

The focus of this volume is B. F. Skinner, and by extension the history
of psychology. I am not a psychologist and not a historian of the subject.
My knowledge of the research activities of Skinner and his colleagues at
Harvard is sketchy at best. But Skinner was a public figure and in fact
presented some of his basic precepts in literary form in *Walden Two*. One
result of my reading of that work is to wonder what Skinner's own attitude
toward history might have been. His appreciation of history presumably
is one reason why he placed his papers in the Harvard Archives. Some
of his earliest work in psychology made significant use of historical analysis of concepts in science.[2] In light of this, one wonders what to make of
the words of Skinner's protagonist Frazier, in *Walden Two*, when he states
"we discourage any sense of history," and later adds: "What we give our
young people in Walden Two is a grasp of the *current* forces which a
culture must deal with. None of your myths, none of your heroes—no
history, no destiny—simply the *Now!*"[3] An archivist and historian cannot

accept that judgment, but still the role of history in Skinner's own work may be worth consideration by some interested and informed scholar.

Although archives can potentially support research in various disciplines (depending on a repository's collecting policy),[4] the traditional and primary use is for historical studies. As background to a more specific discussion of sources for the history of psychology in the Harvard Archives, what follows is a brief overview of Harvard psychology, from the institutional viewpoint. Psychology at Harvard began with the pioneering work of William James. He represented a connection of psychology with philosophy that perhaps at first gave place and credibility to the new field but in the end tended to stifle it. For the institutional history of psychology at Harvard in this century, the university career of Edwin G. Boring is especially germane. Boring came to Harvard with the mission to separate psychology from philosophy, and it took him more than a decade to reach his goal, in 1934.[5] Judging by Skinner's statement that his own 1931 "thesis had only the vaguest of Harvard connections,"[6] and in spite of the problems that Boring saw in the established departmental structure, it appears that the placement of psychology in philosophy before 1934 may have worked to make more permeable the walls between disciplines to the benefit at least of some students.

In the decade after the emergence of psychology from philosophy, the struggle to define it in the university continued. The terms that Boring used in referring to the contending parts were the sociotropes and the biotropes,[7] suggesting an orientation respectively to the social and biological poles of the field. The presence of Henry Murray and the Psychological Clinic also signifies the presence of applied science or psychological practice. The resolution of the rift came in 1946 with the establishment of the Harvard Social Relations Department. That new department included social psychology, along with sociology and social anthropology. The psychologists Gordon Allport and Henry Murray went with Social Relations, and E. G. Boring and Stanley Smith Stevens stayed with the Psychology Department. Soon thereafter Skinner joined them. In 1972, the Psychology Department, and what remained of Social Relations—by then largely psychology—were reunited as the Department of Psychology and Social Relations.[8]

In reading the recollections of the Harvard psychologists, it is clear that space and facilities—a sense of place—played a significant role in the history of the subject. From Emerson Hall the psychologists moved to a laboratory in Memorial Hall as a result of the split in the department that accompanied the establishment of the Social Relations Department. An attempt to mold disciplinary relations was an apparent part of the design of William James Hall which opened in 1965. It seems to have succeeded in that goal only modestly.[9]

Sources for the History of Psychology

Psychology as a field conscious of its own history has made effective use of autobiography, and Skinner has contributed significantly to this literature. Autobiography or recollection is only one form of historical documentation. In my own work as an archivist and historian interested in historiography and historical method, I have come to view documentary sources, considered in their relations to historical events, as predominantly one of three types. First, some documents are themselves "events"—an example is a poem, or even a scientific paper. Second, and most numerous and complex, are documents that have as their intent to bring about some demonstrable action or reaction—a simple example is the writing of a letter requesting a reprint of a scientific paper. The expected outcome is the sending and receipt of the requested item. Third are documents that report on an event that might not otherwise be known to the future in the absence of that report; beyond the act of reporting, the document in this latter case has no role in the event itself.[10] It is apparent that the third category encompasses autobiography, and yet it is equally obvious that history that relies largely on such remembrances of events may miss any chance at objectivity. To adequately document any historical event or period, one has to have access to, and adequate appreciation of, documents from a variety of sources, including all three of the classes just outlined.

The remainder of this essay refers to some of the major collections in the University Archives that support the history of psychology.[11] It should be understood that these are sources more or less specific to the field, but for a researcher interested in certain aspects of history, use of the records of the Office of the President and of the deans, as well as other general resources previously mentioned, also would be appropriate and in some cases imperative. The discussion that follows begins with records of university offices and then moves to collections of personal and professional papers. Some collections have restrictions on access for a stated period of time, and all university records less than fifty years old require the permission of the head of the department or office whose records are involved.

University Records

Insofar as official records are concerned, those of the Department of Philosophy constitute the chronological foundation for the study of psychology at Harvard.[12] They date from the 1890s, when academic departments were first formally recognized at the university (the name was changed to Philosophy and Psychology in 1913). The substantive records such as correspondence of the chair do not start until about 1910. These records, typical for an academic department, include minutes of meetings, correspondence with faculty members and others about departmental business, records concerning appointments, fellowships, and the budget, more or less routine records for the departmental library, and individual student folders (which are closed without special permission for eighty years from the time the student left the university). Among the correspondents in the old Philosophy Department records are E. G. Boring; one would expect this file to support research on Boring's protracted effort to separate psychology from philosophy. Aside from the Boring correspondence, however, some of the more routine papers can give a day-to-day view of how psychology fit into the business and concerns of the department before the separate establishment of psychology in the early 1930s. It is possible that the archives' collections of personal papers of such philosophers as Ralph Barton Perry may also shed light on the general topic of the relations between philosophy and psychology at Harvard.

The records of the Department of Psychology (and after 1972, Psychology and Social Relations) are a substantial collection occupying about 100 linear feet of shelf space (about 250 document boxes). For the official view of Harvard psychology since the 1930s, this is the core collection. The series of departmental minutes dates from 1934 to 1983, and minutes of permanent members from 1952 to 1983. Correspondence and other records of the chair—including E. G. Boring, Gordon Allport, Edwin Newman, and others—begin in the mid-1930s to the 1980s and cover the spectrum of departmental concerns. There also are minutes and other records relating to the departmental Comparative International Studies Program from 1964 to 1970, and Experimental Psychology Program minutes from 1972 to 1980. Other records for the department include correspondence, lists, reports, and curricular material from the Undergraduate Office, as well as folders for individual undergraduate concentrators and graduate students. There are folders for individual faculty members from 1946 to 1982. The archives also has the annual reports for the Psychology Department from 1934 to the early 1970s, and for the Psychological Laboratory for the period 1931–33. The records on finances that have been preserved contain some items for the laboratory, 1924–45; these include correspondence between the departmental chair and the dean of the faculty. Other special series include correspondence and other records, 1956–72, concerning the planning and construction of William James Hall, and correspondence, memorandums, and proposals relating to reorganization of the Departments of Psychology and Social Relations; these cover the period 1963–72.

From 1946 to 1972, materials relating to social psychology, clinical psychology, and related areas are represented in the records of the Department of Social Relations. Again, there are series of departmental minutes, correspondence, student folders, and other records. Because the psychology-related materials are not isolated, a search has to be made for them; but as with philosophy before 1934, such a search shows psychology in the ongoing context of the larger department of social relations. One special series in the Social Relations Department files is the records for the Committee on Nominations to the Cabot Professorship of Social Ethics, 1966–68; the psychologist Gordon Allport was the first to hold the Professorship, in 1966. In addition to the official records of the Department of Social Relations, researchers interested in the establishment and history of that department may want to consult the personal and professional papers of major figures in the department other than psychologists. Most notable here are the very substantial and frequently consulted papers of the sociologist, and first chair of the department, Talcott Parsons. Also of interest is a series of taped interviews done in 1978 by two Harvard undergraduates for their senior honors theses. These tapes are in the archives, with the records of the Department of Psychology, but permission of the interviewees is required for use. Skinner was interviewed but not taped.

In 1964, a Center for the Behavioral Sciences was established as a means of coordinating the use of instructional and research facilities for psychology, sociology, and social anthropology. This event was a consequence of construction of the new William James Hall. The archives' records for the center relate especially to the Committee on the Use of Human Subjects in research. Other special facilities will be referred to subsequently in discussing collections of the papers of individual faculty members.

Faculty Papers Collections

The papers of William James are in Harvard's Houghton Library of Rare Books and Manuscripts. The James collection includes correspondence, diaries, manuscripts and notes, including some on psychology, and other papers. The archives has a small group of papers by students in James's Philosophy 2—psychology—course in 1890–91. The papers of James's successor in psychology at Harvard, Hugo Münsterberg, are in the Boston Public Library. Abraham Roback was an instructor in psychology at Harvard from 1920 to 1923 and published a *History of American Psychology*. The archives has about seven linear feet of Roback's papers, including correspondence, manuscripts, and other items, although most of this material relates to his interests in Yiddish language and literature.

Walter Fenno Dearborn was a professor of education at Harvard from 1917, the year in which he established the Psycho-Educational Clinic. He died in 1955. The archives has the correspondence and other records of the clinic for 1927–46. The file includes what appear to be Dearborn's personal and professional papers, as well as his records as clinic director. There is sensitive content here relating to students, and material on persons psychologically tested, with test data; for these reasons any access for the present would be limited. There also is a very small collection of materials in the archives that concern Dearborn's teaching in the Graduate School of Education.

It is no exaggeration to say that the single most significant collection in the Harvard Archives for the general history of psychology—both for the university and for the discipline—is the papers of Edwin G. Boring. Skinner himself recognized this in a biographical memoir of Boring in 1968. He wrote:

> Boring's influence on psychology was perhaps most effectively exerted through his extensive correspondence. . . . He left the Harvard archives a correspondence of more than 120,000 letters. . . . Only a careful study of this vast material will make it possible to evaluate the full extent of his influence on the psychology of his time.[13]

Skinner has intimated here a truism in regard to manuscript collections. There are figures who may not be of the first order as personal contributors to the intellectual content or ideational structure of their fields, but whose papers are of enormous value because of the person's social function in the discipline. It is probably safe to place Boring in this category. The Boring Papers are extensively used, and yet it seems that relatively very few users are interested primarily in the man himself. They are interested in other topics, and Boring's involvement and insightful commentary on events—and on himself—help to reveal what happened and how a major actor perceived that action. (In contrast, I would suggest that Skinner's own papers will be used by researchers interested especially in his work.) The Boring Papers consist very largely of correspondence, going back to about 1919 when Boring was a professor of experimental psychology at Clark University. There also are subject files, including material relating to research in psychology, course lecture notes, and a series of correspondence dating from Boring's editorship of *Contemporary Psychology* during the period 1956–61.

The papers of Boring's contemporary and sometimes (gentlemanly) antagonist, Gordon Allport, are also in the University Archives. The correspondence dates from about 1930. There also are manuscripts, notes, data and other materials relating to courses, lectures, and publications. Among Allport's interests represented by these materials is the topic of psychology and religion.

Henry Murray, a professor of clinical psychology and director of the Psychological Clinic, placed his papers in the archives. This is a large and varied collection that reflects Murray's many interests. Occupying about 95 feet of shelving, it includes correspondence, manuscripts, notes and data, photographs, and other material. In addition to the papers concerning psychology, a portion of the collection documents Murray's interests in Herman Melville. There is apparently little here that relates to the Psychological Clinic, nor does the archives otherwise have the records of the clinic, which was established in the mid-1920s and which Murray directed for many years. Henry Murray, along with Gordon Allport, went to the Social Relations Department when it was established in 1946, and they represented the clinical and social psychology section of that department.

Edwin Boring's protégé, Stanley Smith Stevens, was a professor of psychology and of psychophysics at Harvard until his death in 1973. The archives has his personal papers, dating from the early 1930s and amounting to about 11 linear feet in size. As with other collections of personal and professional papers in the archives, the Stevens Papers include materials for the history of psychology at Harvard as well as for the field more generally. Materials for the discipline are represented, for example, by correspondence and other papers relating to organizations such as the American Psychological Association, the National Academy of Sciences, and the Acoustical Society of America. S. S. Stevens's presence at the university also is documented by a significant collection of records of the Psycho-Acoustic and, later, the Psycho-Physics Laboratory of which Stevens was director. These records begin during the World War II period when the laboratory was first established. They include correspondence, memos, reports, notes, data, photographs, and other items relating to research contracts, budget, research activities and results, the relation of the laboratory to the Psychology Department at Harvard, and other topics. The Stevens Papers include a small amount of material regarding George von Békésy, senior research fellow in psychophysics. Under von Békésy's own name is a scrapbook of clippings, letters, and other items relating to his 1961 Nobel Prize; the scrapbook came to the Archives with Stevens's papers.

Jerome Bruner, formerly a professor of psychology (in the Social Relations Department), has one of the largest collections in the Harvard Archives. The material that has been archivally processed—that is, arranged and described for research use—is some 90 linear feet and covers the period from about 1940 to 1971; there is about 75 linear feet of material subsequently received but not yet processed and therefore not available. The processed papers contain correspondence, including material relating to the American Psychological Association, the Society for the Psychological Study of Social Issues, and other organizations. There is also a substantial amount of material relating directly to Bruner's research projects, including notes, data, reports, and correspondence, and material relating to courses. Although Bruner left Harvard in 1972, he continues to send his papers to the archives, thus maintaining the continuity and integrity of his life's record. His personal and professional papers are complemented by the records of the Center for Cognitive Studies, which he established and directed at Harvard, from 1961 to 1972. These records include correspondence concerning academic appointments, and budgets and grant records.

George A. Miller was a professor of psychology at Harvard from 1958 to 1968, having earlier served as assistant and associate professor. The archives has a small collection of his correspondence, for the years 1955–57, with some earlier letters. The papers of Prof. Sheldon H. White include miscellaneous correspondence and other material for the period from about 1973 to 1984. Audiotapes of the psychology and social relations lectures of the senior lecturer George Goethals during the years 1975–85 are among the Modern Language Center's records in the University Archives.

A recent acquisition is the papers of David McClelland, who joined the Department of Social Relations as a professor of psychology in 1956, and who served as head of the University's Center for Research in Personality. The McClelland Papers, including correspondence and curricular and other material, amount to about 25 linear feet. The papers are among the currently unprocessed accessions in the archives, and as with other unprocessed collections, McClelland's papers are not available for use at present. Also recently received (but unprocessed) are correspondence and other papers of R. Duncan Luce, chiefly for the period when he was a professor of psychology at Harvard. The Luce papers date from 1976 to the late 1980s. Also presently unprocessed is the extensive collection of the papers of Graduate School of Education professor Lawrence Kohlberg relating to his work in developmental psychology.

Faculty Papers Collections: B. F. Skinner

The papers of B. F. Skinner that the archives now has do not represent the entire Skinner collection. Some materials are only recently received and have not been processed (including correspondence for the early

1980s, and manuscript notes and reflections). Furthermore, additions to the papers are expected in the future. The collection currently available amounts to about 30 linear feet of material. The larger portion is correspondence. For the period before Skinner's return to Harvard as a professor of psychology in 1948, there is relatively little correspondence—of the 30 linear feet for the collection as a whole, only about 2 or 3 feet is correspondence and related documents for the period before 1948. The period of his life before graduate school is essentially undocumented in the collection now in the archives (though it is well represented in Skinner's published autobiographical writings). The vast majority of the collection dates from the 1960s and 1970s.

The correspondence files, overall, have a chronological-alphabetical arrangement, with several overlapping chronologies. This arrangement may present some difficulties for researchers interested in following Skinner's relations with particular correspondents (either persons or organizations) over a period of years. Biographers, on the other hand, could find the arrangement advantageous since they can cover the course of his life through time. The archives, with this collection as with others, has attempted to maintain the original arrangement of the material as much as possible, in order to preserve the historical information implied through the physical relation of one document or folder to another. The correspondence touches on many particular aspects of Skinner's professional life, but the papers may prove interesting especially in the aggregate. That is, they will help to show the impact of his work on a number of persons. For example, a significant part of the collection of correspondence appears to be queries or comments from various quarters, reacting to Skinner's work. In addition to such evidence in the correspondence files, there also are chronologically arranged folders of news clippings and similar items giving public notice of his work.

There are a few folders in the Skinner Papers for individual correspondents, the most notable of which is correspondence with E. G. Boring from the time when Skinner was a graduate student. There also are some letters and other documents arranged or grouped by subject. These include items relating to the Aircrib, speaking and writing engagements (including regrets), correspondence and patents relating to teaching machines, lecture notes and manuscripts, correspondence relating to *Walden Two* (covering the period from about 1946 to 1974), and other topics. A small collection of earlier laboratory and research records, for the years 1929–40, are in the archives. These have been arranged and described by Stephen Coleman, who has published some of the results of his studies.[14]

There are several collections in the archives that might not be noted in a general review of psychological sources, but which are nonetheless relevant for the study of Skinner's work. The archives has the papers of two Harvard professors who were particularly significant in his early development. They perhaps demonstrate also, by not being psychologists, something of the special significance of a university as intellectual community. William J. Crozier, a professor of general physiology, not only influenced the work of the young B. F. Skinner but gave him material aid as a researcher through an allotment of laboratory space for postdoctoral studies. The second collection to be mentioned is the papers of the professor of physics Percy W. Bridgman, whose *Logic of Modern Physics* and ideas on operationism were key encounters for the young psychologist. Also to be mentioned as interesting for a later stage in Skinner's career are the records of the Harvard Committee (subsequently, Office) of Programmed Instruction, with which he was involved as an outgrowth of his work with teaching machines. These files date from the 1960s and are with the records of the Graduate School of Education.

Conclusion

Most of the collections mentioned in this essay include materials relating more or less directly to Skinner's career. Relatively extensive though his own papers are, an adequate historical picture requires that events be examined from various points of view. The collections of the Harvard University Archives not only document the local environment but also connect to larger events and concerns in the discipline and society itself. There will also be relevant and useful supplementary materials in the papers of other persons or institutions, located in other repositories. These may involve correspondence with Skinner that is not represented in his own papers—for example, if letters were written without retaining carbon copies. Other collections might include materials about Skinner, although such subject-oriented materials can be particularly difficult to locate. Collections elsewhere also may prove useful for other aspects of the history of behavioral psychology, aspects in which Skinner and his work were not so directly involved. Furthermore, a full view of his life involves personal and family considerations, and in this regard it should be noted that the Schlesinger Library on the History of Women in America, at Radcliffe College, has a small collection of papers of Skinner's wife, Yvonne Blue Skinner. These include her diaries and other writings.

For an adequate study of Skinner's work, insofar as unpublished material is concerned, it is apparent that his own papers are at the center. Around that core are concentric but connected circles of other sources, as already indicated—the Psychology Department, Harvard colleagues, other collections in the University Archives, and collections in other repositories. All of this suggests a complex array of material, and it is based on an assumption that researchers are also familiar with the published primary and secondary literature. Each of these sources supports the other, and together they hold the key to an adequate reconstruction of the past. What ultimately is done with the sources depends, of course, on the diligence, ingenuity, and imagination of the historians and other scholars who use them.

NOTES

1. Thomas L. Hankins, "In Defence of Biography: The Use of Biography in the History of Science," *History of Science* 17 (1979): 1–16.

2. See, for example, the historical portion of Skinner's doctoral thesis, published in part as B. F. Skinner, "The Concept of the Reflex in the Description of Behavior," *Journal of General Psychology* 5 (1931): 427–58. See also the discussion in Walter C. Stanley, "B. F. Skinner," in *International Encyclopedia of the Social Sciences,* vol. 18, *Biographical Supplement,* ed. David L. Sills (New York: Free Press; London: Collier Macmillan, 1979), pp. 722–29.

3. Skinner, *Walden Two,* with a new introduction by the author (New York: Macmillan, 1976), pp. 221, 224–25.

4. The Harvard University Archives, for example, generally does not accept scientific data files except as a sample or illustration of research procedures or methodology.

5. Patrick L. Schmidt, "Towards a History of the Department of Social Relations: Harvard University, 1946–1972" (unpublished undergraduate thesis, Harvard College, 1978 [copy in Harvard University Archives]), p. 7.

6. "B. F. Skinner," in *A History of Psychology in Autobiography,* vol. 5, ed. Edwin G. Boring and Gardner Lindzey (New York: Appleton-Century-Crofts, 1967), pp. 387–413, on p. 399.

7. Schmidt, "History of the Department of Social Relations," p. 11.

8. Ernest R. Hilgard, *Psychology in America: A Historical Survey* (San Diego, Calif.: Harcourt, 1987), pp. 599–602; and Schmidt, "History of the Department of Social Relations."

9. Hilgard, *Psychology in America,* p. 601.

10. Clark A. Elliott, "Communication and Events in History: Toward a Theory for Documenting the Past," *American Archivist* 48, no. 4 (fall 1985): 365–67 and 49, no. 1 (winter 1986): 95.

11. For an overview of archival sources relating to the history of the sciences at Harvard, see Clark A. Elliott and Margaret W. Rossiter, eds., *Science at Harvard University: Historical Perspectives* (Bethlehem, Pa.: Lehigh University Press; London and Toronto: Associated University Presses, 1992), pp. 314–19.

12. The University Archives, while collecting records for most of Harvard, does not maintain those of the Medical School. Their records are the responsibility of the Medical School itself, namely the Countway Library. Although the Countway's holdings likely contain materials relating to certain aspects of psychology and related areas, they are not reviewed here.

13. Skinner, "Edwin Garrigues Boring (1886–1968)," *Yearbook of the American*

Philosophical Society 1968 (Philadelphia: American Philosophical Society, 1969), p. 114.

14. See, for example, Coleman, "Quantitative Order in B. F. Skinner's Early Research Program, 1928–1931," *The Behavior Analyst* 10 (1987): 47–65; and Coleman, "Skinner's Progress During the 1930s: Reflexes, Operants, and Apparatuses," this volume.

Contributors

DANIEL W. BJORK is professor of history at St. Mary's University in San Antonio, Texas. He has published a biography of William James as well as *B. F. Skinner: A Life,* the first major Skinner biography. He is currently working with Rhonda K. Bjork on *Concord,* a midnineteenth-century historical novel.

RHONDA K. BJORK is a freelance historian in San Antonio, Texas.

JAMES H. CAPSHEW is assistant professor in the Department of History and Philosophy of Science at Indiana University, where he teaches courses that explore the culture of science, past and present. His research in the history of psychology concerns the disciplinary and professional development of the field in the United States. He is completing a book-length study of the impact of World War II on American psychologists and their work.

JOHN J. CERULLO is associate professor of history at the University of New Hampshire at Manchester, specializing in European intellectual history and the history and philosophy of social science. His publications include studies of the social constructionist movement in psychology, and epistemological discourse within radical sociology. He is currently working on a study of the role of French social scientists and other intellectuals in the Dreyfus Affair.

S. R. COLEMAN is professor of psychology at Cleveland State University. His scholarly specialty is the history of psychology, especially of behavioral research and behaviorism. He has published articles on a variety of topics in this area, including several on Skinner's development as a researcher and theorist.

CLARK A. ELLIOTT is associate curator for archives administration and research in the Harvard University Archives. He has published articles on archival topics and historical research methodology and was founding editor of the newsletter, *History of Science in America: News and Views.* His books include *Biographical Dictionary of American Science: The*

Seventeenth Through the Nineteenth Centuries (Westport, Conn.: Green-wood, 1979), and (with coeditor Margaret W. Rossiter) *Science at Harvard University: Historical Perspectives* (Bethlehem, Pa.: Lehigh University Press, 1992).

ELIZABETH A. JORDAN is assistant professor of psychology at Kalamazoo College, Michigan, where she pursues research on the characteristics of parenting and parent-child relationships as they relate to psychosocial development. She was trained in the history of psychology in the University of New Hampshire's program in History and Theory of Psychology.

TERRY J. KNAPP is professor of psychology at the University of Nevada, Las Vegas. He is editor (with Lynn Robertson) of *Approaches to Cognition: Contrasts and Controversies* (Hillsdale, N.J.: Erlbaum, 1985) and *Westphal's "Die Agoraphobie": The Beginnings of Agoraphobia* (Lanham, Md.: University Press of America, 1988). With Robert Epstein, he is working on a guide to the primary and secondary literature on Skinner.

JOHN K. ROBINSON received his Ph.D. in physiological psychology from the University of New Hampshire, where he also participated in the program on History and Theory of Psychology. He is assistant professor of psychology at the State University of New York at Stony Brook where his research uses operant behavioral paradigms to study the neurotransmitter systems involved in learning and remembering.

ECKART SCHEERER is professor of psychology at the University of Oldenburg, Germany, where he is affiliated with the Institute for Cognition Research. He has written extensively on the systematic foundations and historical background of scientific psychology. His publications include *Die Verhaltensanalyse* (Behavior analysis) (Berlin: Springer-Verlag, 1983), a historio-philosophical treatment of Skinnerian behavior analysis.

LAURENCE D. SMITH is associate professor of psychology at the University of Maine. Trained in the history of science at Indiana University and at the University of New Hampshire, he is the author of *Behaviorism and Logical Positivism* (Stanford, Calif.: Stanford University Press, 1986) and of various articles on the history of behaviorism and its philosophical origins.

E. A. VARGAS is professor of behaviorology at West Virginia University. His current interests are instructional systems, university organization, and verbal behavior.

JULIE S. VARGAS is professor of behaviorology in the Department of Educational Psychology and Foundations at West Virginia University. She has written programmed instruction in subjects as diverse as kidney structure and function, and reading comprehension. In addition to this chapter, she has published, jointly with E. A. Vargas, two other articles about programmed instruction.

NILS WIKLANDER received his Ph.D. in the history of science at the University of Göteborg, Sweden, with a dissertation on the historical background of Skinner's utopian social philosophy. He is working on a book-length study, "Management and Community: B. F. Skinner, Behavioral Technology, and Cultural Design."

WILLIAM R. WOODWARD is associate professor of psychology at the University of New Hampshire, where he directs the program on History and Theory of Psychology. Trained in the history of science at Harvard and Yale, he has published widely on the intersection of personal lives and scientific work of psychologists.

Index

Adler, Alfred, 187
Agee, James, 91, 295
Agnew, Spiro, 283, 295, 303
Aircrib (baby-tender): as behavioral engineering, 144; commercial production of, 129, 200, 210n. 11; described, 9, 199; media coverage of, 129, 200, 282–83; motive for, 9, 199; public response to, 200; as social invention, 43; rumors about use of, 9, 200–201, 210–11n. 13, 211n. 14; Skinners' use of, 190, 199–200, 204
Air Force, 239, 245
America: as building site, 42, 296; the depression in, 89–90, 96, 298; as frontier, 51; industrialization of, 46–47; Industrial Revolution in, 297, 299; labor history of, 89; in 1920s, 84–85, 87, 180, 183, 186; urbanization of, 297; as utopia, 296; as wilderness, 57, 296
American Association for Applied Psychology, 96
American culture: advertising in, 73; and "Age of Alfred Adler," 187; and antidemocratic critics, 286; behaviorism in, 17, 89, 298–99, 306–8; characteristics of, as Skinnerian characteristics, 297; child-rearing practices in, 205–7, 209; and freedom, 209, 303, 308; home efficiency movement in, 210n. 2, 298; individual and environment in, 51, 308; individualism in, 303; Jacksonian era in, 48; Lockean themes in, 296–97, 301; meliorism in, 296; modernism in, 85, 87; as one-generation culture, 36; progressivism in, 297–99, 301, 304–5; religious determinism in, 297; science in, 41; scientific management in, 298–99; self-cultivation in, 180, 183, 187, 189–90; Skinner as provocateur

of, 299–304; —, as product of, 296–99; Skinner's influence on, as measured by secondary literature, 273–88; Technocracy movement in, 298–99; technological orientation of, 8, 45–47, 51, 57, 296–99, 306. *See also* individualism; invention and inventors; liberators and traditionalists; pragmatism; small-town life
American Humanist Association, 286
American Mercury, The, 86
American Psychological Association (APA), 21, 96, 121, 145, 245, 285–86
American psychology: during the 1920s, 87, 90; during the depression, 96; growth of applied psychology in, 90, 96; influence of Skinner on, 276–77, 278 fig. 5; rise of humanistic psychology in, 287; Skinnerian behaviorism as school of, 152–53; and World War II, 97. *See also* behaviorism; Harvard psychology; neobehaviorism
apparatuses: as inscription devices, 12; kymographs, 12, 118–19; Skinner's, 13, 42–43, 63, 116–19, 129–31, 210n. 2; social context of, 13. *See also* Aircrib (baby-tender); cumulative recorder and cumulative records; Project Pigeon; Skinner box; teaching machines
appropriate technology, 23, 69, 73, 307
Aristotle, 58–59
Army, 245
Arrowsmith (Lewis), 101n. 27
artificial intelligence, 18–19
artificial/natural distinction, 59, 64, 67–71, 74
Association for Behavior Analysis, 21
Atlantic Monthly, 14, 144, 282, 295
atomic bomb, 41, 69, 144
"autonomous man," 37–38, 301